T0366215

Double Takes

For four decades Professional
Investor and its predecessor,
Investment Analyst, the journal
of The Institute of Investment
Management and Research, has been
publishing sound investment
advice on topical issues from
leading experts in the field.

The articles in this collection
cover financial subjects ranging
from the first introduction of
computers and mathematical
techniques into finance, through
the oil crisis years, to the
valuation of brands, intellectual
property and goodwill. Each
article provides a fascinating
insight both into the subject
concerned and into contemporary
thinking at the time of writing.
All the articles have been
selected for their significance
to the financial world today.
These fascinating articles are as
relevant today as when first
written.

The Institute of Investment
Management and Research (IIMR) is
the professional examining body
for investment analysts and fund
managers in the UK. It provides
the `Threshold Competence'
examination for fund managers and
analysts, in addition to a six
paper Associate examination.

The Institute was founded in 1955
as the Society of Investment
Analysts and changed its name in
1992. It was a founding member of
EFFAS and has close links with
AIMR in the US.

Professional Investor is the
journal of the IIMR and is
published ten times a year.

JOHN GOODCHILD is Joint Editor
of Professional Investor and
has contributed articles on
investment theory and practice
to numerous magazines. He
co-edited, with Paul Hewitt,
a collection of essays on the
Unlisted Securities Market, which
was published by the IIMR.
Originally an analyst with
Mullens & Co., John Goodchild
is now an Associate with KBR, the
London stockbrokers.

CLIVE CALLOW has had widespread
experience in financial business
news, starting as an editorial
assistant in the newsroom of
The Financial Times in the 1960s.
After working for a US based
publication specializing in the
petroleum industry, he joined The
Times, where he covered the early
days of the North Sea oil search.
His book, Power from the Sea,
remains one of the best early
accounts of this major UK
industrial enterprise.
Subsequently he became an oil
analyst, helping to form the
London Oil Analysts Group. Clive
is Joint Editor of Professional
Investor and is also an Associate
of KBR.

Double Takes

Four decades of classic investment writing from
The Investment Analyst and *Professional Investor*

Edited by

John Goodchild and Clive Callow

JOHN WILEY & SONS, LTD

Chichester • New York • Weinheim • Brisbane • Singapore • Toronto

This edition published in 2000 by

John Wiley & Sons Ltd
Baffins Lane, Chichester,
West Sussex, PO19 1UD, England

National   01243 779777
International   (+44) 1243 779777

e-mail (for orders and customer service enquiries):
cs-books@wiley.co.uk
Visit our Home Page on http://www.wiley.co.uk
or http://www.wiley.com

Other Wiley Editorial Offices

John Wiley & Sons, Inc., 605 Third Avenue,
New York, NY 10158-0012, USA

Wiley-VCH Verlag GmbH
D-69469 Weinheim, Germany

Jacaranda Wiley Ltd, 33 Park Road, Milton,
Queensland 4064, Australia

John Wiley & Sons (Asia) Pte Ltd, 2 Clementi Loop #02-01,
Jin Xing Distripark, Singapore 129809

John Wiley & Sons (Canada) Ltd, 22 Worcester Road,
Rexdale, Ontario, M9W 1L1, Canada

Library of Congress Cataloging-in-Publication Data

British Library Cataloguing in Publication Data

A catalogue record for this book is available from the British Library

ISBN 0 471 89313 7

Typeset in 9.5/11.5 Times by Footnote Graphics, Warminster, Wiltshire

This book is printed on acid-free paper responsibly manufactured from sustainable forestry
in which at least two trees are planted for each one used for paper production.

Contents

Introduction

The Society of Investment Analysts was formed in 1955. For some years, there had been concern among those engaged in investment management about the lack of standards in financial analysis and analytical techniques. In the USA, Societies of Financial Analysts had existed in many of the larger cities since before the Second World War; the need for a corporate body in the UK was self-evident.

Exploratory meetings were held in the City of London during the early part of 1955, and eventually the statutory and legal work was put in hand. Board of Trade consent was obtained, and the final Memorandum and Articles of Association were produced. Subscribing members – including J. S. Allison, W. F. Andrews and Sir Henry Warner – were appointed and on 9 May 1955 the Certificate of Incorporation was received.

The inaugural meeting of the Society was held on 26 June 1955 at the offices of the Hudson Bay Company. Among the speakers who addressed the members was Harold Wincott. Future plans were outlined by the Council, and details were given of speakers who had agreed to address the Society. Early participants were S. P. Chambers of Imperial Chemical Industries and Sir Halford Reddish of Rugby Portland Cement.

Initially, then, the Society concentrated on programmes of speakers and company visits, but the Council recognized that this was not enough; the active participation of members was sought, and its successful outcome resulted in the formation of committees to study and report on particular subjects.

From this point, the Society began to grow, and the financial community became more enthusiastic and co-operative – at first, there had been some scepticism and even opposition to its aims. Official recognition came in the form of an invitation to give evidence before the Jenkins Committee – a task undertaken by Sir Henry Warner, the Chairman, and P. W. Freeman, the Chairman of the Technical Studies Committee. This was regarded as the most important event in the Society's early life.

At the beginning of the 1960s, two further developments occurred that were to have long-lasting importance. In 1961, it was decided by the Council to publish a quarterly journal, *The Investment Analyst*. It was an immediate success and quickly attracted subscribers throughout the world. Then, in 1962, the British Society was invited to attend the first conference of European Analysts' Societies in Courchevel. It was a successful venture, and was followed by a second congress in Cambridge in 1963. (Today, the IIMR – as the Society became known in 1992 – is the largest member of the 19-nation European Federation of Financial Analysts' Societies and plays a major part in that organization. There are also strong links with the Institute's American equivalent.)

During the 1970s, presentations, discussion meetings and company visits continued, but the Council began to feel that a professional qualification was required. Consequently, in 1977, a diploma examination was started in three subjects at a level equating to a university pass. An Associate examination was established in five subjects in 1979. It was at this time that the diploma became a Fellowship examination and the Institute membership was divided into three grades: Students (who were attempting the Associate examination), Associates and Fellows. The whole examination structure of the Institute was revised in 1989 when the Fellowship examination was discontinued, and the current Associate examination upgraded to university degree level, with eight examination papers. In 1994, a further change to the Associate examination was made when the regulatory authorities required a competence examination for those in investment management, and the Institute developed the Investment Management Certificate (IMC).

The Institute does more than just offer a qualification, and over the years has given evidence to a number of government enquiries on such subjects as company law, investor protection and criminal justice. It continues this work today, with contributions to the work of the UK Accounting Standards Board and the International Accounting Standards Committee. It is also often called upon to respond to official documents on matters affecting the profession of the investment analyst and fund manager.

The first issue of *The Investment Analyst* was published in November 1961. It contained two forewords: one by Lord Ritchie of Dundee, the Chairman of the Stock Exchange, and the other by Sir Henry Warner, the Chairman of The Society of Investment Analysts. Lord Ritchie wrote that 'an ever higher standard of advice based on detailed and expert research is required today by investors'. Sir Henry stated that the publication of the journal 'marks a decisive step along the road to full professional status'.

The November 1961 issue comprised three articles: 'The Flow of Funds for Investment' by Professor E. V. Morgan; 'Computers As an Aid to Investment Analysis' by J. G. Blease; and 'Some Comments on the Analysis of European Securities' by R. C. Larcier. The issue ran to 32 pages and the format was small, double-column pages. Clearly printed and easy to read, the design remained in use until the 1970s.

From its first edition, the tone and content of *The Investment Analyst* were established under the editorship of Sammy Wainwright. Contributors were given enough space to develop their themes and arguments, and early issues featured many distinguished academics, such as Roy Harrod, George Clayton, Richard Stone, Harold Rose and John Whittaker. Practitioners included R. E. Artus of Prudential ('The Investment Analyst's Materials', December 1963), G. T. Holdsworth of GKN ('Accounting for Inflation', December 1964) and Angus Irvine of stockbrokers Savory Milln ('The Machine Tool Industry', September 1966).

The growing interest in technical analysis was not ignored, and in September 1963 Edward W. Tabell and Anthony W. Tabell published an introduction to the subject. Subsequently, articles by Alec Ellinger, David Damant and Harvey Stewart amplified the topic with great clarity.

During the late 1960s, industry studies appeared regularly, such as Sir Henry Jones on the gas industry (October 1967) and B. D. Costello of Hoare & Co on shipbuilding (December 1969). Theoretical papers reflected the growing awareness of takeover bids and their techniques; the dollar premium and investment policy were scrutinized.

By 1970, the journal had expanded, with each issue containing at least five and often more articles. In the same year it had what was – with hindsight – a scoop: Professor A. A. Walters of the London School of Economics published his thoughts on 'Monetary Policy, Gilts and Equities'.

In 1974, Sammy Wainwright retired as editor. The Journal's success was largely due to his guidance, achieving high standards of writing and breadth of subject matter. His role in the history of *The Investment Analyst* is especially significant. Sammy was succeeded by Colin Leach, then of J. Henry Schroder Wagg. Colin had been a regular contributor for some time, both on such topics as 'The Weight of New Money' – which was to become a series – and as editor of the book pages.

In the 1970s, *The Investment Analyst* continued to reflect the investment community's main preoccupations: inflation accounting was discussed by J. R. Grinyer, R. S. Allen and C. I. P. Roberts; rights issues brought articles from Barry Riley, I. R. Woods and P. A.

Harding; convertible stocks were assessed by A. P. Bird, L. C. L. Skerratt and D. E. Purdy. Throughout the period, the society published its own comments on such matters as the Royal Commission on the Distribution of Income and Wealth, the Morpeth Committee and the Wilson Committee.

Colin Leach remained in the editor's chair until 1979, when he left to take up a post at Pembroke College, Oxford. Paul Richards, a frequent contributor, was appointed as the new editor. Paul had written papers on 'Risk Analysis in the North Sea' (with A. Contesse), 'Investment Pricing in the North Sea' and 'Share Performance Among Pension Funds'. Paul was assisted by Robin Dunham – who wrote on technical developments within the profession – and the latter is still very much involved with *Professional Investor*.

In 1980, the Unlisted Securities Market was launched, and over the next few years several articles were published charting its progress: Messrs Keef, Herbert and Murphy were prominent among the essayists. General Elections and share price performance were discussed in two articles by D. A. Peel, P. F. Pope and K. Walters. Stockbrokers' earnings and profit forecasts were probed by A. E. Cooper and Basil Taylor, P. Atrill and E. McLaney; and technical analysis was not forgotten, with dissertations on the Random Walk Hypothesis by J. C. B. Cooper and Dr J. C. Dodds. Inflation accounting still exercised a number of minds, including those of S. M. Keane and A. P. Thomson.

However, important changes were in the offing. Many members of the Society expressed concern that *The Investment Analyst* had become too 'academic', even esoteric; research papers dominated its pages, with few articles from practitioners. As a result, a committee was appointed under the chairmanship of Paul Richards to investigate means by which the journal could broaden its scope without losing its primary function of producing research-based material.

The committee concluded that a balance of research papers, news, profiles of people within the profession, society activities and overseas developments was both a desirable and a realistic aim.

George Littlejohn's Corporate Finance Publishing gave an impressive presentation, with a clear interpretation of the committee's ideas. Corporate Finance Publishing became the publisher of the renamed *Professional Investor* (*PI*), with George as the editor. It was launched in October 1989. *The Investment Analyst* had appeared quarterly, but the new journal would be published ten times a year.

Over the next three years or so, there were features on the new East European markets, as well as extensive coverage of global security; the pensions industry was analysed and the bond market explained; accounting practice was rigorously examined by Geoffrey Holmes and Alan Sugden, and environmental issues were given greater prominence as we all became more aware of their implications for the investment analyst and fund manager.

Barry Riley, Robert Heller, Anthony Hilton and Stephen Lewis contributed monthly columns, and Robin Griffiths' technical analysis was an excellent counterpoint to the fundamentalist approach. Robin Dunham was news editor during this period, and Colin Leach's perceptive reviews continued to grace the book pages.

But George's editorship ended sadly. Internal problems at Corporate Finance led to the company withdrawing as publishers of *PI*, and George resigned as editor.

Following his departure in 1993, *PI* was produced in-house with Paul Hewitt as editor. Members of the journal committee took responsibility for specific areas: IIMR news, the people page and book reviews. It worked remarkably well, but it was a temporary measure and a new publisher was actively sought. After considering numerous submissions, the committee appointed Blackwell Publishers of Oxford, and they began production in January 1994. Blackwell had an impressive book list – with sundry titles in the business and finance field – and they wanted to expand into financial magazine publication. The omens were good.

Initially, Paul Hewitt remained as editor, but in April 1994 Lynn Strongin Dodds was recruited to the position. An experienced journalist who had worked for Reuters in the USA and had written for many UK newspapers, Lynn joined on a part-time basis, but soon became the full-time editor.

Unfortunately, the Blackwell connection was brief, and the company resigned as publishers in the summer of 1994. Given the experience with external publishers, the Institute's management committee decided to revert to in-house production.

Lynn edited *PI* for three years, and during her tenure coverage of the derivatives market increased – Alex Carpenter contributed a monthly column on the subject – and there were regular features on European and Far Eastern economies. Pension fund performance, venture capital, ethical investment and global custody were prominent on the features pages, and, in the mid-1990s, Eddie George outlined his thinking on EMU. Also, David Smith of the *Sunday Times* became a regular columnist on economic matters.

In 1997, John Goodchild and Clive Callow were appointed joint editors, and production of *PI* shifted to the Institute's headquarters in Ironmonger Lane. The design and production editor is now Catriona Dickson, who originally worked on *PI* at Corporate Finance Publishing, and she has helped to give the journal a new, fresher look. The content has expanded to include greater environmental coverage, but the emphasis has remained on high-quality research material from university departments and, increasingly, leading legal and accounting bodies. The reprinting of past articles from the archives of *The Investment Analyst* and *PI* has led directly to the preparation of this collection of essays.

From its first issue, *The Investment Analyst* provided a forum for the discussion of new ideas; *PI* inherited that mantle. The quality of the published research – both theoretical and applied – has been consistently high, with writers ranging from dons to industrialists, politicians to actuaries, and, of course, investment analysts.

Faced with the sheer volume of material that has appeared over a period of nearly 40 years, the task of selection has proved daunting, and unfortunately there are many writers who have been omitted for reasons of space. Hopefully, they will appear in a subsequent collection, for in truth we have been faced with an embarrassment of riches.

Given this dilemma, we applied certain criteria: the importance of the article in the context of its time, and the excellence of the writing. (With regard to the former point, we found that many of the earlier contributions had retained their relevance to current investment thought – for example J. G. Blease's essay on 'Computers as an Aid to Investment Analysis', November 1961.)

During its history, the journal has received brickbats as well as plaudits, and articles have provoked indignation, even wrath. However, it has rarely failed to stimulate. We hope that this collection does likewise.

John Goodchild
Clive Callow
March 2000

Part I
The 1960s

1 Computers as an Aid to Investment Analysis

J. G. BLEASE*

This article was published in The Investment Analyst *in November 1961, at which time there were signs that a combination of changing economic and political conditions would bring a greater competitive edge to trading, and a more scientific approach would be needed in the analysis of individual companies, sectors and the UK economy as a whole. Computers were not unknown in brokers' offices, but their use was limited; the application to analysis and management was negligible. Mr Blease's essay was a timely assessment of their potential in the evaluation of ordinary shares and gilt-edge securities. The result, he concludes, would be an improvement in the quality of investment judgements.*

Graham Blease was an important figure in the early days of The Society of Investment Analysts. He served on the Editorial Committee of the Journal during the late 1960s and early 1970s, and was a leading advocate of the use of computers in the development of investment analysis. When this paper was published, Graham Blease was Investment Officer at the BOAC/BEA Pensions Fund.

At a time when electronic computers have been rapidly gaining acceptance within industry, the City has been noticeably slow to adapt these machines to the various facets of its own work, and it is only during the last year or so that the possibilities for using them in relation to investment analysis, in particular, have been investigated. Nevertheless, a certain amount of useful work is now being undertaken and, of more importance, some of the potentialities for the future are becoming apparent.

In view of these developments it may be appropriate at this stage to summarise briefly what has already been achieved and to consider in general terms a number of possible developments. The use of computers for office work, including the preparation of contract notes and accounting in Brokers and Jobbers' offices, is not included in this survey, nor is the question of calculating portfolio market values. Progress is being made in both these directions but here the computer is considered strictly in relation to how it can help with the problems of investment analysis and management.

WHERE COMPUTERS CAN HELP

The student of investment analysis must be excused a feeling of some disappointment at the present state of the techniques of his trade. There has undoubtedly been progress since the War, particularly as a result of the 1948 Companies Act, but the rate of advancement has been slow. He has to accept that investment analysis is inexact involving ultimately a

* The author is indebted to the Trustees of the BOAC/BEA Pension Fund and to Professor Richard Stone for permission to publish some of the material contained in this article.

judgement, but he may be startled by the unscientific approach to the formation of these judgements that characterises much of the work currently undertaken. Too little thought has been given to developing new techniques, progress towards standardisation of terms and methods has been disappointing, too many decisions are made on superficial yardsticks and insufficient use made of the very large flow of statistical information available from industry and the Government; few attempts have been made to rationalise comparative studies in what is, after all, an exercise in alternative choice.

This state of affairs is particularly unfortunate since the problems facing the investment analyst are currently becoming more difficult and the disciplines available will have to meet new challenges. Changing economic and political conditions are promising to bring a degree of competitive trading for industry not previously seen in the post-war period, due to new thinking on liberalising international trade, the crumbling of such defences as restrictive price agreements and re-sale price maintenance, as well as a quickening pace of technological change. The time has passed when a reasonable investment performance could be obtained by purchasing a wide spread of shares in the hope that the effect of failures might be concealed by the whole stock market moving upward under the influence of inflation and an excess level of demand in the economy.

It seems that computers may be able to help in this situation in the following ways:—

(1) They can collate existing information and make it available in a systematic and concise manner enabling it to be assimilated more quickly.
(2) They can produce information not previously attainable due to complexities of calculation, excessive cost and length of time required.
(3) They can attempt to measure the extent that the future is being discounted in the present, giving an indication of the expected performance that is implicitly being accepted in current thinking.

If these three functions of the computer can be developed successfully it could mean an important step forward in analytical techniques, for knowledge of the past and present could be extended, the area of unknowns reduced, future assumptions quantified and judgements made more rational as a result.

Some examples of these functions are tentatively developed in the paragraphs that follow, subdivided between Ordinary Share and Gilt-Edge analysis.

ORDINARY SHARES

Computer applications in Ordinary Share analysis can be most conveniently considered in three principal areas of study – technical analysis, fundamental industry analysis and fundamental company analysis. The following notes deal with each of these in turn.

TECHNICAL ANALYSIS

Technical analysis is assumed to cover the study of the market position of a share, including price, price history, price 'patterns', dividend and earnings indexes, dividend and earnings yields and yield ratios, the changes in status they indicate, and share activity. Work in this area is already being done on a computer by the Investment Department of a large Pension Fund, and a brief summary of the main aspects of this programme may be of interest.

Two principal series of figures are produced once a week, namely indexes and ratios, and representative examples of these are shown in Chart I. The indexes comprise three relatives for price, dividend and earnings for each of 650 companies. On the basis of the '£100 invested' principle they express the current situation as a percentage of a base-date figure which, in this case, is 30 June 1960. The price index shows the true performance in terms of market value of the investor's £100, and is adjusted for all capitalisation changes, including 'rights' issues, where the basis used is the generally accepted principle of reinvesting the proceeds from the sale of 'new' shares; the dividend index gives a true picture of the proportionate growth or decline of the dividend received on this investment, and the earnings index shows the proportionate change in ordinary earnings attributable to the investment after capitalisation changes and, of course, in terms of the last available earnings figures published by the Company. Examples of points illustrated by these statistics can be enumerated:—

(1) the use of indexes and a common base-date for all three variables of price, dividend and earnings facilitates rapid and accurate comparative studies between Companies, taking into account all appropriate adjustments. As an example, the recent figures for a group of Steel companies were as follows:—

	Price Index	Dividend Index	Earnings Index
Colvilles	71.1	115.1	90.2
Dorman Long	62.7	100.0	107.7
Lancashire Steel	70.4	115.8	113.5
SCOW	75.1	111.1	144.2
Stewarts	96.2	142.0	162.6
J. Summers	65.4	103.4	112.0
United Steel	86.7	110.8	123.8

(30.6.60 = 100 in all cases)

They readily illustrate a degree of divergency in performance not easily seen in the more usual figures.

(2) adjustments to historical price 'highs' and 'lows' to allow for capital changes are unnecessary. In the charts for Metal Box, ICI and Bowater, adjustments for rights issues have been incorporated in the price indexes and no further calculations need to be made.

(3) the real value to the investor of a rights issue below the market price accompanied by a maintained dividend or a revised forecast is shown. For instance, the Metal Box rights issue brought a 12½ per cent increase of income and the Bowater issue a 5½ per cent increase.

(4) on the conservative assumption that new money earns nothing, the extent to which rights issues dilute earnings and the length of the interval before these are restored is also shown. In the case of Metal Box the results for the year ended 31 March 1960 showed an increase in earnings of 17 per cent but the index was subsequently reduced to 102.7 by the rights issue in December 1960. The results for the year ended 31 March 1961 restored most of this fall. This was not true for Bowater.

(5) situations where dividends have risen at a faster rate than earnings, or have been unaccompanied by earnings increases, are quickly shown. A general trend of this nature has been a feature of the last few years with increased payout ratios and reduced dividend cover. Such a trend is better shown over a longer period than depicted on the charts, but the tendency is seen short-term in Bowater and APCM.

After the calculation of Company data the next stage in the computer programme is the aggregating of this material into a series of groups to form industry indexes; the result is a group arithmetic average with market value as the basis of individual company weighting.

CHART I.

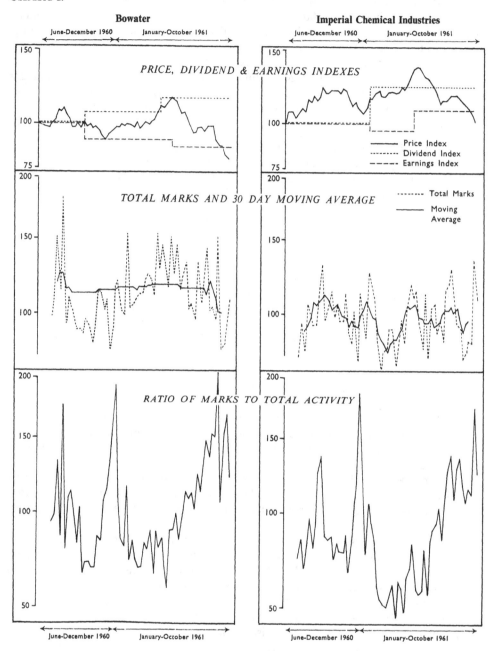

Indexes of price, dividend and earnings are produced for 45 industry groups and examples for the Pharmaceutical and Steel industries are shown in Chart II. The calculation of these figures permits comparison between an individual company and the industry group of which it forms part, and between separate industries.

As a final stage in the construction of the index a further aggregating of the industry groups is undertaken to form a Total Share Index. This comprises nearly all the shares

CHART I.—*contd.*

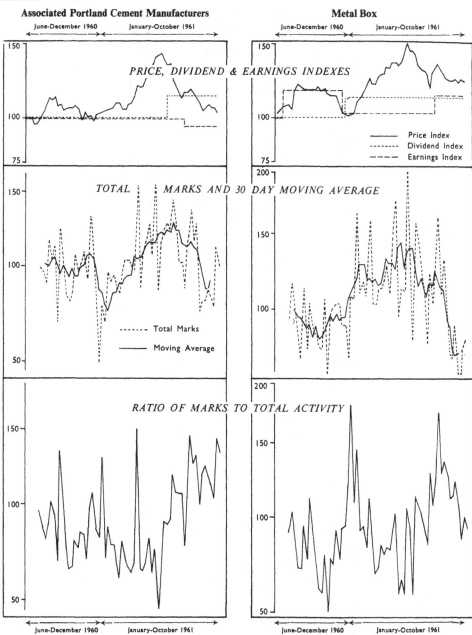

studied in the industry groups and is the most comprehensive index produced in the UK. It is an arithmetic average, weighted in terms of market value, covering just over 80 per cent of the value of the principal ordinary share groups on the London Stock Exchange. The progress of this index since base-date is shown in Chart II. As with the earlier examples Total Dividend and Earnings Indexes are produced as well as a Price Index and these have formed extremely interesting indicators of general trends; it is noteworthy, for instance,

CHART II.

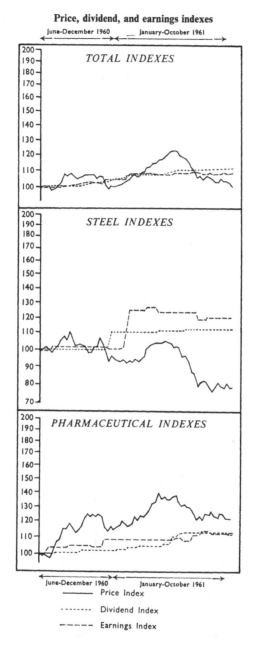

Price, dividend, and earnings indexes

June-December 1960   January-October 1961

TOTAL INDEXES

STEEL INDEXES

PHARMACEUTICAL INDEXES

June-December 1960   January-October 1961

——————— Price Index

· · · · · · · · · Dividend Index

— — — — — Earnings Index

that the earnings index flattened out quite early in 1961, preceding the abrupt change of trend in the price index by several months. The dividend index is particularly valuable as it makes available for the first time an indication of the true rate of growth of dividend payments after allowing for new capital issues, tax changes and similar factors. This index approach to the measurement of dividend growth gives results that are rather different than those derived from the Financial Times Summary of Company Accounts, where no such adjustments are made.

Comparable figures from the two sources for the last half of 1960 and the first half of 1961 were:—

	Computer Dividend Index	Financial Times Summary of Company Accounts
	% rise for the period at annual rate	% increase in cash amount of dividends over same period in previous year
July–December 1960	11.8	20.1
January–June 1961	9.4	15.2

Because of its method of construction the computer index has one further important merit – that of providing a realistic yardstick for measuring the performance of portfolios. This applies not only to the price, dividend and earnings indexes of the total Index, but also to the industry sub-group figures.

Apart from this material on indexes, the computer also produces weekly data on yields and yield ratios. For companies, industry groups and the total index, dividend and earnings yields are calculated; subsequently each company yield is expressed as a percentage of the yield on the industry group of which it is a member, and of the yield on the total index. This ratio or status is stored in the 'memory' and a history is built up of the range through which the ratio moves. If the current ratio is at or near a previous 'high' or 'low' the computer programme is instructed to throw up a special signal on the tabulation indicating an extreme position that may be of particular interest. The historical range in the 'memory' can be varied on a basis of calendar years, or for an individual company, the period between dividend declaration dates.

These ratios are calculated for dividend and earnings yields and examples of the ratios against the total index are shown on Chart III for the period since 30 June 1960; additionally, annual ranges of dividend yield ratios are shown for the 4½ preceding years. The use of dividend yield ratios as a measure of relative status and as an indication of change of status is becoming more widely accepted. Examples of uses are:—

(i) The extent of the price movement required to restore the position, following, say, a dividend change or a rights issue, can be estimated. The Metal Box dividend ratio illustrates this point, for after the rise in the ratio during ex-rights dealings, the price moved quite quickly to restore the original relative position.

(ii) The ratio can be used as a basis for estimating the extent of a dividend change discounted by the market. Immediately prior to the APCM dividend announcement the price appeared to be discounting a 12 per cent to 15 per cent increase in payment. The actual increase was 14 per cent.

(iii) Movements of share prices involving a sudden change of status become quickly apparent and can be followed by an immediate investigation of all relevant material available to the analyst. This signal may, therefore, reveal a special short-term opportunity, or the first move in a general change of status for the share. The analyst with his background knowledge derived from a study of the industry and company position must decide which of these alternatives is the most likely. The ratio movement has merely drawn his attention to the changed situation.

CHART III.

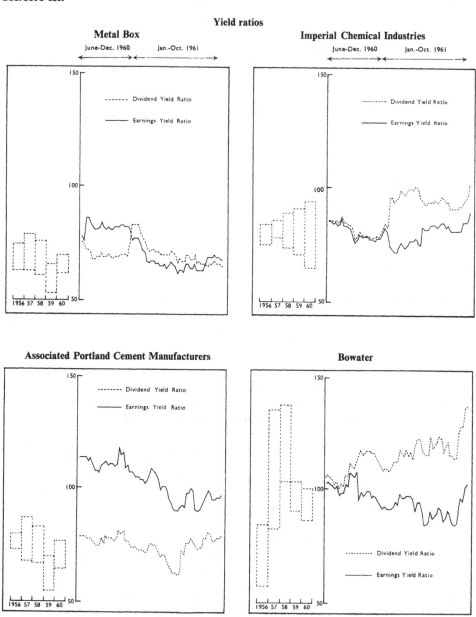

These considerations apply to dividend yield ratios; earnings yield ratios are not so widely used and they have been calculated only recently for the first time. The scant attention afforded to earnings yields is borne out in the charts showing earnings yield ratios; shares are clearly not yet being valued on the basis of any rational earnings capitalisation rate. In the case of Bowater no dividend increase is being anticipated and status is deteriorating, but in terms of earnings an optimistic view is implied with an indication of maintained or slightly increased figures.

Quite apart from the regular compilation of the data described above, the existence of the basic material in card form has enabled a number of supplementary exercises to be undertaken with little extra effort. One field of activity has been the preparation of lists of all the constituent Companies of the Index in order of descending or ascending price indexes since base-date, to show the best performing shares. This is varied to show lists of proportionate movements between any two dates, covering periods of, say, sharply rising or falling prices and demonstrating performance under differing market conditions. Similar lists are constructed classifying the Companies in order of ascending dividend and earnings yields. These are essentially sorting operations but produce interesting results without the tedious and expensive clerical effort normally involved in this type of work.

A second supplementary activity has been the construction of a series of indexes to show trends in groups of shares classified in accordance with certain criteria, in an endeavour to throw light on Stock Market behaviour and to test some of the widely held beliefs on yield, cover, growth and similar dogma. The criteria used for selecting the groups are shown in Table I together with results including yields at base-date; indexes for price, dividend and earnings have been constructed in a similar manner to those mentioned earlier and in all cases the results are for June 1961 with June 1960 as base-date. This test period is clearly too short a time on which to base any firm conclusions, but the results of the exercise have been included as an example of the scope of computer applications.

TABLE I. Special indexes.

Share Characteristics at Base-Date (30.6.60)	Base-Date Dividend Yield	Base-Date Earnings Yield	Indexes at June 1961 Price	Dividend	Earnings
1. Low dividend yields (up to 3¼%)	2.78	6.7	135.5	119.9	113.8
2. High dividend yields (over 5½%)	6.34	10.7	100.1	101.8	110.6
3. Low earnings yields (up to 7%)	3.59	5.7	127.6	112.8	119.1
4. High earnings yields (over 12%)	4.93	14.4	106.0	109.7	106.8
5. Small companies (Net Tangible Assets from £2.43m. to £4m.)	4.38	9.7	114.5	115.0	109.1
6. Large companies (Net Tangible Assets over £15m.)	4.06	8.5	118.5	112.5	115.3
7. High growth companies (Five year compound dividend growth rates of over 14 per cent p.a.)	3.77	8.5	124.4	114.5	115.6
8. Low growth companies (Five year compound dividend growth rates of under 5 per cent p.a.)	5.35	9.2	106.0	103.1	110.4
Total Index	**4.12**	**9.2**	**119.6**	**111.8**	**109.7**

Some comments on the results can be made:—

(1) The performance of the low yielders exceeded that of the high yielders by a substantial margin in terms of capital value and dividend increases, but, significantly, the difference in earnings performance was far less marked.

(2) Low earnings yield shares beat high earnings yield shares on all counts. It is difficult to reconcile this with advice to buy high earnings yields that is sometimes proffered.

(3) The comparison of small and large companies is interesting. At base-date the larger companies offered slightly lower dividend and earnings yields, and they sub-

TABLE II. Special Indexes.

Base-Date 30.6.60 Share Characteristics	Dividend Yield	Earnings Yield	Market 'High' 17.5.61					Market 'Low' 12.7.61					% Change in Price Index
			Dividend Yield	Earnings Yield	Price Index	Dividend Index	Earnings Index	Dividend Yield	Earnings Yield	Price Index	Dividend Index	Earnings Index	
Low Dividend Yields (up to 3¼%)	2.78	6.7	2.35	5.3	141.1	119.7	111.4	2.72	6.2	122.6	120.1	112.7	−13.1
High Dividend Yields (over 5½%)	6.34	10.7	6.13	11.5	103.1	102.1	109.9	6.95	13.1	91.0	101.6	110.8	−11.7
Minimum Ratios (near to minimum dividend yield ratios at 30.6.60)	3.17	8.5	2.91	7.8	133.7	122.7	121.8	3.67	8.8	110.1	127.3	113.0	−17.7
Maximum Ratios (near to maximum dividend yield ratios at 30.6.60)	5.26	10.1	4.63	9.2	116.7	104.3	106.3	5.33	10.5	101.6	104.3	105.7	−12.9
Total Index	**4.12**	**9.2**	**3.66**	**8.2**	**124.4**	**111.2**	**109.6**	**4.30**	**9.5**	**106.9**	**112.2**	**109.9**	**−14.1**

sequently provided a superior capital appreciation. In distribution terms the small companies paid out increased dividends that were not matched by the same increase in earnings, whereas the larger companies followed a more cautious policy paying out a smaller dividend increase but one that was more than matched by the rise in earnings. They achieved a larger increase in earnings than the small companies and a larger increase than the market average. There is little in these figures to support a general policy of buying a range of small companies.

A further series of indexes has been constructed in Table II to show comparative performance at different market levels of four groups of shares with varying characteristics at base-date; the criteria selected and the figures for base-date are shown on the left, the second series of figures reflect the peak in the market reached in May 1961, and the third series are for July 1961, by which time a sharp setback had removed a large part of the earlier gain. Interest here centres on the price indexes, and percentage price falls for the four groups between May and July are given in the right-hand column. The low yielders showed an impressive performance in the boom but were, surprisingly, only slightly more vulnerable in the fall than the high yielders, with the result that by July they could still show a useful appreciation of 22.6 per cent against a loss of 9 per cent for the high yielders. This is all the more surprising when the earnings figures are compared. The comparison of groups based on shares giving, respectively, maximum and minimum ratios at base-date is not conclusive. Minimum ratio companies provided the better price performance and a much superior dividend growth, but were very much more volatile in falling markets and suffered in particular from a fall in earnings. The maximum ratio companies improved their status slightly over the period (dividend yield ratio falling from 128 to 124) but the minimum companies lost status (the ratio rising from 77 to 85). It must be remembered here that the sole criteria for inclusion in these groups was the yield ratio position at base-date and that no further selectivity on grounds of quality or judgement was undertaken.

The above outlines some of the work already being done on a regular basis with the aid of a computer but it is possible that much more can be done to help the technical analyst.

One area for further study is share activity. The absence of volume figures for the London Stock Exchange has inhibited work in this direction and there is a widespread belief that very little can be learned from the information available on marks. But it can be argued that an investigation into marks and their correlation with price movements may yet yield something of interest. Data on activity based on marks is shown for four companies in Chart I. Three series of figures are produced:—

(a) A weekly total of marks as a percentage of a base-date period. This produces a curve with extreme fluctuations.

(b) A moving average of these figures designed to eliminate the larger movements.

(c) A curve expressing the company's figures as a proportion of the total market, thereby eliminating the effect of general trends from the individual company picture.

This is an ideal computer application because very large numbers of calculations are necessary if a useful range of companies is included in the survey. It is difficult to draw conclusions from the small pilot study so far undertaken but these are some interesting points:—

(1) expressing marks as a ratio of a base-date period permits easier comparisons between stocks that could not be undertaken by reference to the actual figures;

(2) the Companies shown are four market leaders and it is noteworthy that in terms of relative activity, interest in these stocks did not decline so much as in the general market during the fall in activity at the end of 1960;

(3) activity in these shares did not rise in line with the general trend in the boom that lasted until May 1961 – the relative figures all declined during this period;

(4) similarly, when the general level of activity started to decline after May, activity in these leaders fell very much less.

This work is at an early stage of development, but it is hoped that further experiments can be undertaken with the aid of a computer, and that perhaps in due course it may be possible to incorporate volume figures if they are made available.

Other possibilities in the area of technical analysis include further calculations derived from price movements, comprising ratios between the Company price index and the Total price index, moving averages of these indexes, comparisons with historical ranges, correlation of market performance with dividend and earnings growth, and correlation of changes of status with dividend changes.

In this field of technical analysis it is not suggested that the material being produced on existing programmes, or the further developments envisaged, are in any way original, or that new techniques are involved. The importance of computers in this field lies, rather, in the fact that an extensive volume of data can be presented quickly, systematically, in an easily assimilated form, and that it would be impossible to produce this regularly for the large number of companies covered, without the aid of electronic equipment.

FUNDAMENTAL INDUSTRY ANALYSIS

For the purpose of these notes this area of fundamental analysis is defined as the study of industries and products with which the company is concerned, embracing technical and financial history, the current situation and the prospects. Evaluation of the current situation involves the consideration of such basic elements as the nature of the production system, optimum sizes, cost structures, price structures, import and export relationships and tariffs, and the very large amount of data made available by industry and the Government on costs, volume and stock changes of inputs, price, volume and stock changes of outputs and demand changes in principal markets. An assessment of the prospects includes consideration of technological innovation, changing patterns of expenditure, substitution between products, the consequences of price and income elasticities of demand, barriers to the flow of capital, and the effects of known plans to expand capacity.

In many of these areas a computer, adequately backed by appropriate ancillary equipment, can make an important contribution to extending the knowledge of the investment analyst. In relation to the current situation in industry the flow of statistics is such that the point has now been reached where it is quite impossible for an Investment Manager to keep abreast of all the data covering the companies in his portfolio, let alone companies where he may wish to acquire an interest. It seems that his task would be made easier and the quality of his decisions improved if he is assisted by a team of analysts working with a computer which performs a 'monitoring' function on this flow of material. Similarly, his assessment of the long-term prospects may be improved by the use of rather complicated mathematical and econometric techniques now being developed with the aid of computers.

These concepts of monitoring and forecasting are described in more detail below, together with some of the obvious difficulties.

'MONITORING'

The possibilities under this heading are almost limitless, subject only to the power and capacity of the computer and the consequent cost of operation. Basically, the programme would consist of feeding into the computer all available industrial information relating to a comparatively large number of companies. This would consist of an extensive series of statistical tables relating to production, costs, prices, exports, etc. of the appropriate products, each being updated as fresh information became available, in most cases on a monthly basis. By means of a random access installation or high speed sorting equipment, all the material appertaining to a particular company could be selected and presented at short notice. Further refinements are clearly possible; the computer could not merely store the material but it could check trends, produce moving averages, compare current statistics with previous series, calculate percentage variations and throw up special signals where extreme movements occur. For an individual company the material could thus appear in a concise summary showing percentage movements in a large number of variables tailored to show the current financial year compared with the previous period. In cases where a weighting of input figures is available from the Census of Production, it is quite possible to construct individual indexes of production costs as a further development.

An example of the type of information that can be produced is illustrated in Table III in respect of British Insulated Callender's Cables Ltd. One series of figures compares 1960 with 1959, and a second series shows the first half of 1961 against the first half of 1960. In this case construction of a weighted input cost index has been possible and its use in conjunction with other material as part of a technique for forecasting profits has given reasonably satisfactory results.

Undoubtedly more material could be assembled with further research, but tables of this type can at least suggest something of the general condition existing in a particular industry, and although the extent to which they can be related to a company must vary with individual cases, they provide an extension to background knowledge that would be most valuable in situations where quick decisions are necessary.

There are obvious difficulties in such a system apart from cost and the physical effort of preparing a large volume of input material for the computer. Many of the statistics appear only after a considerable time lag, periods covered vary from monthly to quarterly, there are the problems of multi-product firms and there may be a tendency to expect too close a correlation between what are basically industry figures and an individual company's performance. Nevertheless, the advantages appear to outweigh these factors and a certain amount of tentative experimental work is proceeding along these lines.

FORECASTING

High speed computers are now being used both at Oxford and Cambridge to forecast trends by means of econometric models. Professor Richard Stone of the Department of Applied Economics at Cambridge has constructed an econometric model of growth of the UK economy over the next ten years, and although this valuable work is still at an experimental stage a brief description of the procedure is set out below in view of its very great interest to analysts.

The object of the model is to study the effects on different sectors of the economy and on import/export relationships of various assumed rates of overall growth of consumption. The model proceeds in the following way. Consumption is assumed to grow by a given amount, of, say, 3 per cent per annum. The resultant total figure of consumption in 1970 is then subdivided between the principal classifications of public and private sector expenditure including food, drink, housing, durables, motors, clothing, education, health, roads, police, etc., and additionally, exports and capital investment. The effects of this pattern of consumption on final demands on industry is then worked back by means of an advanced computer technique using input-output tables and demand and production functions, so that growth rates, assuming a balanced overseas payments position, are obtained for seventeen industry groups.

TABLE III. Industry statistics. British Insulated Callender's Cables Ltd.

		ANNUAL FIGURES			HALF YEARLY FIGURES			Source Number
	Unit	Year to Dec. 1959	Year to Dec. 1960	% Change 1959–1960	6 months to June 1960	6 months to June 1961	% Change 1960–1961	
SERIES I – INPUTS								
(a) Prices								
Average price of spot copper	£ per ton	237.8	245.8	+3.4	256.1	229.3	–10.5	1
Average price of lead and alloys	£ per ton	70.8	72.1	+1.8	75.6	65.5	–13.4	1
Average price of aluminium	£ per ton	180.0	186.0	+3.3	186.0	186.0	–	1
Average price of rubber	d. per lb.	30.0	32.2	+7.3	36.1	25.3	–29.9	1
Price index of iron and steel	Index No.	128.9	128.5	–0.3	128.3	129.0	+0.5	2
Price index of paper and board	Index No.	108.8	108.6	–0.2	108.4	109.9	+1.4	2
Price index of plastics and synthetic resins	Index No.	90.3	88.8	–1.7	89.4	86.5	–3.2	2
Price index of other materials	Index No.	115.6	116.8	+1.0	116.9	117.5	+0.5	2
Wages index	Index No.	173.5	185.3	+6.8	173.5	185.3	+6.8	3
Weighted price index of inputs		100	103.5	+3.5	100	95.2	–4.8	
(b) Volume								
Labour employed in industry	000's	60.5	61.2	+1.2	61.4	61.9	+8.1	4
Total UK consumption of copper	Tons	633,166	722,593	+14.1	374,620	356,058	–5.0	5
Total UK imports of copper	Tons	556,373	439,972	–21.9	274,734	287,537	+4.7	6
Imports of copper from Canada	Tons	75,055	106,479	+41.9	53,109	53,867	+1.4	6
Imports of copper from Rhodesia	Tons	228,249	248,967	+9.1	124,060	140,070	+12.9	6
Deliveries of aluminium wire in UK	Tons	24,250	19,194	–20.9	10,031	9,991	–0.4	5
Deliveries of aluminium bars, rods and sections in UK	Tons	38,293	48,857	+27.6	24,238	24,237	–	5
(c) Stocks								
Change in stocks of copper during period	% change Tons	–7.0	+108.1	N/A	+29.8	+26.9	N/A	5

SERIES II – OUTPUT

(a) Value or Quantity

UK deliveries of insulated wires and cables	£M.	116.8	135.5	+16.0	67.1	75.5	+12.5	1
UK exports of cables—								
All cables	Tons	85,601	74,074	-13.5	40,903	38,794	-5.2	6
Telephone cables	Tons	30,752	16,617	-46.0	10,597	7,855	-25.9	6
Paper insulated cables	Tons	29,180	29,914	+2.5	15,975	14,823	-7.2	6
Rubber insulated cables	Tons	10,797	9,452	-22.5	4,879	5,259	+7.8	6
Thermoplastic insulated cables	Tons	8,141	9,284	+14.0	5,375	5,688	+5.8	6
UK production of copper wire	Tons	231,062	271,279	+17.4	145,258	131,814	-9.3	5
UK production of copper rods, bars and sections								
(a) rolled	Tons	5,989	6,004	+0.3	3,011	2,338	-22.4	5
(b) extruded	Tons	13,637	15,260	+11.9	7,762	9,327	+20.2	5
(b) Stocks	% change							
Change in stocks of copper wire rods during period	tons	-25.3	+22.9		-24.0	-22.2		5
Change in stocks of refined copper wire during year	Tons	-43.3	+149.3		+69.8	+27.3		5

SERIES III – SELECTED FINAL DEMAND INDICATORS

UK consumption of copper wire rods	Tons	218,973	232,485	+6.2	120,468	125,136	+3.9	5
Deliveries of electric generating plant and associated equipment	£M.	295.5	312.0	+5.6	154.2	–	–	1
Completed houses in UK	No.	281,568	304,255	+8.1	146,969	147,762	+0.5	1

(1) Sources: 1 = *Monthly Digest of Statistics*.
2 = *Board of Trade Journal*.
3 = *Guardian Wage Index* (based on wage rates not earnings).
4 = *Ministry of Labour Gazette*.
5 = *British Bureau of Non-Ferrous Metal Statistics*.
6 = *Trade and Navigation Accounts*.
(2) Weighting in price index of inputs is based on 1954 Census of Production.
Note: Wages
Since annual averages are not available the wage indexes quoted for 1959 and 1960 are those prevailing in January 1960 and 1961 respectively. The rates used in the half year calculations are those applying to June 1960 and June 1961. The apparent inconsistency is therefore explained by the timing of the increase in wage rates.

Further development of the techniques and improvement of the relationships, particularly regarding substitution and productivity, is foreseen, and clearly much experimental work remains to be done. Nevertheless, the merits of such an exercise are obvious; the effects on industries and on the level of capital investment of a range of alternative overall growth rates and a choice of consumer expenditure patterns can be studied. It can show how indicated growth in different sectors compares with known expansion plans, it draws attention to the possibility of bottlenecks in the system, and conceivably it could go some way to preventing excesses or shortages of productive capacity in some areas of industry. Perhaps this information may lead to a faster growth of the economy and, in any event, it will be important in the context of the present swing towards 'decentralised planning'.

The value to investment analysts is two-fold. Estimates of growth rates in certain industries for given rates of expansion of the economy are important, and conversely, where expansion plans are known, for example, in motors, the model could be made to demonstrate the overall growth of GNP, the patterns of consumer expenditure needed and the effects on other industries, if this planned capacity is to be fully used.

Given the great amount of development still required on the model, is it possible that in the future an exercise of this kind will provide a basis for planning the proportions of investment portfolios held in each industry group? It would certainly seem to be a more reasonable approach than the past or present pattern of industry that is now used as a basis for investment targets by many Funds.

Under fundamental industry analysis the functions of monitoring and forecasting have been considered. Computers may also be of service to analysts in another more remote area, that of collection and interpretation of statistics by Government Departments, including the Board of Trade and the Central Statistical Office. If material on the economic and industrial situation could be made available more quickly, the value of the services would be immeasurably improved. It is to be hoped that studies on the use of computers by these bodies will quickly reach fruition.

FUNDAMENTAL COMPANY ANALYSIS

For the purpose of this discussion fundamental company analysis is defined as a study of factors concerning the companies' financial position including historical, current and projected trends. This area covers all the conventional measures and ratios, including growth of dividends, earnings, history of Profit and Loss Accounts and Balance Sheets, gearing, liquidity, taxation matters, trade investments, cash flows, sources and uses of cash, pay out ratios, earnings on capital employed and so on.

At first sight this does not appear to be a promising field for computer work but useful, if limited, applications seem possible in certain areas; three uses in relation to historical, current and projected situations are briefly considered below.

An historical application now being undertaken is the monitoring of the financial records of a very large number of Companies in order to select smaller groups that have certain characteristics in common. Once the historical records have been incorporated in the programme any number of groups based on different criteria can be selected. An example has been a study of Companies of over a certain size, giving continuity of dividend payments and an average annual growth rate of adjusted earnings that exceeds the average market performance by a predetermined amount. The programme can be designed to eliminate Companies where there have been severe fluctuations in earnings or where the recent trend has been downward although the overall performance is satisfactory. A further development follows from a regular repetition of the monitoring so that new Companies qualifying by virtue of improving performance can be admitted to the list and others removed where growth has been checked. The result is a constantly up-dated record of Companies giving an above-average performance in terms of recent financial history.

Applications of computers to current financial statistics are less easy but one field is being developed which will make available a range of figures permitting new forms of inter-company comparisons of financial data. Fundamentally, the programme will link Profit and Loss Account data and Balance Sheet data to market price by expressing statistics derived from these sources in terms of a '£100 invested'; as the market price fluctuates such figures as turnover, depreciation, cash flow, capital expenditure, operating assets, quick assets and other factors can be expressed in terms of the amount obtained for the £100 investment. In certain cases of single product firms, the exercise can extend to physical capacity, such as tons of steel, tons of cement, numbers of motor cars and barrels of oil per day, where these figures are obtainable. The value of these statistics will lie in the facility they offer for Company comparisons on the basis of new criteria, providing a further technique of price assessment. In view of the large number of calculations necessary, this would be a difficult task without a computer.

The area of projection analysis appears to be a fruitful field of application for computers although development work is only just starting. The task is not to attempt a forecast of a company's growth but to develop techniques for assessing rates of dividend growth implied in current prices, or rates of dividend growth needed to reach certain targets. When these have been established it is logical to work back from the future dividend expected to the rate of earnings required to support this level of payment and in turn the growth of assets and profitability rates on assets that are required. It then falls to the analyst to attempt a judgement on the feasibility of this rate of growth of assets and profitability level, given his knowledge of the company's past growth, the industry situation and management attitudes. Surprisingly, this technique appears to be amenable to computer programming and from the work done so far, some very interesting results are likely to develop.

These points have served to illustrate the type of work that a computer may be able to do in the area of fundamental Company analysis. They can be criticised, justifiably, on several grounds, and much development work remains to be done. But they constitute an example of where much thought and research by the analyst may prove rewarding. There are many other instances, such as adaptations of the work of Markowitz, and of von Neumann and Morgenstern on the Theory of Games, and it is to be hoped that effort continues to be applied both in London and New York to the development of these ideas.

GILT-EDGE ANALYSIS

It is probably true that more work is being done on gilt-edge statistics by computers than on any other aspect of the Stock Market. It will suffice here to mention briefly the figures now being regularly computed and to indicate some further developments that have been considered.

Redemption yields, price and yield differences, and price ratios are now being calculated regularly, and are a relatively straightforward application of computers. One result of this work has been that gilt-edge statistics are now available within a larger number of broker firms and little effort is required to obtain the historical records. Surprisingly, computation of the daily gilt-edge price and yield list on a centralised basis, possibly at a computer service bureau, has not yet been achieved. A great deal of competitive and wasteful effort is still expended by many brokers all preparing individual but similar lists.

Other gilt-edge applications designed to assist 'switching' operations are likely to be developed, including new methods of studying relative positions of stocks. Perhaps the most interesting of these is a projection exercise enabling the performance of stocks in terms of capital and income to be compared under various market conditions. Yield curves of different shapes and levels can be postulated at successive intervals in the future and the proportionate price changes easily demonstrated, allowing for variations in coupons and maturity dates. The analyst must decide the possible future shape and level of the curve on the basis of his own judgement.

Another development under the same heading is the calculation of 're-investment' yields, which are an accepted criteria for assessing the advisability of switching between stocks of widely differing maturity dates. They involve the calculation of the price at which a longer dated stock must stand when a shorter stock matures, in order to ensure that a switch between the two 'breaks even' at the earlier maturity date. Again, the analyst must decide for himself whether or not the price and the consequent yield are reasonable.

It can be seen from these examples that the application of the computer to the Gilt-Edge market does not merely alleviate the drudgery of extensive routine calculations but it also enables the production at frequent intervals of complicated statistical material not previously available.

CONCLUSION

Sceptics will suggest that attempts to introduce computers into investment analysis over-simplify the problems facing investors and that no substitute is available for flair, judgement and sense of timing. The importance of these qualities is unreservedly accepted but if some of the techniques discussed here can be further developed, they will have the effect of presenting more information in a logical and easily assimilated form, enabling the quality of judgements to be improved and perhaps making a small contribution towards raising the standard of investment management.

2 Economic Forecasting and Investment Analysis

J. G. MORRELL

This article appeared in The Investment Analyst *in December 1962. James Morrell writes: The article was written to illustrate some of the features of the mooted and ill-fated national plan. Politicians (and forecasters) seldom make allowance for unforseen shocks, which turn up on average every four years. The national statistics contain as many hazards now – if not more – as then, and my pious hope in the last paragraph about computers is still thwarted by the shortage of hard facts. At the time, I was under the spell of Richard Stone's Cambridge computer growth model.*

James Morrell began his forecasting career with Ford in 1955. He joined Phillips & Drew in 1957, and began collaborating with economists in other firms to produce forecasts. He went on to form his own forecasting company and then the Henley Centre for Forecasting in 1974. He served as economic adviser to the Charterhouse Group for over 30 years. He has published extensively, recently completing A Short Guide to the 21st Century.

'There is no reason for the defeatist view that to make the effort and get the wrong answer will lead to a worse result than if no effort at all were made. We have to risk such a result, in all economic policy as well as in much else of life. Most capital planning, both public and private, has to be based on assumptions equally shrouded in the mists of time.'

Thus wrote Professor Sayers in a recent article[1] on forecasting the 'equilibrium' rate of interest some years ahead. These remarks apply equally well to the whole field of economic forecasting.

For the investment analyst, every judgement about the price of a security involves a view about the future, and whether this is consciously admitted or not each man's assumptions are part of his own private economic forecast. These notions are seldom rationalised, most of us absorbing a climate of opinion from the flow of articles in the financial press. Yet every serious contributor, looking forward at some aspect of the economy, has his own underlying set of assumptions about the economy as a whole. Mr. Harold Rose, for example, showed in the previous issue of this journal[2] projections of company earnings to 1965. Although these were not stated, obviously an economic forecast of the period to 1965 is implicit in each set of estimates.

Of particular interest, we have now been given a preview of the kind of targets which the Office of the National Economic Development Council has so far suggested to match an overall growth rate of 4 per cent per annum for the five year period to 1966. A more elaborate set of assumptions and targets will presumably be available to us in a few months'

---

[1] 'English Policy on Interest Rates, 1958–1962', Banca Nationale del Lavoro Review, June 1962.
[2] 'Company Liquidity Under Strain', August 1962.

time, and one of the objects of this article is to suggest an independent assessment of Britain's economic prospects.

There will be no need to recommend caution to the investment analyst where forecasts are concerned. Most of us have been healthily inoculated with scepticism. Nevertheless, it is as well to make clear at the outset that we do not dispute the ability of that class of investor which 'plays by ear' or 'keeps its nose to the ground'. The 'smell' of the market tells a good bloodhound much of what he wants to know. But the fact is that few investors are 'bloodhounds' and the majority of analysts are compelled to adopt assumptions about the future in order to set the investment scene. Even so some situations, involving small companies for example, may well be analysed without reference to the economic framework at large. We do not claim, therefore, that nothing can be done without an economic forecast. We are concerned here with broader questions, with investment analysis in the round and the problems facing the investment manager charged with framing policy in all spheres.

THE OBJECT OF FORECASTING

The general questions confronting the investment analyst may be summarised as follows:—

  (i)   what is the course of interest rates
  (ii) how is the price level of goods and services likely to move
 (iii) what levels of company profits may be expected
 (iv) how will new issues dilute company earnings
  (v) what relationship will obtain between fixed interest and equity markets
 (vi) do international considerations, such as exchange rates, affect the picture, and
(vii) what kind of timetable is to be expected.

This set of questions involves the whole economy and for an answer we must turn to a second set of questions, namely

 (a) what are the balance of payments prospects
 (b) what is the labour productivity outlook
 (c) what economic growth rate is likely
 (d) what pattern of expenditure may be expected
 (e) what are the trends in saving and investment.

The pattern is a familiar one and there are already a number of forecasts available. As mentioned above, the NEDC has begun to fill in some of the numbers for this kind of model. Yet this is where the problem begins for the NEDC estimates are not forecasts and if they were, should we accept them? In any event we must seriously examine the likelihood of target growth rates being attained. We must test the major assumptions used and where necessary substitute alternatives.

This is of particular importance for there are some astonishing differences of view among experts. To cite instances, Mr. Deakin[1] finds evidence of a declining trend in labour productivity growth in the UK in the period 1948 to 1960. More recently, Professor Paish[2] finds evidence of a rising trend, and employing these trends both authorities are led to quite different conclusions about the future. Without quantifying his views, Mr. Duncan Burn[3] outlines a gloomy panorama of British industry which scarcely accords with Professor

---

[1] 'Exercise in Forecasting the Gross Domestic Product of the United Kingdom to 1970', B. M. Deakin, from 'Europe's Future in Figures', edited R. C. Geary.
[2] 'The Economic Position of the United Kingdom', F. W. Paish, Westminster Bank Review, August 1962.
[3] 'Investment, Innovation and Planning in the United Kingdom', Duncan Burn in 'Progress', the Unilever quarterly, Volume 49, No. 274.

Paish's optimism; whereas Mr. C. T. Saunders[1] in a projection (not a forecast) shows a figure for growth in labour productivity between 1950 and 1960 more optimistic than Mr. Deakin's and finds evidence of a more cheerful nature than Mr. Burn for the future growth in productivity.

Having enjoyed his laugh at the expense of the economists the investment analyst ought at least to attempt to unravel the reasons for these differences and to satisfy himself as to the most probable course of events. The seasoned analyst will have learned the limitations of non-monetary statistics. Periodic revisions of indices, such as the index of industrial production, serve to remind us of the dangers of crediting some of these measures with a spurious accuracy. For this reason the reliability of a series should always be checked before hanging an argument upon it and, in forecasting the gross domestic product, cross checks by other methods are necessary. In the instances referred to above it is possible to work back through the statistics to find both the sources and methods used. Differences in time, later revisions to published statistics, the use of alternative series and the appearance of new series have all contributed to these differences. Once this is understood it is possible to frame independent assumptions and to make independent forecasts.

The usefulness of a forecast for the investment analyst lies, as much as anything, in the lessons learned in handling the sources of information. The methods used in compiling the annual National Income Blue Book are outlined in 'National Income and Statistics: Sources and Methods', prepared by the Central Statistical Office, and although methods of statistical collection are improving many imperfections remain. The positive usefulness of a forecast, however, arises from the attempt to achieve consistency. As instances of this the analyst will be familiar with the arguments concerning the growth potential of the market for consumer durables and the extreme optimism of manufacturers in planning future capacity. In the last year or two many shortages have been eliminated and surplus capacity has emerged. Such situations were foreseeable yet were not foreseen by many investors. Likewise important changes in the public sector are highly probable in the next few years. Changes in this field are not evident until a forecast is constructed and in aggregate are of such importance as to present serious implications for future levels of activity.

THE MAJOR ASSUMPTIONS

The starting point of the forecast must be a statement of assumptions. The NEDC will have been presented with a full statement of assumptions in the first exercise prepared by its officers. For example, it has been assumed that Britain joins the Common Market, that the terms of trade remain level and that we have a balance of payments surplus of £300 million on current account in 1966. Other assumptions may be inferred from the figures released to the press. A substantial rise in labour productivity has been assumed and the next five years are obviously seen as a period of peace. Few people would wish to quarrel with such assumptions at this stage although it would be interesting to know whether a private set of estimates exist, based on an assumption that we do not enter the Common Market. Similarly, alternative assumptions about the terms of trade are necessary. The growing awareness of the dangers to world trade arising from inadequate growth in export income of the world's primary producers may lead to revised marketing systems and an adverse change in the UK's terms of trade.

The assumption about peace is critical. During the 1950's growth rates were low. Yet in the first half of the decade the Korean War had a dramatic impact on the economy. The defence effort of those years strained the economy and checked the rise in productive

---

[1] 'A Ten Year Projection for the British Economy', C. T. Saunders, from 'Europe's Future in Figures'.

investment. In addition the balance of payments suffered acutely from the sharp rise in commodity prices. In the second half of the decade the Suez affair made a further impact on our economic performance. Apart from some distortion of trade a number of highly dubious investment decisions in the energy field were taken in the wake of Suez. If one reckons without such episodes in the future a higher growth rate may appear plausible. On the larger view, however, greater caution should prevail. A glance at a time chart of British history over the past three or four hundred years shows involvement in wars of one kind or another in most decades. We may hope that the growing destructiveness of modern arms may make even localised conflicts less likely in the future, but so far the evidence for such a hope being fulfilled is impressively slender. The Cuban situation is a case in point for an optimistic view whereas the Sino-Indian dispute confirms the dangers at large in the modern world.

A FORECAST BASED ON LABOUR PRODUCTIVITY

Taking the optimistic view of the world situation, what are the chances of attaining a 4 per cent growth rate in the near future? A first approach is to examine what has been happening in terms of output per unit of labour. In the current issue of the Blue Book (National Income and Expenditure, 1962) we find two series of index numbers for gross domestic product at constant prices. These are shown below.

Both methods of measuring GDP have their limitations and it is by no means clear which method is likely to produce the more accurate result. It will be noted that the output method suggests a faster rise in GDP since 1956 than the expenditure method, so much so that if Table 14 alone was consulted it would appear that the growth rate has significantly increased. The more prudent course is to examine an average of the two sets of figures.

Gross domestic product at 1958 factor cost

	Table 13 (expenditure)	Table 14 (output)		Table 13 (expenditure)	Table 14 (output)
1951	86.3	87.0	1957	100.3	99.9
1952	86.4	86.4	1958	100.0	100.0
1953	89.9	89.9	1959	103.2	104.6
1954	93.4	93.8	1960	107.7	109.9
1955	96.4	97.1	1961	110.1	112.1
1956	98.7	98.1			

The GDP series must now be married up with the figures for labour. A new publication, 'Statistics on Incomes, Prices, Employment and Productions'[1], provides much of the raw material including an index of total hours worked. During the 1950's the labour force increased in size, part of the increase being offset by a modest decline in the second half of the decade in the length of the working week. One factor is still missing, namely an estimate of the average number of weeks worked in a year. Here we may only generalise, a movement from one to two weeks' paid holiday a year becoming general early in the 1950's and a gradual trend towards a third week's holiday beginning at the end of the decade.

Taking these factors into account output per manhour increased by 2.3 per cent a year between 1951 and 1961. But in the last five years, between 1956 and 1961, it looks as though

---

[1] A Ministry of Labour publication issued at four monthly intervals to assist those engaged in pay negotiations.

the growth rate rose significantly to 2.7 per cent annum. If the next five years are politically less difficult than the 1950's the growth in labour productivity may rise to between 3.0 and 3.5 per cent per annum, depending of course upon both the quantity and quality of investment and on success in export markets.

For the next decade the Ministry of Labour has provided us with estimates year by year of the size of the labour force. These are based on the Registrar General's estimates of population levels by age groups and the Ministry of Labour's estimates of participation rates for each age group. There will be a useful increase in the labour force in the next few years but in the second half of the decade the rise will virtually cease. In addition to this, some allowance must be made for a shortening of the labour year. Hours worked are slightly longer here than in the Common Market and in every country except Holland there are more statutory paid holidays. Although the Ministry of Labour does not see this as a significant trend[1] we believe that British practice will gradually provide more leisure. Summing these assumptions it appears that over the five year period of the NEDC forecast, 1962–1966, GDP may rise between 3¼ and 3¾ per cent per annum.

THE BALANCE OF PAYMENTS

In theory it ought to be possible to check this estimate against a projection based on capital/output ratios. The difficulty, as the investment analyst knows full well, lies in setting values on the nation's stock of capital. Published estimates so far available are helpful but insufficiently dependable for work of this nature.[2] Therefore our first check on the forecast has to be through a construction of the balance of payments.

The main feature of the British balance of payments is the heavy dependence on the export of manufactured goods. If we first examine exports, particularly of manufactured goods, and estimate likely levels of income from total exports of goods and services we may calculate the level of imports which can be sustained and the volume of GDP which such an import would allow, after providing for a surplus. The pressure to provide aid to under-developed countries seems likely to increase and the need to push up the gold and foreign currency reserves to a safer level in relationship to the sterling area's rising level of trade suggests the need to budget for a large current surplus. The NEDC figure of £300 million is not excessive.

World trade in manufactured goods has been rising rapidly since the War. At the same time the British share of that trade has been steadily declining. In 1962, however, there are indications that the UK is now holding its share of world trade (see the table at the top of the next page).

If British exports have become more competitive and we succeed in holding our present share in aggregate then the prospects are for a much faster rate of growth in exports. Unfortunately the possibility cannot be ruled out that the rate of growth in world trade in manufactured goods will slow down. The great shortage of capital resulting from the Second World War is now coming to an end and over the next five years the growth rate for world imports of manufactured goods may ease back. On a market by market survey it appears that British exports could grow at about 5 per cent per annum in total, permitting a rise in imports of about 3¾ per cent per annum.

Imports must now be analysed by major classes. Manufactured imports tend to rise at

---

[1] See 'Statistics, Incomes, Prices, Employment and Production', September 1962, Section D.7 'Holidays With Pay'.

[2] See 'Net Investment in Fixed Assets in the United Kingdom, 1938–1953', by Philip Redfern, Journal of the Royal Statistical Society, Part 2, 1955, and 'The Replacement Cost of Fixed Assets in British Manufacturing Industry in 1955', by T. Barna, Journal of the Royal Statistical Society, Part 1, 1957.

UK share of total value of exports of manufactures.

	per cent			per cent
1956	18.7	1960	I	16.6
1957	17.8		II	16.2
1958	17.7		III	15.6
1959	17.3		IV	15.5
1960	15.9	1961	I	16.1
1961	15.7		II	15.9
			III	15.7
			IV	15.4
		1962	I	15.1
			II	15.3
			III	15.3

Source: *NIESR review*, Table 23, November, 1962.

substantially above the average rate of growth, food imports nearly in line with population and raw materials, including semi-manufactures, in line with production. Fuel imports rise at a faster rate. This complex of assumptions sets the limit on the rate of growth in GDP permitted by our assumed export performance at 3¼ per cent per annum.

A FORECAST BASED ON EXPENDITURE

In brief we have constructed a picture of the growth in total output. We may now break down the total, compiling separate estimates of the components of expenditure as shown in Table 13 of the Blue Book, backing these with detailed estimates of consumers' expenditure by classes (Table 19), public authorities' expenditure (Departmental white papers), and gross fixed capital formation (Tables 51, 55 and 57). Further reconciliations are involved in each stage but at this point we now have material of real use to the investment analyst.

To take consumers' expenditure, for example, we have expenditure in current prices (Table 18), in 1958 prices (Table 19) and index numbers of prices (Table 20). Apart from the trends in the volume of consumption the relative price movements tell us a great deal, and since trends change gradually rather than suddenly we get useful industry pointers for the future. The following table shows various price indices against an index of all goods and services sold on the home market.

Index Numbers of Prices, 1958 = 100.

	Housing[1]	Motor Vehicles	Running Costs of Vehicles	All Items
1951	67	84	84	78
1953	74	87	94	84
1955	78	88	94	89
1957	87	99	102	97
1959	107	97	101	101
1961	115	94	105	105

[1] Excludes maintenance and improvements, but includes rates and water charges.

The prices of motor vehicles have not risen appreciably because of the strong rise in volume of output and the intensive use of capital. On the other hand the running costs of vehicles, having a higher labour service content, have been close to the average, whereas housing prices have risen more sharply than any other major class of expenditure.

This last point is of extreme importance and a recent article on future housing problems[1] clearly indicated that the movement of housing costs relative to income would effectively limit the demand for new housing unless far-reaching political action is taken to facilitate easier purchase and rentals. A study of the age structure of British housing suggests that by modern social standards a rate of house construction of 400,000 units a year is necessary. If such a rate was established house building and all the associated demand arising from new housing would go a good way towards raising the overall growth rate. The point is worth making since it illustrates the importance of political decisions. Local authorities need greatly increased powers and substantial aid from the central government to facilitate redevelopment of decaying town centres. Therefore higher rates of house building will hinge on effective political action in this field.

HOW MUCH INFLATION?

Movements in relative costs to the consumer are important but to fix the magnitude of price changes we must have some idea of the overall trend in the price level. When external factors such as the 1949 devaluation and the rise of import prices following the Korean War are eliminated and allowance is made for the high degree of post-War liquidity and the low, or negative, level of personal savings in this period, the rates of inflation of the post-War period must be regarded as exceptional. The prospect for the 1960's is for less inflation and for the following reasons:—

(*a*) the marginal propensity to save is rising,
(*b*) public sector savings, notably profit retentions of the nationalized industries, are likely to be at higher levels,
(*c*) the national product is likely to increase at a faster rate, and
(*d*) some form of incomes policy is likely to be introduced.

Even if personal income continues to rise at about the same rate as in the last five years the gap between the gross national money income and the real gross national income is unlikely to average more than 1½ per cent per annum.

Given an assumption as to the overall rate of price change, the changes in prices and expenditure for individual items may be estimated and broadly reconciled. For the analyst it is important to move from estimates at fixed prices into estimates at current prices since a vital aspect of policy is the relationship between equities and fixed interest stocks. If the rate of inflation declines then in order to maintain the same income attraction vis a vis fixed income stocks as in the 1950's the rate of real growth underlying earnings per share must be increased. To judge by equity and fixed interest price movements in recent months the stock market has already made an adjustment in its outlook so far as inflation is concerned. The expectation is for more stable prices of goods and services and a slower rate of profits growth.

---

[1] 'A Long Term View of Housing', L. Needleman, N.I.E.S.R. Review, No. 18, November 1961.

Personal savings (five year aggregates).

Mid Year	Disposable Personal Income	Personal Savings	Savings Ratio	Marginal Increase in		Marginal Propensity to Save
				Income	Savings	
	£000 million		per cent	£000 million		per cent
1948	42.9	0.6	1.5			
1949	45.7	0.5	1.1	2.9	–0.1	–3.9
1951	51.7	1.3	2.5	3.0	0.5	17.9
1953	59.5	2.2	3.7	4.2	0.5	12.6
1955	68.1	3.5	5.1	4.3	0.5	12.4
1957	76.7	4.2	5.5	4.4	0.5	12.0
1959	86.0	6.3	7.3	4.7	1.1	24.0

SAVINGS AND INVESTMENT

Having reconstructed the whole forecast in current prices we may now proceed to an estimation of savings and investment. The financing of investment is summarised in Table 48 of
the Blue Book. An important weakness here is that the figures given for personal savings are
residual items and since the evident strong upward trend is of such great consequence the
series must be treated with considerable caution. The errors can perhaps be minimised by
looking at disposable personal income and personal savings in moving five year aggregates.

The savings ratios given by this method and the marginal propensity to save can both be
seen to be moving comfortably upwards and even on a conservative assumption that the
marginal propensity to save is at a lower level it is still probable that the savings ratio will
rise and the level of personal savings increase.

From an estimate of personal savings we move to an estimate of public authority savings.
The future policies of the Boards of nationalised industries may be inferred from official
pronouncements over the last two years indicating a more commercial attitude towards
investment decisions and financing. Local authorities are unlikely to increase the level of
their savings whilst the Central government, apart from cyclical pump-priming requirements, may be expected on average to increase the proportion of investment to be financed
out of taxation.

On the other side of the account gross fixed capital formation, investment in stocks and
net overseas investment have already been estimated. By implication, therefore, company
savings are derived as the residual item required to finance capital formation, and if the
rising levels of depreciation associated with the rise in gross fixed capital formation are
taken into account, a crude figure for company retained earnings emerges. Although company saving and investment was roughly in balance in 1961, by 1966 the need for new
financing is likely to have risen substantially. Taking all aspects of new issue business into
account the level of net borrowing of the public sector appears unlikely to increase, so that
if savings continue to increase through the national savings movement there are strong
grounds for assuming that net new issues of government securities through the open market
will not be particularly significant. On the other hand the demand for stock is likely to
support any official moves to raise bond prices and depress interest rates.

Conversely new issues by companies are likely to exceed £1,000 million. Company
financing and future profitability was discussed in detail by Mr. Harold Rose[1] and also by

---

[1] 'Company Liquidity Under Strain'.

Professor Paish[1] in recent articles and it is not appropriate to cover the same ground here. It remains for the analyst, however, to break the global estimates down into industry components and to distinguish between the private and public quoted company sectors.

Finally, the most useful piece of reconciliation can be achieved by an examination of the trends in the return on capital employed industry by industry. If these are taken out on a five year moving average some useful leads emerge and if the industry factors already considered in compiling the forecast are taken in conjunction with estimates of company profits, depreciation, rates of earnings on capital and financing requirements it is possible to arrive at indications not only of future aggregates of earnings for ordinary but of earnings per share. A broad cross check of these trends is given by examining trends for the whole quoted company sector.

Earnings on mean capital employed
(After depreciation and before tax).

Mid Year	Five-Year Moving Average per cent.
1951	18.3
1953	18.3
1955	17.1
1957	16.3
1959	15.2

The decline in return indicated in the above series is undoubtedly overstated since assets were substantially undervalued in earlier years and are much less so now. The real decline was therefore relatively modest and if we assume that the future rate of return stabilises at around 15 per cent future dividend growth may be represented as follows:—

	per cent
Return on capital employed	15.0
Less: Prior charges	1.0
	14.0
Less: Tax at (say) 50 per cent	7.0
Available for ordinary	7.0
Distributed in dividends (say) 50 percent	3.5
Net retention and growth rate	3.5

A more or less consistent result is obtained when the above method is applied to earlier periods and checked against results.

No one, of course, will assume that we have achieved a precise forecast for that is not the object of the exercise. It is apparent that the complex network of assumptions allows of a nearly infinite number of permutations. Yet in some areas under discussion the analyst will find himself confronted with an unfamiliar view of an industry and its prospects. The further probing prompted by such discoveries may prove the worth of the exercise as a whole.

CYCLICAL MOVEMENTS

The present uncertainties concerning entry to the Common Market are sufficient warning of the difficulties in estimating the likely timing of changes in course for the economy. At

[1] 'Profits and Dividends – The Next Five Years', F. W. Paish, The Banker, August 1962.

the best of times one cannot see very far ahead and for the moment it is nearly impossible to see beyond the end of 1963. Short-term forecasts for a year ahead ought to have a great deal more precision than the longer-term forecast discussed above. Apart from movements in stocks and work in progress the other major components of expenditure may be estimated with much more confidence. Useful data for orders on hand and work under construction give good leads for capital expenditure. Consumers' expenditure is not very volatile and government expenditure is at least subject to public budgeting. Even in export markets some kind of forward lead may be obtained for the major markets and the general drift perceived. Forecasts of this nature may yield indications of balance of payments trends with the almost certain knowledge that a deterioration will lead to government action and to an adverse movement in stock markets.

Likewise, Wall Street has given us a particularly useful indicator of approaching recession in the United States throughout the post-War period and this should also be consulted in appraising British prospects in the short run.

IS THE EFFORT WORTHWHILE?

Since we have no claims to achieve any kind of precision or exactitude in economic forecasting, is so much effort worthwhile? To cite our own experience the laborious task of working through the sources and of repeatedly going back to revise earlier stages in the work has proved highly educational. The familiarity gained with sources of statistics and of their reliability is of first practical importance. Secondly, the construction of a model intended to be consistent in its component parts gives considerable confidence in the handling of relationships between various sectors. One may see, for example, the implications for consumers' expenditure arising from a fast rise in commitments for house purchase and hire purchase repayments. It is possible to talk with greater confidence and authority about future price levels and it becomes much easier to trace the likely effects of political action. A particularly rewarding result is the ability to cross-check the authoritive views presented in the financial press and which have such a strong influence upon stock market sentiment.

As mentioned at the outset of this article it will be necessary to cast a quizzical eye over the targets suggested by the NEDC from time to time and an acquaintance with the patterns and trends of the economy will help set things in a reasonable political perspective.

THE USE OF A COMPUTER

It will have been apparent throughout this discussion that the number of variables and the vast range of alternative assumptions can only be effectively explored with aid of an electronic computer. A great deal of work of this nature has already been undertaken at the Department of Applied Economics at Cambridge and described in a number of articles.[1] It will not be appropriate for the investment analyst to consider a task of such complexity unless as member of a team handling a considerable investment portfolio. Even so, narrower aspects of the forecast do lend themselves to analysis with the aid of a computer and there can be no doubt that the investment analyst of the future will be able to equip himself with a great range of statistical material marshalled into good order by the machine.

---

[1] See 'A Long-Term Growth Model for the British Economy', Richard Stone and J. A. C. Brown, from 'Europe's Future in Figures'.

3 Personal Saving and Business Profit

R. HARROD

This article was published in The Investment Analyst *in September 1963. Against a background of rapid change in society and politics, Roy Harrod points the way to achieving a balance between personal savings and business borrowings. The role of government authorities is also questioned. The problem of external balances and the possibility of import controls is discussed. (How today's UK consumers would cope with import controls would probably spell doom for any political party à la Heath's three-day week in the 1970s.)*

In 1963, Roy Harrod was a Student of Christ Church, Oxford, where he was the senior economics tutor. He had been there for nearly 40 years. By this time, he was already Sir Roy and had been unofficial adviser to several post-war governments.

Sir Roy wrote the biography of John Maynard Keynes in the 1950s as well as many other works on economics. He was also a regular contributor to the Financial Times. *He died in 1978.*

It is the purpose of this article to show the relation between the course of personal saving and the squeeze on business profit during 1961 and 1962.

It may be well first to set out the principles on which the analysis is based. The costs of business consist, in the last analysis, of incomes paid out to those who co-operate in the productive process; the costs of materials, components, etc., may be reduced to incomes paid out at an earlier stage of production. (For the question of imports and exports, see below.) Business also pays out part of its profit by way of incomes to shareholders, etc. Much, but not all, of the incomes so paid out come back to business in the demand for goods and services. Some part of the incomes paid out are held back by their receivers, and constitute saving. On the other hand, the demand for goods and services constituted by the spending of incomes is supplemented by a demand for goods on capital account. If the amount held back by persons receiving income (saving) were equal to the amount of outlay on capital account, the total demand for goods and services from business would be exactly equal, neither more nor less, to the amount paid out by business by way of costs and distributed profit.

The governmental authorities also undertake some saving, and, for the moment, this saving may be regarded as a supplement to personal saving, and be added to it. In some respects, it is true, governmental saving resembles business saving in being the unintended consequence of the functioning of the economy during a given period, e.g., as when tax revenues exceed or fall short of what are budgeted for; we shall waive that point for the moment.

If personal and governmental savings together were exactly equal to the capital outlays authorized in any period, the amount coming back to business by way of demand for its goods and services would be exactly equal to the amount that it paid out by way of costs and distributed profit. This would by no means be a satisfactory state of affairs for business. The representative business hopes in each period to receive back somewhat more than it paid out in the previous period by way of costs and distributed profit. It may need to enlarge the amount of profit distributed, to the extent that in each succeeding period it is working with a larger capital. Much more important, it hopes to receive somewhat more in each period than it paid out in the preceding period, so as to plough it back, in the form of undistributed profit for the enlargement of its own capital. Thus it is expedient that personal and governmental saving together should constitute a proportion only of the total amount of new capital outlay in the economy. If the whole of the capital outlay was always covered by personal and governmental saving, business would never be able to set aside anything to reserve at all, for the simple reason that the money it got back would be no more than the money that it was paying out by way of costs and profit distributed.

This would be an unhealthy state of affairs. It is desirable that businesses should be able to rely, in part at least, on profits ploughed back for the extension of their own operations. It would be a bad thing if businesses had to go to the outside capital market for every little bit of extra capital needed for any extension.

There is, of course, in this matter a golden mean. If persons and the governmental authorities saved too little in relation to fresh capital outlays proceeding in the economy, so that the inflow of the aggregate money demand for goods and services was too great, profits would be unhealthily inflated. What is wanted is that some 'right' proportion of the fresh capital outlays should be financed by personal and governmental saving, leaving the rest to be financed by business profits ploughed back. What that 'right' proportion is cannot be stated *a priori*.

This theory of the circular flow of income is evidently analogous to the theory of full employment. If all incomes received were expended on consumer goods and there was, at the same time, some demand for fresh capital goods, the aggregate demand for goods and services would be more than the community could provide, and demand inflation would arise. On the other hand, if the excess of incomes paid out over incomes spent on consumer goods were greater than the total demand for fresh capital goods, the aggregate demand for all goods would fall below the supply potential of the economy, and a recession would set in. It is important to stress that personal plus governmental saving alone should not be as great as the fresh demand for capital goods, since that would leave no scope for the provision for saving by businesses themselves, and indeed would prevent their making any savings, since they would not be getting enough money in to be able to do so.

A demand inflation generated by deficient personal and governmental saving relative to fresh capital outlay must be sharply distinguished from a cost inflation caused by money incomes paid out rising more quickly than productivity (output per person). It is quite possible, and in recent years has been quite common in Britain and the United States, to have a cost inflation in periods when demand was deficient. It may be thought that the authorities have at times misjudged the situation in this respect, wrongly inferring demand inflation from the existence of a cost and price inflation. To the extent that this mistake was made, the cost and price inflation may well have been accentuated, since the low demand prevented productivity increasing as much as it could otherwise have done.

It is sometimes said that the responsibility for a price inflation, when no excess demand is present, lies not only with the granting of excess income increases relatively to productivity increases, but also to the maintenance of what the Americans call 'administered prices' at an excessive level. It is to be noted that when demand is deficient and profit is consequently being squeezed, the representative business will be especially reluctant to reduce an 'administered price'.

To summarize, we may say that, for equilibrium, there is a certain 'right' proportion of current fresh capital outlay that should be financed out of personal and governmental saving, and that, if this proportion becomes too high, business will find its profits reduced below the satisfactory level.

The following analysis depends on our National Income statistics. It is to be remembered that these have margins of error. But it will become apparent that the pattern of development in recent years stands out clearly, even if there are substantial errors in the statistics.

In what follows I shall work mainly in terms of money values. This will not affect the argument, since I shall be concerned with the changes from year to year in ratios, e.g., between personal saving and investment. It would be difficult to reduce the values to 'real' terms, as the choice of appropriate index numbers would be difficult. For example, one might think it appropriate to apply to savings the index number for consumer prices, since savings represent consumer goods foregone; on the other hand, if savings are to be used for the order of capital goods, the index number of capital goods prices might seem appropriate.

However, in order to safeguard against exaggerated ideas about the increase of investment in recent years, a preliminary table is given comparing total investment in money terms with the total investment in 'real' terms, i.e., after deflating it for the rise in prices.

TABLE I. Total investment.

Index numbers
1952–1955 (average = 100)

	Total Investment (money)	Price Index (fixed assets)	Total investment (real)
1956–1958 (annual average)	142.1	111.5	127.5
1959	151.0	115.0	131.3
1960	165.6	116.1	142.7
1961	181.3	119.5	151.7
1962	180.0	123.1	146.2

* Figures in these and the following tables are derived from the Blue Books on National Income and Expenditure. The Preliminary Estimates (Cmnd. 1984) are used for 1962 and also, where possible, for other years, since these give the most recently revised figures.

In the preliminary analysis abstraction was made from the influence of exports and imports on the circular flow. If exports exactly balanced imports, their influence could be ignored. An excess of exports (of all goods and services) over imports (ditto) has the same effect on the circular flow as additional capital outlay of that amount. An excess of exports is equivalent to investment abroad (in the simplest case it might be investment in an additional stock of gold which, is an international asset); and conversely. In the above table, and in all the tables that follow, total investment includes investment abroad (or disinvestment abroad).

The next table sets out the course of personal saving over an 11 year period and compares it with the course of total gross investment.

The greatly superior increase in personal saving is evident. It could be argued that personal saving was somewhat below the 'right' level in the 4 year period 1952 to 1955. It is

TABLE II. Personal saving and total investment.

	Personal* saving (£ million)	Personal* saving (Index numbers)	Total gross investment (£ million)	Total gross investment (index numbers)
1952–1955 (annual average)	483	100.0	2,652	100.0
1956–1958 (annual average)	837	173.3	3,768	142.1
1959	905	191.3	4,005	151.0
1960	1,463	303.0	4.390	165.6
1961	1,910	395.5	4,800	181.3
1962	1,752	362.7	4,772	180.0

* Personal saving minus stock appreciation attributable to persons plus additions to personal tax reserves.

Table III. Adjusted personal saving and total investment.

	Personal saving +Residual Error (£ million)	Personal saving +Residual Error (index numbers)	Total gross investment (index numbers)
1952–1955 (annual average)	550	100.0	100.0
1956–1958 (annual average)	1,077	195.8	142.1
1959	1,034	188.0	151.0
1960	1,214	220.7	165.6
1961	1,922	349.3	181.3
1962	1,626	295.6	180.0

most unlikely that it was so in the following 3 year period, when the economy was flat, and in 1958 tending to recession. The very sharp upsurge after 1959 may be noted. The small drop in 1962 is discussed below.

The figure supplied for personal saving in the National Income statistics may be a somewhat precarious one. Those statistics contain a 'residual error'. In the tables that follow the whole of the residual error is credited (or debited) to personal saving. This goes against the trend of the argument, since it somewhat flattens out the rise in personal saving shown in Table II. Since there may be errors in other items, plus or minus, it may be wrong to attribute the whole of the residual error to personal saving. The truth may lie somewhere between the figures shown in Table II and those shown in Table III; but the figures in Table III are used in what follows, precisely because they go against the trend of the argument.

Next it is necessary to take account of governmental saving. This is done in Table IV.

It is to be noted that the strong increase in personal saving in 1960 and 1961 was in part offset by a decline in governmental saving, although the point explained in the footnote somewhat obscures the pattern. In any case in 1961 the status of governmental saving was

Table IV. Governmental saving and adjusted personal saving and total investment.

	£ million		
	Governmental saving[1]	Governmental saving plus adjusted personal saving	Total gross investment
1952–1955 (annual average)	480	1,070	2,652
1956–1958 (annual average)	647	1,724	3,768
1959	684	1,728	4,005
1960	430	1,644	4,390
		(697)*	(1,911)*
1961	462	2,384	4,800
1962	853	2,479	4,772

[1] Central Government:– adjusted surplus on revenue account minus taxes on capital plus transfers to capital accounts. Plus savings of local authorities. Minus stock appreciation attributable to government. Plus 'other central government receipts'.
* For some reason, perhaps owing to a lack of liquidity in a time of expansion, companies appear not to have paid taxes promptly in 1960. The pattern was as follows:-

	1959	1960	1961	1962
Taxes paid	968	705	828	1.004
Additions to tax reserves	–196	267	91	–71
	772	972	919	933

The bracketed figures show position if companies had made no addition to tax reserves in 1960.

by no means adapted to the large increase in personal saving. In 1962 there was a large increase in governmental saving which was altogether inappropriate. It was doubtless largely due to policies adopted during 1961. It is to be noted that these tables relate to the calendar, and not to the fiscal year.

The next table shows the relation of governmental and personal saving together to total investment.

TABLE V. Government Saving plus Adjusted Personal Saving as Percentage of Total Investment

1952–1955 (annual average)	40.35
1956–58 (annual average)	45.75
1959	43.14
1960	37.44
	(43.52)*
1961	49.67
1962	50.77

* See footnote on Table IV. The bracketed figure probably represents the situation better.

The matter may be illustrated much more clearly by reference increments. This is done in the following table.

TABLE VI. Contributions to Increments of Investment by Governmental Saving plus Adjusted Personal Saving

	(i) Increment of gross investment (£ million)	(ii) Increment of governmental saving plus adjusted personal saving (£ million)	(iii) (ii) as percentage of (i)	(iv) Increase of saving by companies and corporations
Value in 1959 minus value in 1952	+1,689	+707	41.85	+982
Value in 1962 minus value in 1959	+767	+766	100.0	0
Value in 1962 minus value in 1960	+382	+835 (+568)*	218.6 (148.7)*	−453 (−186)*

* See footnote on Table IV.

In 1959 the value of total investment exceeded its value in 1952 by £1,689 million; the value of personal and governmental saving together in 1959 exceeded its value in 1952 by £707 million. The increase in these values was naturally not steady year by year. But if we take the period as a whole, the contribution of the increase of governmental and personal saving together to the increase of gross investment was 41.85 per cent. of the latter. This 7 year period includes years of demand-inflationary pressure (1954–1955), in which it could be argued that personal and governmental savings were insufficient. It also includes 1953, a year of revival, in which the economy was by no means fully stretched, and the years 1956 to 1958 when the economy was flat. 1959 was a year of revival, but by no means one of very full demand. Thus we may think that the contribution by persons and governmental authorities to increased capital requirements was not deficient at 42 per cent. The savings of companies and public corporations increased by £982 million, thus contributing 58 per cent. to increased capital requirements. There is nothing final about this figure. But we may think that this is a reasonable proportion for business to contribute to capital requirements. Given investment requirements, had personal and governmental savings been higher, companies and public corporations would not have been able to plough back so much profit to the expansion of business, for the simple reason that they would not have had enough profit thus to plough back.

Between 1959 and 1962 the increase in personal and governmental saving together was equal to the whole of the increase of total investment, companies and public corporations together contributing nothing. It is to be stressed again that, given capital requirements, given the level of personal saving, and given governmental policy, it was physically impossible for companies and public corporations together to save anything. This was surely an unhealthy state of affairs.

Between 1960 and 1962, the pattern becomes still more striking as shown in the third line. There remains some obscurity owing to the distorted relation between taxes paid and additions to tax reserves in 1960. However that may be, persons and governmental authorities together increased their savings by much more than was required for the increase of investment, thereby compelling companies and public corporations together to reduce their savings. This was evidently a highly unsatisfactory state of affairs.

The next table shows the gross trading profits of companies and the surpluses of public corporations. The former grew healthily until 1960, with a small setback during the

TABLE VII. Gross Trading Profits of Companies and Surpluses of Public Corporations

| | £ million | | |
	(i) Gross Trading Profits of Companies	(ii) Surpluses of Public Corporations	(iii) (i) plus (ii)
1952–1955 (annual average)	2,493	317	2,810
1956–1958 (annual average)	3,032	336	3,368
1959	3,336	391	3,737
1960	3,685	540	4,225
1961	3,487	650	4,137
1962	3,474	757	4,231

recession of 1958. After 1960 there was a serious setback. The reason for this was indubitably the strong increase in personal and governmental saving together, as shown in Table IV, without there being a matching increase in requirements for capital outlay.

The squeeze on profit was somewhat greater than appears in the table. It is to be remembered that the corpus of capital was increasing, so that gross trading profit per £ of capital fell more than is shown. We may also bear in mind the rise of prices. The following table makes an attempt to deflate the figures for 1961 and 1962, to allow for the increase of prices.

It appears from this table that even the total of the gross trading profits of companies and the surpluses of public corporations was substantially lower in 1962 than in 1960.

A word must be said about the surpluses of public corporations. It is to be noted that even in Table VII, i.e., before deflating for the rise of prices, the sum total of the companies' profits and public corporations' surpluses was no higher in 1962 than two years earlier, and this was a most unsatisfactory state of affairs. There should be an increase each year.

It may be thought that out of a static return flow of funds, the trading profits of companies fell because the public corporations took a rising fraction of the monies available for themselves. There may be comething in this. They may have taken advantage of their monopolistic position and the inelastic demand for the services that they provide to bolster their revenues.

In this connection it is appropriate to call attention to the White Paper Cmnd. 1337, published in April 1961, and presenting, as the basis of its arguments, statistics up to 1959. The general tenor of its recommendations is that the public corporations should meet a larger part of their capital requirements out of their own surpluses. The historic background

TABLE VIII. Gross Trading Profits of Companies and Surpluses of Public Corporations at 1960 prices

| | £ million | | |
	(i) Gross Trading Profits of Companies	(ii) Surpluses of Public Corporations	(iii) (i) plus (ii)
1960	3,685	540	4,225
1961*	3,388	631	4,019
1962†	3,330	726	4,056

of this is well-known. Any capital required by these corporations, over and above what they can find for themselves, has to be provided by the government "below-the-line". Prior to 1961 the government had been in a dilemma. If it sought to cover these below-the-line items by taxation, this might require the jacking up of taxation to an unsatisfactorily high level from the incentive point of view and to a level which, anyhow iin certain years, would have deflationary effects. Alternatively it could raise the money by borrowing; but in certain years this was difficult, owing to the weakness of the market for gilt-edged stock, without resort to such an increase in the floating debt as might have undesirable inflationary repercussions. Therefore the right answer *at that time* seemed to be to encourage the public corporations to enlarge their 'surpluses' in order to have more to plough back into capital requirements and to be less dependent on government finance.

But the rise in personal savings since 1959 has entirely transformed the situation. There is now quite enough personal saving to provide a reasonable proportion of the capital requirements of the public corporations. It is true that there may be insufficient appetite for gilt-edged stock. This is an awkward problem. But the major point here is that if, given the present level of personal saving, the public corporations do too much saving on their own account, thus re-duplicating available personal saving, this is bound to have a deflationary effect on the economy as a whole. Furthermore, to the extent that auto-finance causes the public corporations to put up their charges, e.g., electricity charges, above the level that would otherwise be necessary, this has a cost-inflationary effect on the economy and is likely to be deleterious to the success of an 'incomes policy', which is so much needed. We require an authoritative statement that Cmnd 1337 is now out-of-date.

It will have been noted that, although between 1960 and 1962 the rise in governmental and personal saving together so much exceeded that in gross capital outlay, there was not a net reduction in the trading profits of companies and surpluses of public corporations together in that period. There was a reduction in their joint savings, which fell wholly on companies. The lack of reduction in profits cum surpluses is to be attributed to the increases of dividends, especially in 1960.

If dividend receivers spent the whole of any increases of dividends in the demand for goods and services, company and corporation receipts together would rise by the whole amount of the increase of dividends. Thus companies could, as a collection, by raising dividends increase their receipts by an equal amount, save to the extent that some of the increased spending was siphoned off by the public corporations. In fact dividend receivers do not spend all their dividend increases. The increased dividends in 1960 were partly, but only partly, responsible for the rise in personal savings. The fact that the increases in dividends occurred particularly in 1960 suggests that the pattern of personal savings shown in Table II is nearer the truth than the pattern shown in Table III, in which they are adjusted for the residual error. Table II should not be completely ignored.

And so it happened that the profits of companies and the surpluses of corporations together were sustained, owing to increased dividend distributions, in a period in which governmental and personal saving exceeded fresh capital outlays. The excess of governmental and personal saving over fresh capital outlays inevitably meant that the savings of companies and corporations declined by an equivalent amount. The dividend distributions protected companies and corporations together from a decline in aggregate profits and surpluses together, but did not protect them from a decline in their joint savings.

Had there been no dividend increases, less would have been spent by persons and less saved. Aggregate company profits would have been lower but aggregate company savings would have been higher.

According to the Budget of last April, government saving in 1963–64 is to be reduced by £621 million compared with 1962–63. In fact it is not likely to be reduced by so much. There appears to be a tendency, which however varies greatly from year to year, for the Budget to underestimate the out-turn. The average figure for the underestimate over the past 14 years is £88 million. If 1963–64 corresponded with the average, government saving in that year would be decreased by £533 million only. But in years of revival the underestimate is usually greater and it is to be hoped that 1963–64 will be a year of revival. It is impossible to be precise about the outcome. The greater the decline in government saving, the greater will be the revival; and the greater the revival the smaller will be the decline in governmental saving. It is a question of simultaneous equations; unfortunately we do not know the values of the parameters.

If all other things remained the same, and if governmental saving declined by the full amount of £533 million, this would give personal and governmental saving together a contribution of 40.8 per cent. towards investment requirements. If we assume personal saving and investment requirements both to rise by 4 per cent, then personal saving plus governmental saving would provide 40.6 per cent towards investment requirements. This would be a sufficiently satisfactory figure. But, as noted above, it is not certain that governmental saving will decline so much.

It is expedient at this point to make a comment on the decline in personal saving in 1962. Some might be inclined to argue therefrom that personal savings were now set on a downward course, or, at least, would not increase. But this would probably be a wrong inference. It appears that, when allowance is made for the rise in retail prices in 1962, personal income was the same in 1962 as in 1961. It would be against nature for personal spending to flatten out entirely in a particular year in which incomes did not increase. There is bound to be a gentle upward drift, despite the stagnation of incomes. Actually consumer expenditure in real terms rose by the very moderate amount of 1.4 per cent. Money incomes were up by £1,025 million, but disposable incomes (i.e. after taxation and contributions) by £694 million only. Expenditure was up by £856 million (money terms). This would indicate a decline in personal saving by £162 million, which corresponds to the figure shown in Table II.

Thus the various facts do not suggest any decline in the *propensity* to save. If real personal incomes begin to climb again, we may expect an upward trend in personal savings.

If we budget for a decline in governmental saving of £530 million and if we suppose that public corporations siphon off, say, £80 million of this, it would leave, other things being equal, an extra £450 million for the gross trading profits of companies, an increase of 13 per cent.

One final point must be noted. It may happen that, in the 12 months ahead, the external balance on current account will deteriorate. This may not happen very soon. In 1958–9 there was a substantial time lag between the revival of the economy and the increase in the imports of basic materials and manufactures for further processing. If, however, such a deterioration occurs, this will be, pro tanto, a deflationary force. One way of putting it is that the decline on current account is equal to a disinvestment (abroad) of that amount and thus entails a decline in total investment and therefore a decline in the ratio of total investment to governmental and private saving. Looking at the same fact from another point of view, the external deficit decreases government borrowing from the public; the Exchange Equalization Account sells gold for sterling and lends that sterling to the government (against Treasury Bills), whereby the government has to borrow that much less from the public.

Of course, it is possible that the authorities might prevent a decline in the external balance by imposing import restrictions. That would of course prevent the external position from having a deflationary effect and open up a new prospect.

4 Possible Worlds

R. STONE

This article was published in The Investment Analyst *in September 1963. In the article, Professor Stone reported on the quantitative model of the British Economy that he had developed with his colleagues at the Department of Applied Economics in Cambridge. The model consisted of a set of variables, a set of relationships connecting the variables, a set of estimates of the parameters in the relationships, and a computing format to solve equations based on different initial assumptions. The underlying purpose was to examine the limits imposed by social and economic considerations to economic growth.*

The early model did not contain any financial relationships, but further research on this aspect of economic life was planned as the original article went to press. Meanwhile, the preliminary work provided the basis for a 'new piece of economic machinery' and underlined Professor Stone's belief in systems analysis.

Professor Sir John Richard Stone won the Nobel Prize for Economics in 1984. Formerly Director of the Department of Applied Economics at Cambridge University, he held many academic posts including the P. D. Leake Professorship of Finance and Accounting. He was awarded Honorary Doctorates from the universities of Oslo, Brussels, Geneva, Warwick, Bristol and the Sorbonne. He was a Fellow of Gonville and Caius College, Cambridge University. Professor Stone died in 1991.

1. INTRODUCTION

Some thirty-five years ago the biologist J. B. S. Haldane wrote a book called *Possible Worlds*, in which he examined the limits set by biological considerations to size, growth and form: could we, say, contemplate an elephant ten times as big as those we know? Could its bones bear its weight? In a similar way I am interested in the limits set by social and economic considerations to economic growth: could we, say, contemplate a rate of economic growth twice or three times as fast as the present one? Could the socio-economic system bear the strain? To answer this we must first find out how the system works.

An economy, like any other system, works by means of decisions which relate a flow of information to a set of objectives. Given the objectives, a system will work better the more relevant, accurate and prompt is the information flowing into the different centres of decision. In recent years a whole host of new techniques has been developed to improve this flow: market research, input-output analysis, programming, investment analysis and so on. But these techniques only provide partial information. They lack an organising principle.

For example, most business concerns are simply not large enough to make their own market, so they try to adapt themselves to the market as it is, and in planning ahead they try to follow whatever trend the market seems to be following. But the observation of trends is no more than the observation of the past. And so a given growth rate tends to get built into an economy: people tend to act as if the growth rate they have observed in the past from their particular corner of the system would continue unchanged into the future, and of course by so doing they perpetuate it.

This is not surprising. However energetic a producer may be, what is the point of his doubling his output unless he is sure that the buying capacity of his clients will also double? And how can he contemplate doing it unless he is sure that he can obtain the necessary amount of raw materials, machinery, labour, etc.?

Doubts of this kind can only be resolved by systems analysis, which in this context means a detailed study of the economy as a whole. Instead of asking, how fast can this bit of the system grow if nothing else in the system changes, systems analysis asks, what would happen to each bit of the system if the whole system started to grow much faster; where would the strains come; which would the breaking points be; and what are the ultimate limits beyond which it cannot expand?

In other words, systems analysis sets out to examine not only how a system operates but how it might operate, and relates the performance of the component parts to the needs of the system as a whole. By means of it we could examine the implications not just of one but of many growth rates. Once we had agreed on which of them seemed possible as well as desirable, potential expansion, at present held back by uncertainty and individual caution, might become a reality. Within limits, we could make our own future and not simply adapt ourselves to a perpetuation of the past.

2. A MODEL OF THE ECONOMY

For the last three years a group of us at the Department of Applied Economics in Cambridge have been working on a large, quantitative model of the British economy which is designed to throw light on growth possibilities and problems. Here I can only give a very general outline of our objects, methods and results. A detailed account of our work is being published in a series entitled *A Programme for Growth*, of which three issues have so far appeared [2,3,4]. A statement of our first, very tentative, results can be found in the report of the BACIE Spring conference for 1963 [1].

A model, in the sense in which I am using the word, consists of a set of variables, a set of relationships connecting these variables, a set of estimates of the parameters in these relationships, and a computing lay-out which provides the means of solving the equations according to different initial assumptions. Let us first glance at each of these components.

(a) Variables The main variables of our model as it stands at present are the quantities, prices and values relating to production, consumption, accumulation and foreign trade in different branches of the economy. A distinction is made between flows of product and flows of finance. For the moment our treatment of product flows is much more developed than our treatment of financial flows, but we are on the point of expanding this side of the model too, as I shall explain in section 5 below.

To deal with the product flows, we distinguish thirty-one industries, thirty-one commodity groups, forty categories of goods and services bought by private consumers and twelve government 'purposes'. To deal with the financial flows we distinguish five institutional sectors, two private and three public.

The resulting information is brought together in a system of accounts, or social accounting matrix as it is called. The present matrix, consisting of 253 accounts, is set out in detail for our base year, 1960, in the second volume of our series [3].

(b) Relationships   The variables are connected by a number of relationships in addition to arithmetical and accounting identities. These additional relationships refer to aspects either of human behaviour or of technology. For example, if we study the behaviour of private consumers, we find that on the average their outlays on different goods and services depend on the amount of money they have to spend, the structure of relative prices and the state of their preferences, which tend to change over time. Thus, as far as we can see, the saturation level for food has not varied appreciably over the last fifty years, but the average consumer is much nearer to this level than he used to be and the composition of his food basket has changed accordingly. In the case of transport, on the other hand, the saturation level has been rising, largely as a consequence of the invention of the motorcar; of course the composition of expenditure on travel has changed too.

Similar variations have been taking place on the productive side of the economy. With changing prices and changing technologies, and with the development of new products and new industries, cost structures and sales structures have varied systematically. The first step, then, is to formulate a set of relationships connecting the variables in the social accounting matrix in various ways. These relationships can then be used to determine values for the variables which are compatible with one another, to pin-point, that is to say, possible worlds.

(c) Parameters   Most relationships contain parameters, or constants, as well as variables. Examples of parameters are the numbers which express the response of consumers to a change in income or prices, or the ratios which relate the inputs needed by a producer to his output.

Such constants have to be estimated empirically. We have based our estimates in the first place on econometric studies of the past, taking care as far as possible to find out not only what the parameters were at any particular point in time, but also how they have been changing. This provides a consistent body of empirical relationships, from which answers about compatibility can be derived. The next step is to discuss these answers and the relationships on which they are based with people engaged in various branches of economic activity. In this way we hope to ensure that our figures are realistic as well as consistent.

(d) Computability   Our model involves formidable computing problems in processing basic data, in estimating the parameters, in obtaining solutions and in absorbing new information. For this reason we have set it up so as to take full advantage of the computing facilities at our disposal, and have tried to design a computing lay-out which would ensure as much flexibility as possible.

3. A PROGRAMME FOR GROWTH

Once we have decided on the variables, formulated the relationships, estimated the parameters and devised the computing lay-out, the model is ready to work. In order to set it in motion we must now feed into it a number of assumptions about the future. Our starting assumptions are: (i) a certain level of private consumers' expenditure in 1970; and (ii) a certain rate of growth of this expenditure from 1970 onwards. We then work out the composition of consumers' expenditure and the rates at which the components might be expected to grow if the total grew at the rate assumed. Similar estimates are made for public consumption, for investment in consumers' durable goods, housing and social capital, and for exports. All these demands for goods and services are then converted into direct demands for the products of our thirty-one industries. This is the first step in our calculations.

But in order to satisfy these direct demands, the productive system must also supply: (i) the capital goods needed to maintain and increase capacity in all branches of production, and (ii) all the raw materials, fuels and semi-finished products needed for current production. The second step is therefore to use the relationships of the model to work out these indirect demands and see how far they could be met by domestic production and how far they could be met by imports, given a certain level of the balance of trade. For this purpose we divide imports into two classes. The first class, complementary imports, consists of goods which cannot be produced in Britain, such as raw cotton or crude oil. These goods we assume to be needed by the different industries in fixed proportions to output. The second class, competitive imports, consists of goods which are produced in Britain but also come from abroad, such as motorcars and clothing. These goods we assume to be imported according to: (i) the amount of money available given a certain level of exports, a certain level of complementary imports and a certain level of the balance of trade; and (ii) the sensitivity they have shown in the recent past to the state of the balance of payments.

Thus once we have decided what initial assumptions to feed into it, the model enables us to work out in a fair degree of detail their implications for domestic production and foreign trade. But how, it may be asked, do we know whether our assumptions are realistic? Only by working out their implications and then submitting these to the judgment of outside opinion. For this reason I must emphasise that the growth rates we have assumed for our first exercise, which I am going to describe below, are in no sense predictions; they are made simply in order to trace their implications. When we have perfected our techniques and collected more information, we shall repeat the exercise taking other growth rates as a starting point. Of course, as we change our initial assumptions, so we shall find that output levels, capital expenditures, labour requirements, imports etc. change with them. When we have worked out a certain number of possible programmes, it will be up to the public to choose the one they think the best.

4. SOME PRELIMINARY RESULTS

The initial assumptions we have made in order to carry out our first 'programme for growth' are: (i) that during the 1960's private consumers' expenditure, including expenditure on durable goods, would grow at an average annual rate of 3.2 per cent per head, reaching in 1970 a level 47 per cent higher than that attained in 1960; and (ii) that from 1970 onwards this annual rate of growth would rise to 4 per cent. We further assumed that between 1960 and 1970 public consumption would rise by 42 per cent; public investment in social capital would rise by 100 per cent, including for example an increase of 88 per cent in educational facilities and an increase of 200 per cent in road expenditure; and, finally, exports would rise by 50 per cent, increases above the average being expected in chemicals, oil and transport equipment, and a fall being expected in textiles and clothing.

When all the direct and indirect demands implied by these growth rates had been worked out and added together industry by industry, and competitive imports had been subtracted, we found that the implied percentage increases in the outputs of the different industry groups ranged from 0 to over 100 per cent. At the top of the list, with increases in the decade of 75 per cent or more, we find electricity, motor vehicles, mineral oil refining, 'other manufacturing', and leather, clothing and footwear. The next group, with increases ranging between 50 and 75 per cent, contains chemicals, aircraft, metals and metal goods, distributive and other services, and engineering and electrical goods. The third category, with increases ranging between 25 and 50 per cent, contains the timber trades, construction, textiles, gas, the paper trades, coal and other mining, building materials, transport and communications, agriculture, and water. Finally, the lowest increases are found in food, drink and tobacco, pottery and glass, coke ovens, locomotives, and shipbuilding.

These are preliminary results which need to be discussed and checked. All that can be claimed at the moment is that they form part of a consistent picture: buyers exist on paper for everything that is produced and sellers exist on paper for all the inputs that are wanted. The next thing to do, therefore, is to discuss these results with the different industries and see what they have to say about the possibility of producing the output we have estimated, and producing it with the inputs we have ascribed to them.

In carrying out these checks there is another aspect of the productive process which is very important in a country with a slow-growing and fully employed labour force: productivity and labour mobility. The figures I have just given imply for 1970 an increase in the net output of the thirty-one industries taken together of about 50 per cent above the 1960 output levels. Our estimates of the labour force likely to be available to industry as a whole in 1970 suggest an increase of only 5 per cent above the 1960 labour force. On the average, therefore, the productivity of labour must increase by 43 per cent in the decade. What does this imply for individual industries?

This question should be answered by means of production functions. We are working on these at the moment, but for the time being we have had to make use of the simpler method described in the BACIE report [1]. On this basis it turned out that almost the whole of the additional labour force would be absorbed by distributive and other services, leaving the increased needs of other industries to be met by a redistribution of the existing numbers, coupled with considerable increases in labour productivity. For example, in our calculations agriculture would continue to lose labour as it did in the 1950's and its annual growth rate of productivity would have to be 5.7 per cent as against the 4.1 per cent observed in the period 1948–1960. Iron and steel, on the other hand, would gain labour; all the same its annual growth rate of productivity would have to rise from 2.5 per cent to 2.8 per cent. As a final example, electricity would lose a little labour in spite of its large rise in output, and its annual growth rate of productivity would have to rise to 7.3 per cent, as against the 5.3 per cent observed in the period 1948–1960 and the 6.5 per cent observed during the second half of that period, namely 1954–1960.

Are such increases possible in terms of technological developments? Until our work on production functions is complete we cannot give even a *prima facie* answer. But we can begin to find out what some of the people concerned think and what would be involved in terms of human behaviour if an attempt were made to achieve such gains.

There is yet another aspect of the problem which must be considered. Once we start discussing high growth rates in productivity, we have to face not only the question of technical advance in terms of adequate plant and machinery but also the other side of the coin, namely the question of providing adequate skills in the labour force. These questions have already attracted public attention as far as scientists and engineers are concerned, but clearly this qualified manpower must be backed by sufficient numbers of technicians and craftsmen trained in the particular skills that will be needed. We have begun to work on these questions too, and some preliminary results can be found in the BACIE report [1].

5. FINANCIAL RELATIONSHIPS

At present our model does not contain any financial relationships. Being designed to fit into an accounting framework, it automatically generates an amount of income such that when consumption has been paid for, enough money is left over to finance investment. Thus in principle the community could finance the required investment, but whether in practice it would want to divide its income between spending and saving as required is an open question. According to our calculations, in order to provide for domestic net investment plus an assumed £200 million of net investment abroad, the country would have to save 14 per cent of its income instead of the 12 per cent which it saved in 1960.

But even if this rate of saving were achieved, who would do the saving? And what portfolios of assets and claims would arise as a consequence of the productive activity that would be going on? We do not yet know, but thanks to the generosity of the Bank of England and other institutions in the City in response to our appeal for research funds, we are planning to start work on this aspect of economic life in the near future.

This work will take three main forms. First, the integration into our social accounting matrix of flow-of-funds data and sectoral balance sheets. Second, an investigation of behavioural relationships in the financial sphere: saving relationships, preferred portfolio patterns and so on. Finally, the use of this information to throw light on the financing aspects of the possible worlds that emerge from our study of men, materials and machines.

6. CONCLUSION

The work outlined in this paper represents an attempt to construct a new piece of economic machinery which will enable possible worlds to be explored systematically and realistically. Models are a means of starting off this process and ensuring consistency and coherence for it when it is under way. Their success depends on the willingness of people in the practical world to put information into them as well as to take information out of them. Let me conclude by repeating what was said in the first volume of *A Programme for Growth:* 'The only difference a model can make is to change men's minds as to what it is good, sensible, worthwhile or profitable to do. Doing it is up to them'.

7. A LIST OF WORKS CITED

1. BRITISH ASSOCIATION FOR COMMERCIAL AND INDUSTRIAL EDUCATION. *Economic Growth and Manpower.* Report of the Spring Conference 1963, BACIE, London, 1963.
2. CAMBRIDGE, DEPARTMENT OF APPLIED ECONOMICS. *A Computable Model of Economic Growth.* No. 1 in *A Programme for Growth.* Chapman and Hall, London, 1962.
3. CAMBRIDGE, DEPARTMENT OF APPLIED ECONOMICS. *A Social Accounting Matrix for* 1960, No. 2 in *A Programme for Growth.* Chapman and Hall, London, 1962.
4. CAMBRIDGE, DEPARTMENT OF APPLIED ECONOMICS. *Input-Output Relationships:* 1954–1966. No. 3 in *A Programme for Growth.* Chapman and Hall, London, 1963.

5 The Investment Analyst's Materials

R. E. ARTUS

This article was published in December 1963.

Ronald Artus had an immense influence on the development of investment management and analytical research not only in London but throughout the UK and even in financial centres overseas.

Following graduation from Oxford in Philosophy, Politics and Economics, he joined the Economics Intelligence Department of the Prudential Assurance Company in 1954. The next year, he joined the Society of Investment Analysts. At the Second Congress of the European Federation of Financial Analysts' Societies held at Cambridge in 1963, he chaired the Committee responsible for compiling a comprehensive bibliography for each country of sources of statistics and other information useful to analysts.

He was elected to the Council of the Society in September 1964, and became Chairman of Education and Membership in 1966. In 1965, he was appointed to the newly formed Committee for International Liaison outside Europe.

When Ronald Artus was appointed Chief Investment Manager of the Prudential in 1975, he introduced reforms that revolutionized the accepted practises of investment management and research throughout the British financial community. He observed how in the late 1950s the investment trust movement started to change its approach to fund management. It recognized that no manager could oversee a thousand or more companies, and the better performers were achieving this by reducing their holdings to the low hundreds. Secondly, he took the view that if stockbrokers wished to do business with the Pru then they had to have knowledgeable analysts researching the companies that they were recommending. He undertook a series of visits to brokers to meet their staff and judge their quality and their procedures. These measures had a profound influence on performance and the demand for qualified investment analysts, and such practices were soon adopted by other institutional investors.

He retired from the Council in 1976, but continued to work for the improvement of investment analysis and management through service on various committees. He was appointed to the CBI City Industry Taskforce. In 1992, at the behest of the Bank of England, he was a member of the working party that proposed radical reform in the Lloyd's insurance market. He was a Director of the Prudential from 1984 and Deputy Chairman from 1985 to 1990. Ronald Artus died in 1991.

The process of analysis which earns the investment analyst his title is performed upon, and within limits set by, that volume of available information which is relevant to the problems examined. The range of problems which can come within this field is rather daunting, if it is defined as I would define it, as the attempt to make possible in the field of investment decision-taking rational choice on the basis of the best available evidence.

The problems met with may vary from the assessment of the likely overall stock-market performance in the light of any given short-term economic outlook, to a highly technical discussion of the accountancy practices or the taxation provisions of a particular firm. The range of the available information is therefore very considerable, and the task of keeping abreast of what is available throughout the entire field will be attempted only by a few specialised libraries and large institutions. In this article I intend to ignore the more specialised aspects of the field; those who are in need of information as to the source-material for their economic forecasts or for the interpretation of taxation provisions are probably without the technical expertise to make good use of the information even if they had it. But, whilst certain aspects of the work which falls within my definition of investment analysis are clearly the province of those trained in recognised disciplines such as economics and accountancy, there remains an extensive middle area to the subject which is free for all; free for those versed in any one of the relevant disciplines, or in none at all. This area is the study of a company's, or a group of companies', prospects in the general context of the industry within which it (or they) operate(s). It is because the professional freedom of entry into this field is so great that it may be worth while offering this plain man's guide to the relevant source material.

Three broad classes of information sources can be distinguished. These are (a) current statistical sources, (b) reference sources (c) sources of up-to-date comment and information.

(a) CURRENT STATISTICAL SOURCES

By far the bulk of the available statistical information relating to production, investment, sales, stocks, exports, new orders and the like, is nowadays accessible through the principal official statistical publications.

The most important of these are as follows:—

The Monthly Digest of Statistics   A good range of general economic and industrial statistics. Business Monitor – Production Series – a recently introduced series of papers covering a wide range of industries, giving more detailed production series, either monthly or quarterly, than is available in the Monthly Digest.

The Board of Trade Journal   This is the earliest place of publication of a number of interesting series, e.g. those covering the motor industry, new orders in engineering, hire purchase, and the retail trade, some of which are available in more detail here than elsewhere.

The Trade & Navigation Accounts   These give very considerable detail of the export and import trade of the United Kingdom, and are published monthly about four weeks in arrears.

Between them these official publications provide a very considerable body of statistical information. In some fields it is possible, and sometimes important, to supplement it with other statistics. Sometimes, for example, information about exports or imports may be required by classes of goods in more detail than is available from the Trade & Navigation Accounts. On these occasions the information may be available for a small fee from the Statistical Office of the Customs and Excise. This more detailed information later becomes available in the four volume Annual Statement of Trade of the U.K. The practising analyst will probably find it necessary to subscribe regularly to the basic official statistical sources listed above. But it is worth recording that a very comprehensive collection both of British and overseas production and trade statistics is available for use at the Board of Trade's Statistics and Market Intelligence Library at Hillgate House, 35 Old Bailey, E.C.4.

The following list of supplementary sources of statistical information, which is of interest in specific industries, is not presented as being in any way comprehensive or definitive, but rather is of interest for showing the sort of sources which can be tapped.

Building The Cubitt Magazine, the house magazine of Holland & Hannen and Cubitts, contains an index of construction activity and construction costs. The standard source for house price movements, broken down by value, region and whether old or new, is the Occasional Bulletin of the Co-operative Permanent Building Society.

Confectionery Cocoa Market Report by Gill & Duffus Ltd., giving group prospects and usage figures and prices.

Diamonds Quarterly figures of sales through the central selling organisation are released to the Press by De Beers.

Domestic Appliances Sales of gas appliances in its showrooms are given monthly in a statistical release issued by the Gas Council. Odhams Press makes surveys of appliance ownership at irregular intervals, which after a while it makes available on application. These form a standard source for this sort of information.

Electrical Engineering, Cables, Atomic Power & Boilers Central Electricity Generating Board annual reports give detailed statistics of past installations, and the future programme is outlined. Each year the C.E.G.B. also releases details of the commissionings in the past year, including an analysis by manufacturer. These are published during January in the weekly journal Engineering and in the Electrical Review.

Electronics

(i) Domestic Radio & Television Equipment The British Radio Equipment Manufacturers' Association publishes monthly estimates of manufacturers' deliveries of radio and T.V. sets and radiograms, similar to figures which appear later in the Monthly Digest. Figures relating to relay companies' customers, which are not otherwise available, can be obtained from the Relay Services Association.

(ii) Computers The Computer Survey, published quarterly by the United Trade Press gives various figures relating to the installation of computers in the U.K., such as their current use and location.

(iii) Telephone equipment The Post Office Accounts give details of installations of phones, exchanges, etc., and the G.P.O. also publishes an annual White Paper – Post Office Prospects – describing its capital spending plans.

Iron and Steel Iron and Steel Monthly Bulletin, issued jointly by the Iron & Steel Board and the British Iron and Steel Federation gives considerable detail not available elsewhere.

Mining Machinery The National Coal Board's annual reports give details of equipment purchases.

Motors The Society of Motor Manufacturers and Traders publishes Motor Industry of

Great Britain (annual) and a Monthly Statistical Review. Both consist largely of official statistics similar to those available elsewhere, but are given here in more detail than is available in the official publications. They include hire purchase statistics, collected by H.P. Information Ltd., which are of considerable interest as the chief guide to activity in the secondhand car market. These figures are usually given in the press. The Economist Intelligence Unit's quarterly publication, Motor Business, which is available only on subscription, gives an index of used vehicle prices. Non-Ferrous Metal Manufacture – A wide range of statistics on the production and usage of non-ferrous metals is contained in World Non-Ferrous Metal Statistics, published by the British Bureau of Non-Ferrous Metal Statistics.

Oil In this field most of the important sources are outside the field of U.K. official publications. The most valuable sources are (1) Petroleum Press Service, which gives world production and consumption figures, analysed by product and country, refinery building plans etc. (2) Petroleum Information Bureau, in addition to covering some of the same ground as Petroleum Press Service and the Monthly Digest, has an annual release relating to oil reserves. (3) The Chase Manhattan Bank issues a monthly report and annual survey, the former dealing principally with the U.S. oil industry, but the latter covering consumption, supply, refinery construction, reserves, etc., in broad terms. (4) The Oil and Gas Journal, published weekly in the U.S.A., is an important source for up-to-date industry statistics.

Roadbuilding Basic Road Statistics, published by the British Road Federation, annually, collects together into a single place a mass of information which, whilst mostly available elsewhere, would otherwise have been widely diffused.

Rubber Manufacturing, including Tyres The Rubber Statistical Bulletin published monthly by the International Rubber Study Group gives a 6-monthly breakdown of rubber usage by type of product.

Textiles Statistics about this industry, supplementary to those available in official places, are contained in the Cotton Board's Quarterly Statistical Review, the Wool Industry Bureau of Statistics' Monthly Bulletin of Statistics, and the British Man-Made Fibres Federation's Statistical Tables. Tobacco – From time to time the Tobacco Manufacturers' Standing Committee produce an imposing collection of Statistics of Smoking (the last one was published in 1962).

These supplementary statistical sources can be seen to fall chiefly into these rough groups. (1) The accounts and reports of public authorities such as the National Coal Board, the C.E.G.B. and the Post Office. (2) The publications of trade associations. Even where trade associations do not normally publish statistics they may on application give access to statistical material supplementing what is already available. (3) Trade journals and other sources covering international commodities which are not normally sufficiently covered for investment purposes in the standard official British statistical sources. (4) The reproduction in the financial or trade press of information released regularly by some such body as the C.E.G.B. It is important to discover a place where one can rely upon such information being regularly and consistently produced.

(b) REFERENCE SOURCES

Census of Production studies, books and directories, Monopoly Commission reports, reports of productivity commissions, other reports official and unofficial, special supplements in the financial press, and indeed a whole range of publications on industries of more than ephemeral significance, these are all potential grist to the analyst's mill. A handy and useful guide to size in the company sector which is sometimes overlooked is the official publication Company Assets, Income and Finance in 1960, listing some 2,000 of the largest British companies by size of their assets employed.

No generalisations are possible in this field, except to say that even where one's resources permit one to do extensive collecting on one's own account, it still pays to keep in touch with the classification system and storage habits of a large specialised library. The one most likely to be of interest to London members of the Society is the Guildhall Library which has an extensive collection of works in this field.

(c) SOURCE OF UP-TO-DATE COMMENT AND INFORMATION

The requisites for a full scale study of the present position of an industry may be found in the first two categories of information described, but the idea that suggests the probable timeliness of such a study is most likely to come from a careful watch of the day-to-day flow of comment in the financial and trade press. It is from these sources also that the bulk of the information and comment about companies, supplementing that available from chairmen's reports, trade directories and the like, is to be obtained. Over time a collection of references can be built up which will often considerably deepen the knowledge of a company's operations beyond that available from the company's reports. There is no short cut to effectiveness in this aspect of source-collection for investment analysis. The continuing practitioner needs to reconcile himself to the necessity for some effective system for screening the financially orientated dailies and weeklies, and that part of the trade press which is not too hopelessly technical and inward looking. Unless the institution served is a very large one the work involved in covering the ground effectively points strongly to the desirability of specialisation in some limited part of the field. But this is not always possible. In this case it is, of course, true that quarterly indexes to the contents of journals such as the Economist, the Investors' Chronicle and the Stock Exchange Gazette can go some of the way towards replacing the need for a file of cuttings. The range of trade journals which even large institutions will find it worthwhile keeping will be limited. The trade press varies greatly in the frequency with which it contains material of potential interest to the investor. The two largest collections of trade journals likely to be readily available to the London-based analyst are at the Guildhall Library and the very much larger one at the Patent Office Library in Holborn. The Guildhall Library has eschewed the technically-orientated trade press in favour of those journals concentrating on the commercial aspects of business. The Patent Office Library is a much more comprehensive collection of journals, in which leading overseas trade journals are also included. These, and particularly the U.S. journals, can add an interesting extra dimension to any study one is making of conditions and trends in a British industry.

This has been an attempt to suggest the general lines on which a small organisation, with the minimum permanent collection of source material of its own, might, nonetheless, go about finding the information on which to prepare quite ambitious analyses of the investment situation of industries, and of firms within industries. It has been done on the assumption that the attempt will be made without seeking the help of known experts, i.e. solely through the pursuit of publicly available published information. Perhaps one of the chief advantages of the modest operator in this field is that in practice he is very likely to succumb to the temptation to seek expert help, when the research department of the large institution, with its own extensive sources, may be prey to the illusion of self-sufficiency.

6 Taxation, Investment, and Equities under a Labour Government

A. J. MERRETT AND A. SYKES

This article was published in The Investment Analyst *in May 1964. The Labour Government in question was of course the one eventually formed by Mr Harold Wilson. The outgoing Conservative adminstration was described as 'tired' after 13 years in power, and a national perception of this characteristic was the main reason for their defeat in October 1964.*

The market was fearful that Mr Wilson's Government was planning harsher capital gains tax, a new profits tax and other restrictions. In fact, most of their fears proved unfounded. The authors note that the existing taxation and capital allowances were valuable assets and premature scrapping could be risky.

Ironically, the authors conclude that the 'lack of progress from amateurism to professionalism in the direction of Britain's tax affairs' is 'profoundly disheartening'.

A. J. Merrett and Allen Sykes were, respectively, Professor of Applied Economics at the University of Sheffield and Executive in the Treasurer's Department of Rio Tinto Zinc Ltd. at the time of publication.

I. INTRODUCTION

In his speech at Swansea on the 25th January, Mr. Harold Wilson outlined in some detail the economic policy the Labour Party proposed to follow if it wins the general election. The main objective of the Labour Party's economic policy is to expand national production, particularly long term national production, as fast as possible, and certainly much faster than in the past. An associated objective is to ease the burden of personal taxation, particularly on earned incomes. Three of the more important proposals for achieving these objectives may be summarised as follows:—

1. Providing selective investment allowances, speedier write-off provisions, and direct capital subventions for selected industries (and even selected *firms!*); four possible beneficiaries were named:—
   (a) those with export potential,
   (b) those with import-saving potential,
   (c) those producing 'named types of automative equipment', and
   (d) new publicly owned firms or industries 'based on science'.

   In short, generally to favour 'useful' and 'energetic' companies.
2. To redistribute the tax burden between individuals and companies to favour individuals. This will involve an increase in company taxation generally, with a 'return to the pre-1958 system of discriminating sharply between distributed and non-distributed profits'.
3. To introduce an effective capital gains tax.

This article is not concerned with the administrative or political practicability of these measures (the extent to which they could be operated efficiently and kept out of the political pork barrel) but only with their economic justification and effects. The measures will be considered in the order given above; readers primarily concerned with the effect on company results may, however, prefer to refer directly to section III below, which deals with this subject. For simplicity the discussion will be confined to quoted companies subject to the full marginal tax rate of 53.75 per cent.

II. HIGHER CAPITAL ALLOWANCES AND COMPANY TAXATION

Higher capital allowances are, of course, essentially an entitlement to lower effective rates of taxation contingent on the level and type of investment undertaken. (With the special tax concessions available in the Development Areas capital allowances also depend on *where* investment occurs.) As such their effect on company results will depend on the general new company tax structure discussed below. A general economic consideration, however, is the effect on investment decisions of high capital allowances combined with high rates of company taxation. British capital allowances are already the highest of any major industrialised country—investment allowances on much capital equipment is allowed at 30 per cent, and tax depreciation is allowed at between 35 per cent and 25 per cent in the first year, and between 25 per cent and 15 per cent per annum thereafter on the undepreciated balance. In the case of ships the 40 per cent investment allowance represents a direct government subsidy of 21.5 per cent (the 53.75 per cent tax rate times 40 per cent) of the capital cost. The superficial economic justification for raising these allowances still further is presumably that it will encourage investment in the selected industries.

Investment, however, is an economic activity and as such it is not desirable irrespective of cost. The questions to be asked are (i) what are the costs, and (ii) what level of costs would make such investment an economically advantageous activity from the *national* viewpoint. There is, unhappily, little evidence that either of these questions has been seriously considered.

That there is an obvious point at which capital allowances are undesirable can be seen by considering the effect on investment if capital allowances totalled 167 per cent of capital cost and the company tax rate was 60 per cent (a situation not so remote from that which exists with our present maximum for capital allowances of 140 per cent and tax rates of 53.75 per cent). Under these conditions the Revenue would pay 60 per cent of 167 per cent = 100 per cent of the capital cost of assets in tax reliefs. If these tax reliefs were granted immediately on purchase of the asset, a situation would be created in which it would never pay to operate any asset which had higher operating costs than a new asset. The capital cost of the new asset would be immaterial since the government would be paying for it—hence it would be worth getting a machine which cost £500,000 in order to save £1 a year in operating costs! It would also never pay to undertake non-capital repairs on assets—rather than clean their windows, lorries should be thrown away!

Similarly the most capital intensive methods of production would be employed; since the government would be footing the bill it would pay to spend any amount of capital in order to save on the operating costs. The only check on this economic absurdity would be that companies would ultimately all fall out of a tax paying position and the whole system of capital allowances would be negated (as would incidentally the whole system of company taxation).

To put it no higher, there is at least the danger that our existing levels of capital allowances are in a similar way causing serious wastage of capital assets by unjustifiably foreshortening their economic lives; this danger results from the *combination* of high capital allowances *and* high rates of company taxation.

Many complex issues are involved in determining the right levels and patterns of capital allowances, in particular (a) the extent to which companies are responsive to incentives of this kind, (b) the extent to which capital intensive methods should be encouraged to save labour (although it would also be necessary to take into account the labour intensive character of the actual production of such labour saving capital equipment).

It is hoped, however, that sufficient has been said of the dangers inherent in our existing level of capital allowances at our present level of taxation, to indicate the need for a most careful and searching analytical and empirical investigation before the present allowances are accepted as desirable, and certainly such investigation is imperative before any increases should be considered.

III. THE TWO-TIER PROFITS TAX

It is not known at the present time what the rates of tax would be under the new two-tier system. The following analysis is devoted primarily to considering the effects of 'sharp' discrimination on the 1958 scale.

1. SHORT-TERM EFFECTS

(a) 1958 Rates   By short-term we mean in this context one to two years. Barring soft competitive conditions that might be produced by excess demand and boom conditions in this period, it is unlikely that companies will be able in the short-term to pass on much, if any, additional tax burden. If the proposed tax is a reversion to the system in operation before 1958, it will broadly operate as follows. Like the present flat 15 per cent profits tax, the two-tier profits tax would operate only on taxable profits, that is profits as defined for tax purposes net of capital allowances, etc. (We assume that taxable profits are the same for both income tax and profits tax.) Assuming tax rates as in the pre-1958 system, namely 3 per cent on undistributed profits and 30 per cent on distributed profits, the tax computation would work as follows as regards a company with a reported profit of £150,000, net taxable profits of £100,000, and paying a dividend of £66,000 gross of income tax.

	Present System £000's	New System £000's
(1) Reported Profits	150.00	150.00
(2) Taxable Profits	100.00	100.00
(3) Profits Tax	15.00	30.00
(4) Income Tax	38.75	38.75
(5) Dividends (net of tax)	40.43	40.43
(6) Dividends (gross of tax)	66.00	66.00
$\qquad = \dfrac{40.43}{(1-.3875)}$		
(7) Undistributed Profits Tax Relief	(not applicable)	9.18*
(8) Net of Tax Retained Profits $=(1)-(3)-(4)-(5)+(7)$	55.82	50.00

* (This is computed as 27% (30%–3%) of (2)–(6))

It is clear from this simple example that the immediate additional burden or relief resulting from the new tax system will depend (a) on the ratio of reported profits to taxable profits, and (b) on the proportion of profits distributed as dividends. Taxable profits are not given in the ordinary course of company reports and accounts, but a rough estimate from the 3,000 largest quoted companies whose profits are recorded by the Board of Trade suggests that over the last 3 years taxable profits have been about 65 per cent of reported profits. This percentage will, of course, vary markedly with the different types of companies, depending on their particular accounting conventions, tax losses carried forward, the magnitude and type of their investment and the levels of capital allowances to which they are entitled given the particular nature and location of their investments, etc. Taking the average figure of 65 per cent, however, we might consider first the minimum present level of times covered (ratio of net of tax earnings to net of tax dividends) that would be required to maintain the existing level of dividends under the new tax system, assuming tax rates of 3 per cent on undistributed profits and 30 per cent on distributed profits. This times-covered ratio is about 1.17—well below the present average times-covered ratio of 1.725 on the Financial Times and Actuaries 500 index. Hence few companies are likely to be unable to maintain their present dividends.

It is to be expected that, as far as possible, companies would wish to maintain their existing level of dividends. As we have seen, however, a minimum present times-covered ratio of 1.17 would be required for this and it would probably be rather unusual for any company to be prepared to exhaust entirely its net of tax profits in dividends. The 1.17 times-covered figure would, in fact, leave the company with zero retained profits under the assumed new tax rates. A more realistic basis would probably be to assume that companies would wish to maintain a times-covered ratio of at least 1.5 under the new tax rates—that is, companies would retain £1 net of tax for every £2 net of tax that they distributed as dividends. (This would not, of course, mean that they literally had a times-covered ratio of 1.5 in the sense that they could increase dividends by 50 per cent, since the distributed profits tax in this case would be higher and hence they would lose more of their earnings in taxation). The level of times covered which they would require under the present tax dispensation to achieve this 1.5 times covered under the new tax dispensation (assuming again a reversion to the 3 per cent and 30 per cent rates) is about 1.74. This is about the average times-covered ratio; hence firms with dividends less than average times covered may be under some pressure to reduce dividends.

Some more general characteristics of the immediate impact of the two-tier tax are illustrated in the accompanying diagram. This shows on the horizontal axis the times-covered ratio under the present tax dispensation, and on the vertical axis the ratio of net of tax profits under the new dispensation to net of tax profits under the old (the present) dispensation. Each of the curves in the diagram represents a different ratio of taxable to reported profits—thus the curve marked $q = .65$ is the curve which relates to companies with a ratio of taxable to reported profits of .65, the present estimated average. (This diagram can also be used to show the effect on companies with preference shares. The dividend cover should be regarded as including the preference dividend as well as the equity.)

The diagram is based on the following assumptions:—

(i)   Gross profits before and after the new tax are constant;
(ii) The ratio of taxable to reported profits is constant;
(iii) Net of tax dividends are maintained at the present level; and
(iv) the standard rate of income tax is unchanged at 38.75 per cent.

Thus in the simplest case where a company is paying no taxes (the curve marked $q = 0$) because of sufficiently large capital allowances, etc., the new tax will evidently have no effect whatever and the ratio of net of tax profits under the new dispensation to net of tax profits under the old dispensation will be one. For companies with a ratio of taxable to

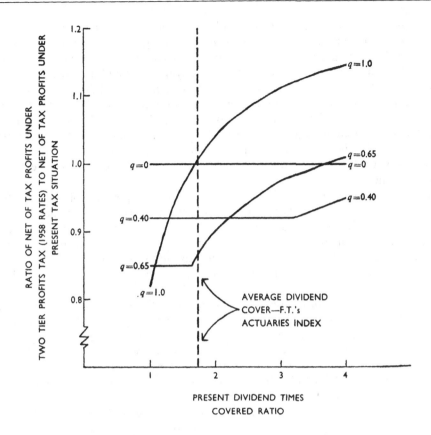

reported profits of .65, however, there will be an appreciable reduction in net of tax profits wherever the present times covered level is much less than 3. Thus companies with a present times covered of 1.72 (the current average on the Financial Times and Actuaries 500 index) will show a ratio of net of tax profits under the new dispensation to net of tax profits under the old dispensation of 86 per cent—that is net of tax profits will be reduced 14 per cent if these companies maintain their dividend at the present level. Strangely enough, companies with a relatively high times-covered ratio and a high proportion of taxable profits will positively benefit from the tax in the sense that their net of tax income will be higher under the new tax dispensation than under the old. Thus, companies with a ratio of taxable to reported profits of 1.0 and a times covered of 3 would show an 11.3 per cent increase in their net of tax profits.

Moreover, as is seen from the diagram, companies with a high ratio of taxable profits to reported profits—for example those companies for whom this ratio is equal to 1—will be almost uniformly better off than companies with a ratio of taxable to reported profits of .65. Companies in the former category would, in fact, be unaffected by the new taxes if they had a times-covered ratio now of 1.72 per cent (the average times-covered) even if they maintained their present level of dividends. If such companies had a times-covered ratio in excess of 1.72 they would gain appreciably from the proposed change in taxation.

There is, therefore, the bizarre result of the proposed new taxation that, in the short-term, both companies with a relatively high ratio of taxable to reported profits and companies with a relatively low ratio of taxable to reported profits would be relatively little affected by the new tax and in some cases would positively gain. On the other hand the company with about the average ratio of taxable to reported profits (of 65 per cent) would suffer substantially. (The reason for this rather extraordinary phenomena is simply that there are countervailing factors—if a company has a high ratio of taxable to reported profits, the disadvantages it would suffer from the high taxation of dividends would be offset by the reduction in the tax which it is now paying on its undistributed profits: but if the ratio of taxable to reported profits is relatively low, then the liability to higher taxation on dividends will be nullified since dividends will come from untaxed profits to a large extent and so will escape much of the new tax burden.) The varying impact of the new tax system has superimposed on it further variability resulting from differences in the times-covered ratio of different companies—the lower the present times-covered ratio the harder hit companies will be by the new tax system if they endeavour to maintain their present level of dividends.

Now it will be apparent that the proportion of taxable to reported profits and the times-covered ratio obtaining at the date of inception of the new tax are both largely fortuitous and may be due to factors quite unrelated in any way to the 'desirability' of the companies gaining or losing from the new taxes. There is, for example, no obvious reason why companies with the average ratio of taxable to reported profits should be worse treated than companies whose ratios are either very high *or* very low, although this, in fact, is what would happen.

There may appear a *prime facie* case for contending that companies with a relatively high ratio of distributed to undistributed profits should be penalised; but it should be appreciated that many of the companies which have such high ratios will be going through a phase of relatively low profitability and are trying to maintain some historic level of dividend payments. It will typically be the case in such instances that their shareholders have, on the whole, done rather badly out of such companies and it would seem somewhat odd, to say the least, to single them out for further sacrifices.

It is only possible to conclude that in the short term, if the burden of taxes could not be shifted on to consumers, the incidence of the new tax would be highly arbitrary if not, in many cases, tending to be systematically unfair and wanting in particular economic justification.

This would not be the case, however, with a straightforward increase in company taxation with no discrimination against dividends. In this case the net short run burden of the additional tax would simply be *directly* proportional to the ratio of taxable to reported profits and for this there may be some reasonable economic justification. Such a tax would not, like the two-tier tax, arbitrarily favour firms at *either* of the extremes of being non-tax paying and fully tax paying, or according to their high existing dividend cover.

(b) The effect of Rates other than the 1958 Rates

The analysis in (a) above was based on the assumption that the exact 1958 *rates* of profits tax will obtain. Sharper discrimination will result in greater arbitrariness, depending upon the proportion of taxable to reported profits. Indeed, only greatly reducing the sharpness of the discrimination will significantly reduce the arbitrariness, but with greatly reduced discrimination it is questionable whether it would be sufficiently effective in reducing dividends to be worth introducing at all.

The above discussion emphasizes the need for companies to publish both the amount of their taxable profits compared to their total profits, and true dividend cover. Without such information investment analysis is significantly handicapped.

2. LONG-TERM EFFECTS

The long-term effect of the two-tier tax and indeed any increase in corporate taxes depends largely on the assumptions that can reasonably be made about the effect such taxation will have on company profitability. We would argue that there is fairly strong evidence to the effect that the net of tax rate of return achieved by *companies* over periods of a decade or so, and barring any major economic upheavals (such as runaway inflation, deflation or price controls), tends to remain relatively constant between 8 per cent and 10 per cent in real terms after profits tax and tax at the standard rate.* It is particularly significant in this connection that in the United States, where corporate taxes have been in the 50/52 per cent range and heavy additional personal taxation has been imposed on dividends in the hands of shareholders, the next tax rate of return to equity capital has been within a similar range. There are obvious exceptions to the generalisation that company taxation is passed on by prices being higher than they otherwise would: industries with heavy excess capacity or industries in competition with foreign countries (for example, ship building and shipping) are unlikely to be able to pass on increases in taxation in this way.

In the past, there has been an identity of interest, as regards taxation, between the shareholder paying tax at the standard rate and companies. As companies tended to maintain their net of tax profits intact despite changes in the standard rate of taxation (which, of course, applies to all company profits) they were in a position to maintain net of tax dividends in the hands of the shareholder paying tax at the standard rate, irrespective of these changes in the standard rate of taxation.

The differential taxation of dividends, however, would effectively eliminate some of this identity of interests between the shareholder paying taxes at the standard rate and the company. For these tax proposals effectively make the company's tax bill, and hence the net of tax profits, variable according to the proportion of profits paid out as dividends. Thus, to keep its net of tax rate of return intact, a company might pay out a reduced proportion of its earnings as dividends so as to reduce its relative tax burden and hence keep its rate of return constant. If this happened then the shareholders' dividend would be reduced by the amount necessary to pay the additional taxes on distributed profits.

Given, however, that most firms which have the earnings cover to enable them to do so will be trying to maintain their existing level of dividends intact, and the rate of growth of profits is generally not sufficiently fast to permit a *rapidly* diminishing proportion of profits to be paid out as dividend without actually reducing the amount of dividend, then we would expect the burden of the increase in taxation to be shared between the consumer and the shareholder in the form of product prices being higher and dividends being lower than they otherwise would. On balance, it seems probable that the excess demand and inflationary conditions, which would seem an inevitable concomitant of the pursuit of high rates of growth (particularly the Labour Party's less qualified commitment to this objective), would be likely to result in the main burden of the higher taxation being borne by the consumer in the form of higher product prices. This conclusion would apply rather more strongly to actual increases in the overall level of corporate taxation.

The exceptions, of course, will be those companies which are already depressed or in severe competition in international markets. These companies would have very limited opportunities to pass on the burden of taxation in higher prices. Moreover, as we have seen earlier, if these companies have a relatively low ratio of taxable to reported profits (as may be fairly common given the often lower rates of profits of such companies) it would be necessary, as far as possible, to relieve these companies of the burden of additional taxation by further investment allowances, etc. The main outcome of the proposed taxation would, therefore, seem to be that in the sheltered home markets much of the burden would be borne by consumers in the form of higher prices, while companies in the more competitive

---

* See 'Incomes Policy and Company Profitability' and 'Return on Equities and Fixed Interest Securities 1919–1962' by A. J. Merrett and Allen Sykes, District Bank Review, September and December, 1963.

international markets would effectively need to be relieved of the additional burden of taxation if they were not to be placed at a most undesirable disadvantage relative to companies operating to a larger degree in the more sheltered home markets.

3. GENERAL ECONOMIC EFFECTS

Even though the whole burden of the additional taxation may be passed on in consumer prices, it is still possible that the change in taxation will have some differential effects on company financing, investment policy, etc. Thus, companies might obtain higher levels of profit in order to offset additional taxation, but might still be inclined towards a higher level of retained profits owing to the effect of the differential profits taxation.

The tendency of higher taxation of distributed profits to result in higher levels of retained earnings is frequently opposed on the grounds

(a) that it restricts the flow of capital, particularly 'risk' capital, by locking it up in companies which have earned it, irrespective of the opportunity to invest it, and
(b) that the funds retained will strengthen inefficient and complacent managements.

Argument (a) is certainly not literally true since companies with excess cash typically invest it in the fixed-interest securities of the central and local governments. If this investment were the only result of the excess cash arising from the distributed profits tax, the latter might be looked on as an inducement to make firms lend their shareholders' money (money that would otherwise be dividends) to the Government. Moreover, if the Government and local governments are not prepared to absorb the additional cash, it must force other lenders to the central and local governments to move out of this part of the fixed-interest capital market and lend more to commercial and domestic borrowers. (It would certainly seem most unlikely that the banks and the major institutions in the short-term money market would ever be prepared to keep their cash idle.) Thus, the argument against retained earnings in this context must be that the utilisation and circulation of this element of retained profits through the fixed-interest markets is less desirable than the utilisation and circulation that would result from this cash being paid out as dividends to shareholders.

This is basically a question of fact and serious empirical enquiry should be able to produce a fairly conclusive answer. The first question is the extent to which new issues and rights issues are financed, directly or indirectly, by funds emanating from dividend payments and the capital gains to which increased dividend payments lead. Second, we need to know the extent to which a reduction in the flow of funds coming into the market as a result of lower dividends would restrict investment significantly and the type of investment which would be so restricted. (It is evidently possible that the companies whose investments are restricted by want of funds are those companies which are in themselves only marginally profitable.) We would, however, incline to the view that the reduction in dividends plus capital gains will be insufficiently large and will be offset by the indirect flow of retained profits into the debt capital market to an extent that will make the net effect under (a) of negligible importance (particularly since the main risky investments are nowadays undertaken by major companies and the smaller companies rely heavily on debt capital and retained earnings).

Argument (b), that high retained earnings strengthen inefficient and complacent managements, is again a question of fact which could be evaluated by a careful analysis of companies which have had high retained earnings in say the last ten years. Common observation suggests that this argument is true—certainly the view is very widely held in industry. Hence argument (b) is almost certainly an adverse feature of heavier taxation of distributed profits: the only question is simply how common and how important are its effects.

The arguments in favour of higher retained profits, and hence higher taxation of distributed profits, are presumably (c) that they might increase the rate of saving, (d) that they might increase the rate of investment, and (e) that they would help in bargaining with organised labour over incomes policy.

Argument (c) is again a question of fact. The main question which needs to be answered is the extent to which the combined savings of companies and shareholders is influenced by the choice between retained profits and dividends. At one extreme the retained profits might be a net addition to the savings of the community, since the distribution of such profits as dividends may normally result in their being entirely utilised by shareholders for consumption. At the other extreme it may be the case that shareholders normally save a high proportion of dividends. Again, it may be the case that the choice between retaining or distributing profits has no effect on savings at all since the retained earnings result in higher capital gains and shareholders maintain their consumption either by realising some of these capital gains or, alternatively, spend on consumption some money they would otherwise have invested, had it not been for their wealth being increased by capital gains. Modern sample survey methods should make it possible to answer this question to a useful degree of accuracy. All that can be said at the moment is simply that there is not sufficient data to come to any firm conclusion.

As regards argument (d), the possibility that higher retained profits would stimulate investment, there should certainly be some effect in this direction. The magnitude of this effect, however, would probably be rather small since the main managements that would probably be induced to retain more of their profit under the differential profits tax will tend to be the financially conservative managements which are generally most inflexible in demanding high levels of safe return. It will also clearly be the case that the companies described earlier which will end up bearing a higher level of taxation (companies with relatively low profits or those competing in international markets) will not be stimulated to higher levels of investment. When account is taken of these factors and the economic losses through reckless and ill-conceived investments which the less capable and less efficient companies will undertake as a result of the pressure from excess cash, it is hard to believe that there will be any net advantage under this head.

On argument (e), that such differential taxation will better enable a bargain to be made with the trade unions as regards an incomes policy, this may be true, although it needs to be evaluated in the light of alternative, less economically harmful methods of achieving such an effect.

IV. EFFECT ON MONETARY POLICY

The most serious effect of the proposed legislation—if it is effective in its object of making firms retain a higher proportion of their earnings—may well be on monetary policy and growth. High levels of self-financing creates situations in which firms are, to a substantial degree, 'their own bankers' with sufficient cash generation and liquid assets to enable them to ignore the efforts of monetary policy to restrain excessive investment booms from developing. This, of course, negates monetary policy and throws the burden of adjustment on those sectors which can be controlled by statute—e.g., hire purchase and public investment. It is possible that this weakening of monetary policy will force the Labour Party towards the very 'stop-go' policies they wish to avoid.

V. CAPITAL GAINS TAXATION

The socialist minority report of the 1952 Royal Commission on Taxation recommended that 'after introduction of a capital gains tax the corporation profits tax should be charged at a uniform rate on the whole income of companies', on the grounds that such a tax would be most conductive to the efficiency of a private enterprise economy and the advantages accruing to shareholders would be offset by the capital gains tax. This flies in the face of Mr. Wilson's latest proposals.

The argument for some form of capital gains tax from the standpoint of equity seems unanswerable, but the question of the rates and methods of assessment are matters of crucial importance. The American system leaves much to be desired since a flat rate combined with a tax assessment only at the time of realisation perpetuates much of the existing inequities and makes the incidence of the tax, particularly its burden in real terms (i.e. its cost in real terms taking into account both the delay in actual payment and the effect of inflation) highly uncertain.

Rather than copying the imperfect American system we should seriously consider the possibility of taxing accrued gains (that is unrealised gains) at income and surtax rates but on the basis of an accrued (not immediately paid) tax liability. Payment of the accrued liability should then be made, say, proportionate to the proportion of the assets realised.[1]

This system, which obviously cannot be discussed in detail here, would appear to have considerable advantages of equity and flexibility over the flat rate system, and would probably be no more expensive to administer.

VI. CONCLUSIONS

Our conclusions are as follows:

1. The existing system of company taxation and capital allowances is such that there is a serious danger of the premature scrapping of valuable assets if the investment allowances are further increased and/or company taxation increased).

2. The short-term effect of the two-tier profits tax would be highly arbitrary, favouring companies with low or high taxable profits or companies with a high times-covered ratio, and penalising the more 'average' firms. In the longer term, with certain important exceptions, the higher taxation would probably be passed on to consumers in higher prices. The most important consideration may be the effects on monetary policy. The general economic effect of the two-tier profits tax would certainly be harmful in some respects, but serious assessment turns largely on unresolved questions of fact and analysis.

3. Given the need for serious reform in our tax system, but given also that the number of major changes that can be undertaken is obviously limited, it should be the subject of great concern to ensure that Mr. Wilson's proposals are given a most careful professional and public examination and evaluation before being implemented.

4. The most significant conclusion, however, is to be drawn from the large number of, and the apparent indifference to, unanswered questions of fact on which the proposals turn, and the absence—either from the Labour Party or any other quarter—of a detailed objective evaluation of the net advantages of the proposed legislation. The conclusion which must be drawn is the profoundly disheartening one of the lack of any real progress from amateurism to professionalism in the direction of Britain's tax affairs.

---

[1] This proposal will be considered more fully in a forthcoming article by A. J. Merrett in 'The Oxford Economic Papers', July 1964.

7 Random Walks in Stock Market Prices

E. F. FAMA

This article was published in The Investment Analyst *in December 1965. It provided a timely introduction to the theory of random walks. Previously, much of the discussion of the subject had taken place in technical journals; this paper provided a lucid assessment of the implications for market analysts.*

Eugene F. Fama was Assistant Professor of Finance, Graduate School of Business, The University of Chicago at the time of publication.

For many years economists, statisticians, and teachers of finance have been interested in developing and testing models of stock price behavior. One important model that has evolved from this research is the theory of random walks. This theory casts serious doubt on many other methods for describing and predicting stock price behavior—methods that have considerable popularity outside the academic world. For example, we shall see later that if the random walk theory is an accurate description of reality, then the various "technical" or "chartist" procedures for predicting stock prices are completely without value.

In general the theory of random walks raises challenging questions for anyone who has more than a passing interest in understanding the behavior of stock prices. Unfortunately, however, most discussions of the theory have appeared in technical academic journals and in a form which the non-mathematician would usually find incomprehensible. This article describes, briefly and simply, the theory of random walks and some of the important issues it raises concerning the work of market analysts. To preserve brevity some aspects of the theory and its implications are omitted. More complete (and also more technical) discussions of the theory of random walks are available elsewhere; hopefully the introduction provided here will encourage the reader to examine one of the more rigorous and lengthy works listed at the end of this article.

COMMON TECHNIQUES FOR PREDICTING STOCK MARKET PRICES

In order to put the theory of random walks into perspective we first discuss, in brief and general terms, the two approaches to predicting stock prices that are commonly espoused by market professionals. These are (1) "chartist" or "technical" theories and (2) the theory of fundamental or intrinsic value analysis.

The basic assumption of all the chartist or technical theories is that history tends to repeat itself, i.e., past patterns of price behavior in individual securities will tend to recur in the

The author is indebted to his colleagues William Alberts, David Green, Merton Miller, and Harry Roberts for their helpful comments and criticisms.

future. Thus the way to predict stock prices (and, of course, increase one's potential gains) is to develop a familiarity with past patterns of price behavior in order to recognize situations of likely recurrence.

Essentially, then, chartist techniques attempt to use knowledge of the past behavior of a price series to predict the probable future behavior of the series. A statistician would characterize such techniques as assuming that successive price changes in individual securities are dependent. That is, the various chartist theories assume that the *sequence* of price changes prior to any given day is important in predicting the price change for that day.[1]

The techniques of the chartist have always been surrounded by a certain degree of mysticism, however, and as a result most market professionals have found them suspect. Thus it is probably safe to say that the pure chartist is relatively rare among stock market analysts. Rather the typical analyst adheres to a technique known as fundamental analysis or the intrinsic value method. The assumption of the fundamental analysis approach is that at any point in time an individual security has an intrinsic value (or in the terms of the economist, an equilibrium price) which depends on the earning potential of the security. The earning potential of the security depends in turn on such fundamental factors as quality of management, outlook for the industry and the economy, etc.

Through a careful study of these fundamental factors the analyst should, in principle, be able to determine whether the actual price of a security is above or below its intrinsic value. If actual prices tend to move toward intrinsic values, then attempting to determine the intrinsic value of a security is equivalent to making a prediction of its future price; and this is the essence of the predictive procedure implicit in fundamental analysis.

THE THEORY OF RANDOM WALKS

Chartist theories and the theory of fundamental analysis are really the province of the market professional and to a large extent teachers of finance. Historically, however, there has been a large body of academic people, primarily economists and statisticians, who adhere to a radically different approach to market analysis—the theory of random walks in stock market prices. The remainder of this article will be devoted to a discussion of this theory and its major implications.

Random walk theorists usually start from the premise that the major security exchanges are good examples of "efficient" markets. An "efficient" market is defined as a market where there are large numbers of rational, profit-maximizers actively competing, with each trying to predict future market values of individual securities, and where important current information is almost freely available to all participants.

In an efficient market, competition among the many intelligent participants leads to a situation where, at any point in time, actual prices of individual securities already reflect the effects of information based both on events that have already occurred and on events which, as of now, the market expects to take place in the future. In other words, in an efficient market at any point in time the actual price of a security will be a good estimate of its intrinsic value.

Now in an uncertain world the intrinsic value of a security can never be determined exactly. Thus there is always room for disagreement among market participants concerning just what the intrinsic value of an individual security is, and such disagreement will give rise to discrepancies between actual prices and intrinsic values. In an efficient market, however,

---

[1] Probably the best known example of the chartist approach to predicting stock prices is the Dow Theory.

the actions of the many competing participants should cause the actual price of a security to wander randomly about its intrinsic value. If the discrepancies between actual prices and intrinsic values are systematic rather than random in nature, then knowledge of this should help intelligent market participants to better predict the path by which actual prices will move towards intrinsic values. When the many intelligent traders attempt to take advantage of this knowledge, however, they will tend to neutralize such systematic behavior in price series. Although uncertainty concerning intrinsic values will remain, actual prices of securities will wander randomly about their intrinsic values.

Of course intrinsic values can themselves change across time as a result of new information. The new information may involve such things as the success of a current research and development project, a change in management, a tariff imposed on the industry's product by a foreign country, an increase in industrial production or any other *actual or anticipated* change in a factor which is likely to affect the company's prospects.

In an efficient market, *on the average*, competition will cause the full effects of new information on intrinsic values to be reflected "instantaneously" in actual prices. In fact, however, because there is vagueness or uncertainty surrounding new information, "instantaneous adjustment" really has two implications. First, actual prices will initially overadjust to changes in intrinsic values as often as they will underadjust. Second, the lag in the complete adjustment of actual prices to successive new intrinsic values will itself be an independent, random variable with the adjustment of actual prices sometimes preceding the occurrence of the event which is the basis of the change in intrinsic values (i.e., when the event is anticipated by the market before it actually occurs) and sometimes following.

This means that the "instantaneous adjustment" property of an efficient market implies that successive price changes in individual securities will be independent. A market where successive price changes in individual securities are independent is, by definition, a random walk market. Most simply the theory of random walks implies that a series of stock price changes has no memory—the past history of the series cannot be used to predict the future in any meaningful way. The future path of the price level of a security is no more predictable than the path of a series of cumulated random numbers.

It is unlikely that the random walk hypothesis provides an exact description of the behavior of stock market prices. For practical purposes, however, the model may be acceptable even though it does not fit the facts exactly. Thus although successive price changes may not be strictly independent, the actual amount of dependence may be so small as to be unimportant.

What should be classified as unimportant depends, of course, on the question at hand. For the stock market trader or investor the criterion is obvious: The independence assumption of the random walk model is valid as long as knowledge of the past behavior of the series of price changes cannot be used to increase expected gains. More specifically, if successive price changes for a given security are independent, there is no problem in timing purchases and sales of that security. A simple policy of buying and holding the security will be as good as any more complicated mechanical procedure for timing purchases and sales. This implies that, for investment purposes, the independence assumption of the random walk model is an adequate description of reality as long as the actual degree of dependence in series of price changes is not sufficient to make the expected profits of any more "sophisticated" mechanical trading rule or chartist technique greater than the expected profits under a naive buy-and-hold policy.

EMPIRICAL EVIDENCE ON INDEPENDENCE

Over the years a number of empirical tests of the random walk theory have been performed; indeed, so many that it is not possible to discuss them adequately here. Therefore in describing the empirical evidence we limit ourselves to a brief discussion of the different approaches employed and the general conclusions that have evolved.

The main concern of empirical research on the random walk model has been to test the hypothesis that successive price changes are independent. Two different approaches have been followed. First there is the approach that relies primarily on common statistical tools such as serial correlation coefficients and analysis of runs of consecutive price changes of the same sign. If the statistical tests tend to support the assumption of independence, one then *infers* that there are probably no mechanical trading rules or chartist techniques, based solely on patterns in the past history of price changes, which would make the expected profits of the investor greater than they would be with a simple buy-and-hold policy. The second approach to testing independence proceeds by testing directly different mechanical trading rules to see whether or not they provide profits greater than buy-and-hold.

Research to date has tended to concentrate on the first or statistical approach to testing independence; the results have been consistent and impressive. I know of no study in which standard statistical tools have produced evidence of *important* dependence in series of successive price changes. In general, these studies (and there are many of them) have tended to uphold the theory of random walks. This is true, for example, of the serial correlation tests of Cootner [4],[1] Fama [5], Kendall [9], and Moore [10]. In all of these studies, the sample serial correlation coefficients computed for successive price changes were extremely close to zero, which is evidence against important dependence in the changes. Similarly, Fama's [5] analysis of runs of successive price changes of the same sign, and the spectral analysis techniques of Granger and Morgenstern [8], and Godfrey, Granger and Morgenstern [7] also support the independence assumption of the random walk model.

We should emphasize, however, that although the statistical techniques mentioned above have been the common tools used in testing independence, the chartist or technical theorist probably would not consider them adequate. For example, he would not consider either serial correlations or runs analyses as adequate tests of whether the past history of series of price changes can be used to increase the investor's expected profits. The simple linear relationships that underlie the serial correlation model are much too unsophisticated to pick up the complicated "patterns" that the chartist sees in stock prices. Similarly, the runs tests are much too rigid in their manner of determining the duration of upward and downward movements in prices. In particular: in runs-testing, a run is considered as terminated whenever there is a change in sign in the sequence of successive price changes, regardless of the size of the price change that causes the change in sign. The chartist would like to have a more sophisticated method for identifying movements—a method which does not always predict the termination of the movement simply because the price level has temporarily changed direction.

These criticisms of common statistical tools have not gone unheeded, however. For example, Alexander's filter technique [1,2] is an attempt to apply more sophisticated criteria to the identification of moves. Although the filter technique does not correspond exactly to any well-known chartist theory, it is closely related to such things as the Dow Theory. Thus, the profitability of the filter technique can be used to make inferences concerning the potential profitability of other mechanical trading rules.

A filter of, say, 5 per cent is defined as follows: if the daily closing price of a particular security moves up at least 5 per cent, buy and hold the security until its price moves down at least 5 per cent from a subsequent high, at which time simultaneously sell and go short. The

---

[1] See References at article's end.

short position is maintained until the daily closing price rises at least 5 per cent above a subsequent low, at which time one should simultaneously cover and buy. Moves less than 5 per cent in either direction are ignored.

It is, of course, unnecessary to limit the size of the filter to 5 per cent. In fact, Professor Alexander has reported tests of the filter technique for filters ranging in size from 1 per cent to 50 per cent. The tests cover different time periods from 1897 to 1959 and involve daily closing prices for two indices, the Dow-Jones Industrials from 1897 to 1929 and Standard and Poor's Industrials from 1929 to 1959. In Alexander's latest work [2], it turns out that even when the higher broker's commissions incurred under the filter rule are ignored, the filter technique can not consistently beat the simple policy of buying and holding the indices for the different periods tested. Elsewhere I have tested the filter technique on individual securities. Again the simple buy-and-hold method consistently beats the profits produced by different size filters. It seems, then, that at least for the purposes of the individual trader or investor, tests of the filter technique also tend to support the random walk model.

IMPLICATIONS OF THE RANDOM WALK THEORY FOR CHARTIST AND INTRINSIC VALUE ANALYSIS

As stated earlier, chartist theories implicitly assume that there is dependence in series of successive price changes. That is, the history of the series can be used to make meaningful predictions concerning the future. On the other hand, the theory of random walks says that successive price changes are independent, i.e., the past cannot be used to predict the future. Thus the two theories are diametrically opposed, and if, as the empirical evidence seems to suggest, the random walk theory is valid, then chartist theories are akin to astrology and of no real value to the investor.

In an uncertain world, however, no amount of empirical testing is sufficient to establish the validity of a hypothesis beyond any shadow of doubt. The chartist or technical theorist always has the option of declaring that the evidence in support of the random walk theory is not sufficient to validate the theory. On the other hand, the chartist must admit that the evidence in favor of the random walk model is both consistent and voluminous, whereas there is precious little published discussion of rigorous empirical tests of the various technical theories. If the chartist rejects the evidence in favor of the random walk model, his position is weak if his own theories have not been subjected to equally rigorous tests. This, I believe, is the challenge that the random walk theory makes to the technician.

There is nothing in the above discussion, however, which suggests that superior fundamental or intrinsic value analysis is useless in a random walk-efficient market. In fact the analyst will do better than the investor who follows a simple buy-and-hold policy as long as he can more quickly identify situations where there are non-negligible discrepancies between actual prices and intrinsic values than other analysts and investors, and if he is better able to predict the occurrence of important events and evaluate their effects on intrinsic values.

If there are many analysts who are pretty good at this sort of thing, however, and if they have considerable resources at their disposal, they help narrow discrepancies between actual prices and intrinsic values and cause actual prices, on the average, to adjust "instantaneously" to changes in intrinsic values. That is, the existence of many sophisticated analysts helps make the market more efficient which in turn implies a market which conforms more closely to the random walk model. Although the returns to these sophisticated analysts may be quite high, they establish a market in which fundamental analysis is a fairly useless procedure both for the average analyst and the average investor. That is, in a random walk-efficient market, on the average, a security chosen by a mediocre analyst will produce a return no better than that obtained from a randomly selected security of the same general riskiness.

There probably aren't many analysts (in fact, I know of none) who would willingly concede that they are no better than the "average" analyst. If all analysts think they are better than average, however, this only means that their estimate of the average is biased downward. Fortunately, it is not necessary to judge an analyst solely by his claims. The discussion above provides a natural benchmark with which we can evaluate his performance.

In a random walk-efficient market at any point in time the market price of a security will already reflect the judgments of many analysts concerning the relevance of currently available information to the prospects of that security. Now an individual analyst may feel that he has better insights than those that are already implicit in the market price. For example, he may feel that a discrepancy between market price and intrinsic value exists for some security, or he may think the intrinsic value of the security is itself about to change because of some impending piece of new information which is not yet generally available.

These "insights" of the analyst are of no real value, however, unless they are eventually borne out in the market, that is, unless the actual market price eventually moves in the predicted direction. In other words, if the analyst can make meaningful judgments concerning the purchase and sale of individual securities, his choices should consistently outperform randomly selected securities of the same general riskiness. It must be stressed, however, that the analyst must *consistently* produce results better than random selection, since, by the nature of uncertainty, for any given time period he has about a 50 per cent chance of doing better than random selection even if his powers of analysis are completely non-existent. Moreover, not only must the analyst do consistently better than random selection, but he must beat random selection by an amount which is at least sufficient to cover the cost of the resources (including his own time) which are expended in the process of carrying out his more complicated selection procedures.

What we propose, then, is that the analyst subject his performance to a rigorous comparison with a random selection procedure. One simple practical way of comparing the results produced by an analyst with a random selection procedure is the following: Every time the analyst recommends a security for purchase (or sale), another security of the same general riskiness is chosen randomly. A future date is then chosen at which time the results produced by the two securities will be compared. Even if the analyst is no better than the random selection procedure, in any given comparison there is still a 50 per cent chance that the security he has chosen will out-perform the randomly selected security. After the game has been played for a while, however, and the results of many different comparisons are accumulated, then it will become clear whether the analyst is worth his salt or not.

In many circumstances, however, the primary concern is with the performance of a portfolio rather than with the performance of individual securities in the portfolio. In this situation one would want to compare the performance of the portfolio in question with that of a portfolio of randomly selected securities. A useful benchmark for randomly selected portfolios has been provided by Fisher and Lore[6]. They computed rates of return for investments in common stocks on the New York Stock Exchange for various time periods from 1926 to 1960. The basic assumption in all of their computations is that at the beginning of each period studied the investor puts an equal amount of money in each common stock listed at that time on the Exchange. This amounts to random sampling where the sampling is, of course, exhaustive. Different rates of return are then computed for different possible tax brackets of the investor, first under the assumption that all dividends are reinvested in the month paid, and then under the assumption that dividends are not reinvested.

A possible procedure for the analyst is to compare returns for given time periods earned by portfolios he has managed with the returns earned for the same time periods by the

Fisher-Lorie "randomly selected" portfolios. It is important to note, however, that this will be a valid test procedure only if the portfolios managed by the analyst had about the same degree of riskiness as the Fisher-Lorie "market" portfolios. If this is not the case, the Fisher-Lorie results will not provide a proper benchmark. In order to make a proper comparison between the results produced by the analyst and a random selection policy, it will be necessary to define and study the behavior of portfolios of randomly selected securities, where these portfolios are selected in such a way that they have about the same degree of riskiness as those managed by the analyst.

If the claims of analysts concerning the advantages of fundamental analysis have any basis in fact, the tests suggested above would seem to be easy to pass. In fact, however, the only "analysts" that have so far undergone these tests are open end mutual funds. In their appeals to the public, mutual funds usually make two basic claims: (1) because it pools the resources of many individuals, a fund can diversify much more effectively than the average, small investor; and (2) because of its management's closeness to the market, the fund is better able to detect "good buys" in individual securities. In most cases the first claim is probably true. The second, however, implies that mutual funds provide a higher return than would be earned by a portfolio of randomly selected securities. In a separate paper [5] I reported the results of a study which suggest that if the initial loading charges of mutual funds are ignored, on the average the funds do about as well as a randomly selected portfolio. If one takes into account the higher initial loading charges of the funds, however, on the average the random investment policy outperforms the funds. In addition, these results would seem to be consistent with those of the now famous Wharton study of mutual funds [11].

These adverse results with respect to mutual funds have tended to lead random walk theorists to feel that other financial institutions, and most professional investment advisers as well, probably do no better than random selection. Institutions and analysts can only dispel such doubts by submitting their performance to a rigorous comparison with a random selection procedure.

CONCLUSION

In sum the theory of random walks in stock market prices presents important challenges to both the chartist and the proponent of fundamental analysis. For the chartist, the challenge is straightforward. If the random walk model is a valid description of reality, the work of the chartist, like that of the astrologer, is of no real value in stock market analysis. The empirical evidence to date provides strong support for the random walk model. In this light the only way the chartist can vindicate his position is to *show* that he can *consistently* use his techniques to make better than chance predictions of stock prices. It is not enough for him to talk mystically about patterns that he sees in the data. He must show that he can consistently use these patterns to make meaningful predictions of future prices.

The challenge of the theory of random walks to the proponent of fundamental analysis, however, is more involved. If the random walk theory is valid and if security exchanges are "efficient" markets, then stock prices at any point in time will represent good estimates of intrinsic or fundamental values. Thus, additional fundamental analysis is of value only when the analyst has new information which was not fully considered in forming current market prices, or has new insights concerning the effects of generally available information which are not already implicit in current prices. If the analyst has neither better insights nor new information, he may as well forget about fundamental analysis and choose securities by some random selection procedure.

In essence, the challenge of the random walk theory to the proponent of fundamental analysis is to show that his more complicated procedures are actually more profitable than a simple random selection policy. As in the case of the chartist, the challenge is an empirical one. The analyst cannot merely protest that he thinks the securities he selects do better than randomly selected securities; he must demonstrate that this is in fact the case.

REFERENCES

1. Alexander, Sidney S. "Price Movements in Speculative Markets: Trends or Random Walks," *Industrial Management Review*, II (May, 1961), 7–26.
2. Alexander, Sidney S. "Price Movements in Speculative Markets: Trends or Random Walks, Number 2," *Industrial Management Review*, V (Spring, 1964) 25–46.
3. Cootner, Paul H. (editor). *The Random Character of Stock Market Prices.* Cambridge: M.I.T. Press, 1964. An excellent compilation of research on the theory of random walks completed prior to mid-1963.
4. Cootner, Paul H. "Stock Prices: Random vs. Systematic Changes," *Industrial Management Review*, III (Spring, 1962), 24–25.
5. Fama, Eugene F. "The Behavior of Stock Market Prices," *Journal of Business*, XXXVIII (January, 1965), 34–105.
6. Fisher, L. and Lorie, J. H. "Rates of Return on Investments in Common Stocks," *Journal of Business*, (January, 1964), 1–21.
7. Godfrey, Michael D., Granger, Clive W. J., and Morgenstern, Oskar. "The Random Walk Hypothesis of Stock Market Behavior," *Kyklos*, XVII (January, 1964), 1–30.
8. Granger, Clive W. J. and Morgenstern, O. "Spectral Analysis of New York Stock Market Prices," *Kyklos*, XVI (January, 1963), 1–27.
9. Kendall, M. G. "The Analysis of Economic Time Series," *Journal of the Royal Statistical Society* (Series A), XCVI (1953), 11–25.
10. Moore, Arnold. "A Statistical Analysis of Common Stock Prices," unpublished Ph.D. dissertation, Graduate School of Business, University of Chicago (1962).
11. 'A Study of Mutual Funds," prepared for the Securities and Exchange Commission by the Wharton School of Finance and Commerce. Report of the Committee on Interstate and Foreign Commerce. Washington: U.S. Government Printing Office, 1962.

8 Security Price Behaviour

A. G. ELLINGER

This article appeared in The Investment Analyst *in May 1966. In his riposte to Professor Fama's article on random walks in stock market prices, Alec Ellinger finds some illumination, but too much pessimism. He also detects a misunderstanding of the aims of technical analysts.*

Alec Ellinger began Investment Research in Cambridge in 1944. The company become the forerunner of technical analysis in Europe. Alec was one of the first analysts to advise investment in equities, in preference to gilts, in the post-war era. He was also one of the first to recognize the seriousness of the oil crisis of 1974. Alec become a founder of the Society of Technical Analysts and the only person to be elected a Fellow both of that Society and of the Society of Investment Analysts (now the IIMR). His book The Art of Investment *was a best seller. Alec retired in the late 1970s and died in 1990.*

Professor Fama's article about Random Walks was both illuminating and infuriating—and, though it was very well discussed by Austin Friars in two successive issues of the *Investors Chronicle* in January, some further comment is desirable. It seems best to deal first with the infuriating aspects of the random walk theory; we can then turn to the illuminating aspects.

Professor Fama derives the random nature of security price movements from the "efficiency" of the stock market. This seems to imply that attention should be paid to the Analysts: Listed Stocks ratio; when this ratio rises above a certain level analysis becomes valueless to the analyst's employer and he should employ a secretary with a pin for stock selection but when enough of his competitors grasp the splendid economies of pin analysis the ratio will decline below the level at which it once again becomes profitable to employ an analyst. The situation is flattering to fundamental analysts who may be deemed to be of value some of the time but unflattering to technical analysts, who would never have any place. The fundamental and the technical analysts both base their beliefs on characteristics which they believe are permanent in the market; the adherents of the Random Walk have to rely on the market's having reached and thereafter continued to maintain a level of what they call "efficiency".

Technical analysts will be unanimous, and they will have the support of most fundamental analysts, in denying that investors act rationally. For investors investment seems about as rational as marriage (statisticians, particularly random walkers, may, for all investors know, conduct their marital affairs on a rational basis). The British investor now finds it difficult to believe that his buying of industrial shares in the first five months of 1961, or of insurance, stores and property shares in the first four months of 1962, was in any way rational. Analysts will agree that investors think, at the time when decisions are being taken, that they are being taken on rational grounds; but most investors must have had subsequent doubts of the rationality of at least some of their earlier decisions.

Analysts may be far less unanimous about the notion of "intrinsic value". No chartist can believe in it; and no fundamental analyst need. But Professor Fama's "intrinsic value" appears to be the price which ought to be paid in the market in the light of all the known infromation, not the price which ought to be paid if all that should have been known were known. This is an important distinction; for Professor Fama the price of Kreuger & Toll the day before Kreuger shot himself may have been very close to the "intrinsic value". To analysts the whole distinction between price and value is unhelpful; and if one pursues the matter further into the philosophy of investment one becomes very doubtful whether the concept of value has any validity.

When Professor Fama writes "in an efficient market, however, the actions of the many competing participants should cause the actual price of a security to wander randomly about its intrinsic value", he is to some extent illuminating. Investors who reject the notion of the rational market and of intrinsic value can still agree that the actual price of a security is likely to be wandering randomly towards something—and that something may well be described as a "target price" (the image is of anti-aircraft gunners aiming at a "drogue" towed at a safe distance behind an aircraft). What fundamental analysts try to do is to estimate the earnings of a company over the years ahead and to apply to those future earnings an appropriate multiple to determine the future price which they should now be expecting. As time passes the estimates both of the earning and of the multiple for the appropriate interval ahead are liable to change; and so the actual price pursues not a fixed, intrinsic value but a moving target. The random movements described by Professor Fama, once they are attributed to a price in pursuit of its target, seem to correspond very closely with the movements of stock prices as we know them.

Professor Fama's attack on the technical analysts seems to be based on a deep misunderstanding of what technical analysts are trying to do. The chartist looks on price movement as an essentially human phenomenon, because buying and selling decisions are made by men and women in response to human needs and human emotions as well as human reasoning. "The theory of random walk implies that a series of stock price changes has no memory—the past history of the series cannot be used to predict the future in any meaningful way". The chartist will argue that in certain price movements he can anticipate the appearance of buyers or sellers at certain points; but he will agree that he cannot predict with any certainty whether enough buyers or sellers will appear at the level stated to reverse the previous movement. The writer tried a simple experiment. He went through his daily chart book for the early sixties from the beginning of Banks to the middle of Commercial & Induustrial, examining the patterns for a well-known "support" phenomenon. First he noted the high point for the first six months of 1961. Next he eliminated all stock which did not later rise 10 per cent or more above that level. Next he eliminated all those which did not suffer a subsequent decline down to or below the early 1961 high. This reduced his 114 stocks to 41. The theory of Support & Resistance expects that, after a decline and subsequent rise higher, in a new decline support will appear at the old high level. In 25 out of 41 cases a rally sprang from the appropriate region. Clearly in 25 out of 41 cases there were buyers at the support level. In the remaining 16 cases there may or may not have been extra buyers. The theory of random walk seems to imply that at any point in a price series it is equally likely that the next change will be up or down. Neither the sample nor the predominance seems large enough to prove that the market, in this situation, has any memory; further statistical investigations are needed. But the chartists insist that market movements represent the decisions of people and that people have memories.

Analysts are entitled to be angered by Professor Fama's misrepresentation of their tenets. "The basic assumption of all the chartist or technical theories is that history tends to repeat itself, i.e. past patterns of price behaviour in individual securities will tend to recur in the future". It is not clear whether he means that chartists expect the past pattern of a given stock to be repeated in the future in the same stock or whether they expect the pattern seen in one stock in the past to recur in some other stock at some later date. The chartist knows well enough that times change and stocks change with them. He does not expect lightning to strike twice in the same place and looks on a repetition of pattern in the same stock, as in Gas Purification, as a blessed statistical miracle. What charts show him is how people behave in certain investment situations; and he looks at the past behaviour of one price series to throw light on the possible future behaviour of another. He will be a very bold and arrogant chartist who claims, in Professor Fama's words, that the sequence of price changes prior to any given day is important in predicting the price change for that day; but the modest chartist will argue that the sequence of price changes prior to a very few days in very few cases is important in predicting the price change for the day.

We should be very grateful to Professor Fama for the illumination which he has thrown on security prices. The multiplication of analysts in Britain since the founding of the Society of Investment Analysts is an important factor in the changing of the market's character. Prices do move from day to day generally in a random manner; and the notion of random pursuit of a value is useful, provided that we do not fall into the trap of believing in an intrinsic value. But we cannot accept Professor Fama's model for the making of security prices, nor the rationality of the investor nor his other lacks of human characteristics; least of all should we accept Professor Fama's descriptions of the techniques of various kinds of analysts. Finally we must reject his pessimism; the business of an analyst is to try to improve his analysing, not to leave the work to his competitors and average out their efforts with a divining pin.

9 Investment Analysis – The Need for Professionalisation

R. J. BRISTON

This article was published in The Investment Analyst *in December 1968. Bids and mergers dominated the London stock market in 1968 and the FT30 Share Index hit a new peak of 521.9 in September. James Hanson expanded his activities and Slater Walker continued its policy of acquisitions (merchant banks were the top-performing sector, with a rise of 110%).*

It was also the year of the Poseidon 'bubble' and the Cyril Lord collapse. The author's call for a more professional approach to analysis was very timely.

Richard Briston is Professor of Accounting and Finance and Acting Director of the Graduate Management Centre at the University of Hull. His main field of interest is international accounting, with particular reference to developing countries. He has published extensively in academic and professional journals, and is the author of several books, including The Stock Exchange and Investment Analysis *and* An Introduction to Accounting and Finance.

The subject of investment analysis barely exists in this country at either the professional or the academic level. The word "investment" is used almost exclusively by academics to describe industrial capital projects, while investment analysis is regarded by many as a synonym for capital budgeting. The problems and techniques of the external investor in assessing the value of the shares of a company tend to be ignored and the only subject relevant to the external appraisal of a company which is taught at all generally is the interpretation of accounts. The availability and methods of analysis of other, often more important information is disregarded.

This problem was recently brought home to me very forcibly when I was asked by a publisher for a list of professional bodies, universities and colleges which provided courses for which a book entitled "The Stock Exchange and Investment Analysis" might be recommendable. A brief perusal of the examination syllabuses of a few likely organisations showed such a lack of interest in the subject of investment analysis that I thought it would be revealing to ascertain the exact extent to which it is taught and examined at all levels.

A letter was sent to all appropriate professional organisations, to all universities and polytechnics and to about five hundred colleges of commerce, technical colleges and colleges of further education requesting details of their courses and examination requirements in the field of management studies, accounting and finance. These rather broad subject headings were necessary because of the tremendous variety of titles under which investment analysis is dealt with, however briefly.

The response of the bodies concerned was very prompt and co-operative and, notwithstanding the lack of detail of some of the course and examination syllabuses, a fairly comprehensive analysis of teaching of investment at all levels has been undertaken. This has shown that investment analysis is, with a few notable exceptions, regarded neither as a professional subject nor as an academic discipline. It is consequently ignored by virtually all teaching institutions.

The results of the survey are analysed under five headings:

(1) Universities; (2) Professional bodies; (3) Other examining bodies; (4) Colleges of further education; and (5) Prospects for the future.

(1) INVESTMENT COURSES AT UNIVERSITIES

This part of the survey was made difficult by the failure of three universities to supply a prospectus or syllabus and by the lack of detail in many of the brochures regarding course content. However, other sources such as the UCCA Handbook and the publication "The Universities and the Accountancy Profession" were used to supplement the information supplied by the universities and it is believed that the analysis in Appendix I is complete and accurate.

The most alarming feature is that only one university (Strathclyde) provides an under-graduate course which is directly related to investment analysis. This course, Business Finance II, consists of two papers and has the following syllabus:

"Interpretation of company accounts: Accounting theory and conventions—the revenue account and balance sheet for various types of undertaking—the interpretation of accounts—published accounts.

"Security analysis: Study of current trends in disclosure of information—principles and technique (sic) of security valuation—comparative study of stock markets in U.S.A. and Europe".

Almost all of the courses specialising in accountancy deal quite comprehensively with the interpretation of accounting information and are thus very relevant to investment analysts. The courses on business subjects are rather less relevant for they are concerned primarily with the internal problems of the firm. The subject of business finance is perhaps the most useful of these for the investment analyst. The traditional content of this course is explained by the following syllabus:

"Sources of capital, dealing with financial institutions including the Stock Exchanges. The theory of the financial administration of companies. The finance of companies, equity shares and loan capital. Long-term and short-term finance. Profits and dividends. Revenue and capital profits and dividends. The management of a company's internal finance, stock control, debtors, creditors and cash balances. The effect of taxes on company finance."

A rather more modern approach is suggested by another syllabus for the same subject:

"The time value of money, risk and uncertainty, and the inflation factor. Sources and costs of capital. The roles and facilities of relevant financial institutions. Gearing and optional financing. Timing, strategy, and planning in company finance. Valuation depreciation and taxation aspects of investment and financing. Accounting data and analysis of costs and revenues relevant to cash flow and liquidity, profit planning, and the planning, appraisal and control of capital expenditure."

An interesting feature of the syllabuses for business finance is the extent to which "investment analysis" is used to describe the subject "project appraisal". Although many of their problems are common to both subjects the first is purely external in emphasis while the latter is internal.

Not all universities provide a special course in business finance. However, all universities which award an economics degree teach some or all of the subjects outlined above, the paper involved being entitled Industry and Trade, Economics of Industry, Financial Administration or any other combination of appropriate words.

At the undergraduate level it would seem that a student who had studied accounting, economics, business finance and quantitative methods would be best equipped for a career in investment analysis. He would, however, still need further training in such subjects as stock market behaviour, availability and analysis of information other than published accounts, attitudes and requirements of different categories of investors, formulation of investment policies and portfolio problems.

At the postgraduate level the situation is hardly any better, primarily because there is not an undergraduate base upon which to build. Many universities now provide a taught higher degree or diploma in the field of management studies and though these are again concerned with internal management problems some of them, for example, the B.Phil. at Hull, include a paper on investment analysis.

The extent of research which is being conducted by the universities in subjects related to investment analysis is impossible to ascertain. Again, however, the emphasis appears to be on the internal decisions of the firm and an examination of the research projects which are currently supported by the Social Science Research Council shows none which are directly related to stock exchange investment. Similarly the details of research in British Universities published by the Department of Education and Science and the British Council show that research into investment analysis is being undertaken at Birmingham, Edinburgh, Essex, Hull, Liverpool, Sheffield and Warwick. The number of projects involved is remarkable small compared with the number being carried out in the field of business finance and investment.

Finally, the syllabuses of the graduate business schools at London and Manchester do not reveal any greater coverage of investment analysis for, although advanced courses on such subjects as portfolio investment are provided, they are mostly optional.

The attitude of universities towards investment analysis is thus very discouraging. The establishment of the Esmée Fairbairn Chair at Warwick and of the Research Fellowship at City University is certain to improve matters, but the attitude of the University Grants Committee towards the expansion of business studies in the universities will hinder any such improvement.

(2) THE PROFESSIONS

The extent to which professional bodies require their members to have studied investment analysis is shown in Appendix II. Most members of the general public believe that an accountant, bank manager or solicitor is qualified to give advice on investments. While they may be qualified by experience to give such advice they are clearly not qualified by ex-amination. Only the actuary receives an intensive training in investment analysis. Far behind the actuaries come the members of the Institute of Bankers of Scotland, the holders of the Trustee Diploma of the Institute of Bankers, those members of the Corporation of Secretaries who have passed Secretarial Practice II (Principles and Practice of Investment) and those members of the Institute of Hospital Administrators who opted for Principles and Practice of Investment.

Those bodies which set papers which are partially related to investment cover between them such topics as the interpretation of accounts, the theory of valuation, the organisation of the stock exchange and sources of capital for industry. The manner in which investment is disregarded by professional bodies is demonstrated by its treatment by the groups in the third category of the appendix. The Institute of Chartered Accountants in England and Wales relegates investment to a general paper which also includes public finance, banking, industry and trade, price theory, economic development and national income. The Chartered Institute of Secretaries goes still further and includes investment in an optional paper which has the following amazing syllabus:

"The practical work of the secretary in reference to organisation of meetings and conferences. Insurances—risks to be covered. Investment of funds—types of investment available, relative risks, flat yield and redemption yield, realisability requirements, internal restrictions, fluctuation in market value, stock exchange quotations and terms, transfers and documents of title. Principal commercial functions and consideration of the main factors involved in carrying them out. Exchange—buying and selling. Transport and storage—practice in relation to carriage of goods by land, canal, sea and air; finance and payment, risk bearing, import and export. The services of the banker. Elementary statistics—terminology, methods of presenting statistical information, uses of statistics in management control. Budgetary control, expense and financial budgets, budget administration. Costing—methods, standard costs, etc."

It is thus clear that the actuary is the only professional man who is qualified by examination to speak with any authority on investment analysis. This situation is unlikely to be altered by the examinations which are to be introduced by the Federation of Stock Exchange in Great Britain and Ireland on 1st August, 1971. This examination will contain four papers:

(a) Stock Exchange Practice.
(b) Interpretation of Company Reports and Accounts.
(c) Taxation.
(d) The Techniques of Investment.

As the first paper is entirely descriptive and the paper on the techniques of investment has the stated object of testing the candidate in the application of the knowledge acquired in studying for the other subjects, it is difficult to see how members of the Stock Exchange will be any better qualified by examination than accountants or bankers with regard to investment analysis.

At the present time there are less than one thousand qualified actuaries in practice in England. About 650 of these are employed by life assurance offices, generally in departments other than those concerned with investment, so that there are not many available to enter the profession of investment analyst. As a result investment analysts have to be recruited from other sources, particularly the universities, and need further training after recruitment. Such training is not at the present time defined or examined by any professional organisation.

(3) OTHER EXAMINING BODIES

Several of the G.C.E. examination boards set papers at either ordinary or advanced level in accountancy, commerce and business studies. Investment analysis, however, is entirely ignored. Similarly the syllabuses for both the Ordinary and the Higher National Certificates in Business Studies generally contain accounting and business finance, but not investment, while the Diploma in Management Studies is also biased in the same direction.

The degrees awarded by the Council for National Academic Awards are based upon syllabuses which have been drafted by the teaching colleges and approved by the Council. Those polytechnics, colleges of commerce, etc., which provide such courses have a considerable discretion over their content, and a variety of interesting specialisms and joint subjects have evolved within the business studies degrees. The City of London College offers a degree in business studies and finance, while the Manchester College of Commerce offers economics and finance and the Lanchester College of Technology provides an optional paper in Investment Theory and Analysis within its business studies degree. Apart from these instances, however, the contents of the C.N.A.A. degree courses in business studies are directly aimed at business managers to the exclusion of the external investor.

(4) COLLEGES OF FURTHER EDUCATION

Under this broad heading are included polytechnics, colleges of technology, technical colleges, colleges of commerce and colleges of further education. These colleges are primarily concerned with providing courses for the examinations of professional bodies and other examining bodies. Because of the omission of investment analysis from examination syllabuses the subject is not taught formally by the colleges and they have had no incentive to recruit investment analysts on to their staffs. This probably explains why those colleges which have developed syllabuses for the C.N.A.A. degrees have concentrated entirely upon the business subjects which they already teach for the Higher National Certificate in Business Studies and the Diploma in Management Studies and for which they already have a suitably qualified staff.

Nevertheless, as indicated in Appendix III, many colleges provide courses on investment for the general public. Similar classes are given by the extra-mural departments of some universities and are often sponsored by the W.E.A. These courses, however, are very elementary and cannot be regarded as a substitute for formal tuition in investment analysis. Finally, the two-year course which the City of London College provides for Stock Exchange personnel touches upon investment analysis and will presumably form the basis of education for the examinations of the Federation of Stock Exchanges.

(5) PROSPECTS FOR THE FUTURE

The immediate need would seem to be a definition of investment analysis. The definition of "financial analysis" provided by Donald H. Randell[1] applies equally well to "investment analysis", the term used by the Society of Investment Analysts:

"As set forth in more detail later, there are several facets to the profession of Security or Financial Analysis. While the terms are used somewhat interchangeably, the author feels that Security Analysis generally refers primarily to the study of individual or related industry groups of securities and the determination of their relative attractiveness as separate investment media based primarily on the study of their past performance.

"Financial Analysis, on the other hand, seems to accent the anticipation of conditions to be expected in the future and the tailoring of investment programmes designed to fit the needs of the individual whose funds are being committed now to provide for that future.

"Whatever the distinction, and regardless of minor quirks of terminology, an analyst has but a single aim. Essentially, he has to master whatever tools are needed for a sufficient understanding of the financial past so as to be able to anticipate which securities will or will not command a premium later on."

Although a knowledge of accounting and business finance is essential for an investment analyst, he needs training in many other fields for the proper performance of his task. In particular he needs to understand the analysis of economic data, statistical forecasting, stock market psychology, investor requirements and portfolio selection. Many of these subjects are not examined either by universities or by professional bodies and the need for the establishment of investment analysis as a profession with its own academic standards appears to be self-evident. The investment analyst would certainly be operating in a growth market, as is evidenced by the growth of the New York Society of Security Analysts from a membership of 20 in 1937 to over 4,300 in 1968. In March 1968 the total membership of the Financial Analysts Federation in the United States and Canada, was 11,649. Nearly 2,000 of

[1] 'Evolution of the Analyst". *Financial Analysts Journal*, March-April, 1961.

these members had passed the examination of the Institute of Chartered Financial Analysts, a body established by the Federation in 1962 with the following syllabus:[2]

"Part I: This will cover the basic skills and the basic sources of economic and financial information used in security analysis. At least 4 areas should be covered:
1. Financial Accounting.
2. Elementary Statistics and financial mathematics.
3. The major economic variables and institutions in the American economy.
4. Instruments and institutions in the securities markets.

Part II: This will cover the application of skills and information to security analysis. The areas covered by this examination will be:
1. Economic growth and fluctuations.
2. Industry and regional analysis.
3. Financial and security analysis.

Part III: This will cover the problems involved in setting investment policy and making decisions to carry these out. The areas are:
1. The determination of investment goals.
2. Investment timing and portfolio balance.
3. The selection of industries and securities."

There appears to be no reason why the Society of Investment Analysts should not establish professional examinations on a similar basis. If a syllabus like that of the C.F.A. were adopted graduates could be encouraged to enter the profession by offering exemptions from Part I to those with a degree in economics and accounting. The other two parts of the examination, being concerned with more specialised problems, could be attempted during a period of practical training. With the present expansion of the C.N.A.A. degrees and their superior flexibility to many university degrees the profession might well be able to encourage some of the London polytechnics to introduce degree courses with the required combinations of subjects with beneficial results for both the profession and the academic acceptance of investment analysis.

APPENDIX I

Teaching of Subjects Allied to Investment at Universities

(1) Universities providing courses on accountancy and business subjects which are approved by the major accounting professional bodies and give exemption from their intermediate examinations.

(a) England and Wales

Aston in Birmingham	Leeds
Bath	Liverpool
Birmingham	London School of Economics
Bradford	
Bristol	Manchester
Hull	Newcastle
Kent at Canterbury	Nottingham
Lancaster (approval pending)	Sheffield
	Southampton

University College of South Wales and Monmouthshire, Cardiff.
University College of Wales, Aberystwyth.
University of Wales Institute of Science and Technology, Cardiff.

---

[2] 'Evolution of the Analyst". *Financial Analysts Journal*, March-April, 1961.

(b) Ireland

Dublin	University College,
Queen's University,	Cork
Belfast	University College, Galway

(c) Scotland

Aberdeen	Heriot-Watt
Dundee	Stirling*
Edinburgh	Strathclyde
Glasgow	

(2) Universities which do not teach accountancy but which provide courses on economics, including subjects related to industry.

Bangor	Oxford
Brunel	Queen Mary College
Cambridge	(University of London)
Durham	Reading
East Anglia	St. Andrews
Essex	Salford
Exeter	Sussex
Keele	University College, London
Leicester	Warwick
	York

APPENDIX II

Coverage of Investment in the Examination of Professional Bodies

(1) Bodies which set a compulsory full paper on investment
Faculty of Actuaries
Institute of Actuaries
Institute of Bankers in Scotland
Institute of Bankers (only for candidates for the Trustee Diploma)

(2) Bodies which set an optional full paper on investment
Corporation of Secretaries
Institute of Hospital Administrators

(3) Bodies which set a paper which relates partially to investment
Association of Certified and Corporate Accountants
Association of International Accountants
British Association of Accountants and Auditors
Chartered Auctioneers and Estate Agents Institute
Chartered Institute of Secretaries
Chartered Insurance Institute
Institute of Chartered Accountants in England and Wales
Institute of Chartered Accountants in Ireland
Institute of Chartered Accountants in Scotland
Institute of Cost and Works Accountants

---

* This university also provides an optional course (Business Finance II) which is devoted to investment analysis.

Institute of Municipal Treasurers and Accountants
Institute of Works Managers
Society of Commercial Accountants

(4) Bodies which set no papers relating to investment
Association of Industrial and Commercial Executive Accountants
Building Societies Institute
Faculty of Secretaries
Incorporated Association of Cost and Industrial Accountants
Incorporated Society of Valuers and Auctioneers
Institute of Bookkeepers
The Law Society
Rating and Valuation Association

APPENDIX III

Colleges of Further Education Which Provide Short Courses on Investment For the General Public

Arnold and Carlton College of Further Education
Bournemouth College of Technology
Bridgnorth College of Further Education
City of Westminster College
Dewsbury and Batley Technical and Art College
East Berks College
East Warwickshire College of Further Education
Ewell County Technical College
Exeter Technical College
Hendon College of Technology
Isleworth Polytechnic
Mid-Cheshire Central College of Further Education
North-West Kent College of Technology
North-Western Polytechnic
Nuneaton Technical College and School of Art
Oxford College of Further Education
St. Albans College of Further Education
Worsley College of Further Education

10 The Value of Research into the Behaviour of Share Prices

R. A. BREALEY

This article was published in The Investment Analyst *in December 1968, Richard Brealey writes: It is always embarrassing to be reminded of things that you wrote many years ago; it is rather like seeing old photos of yourself. So I was somewhat horrified when* The Professional Investor *proposed republishing this article. I did not like it even at the time. I had just joined the London Business School after working in Boston when the journal's editor asked me to write an article. I should have said No, but I did not, and this was the result.*

The article does, however, raise an issue that I believe to be still relevant: management of research involves important agency issues. Managers of investment companies naturally strive for superior performance, and there is nothing they would like more than a simple formula that would tell them which stocks were mispriced. But research cannot presuppose the outcome, and the attempt to second-guess the results encourages bad research. Over the years, investment management companies, brokers and consultancy firms have developed countless models for predicting stock returns. If the majority have failed to live up to their promises, it is partly a consequence of the bad incentive structures for those who were concerned with their development.

Richard Brealey is Special Adviser to the Governor of the Bank of England and a Visiting Professor of Finance at the London Business School. After leaving university, he spent a total of nine years in the investment departments of Sun Life Assurance Company of Canada and Keystone Custodian Funds in Boston. He then joined the Finance Faculty of the London Business School, where he was for some years Deputy Principal and head of the School's Institute of Finance and Accounting.

He is an Honorary Fellow of the IIMR, a fellow of the British Academy, a former director of the American Finance Association and former president of the European Finance Association. He has also served on the editorial boards of most of the principal finance journals.

He has been a director of the Sun Life Assurance Company of Canada (UK), Tokai Derivative Products and The Brattle Group.

His publications include An Introduction to Risk and Return from Common Stocks *(MIT Press, 2nd edn, 1983) and (with Stewart Myers)* Principles of Corporate Finance *(Irwin McGraw-Hill, 6th edn, 2000).*

The next decade can be expected to produce in the U.K. a considerable increase in the total resources devoted by both the financial community and investors to the study of the behaviour of share prices. The reduction in computational costs, the increasing body of data available in machine readable form and the growing number of people with the necessary aptitudes for the work will all encourage this process.

It is, therefore, an appropriate time to consider in quite general terms the benefits that are likely to follow such expenditures. In this respect the interests of the financial community may be different from those of students of the role of the equity market in the wider context of the British economic structure. This article will concentrate exclusively on the possible advantage to financial institutions of such work.

It is one of the main contentions of this article that, where the work has a strong research orientation, the company should as far as possible avoid preconceptions as to the form in which the results should prove useful. If a decision is made as to the use to which results are to be put before those results are known, then almost inevitably it becomes impossible to judge dispassionately the correctness of the original decision. At the same time the possibilities of an alternative use for the findings tend to be ignored and the additional questions that they raise to go unanswered. In this respect the situation is similar to industrial research. The highest returns on such research have always accrued to companies that have been able to keep an open mind about the commercial applications of this work and to seize and develop rapidly any unexpected opportunities that have occurred.

One implication of this fact is that if the full benefits of financial research are to be secured, other members of the financial institution must become quite intimately involved in its progress. The less well equipped the researcher is to detect the commercial value of his work, the more essential this involvement becomes. It follows therefore that the less easy the communication between the two sides, the more the communication is needed. Those American investment companies which, despite lavish expenditures on financial research, have been disappointed in its results have probably not considered the very limited number of circumstances in which they would have benefited.

The above-mentioned preconceptions frequently lead to the research programme actually being planned in terms of the use to which the results are to be put, despite the fact that the nature of the results is not at the time known. In other words research is confused with development. For example, a stockbroker may decide to set up a section with specific instructions to develop a computer programme to filter out those stocks on the basis of past price action which are particularly likely to merit further study by the company's analysts. Presumably, the intended object of such a programme is to distinguish a group of stocks with above average expected returns. This is a very desirable aim, but the project as stated involves the implicit assumption that there is some relationship between the returns of stocks in two successive periods. A project specified in this way will almost inevitably lead to disappointment on the part of the initiator and frustration for the man responsible for having to carry through what may be an impossible task. These problems would be avoided if the original decision was simply to gather evidence as to whether there is any dependence between successive rates of return.

The preceding paragraph should not be construed as a suggestion that research into the behaviour of share prices cannot be directed but only that a clear distinction should be made between the controls appropriate to a research project and those applicable to development work. The decision to allow any characteristic of share price movement to influence one's investments must be postponed until the existence of that characteristic has been established.

The tendency to judge the value of any piece of research by predetermined standards has resulted in the U.S.A. in the loss of a major proportion of the possible pay-off. Much of the money devoted in that country to the search for new investment techniques has been spent on the development of services that seek solely with the aid of published data to obtain superior performance at a given level of risk. Most of these could be classified as technical services. The reason for the proliferation of such effort is not that research on the dependence of successive price changes has provided encouragement for believing that profitable technical schemes can be developed. Instead, the large volume of technical material produced in the U.S.A. appears to have stemmed from the fact that it is trying to provide the information that the investor would most like to have—a simple objective standard for predicting which shares are likely to show the highest appreciation.

While it is difficult to quarrel with the desirability of such a service, two considerations suggest that the chances of its successful development are very low. In the first place, academic studies have supported with considerable unanimity the conclusion that share price changes are approximately random.[1] Recurring patterns do seem to exist, at least in the U.S.A., but there is no evidence that they are sufficiently marked to provide the basis for a worthwhile decision rule. In consequence, in all cases where a technical system has been rigorously tested, the profits have been insufficient to cover transaction costs.[2] The failure of other researchers to discover any marked degree of dependence between successive price changes diminishes the probability that such dependence exists but does not constitute proof of the matter. On the other hand, it is difficult to see how one could expect to obtain the type of evidence that would justify staking money on the continuance of any major market imperfection. To obtain performance that is consistently superior to that of other investors who are incurring similar risks, it is necessary to be aware of some relevant fact that is unknown to the majority of one's rivals. Only in this way can the owner be expected to sell his stock at a price that in retrospect proves too low or can other investors be expected to refrain from competing to purchase it. If this relevant information is based solely on the recurrence of certain characteristic patterns in a body of data that is available to all investors, then those patterns must be either highly complex or short-lived for their existence not to have been already observed. Unfortunately the more complex or the less persistent the pattern the more likely that it was produced by the interplay of chance factors and that it will not therefore recur. Even if it were not the result of a chance occurrence and even if the imperfection remains unnoticed by other investors, the world might change sufficiently rapidly that the circumstances no longer have the same effect. What is needed therefore is an underlying rationale that not only provides confidence that a certain pattern was not a chance event but that the conditions that produced it will have the same effect in the future. Yet any such imperfection will probably be a result of market irrationality, so that it may be equally easy to develop hypotheses to explain both the observed relationship and its opposite. In such a case the system would have to stand on its own feet unbutteressed by a general theory.

The argument, therefore, is not that no imperfections or anomalies occur in share price changes, but rather that, unless such imperfections are trivial in character, it may be difficult to establish their existence until after they have ceased to be of any value.[3] The important thing to realise is that work on technical systems or indeed on any objective method of share price forecasting is a research project with a very uncertain pay-off. Despite widespread claims to the contrary no established technical service has to the author's knowledge been able to produce satisfactory evidence of its liability to provide above average profits *on an ongoing basis for a given level of risk.*

This does not mean that no tangible benefits can yet be derived from the considerable work that has been devoted in the United States to share price behaviour. Although the number of unanswered questions seems to grow much more rapidly than those that have been solved, there is available in the U.S.A. a broad framework establishing the nature and determinants of risk and return from investment in equities. Once one abandons preconceptions as to the way in which such work can be useful, it becomes clear that many of the findings should be influencing investment decisions here today.

This may be illustrated by an example. The risk accepted by an investor can be shown to bear a close relationship to the variability of the rates of return provided by the portfolio.

This in turn depends in part on the number of holdings in a portfolio. The principle of diversification has long been familiar to investors but what has not always been appreciated is how few holdings are required to secure these benefits. It is possible to demonstrate that approximately 90 per cent of the potential benefits of diversification can be secured with just 15 holdings.[4] Furthermore as the number of holdings is increased much beyond this point, the advantages of increasing diversification begin to be outweighed by the concomitant dis-advantages of adding shares which are less desirable in themselves. Very large funds of course cannot limit themselves to such a small number of holdings. However, very widely diversified portfolios are not just a characteristic of large funds and their existence may frequently reflect inefficient risk management.

If a portfolio is diversified, the only risk that the owner bears is that created by uncertainty as to the prospects for the market as a whole. Over what happens to the market the fund manager has no control, but he can influence the degree to which his portfolio can be expected to respond to a market fall. In other words he can alter his risk exposure by buying either aggressive or defensive stocks. The former are shares which are both highly variable and closely dependent on the market. The latter are relatively stable shares that are unaffected by the market. By looking at the behaviour of a share in earlier periods an investor may obtain some guide into which category it fits.[5]

One of the important corollaries of the last paragraph is that the appreciation that should be expected from a diversified portfolio is closely related to the amount of risk that is accepted. This may be demonstrated graphically by Figure 1. The vertical axis measures the risk provided by a portfolio and the horizontal axis the expected returns. If values are plotted for a number of portfolios, they should tend to cluster along an upward sloping line as shown in the diagram. Thus, in one study of 34 U.S. mutual funds nearly three-quarters of the differences between their returns during the period 1954–63 could be explained in terms of differences in the variability of these returns.[6] In contrast the differences in performance between funds with similar degrees of risk are relatively small.

The preceding remarks should not be taken as implying that the fund manager should not bother to strive for performance superior to that of other funds incurring the same risks. It does however stress the importance of a correct and consistent policy towards risk, and point to a somewhat novel interpretation of the fund manager's role. At the same time it

FIGURE 1.

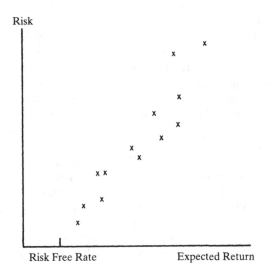

points to the importance of taking into account the risk factor in assessing the portfolio manager's performance.

Since these relationships may be stated in formal ways, they may serve as the basis for a formalised investment approach. For example, if the investor is able to be explicit about both the prospects for the market and the way in which individual shares are likely to respond to market changes, then he may use a portfolio selection model to determine the combination of shares that would provide the highest expected returns for a given degree of risk.[7] Alternatively, if it is desired to assess the past performance of a group of fund managers, formal methods are available for adjusting for differences in the risks that they incurred.[8]

A further example of the valid use of models can be found in the field of share valuation. There have been a number of research studies devoted to the effect on share prices of unexpected changes in earnings and dividends. Thus, in a recent American study, for each of the years 1957–1965 stocks were classified into two portfolios.[9] The first consisted of the stocks of companies whose earnings for the year were above the level predicted by the market twelve months earlier, the second consisted of stocks of companies whose earnings were below expectations. During that twelve-month period, the first portfolio appreciated on the average 17 per cent. more than the second. Such results support the widespread view that superior profits depend to a large extent on the investor's ability to select shares in companies whose earnings will exceed expectations. Share valuation models of the type developed by the Bank of New York[10] and by Philips and Drew[11] have simply formalised these relationships in an attempt to measure the implication for share prices of their analysts' earnings and dividend forecasts.

The remarks of the preceding paragraphs serve to illustrate several conclusions. Firstly the most important value of research into the behaviour of stock market prices lies in the contribution that it makes to our knowledge. This improved awareness must affect the way in which the investor thinks and acts.

These benefits will be wholly missed if financial research is regarded simply as the necessary preparation for a conjuring trick in which undervalued stocks are to be the rabbits. It should also be clear that the investor needs to be fully involved in the process and that communication between the researcher and the investor requires a considerable effort on both sides.

Many of these financial relationships can be reduced to formal models. This procedure is more akin to a development than a research task, in that the aims are established in advance and the value of the model can be assessed by predetermined standards. The model may enhance the value of the research but is unlikely to be necessary to it.

The function of such models is typically to assist the investor to follow through the implications of some piece of information that he already has. Given his expectations for the economy it may be possible to determine which companies have superior earnings prospects. Given his earnings forecasts, a model may be used to distinguish which shares are cheap. Given his expectations for each share it may provide a guide to how much of each should be held. Given the market prospects, it may be possible to assess the prospects for his portfolio. And so on.

The development of such models typically involves considerable problems, and whether they are worth the expense involved will depend on a number of factors. Above all they again require that those who are to provide the inputs and those who are to use the output become fully involved in the process. Otherwise what goes in as human judgment becomes metamorphosed into something wholly inhuman.

The necessity for judgmental inputs into such models means that a brief session with an IBM 360 is no substitute for a prolonged game of golf with the Chairman. The frequently heard antithesis between the role of man and that of the computer in investment analysis misses the point of financial research. It should also be obvious that much of the emphasis on secrecy in such activities is misplaced. Most of the important knowledge on the behaviour of share prices dose not lose its value with its dissemination.

REFERENCES

[1] A valuable collection of articles on the subject is provided by Paul H. Cootner (ed) *The Random Character of Stock Market Prices*, The M.I.T. Press, Cambridge, 1964.

[2] Eugene F. Fama and Marshall E. Blume, "Filter Rules and Stock Market Trading", *Journal of Business*, 39 (January 1966) 226–241.

James C. Van Horne and George G. C. Parker, "The Random Walk Theory: An Empirical Test", *Financial Analysts Journal*, 23 (Nov.-Dec., 1967), 87–92.

Norman Nielsen, John F. Lubin, and D. Teichroew, "An Empirical Evaluation of Technical Stock Market Investment Rules", Working Paper No. 34, Graduate School of Business, Stanford University.

[3] For another reason that dependence between successive price changes may be valueless for prediction, see Benoit Mandelbrot, "Forecasts of Future Prices, Unbiased Markets, and "Martingale Models" " *Journal of Business*, 39 (January, 1966), 242–255.

[4] This figure is based on a theoretical calculation. Empirical support, however, is provided in the U.S.A. by Jack E. Gaumnitz, "Investment Diversification under Uncertainty: An Examination of the Number of Securities in a Diversified Portfolio". Unpublished Ph.D. dissertation, Stanford University, 1967.

[5] Marshall E. Blume, "The Assessment of Portfolio Performance—An Application to Portfolio Theory", Unpublished Ph.D. dissertation, University of Chicago, 1968.

[6] William F. Sharpe, "Mutual Fund Performance", *Journal of Business*, 39 (January, 1966), 119–139.

[7] Harry M. Markowitz, Portfolio Selection: *Efficient Diversification of Investments*, New York: John Wiley & Sons, Inc., 1959.

[8] Jack L. Treynor, "How to rate Management of Investment Funds", *Harvard Business Review*, 43 (Jan.-Feb., 1965), 63–75.

Michael C. Jensen, "The Performance of Mutual Funds in the Period 1945-64", *The Journal of Finance*, 23 (May, 1968), 389–416.

[9] Philip Brown and Ray Ball, "An Empirical Evaluation of Accounting Income Numbers", *Journal of Accounting Research*, 6 (Autumn 1968).

[10] Volbert Whitbeck and Manown Kisor, "A New Tool in Investment Decision Making", *Financial Analysts Journal*, 19 (May-June, 1963), 55–62.

[11] D. Weaver and M. G. Hall, "The Evaluation of Ordinary Shares Using A Computer", *Journal of the Institute of Actuaries*, 93 (1967), 165–203.

Part II
The 1970s

11 Econometric Models and the Stock Market

R. D. NIGHTINGALE and K. VERNON

This article was published in The Investment Analyst *in May 1970. In the early 1970s, econometric models were still a comparatively recent innovation, and had been used primarily in the academic world. However, a growing appreciation by both industry and government of the need to anticipate future trends led to the expansion of models designed to give a picture of the economy in the years ahead. These models provided a useful theoretical aid for decision makers in the private and public sectors. Also, the rapid development of computer technology enabled new data to be incorporated quickly and contribute towards a more accurate overall forecast.*

The authors' main theme is the application of models in a stockmarket environment. They discuss the model pioneered by the Econometrics Unit of Hoare & Co in 1968, and analyse its three main constituents: corporate profits, a weekly update on new data and the inclusion of monetary variables. These aspects of the Hoare & Co model distinguished it from others that were operating at the time.

Although Messrs Nightingale and Vernon make no emphatic claims for models in the context of the stockmarket, they conclude by saying that models do have 'qualities which will prove to be of value in making investment decisions'.

A GENERAL NOTE ON ECONOMIC MODELS

An econometric model is essentially an attempt to systematise and to quantify the various interactions at work within an economy. A model is systematic in that it approaches economic problems through a careful analysis of the functional relationships among groups of variables, and it is quantitative in as far as it ascribes precise arithmetical coefficients to any of the postulated interactions. In recent years there has been a rapid and widespread growth of interest in the development of such models. This interest probably results from the increased awareness on the part of both industry and government that the efficiency with which an organisation operates depends to a considerable extent on anticipating the future trends of the environment in which it works. The real impetus to the recent expansion of models, however, has been provided by the availability of fast, powerful computers. It has been appreciated for many years that an economy is affected by a variety of diverse influences, but it was only with the development of computers that the net effect of the various influences could be traced and quantified. Indeed, the principal advantage that econometric models have over the more traditional methods of anticipating economic trends, lies in the model's ability to deal with a greatly increased number of influences, and in the speed with which it can adjust to meet changing circumstances.

There are three main areas in which econometric models can be employed.

1. Firstly they can be used in the purely academic field of economic theory. This was where econometrics, as such, really began. An investigator would build a model to test, on a statistical basis, the validity of an economic hypothesis. A great deal of valuable work has been, and continues to be, conducted along these lines, and this has greatly improved our understanding of economic concepts.

2. Secondly models can be used to provide forecasts of economic magnitudes. This is the area in which industry is generally most interested since reliable information about, for instance, the likely level of future demand for its products would clearly be of considerable value to a company assessing production schedules or planning capital formation. Moreover an indication of the associated areas of demand which could be expected to grow rapidly would be valuable since such forecasts might enable a company to diversify its product line more quickly than would otherwise be the case.

3. The third major area in which models can make a useful contribution is that of policy formulation. The central authorities are, in particular, interested in applications of this sort. They are currently using, and indeed, continuing to develop, models which analyse the consequences of introducing changes in those economic magnitudes over which they have some measure of control. Adjustments to such factors as Bank rate, Domestic Credit and Public Expenditure might be proposed and the model is used to trace the likely effects of these changes in, for instance, Consumer's Expenditure, the Balance of Payments and the level of Aggregate Demand. Industry, however, is also beginning to study this type of model because of its application in estimating the effects upon profits and turnover of changes in pricing and investment policies.

While models can be classified into the three broad groups outlined above, the underlying structure of most of them is much the same. Despite the increasing sophistication of computers, all models must inevitably provide a simplified picture of an economy. Consequently model builders will attempt to represent the aggregate level of activity, which in reality is the interaction of a very large number of economic influences, by a relatively small number of economic variables. The exact choice, therefore, of the variables that are incorporated, is likely to vary from one model to another and will reflect what the designers of the model regard as being the most significant of the available variables. In general terms, however, it is likely that within any two models of roughly the same size, the differences in the selection of variables will be fairly limited.

A second aspect of the broad similarity of all models lies in the fact that the variables used in any model can be split into two categories, direct and indirect.

(*a*) Direct economic variables are defined as those which are determined largely by other variables within the environment encompassed by the model, and are variables, therefore, about which the model is capable of making sensible forecasts. Consumer's expenditure is an example of a direct variable, since its value is generally thought to be determined by, amongst other things, the level of disposable income and the availability of credit, both of which are variables that are likely to be within the scope of a model.

(*b*) Indirect economic variables can be defined loosely as those about which the model is unable to make sensible forecasts. The model's inability to do so results from the fact that indirect variables are influenced largely by factors which are external to the environment with which the model is concerned. There are three main groups within this category. Firstly there are variables such as Bank Rate and Public Expenditure which are controlled to a considerable extent by some central authority. They are variables whose magnitudes are likely to vary with the political and economic policies which the various authorities choose to pursue, and although it is sometimes possible to anticipate, to some degree, the measures which the authorities will introduce to further their declared policies, the vagaries of political motivation are such that no systematic forecasting procedure is, in general, of any great value. Secondly there are variables over which no indentifiable body appears to exercise control. This group comprises such influences as technological progress, the weater, strikes, natural disasters, as well as demographic characteristics like population growth and marriage rates. A third group contains variables which might, in other circumstances, be of the direct type, but which the designers of the model choose to regard as being outside the scope of their particular model. World trade and world production are examples of such variables. In a very large model these variables might be estimated by looking at, for instance, the growth of demand for, and the capacity to produce, certain categories of commodities in various countries. However, for many models it will be sufficient to arrive at forecasts of such variables by a more intuitive method.

It is, in fact, possible at least in principle, to build a model which uses no indirect variables at all. Where one would otherwise occur, however, it would be necessary to specify some procedure which arrives at an estimate of its future level. The Government policy variables might be forecast through a system which took into account the authorities' current and expected objectives, and which compared these with the current and forecast state of affairs, and which then modified the policy variables in a manner that was likely to achieve the desired objectives. Demographic factors such as the structure of the population are relatively easy to deal with, and many models already incorporate their estimated future levels. Considerable difficulty, however, is likely to arise when an attempt is made to forecast the category of variables which include strikes, technological change and natural disasters. Perhaps the only way to approach such problems would be to measure the frequency of occurrence of these events in the recent past and to use this, together with a "monte-carlo" technique to simulate their occurrence in the future.

A third point of similarity which is common to most models is the procedure by which the individual relationships linking groups of variables are deduced. This is the area of original research which is the essential pre-requisite of any useful model. Usually the designers of the model will propose a specific relationship between certain variables, and then test the adequacy of the relationship on a statistical basis by using historical data. There is a considerable range of statistical tests which the model builders might use. Perhaps the most commonly used technique is stepwise linear regression, however, polynomical regression and time series analysis are also employed sometimes. As an example of the general procedure, it might be supposed that the model builder wished to test the simple Keynesian relationship between consumption and disposable income. Keynes' proposition was that the variables were linked in the following way.

$C = a + bY$
where C is consumption
       Y is disposable income
and a and b are constants.

The statistical test would probably consist of extracting from the National Income Accounts some historical data on the corresponding values of income and consumption, and using this in a regression analysis. The results of the analysis would then tell the model builder two things. Firstly it would reveal the values of a and b which made the proposed relationship most consistent with the historical data. Secondly it would provide a measure of the accuracy of the relationship which incorporated the calculated values of a and b.

Many model builders might feel that the relationship suggested above is not sufficiently accurate. Some may suspect that current consumption should be linked not only to current income, but also to income in some previous period. Alternatively it might be thought that consumption is partly determined by the public's expectations about future levels of income. Other model builders might wish to disaggregate total consumption into expenditure on durables and non-durables, because of the possibility that these elements of expenditure respond to different sets of variables. In any case, as soon as the model builder proposes some specific relationship between groups of variables for which historical data is available, it is possible to quantify that relationship and to test its validity. It is largely the model builder's insight into the interaction of certain economic variables, and his ability to mould these interactions into a usable relationship, which distinguishes a successful model from an unsuccessful one.

The model builder will ultimately bring together the relationships that have been deduced from his research, and the identity relationship which arise from the definitions of the variables he has used. When the total number of such relationships is sufficiently large in comparison with the number of direct variables incorporated in the model, it will be possible to solve the system simultaneously, and thereby to arrive at forecasts of the direct variables.

The existence of non-linearities among the relationships will generally preclude the possibility of solving the system analytically. As a result it will usually be necessary to employ a process of iteration. Firstly, guesses are made of the values of the non-linear direct variables in the period for which forecasts are required. These guesses are then used in the model, together with a technique which measures the extent of the inconsistency that the simultaneous assumption of these values would provide, and an estimate of the corrections that would be necessary in order to achieve consistency. The corrections, obtained in this way, are applied to the original guesses, and the process is repeated to arrive at a further set of corrections. This procedure is continued until, ultimately the corrections are insignificantly small. When this has happened the values of the direct variables will be consistent, and will therefore be the model's forecasts of the direct variables in that period.

A PRACTICAL MODEL

The construction of a model, designed to be of practical assistance in a stock market environment, commenced about two years ago as part of a phased programme by the Econometrics Unit of Hoare & Co. for developing the use of sophisticated computer techniques as aides to investment analysis, particularly in the area of forecasting. This model which is now fully operational, is fairly typical of other models that have been developed in recent years. In consists of about 50 equations and provides forecasts of an equal number of direct variables. Its basic structure is similar to those pioneered in the U.S.A. by Klein and Goldberger and the Wharton School, and in the U.K. by the London Business School. There are, however, three aspects of its construction which distinguish it from most of the others which are operating at the present time.

Firstly its association with a stock market environment requires that it pays rather more attention to an estimation of corporate profits than most other models. Profits, being the residual of two roughly equal magnitudes, are inevitably extremely difficult to forecast. The equations which were eventually incorporated, however, approach the problem, both through a disaggregation of GDP by its income components, and as a residual of revenue and costs. The compromise solution which results from this technique has been found to be reasonably accurate over the period for which it has been tested. Perhaps one of the major advantages that this model had over others in this area, however, was the availability of the historical record of the movements of profits of about 3,000 of the U.K.'s leading quoted companies. It was probably the aggregation of this data into the various components of corporate income which enabled the model to include a reasonably sophisticated explanation of profits. The most difficult problem that was encountered was an estimation of overseas income. Since its level is determined principally by economic activity outside the U.K., the variables that are useful in explaining its movement are largely external to the model, and consequently forecasts of overseas income are necessarily subject to sizeable errors.

When, however, a figure for total income is eventually reached, some attempt is made to arrive at an estimate of net corporate earnings. The procedure involves, in the first place, lagging the income estimates to reflect the delay between the period in which the revenue is earned, and the date on which the results are published, and secondly making the normal accounting deductions. The lagging technique is thought to be reasonably accurate in view of the records that are available for the majority of quoted companies. The accounting deductions, however, are liable to considerable error. The two major elements in the deduction process are depreciation and taxation. The depreciation figure is derived from the levels of capital investment in recent years and the current situation with regard to investment grants. The taxation figure must take account of not only the U.K. and foreign rates of company taxation, but also the accrued level of tax credits that the corporate sector might have. Ultimately it is possible to arrive at an estimate of earnings, and thereby prospective levels of the stock market's average Price Earnings Ratio, given present price levels.

A second distinguishing characteristic of the model is the facility that enables it to make use of the very latest published data. While its basic structure was designed for use with the authorities' quarterly, expenditure-based, breakdown of demand, it nevertheless takes account of a variety of monthly and even weekly data. The procedure that is used can perhaps best be explained through the following example.

At the end of October, the second quarter's expenditure based figures for demand are made available. This data is incorporated in the model, which then produces forecasts of the direct variables for the rest of that year, and for subsequent years. However, before the publication of the third quarter's figures in the following January, monthly statistics relating to, for instance, industrial production, retail prices, and overseas trade, in the third and even the fourth quarters are released. These figures are used by the model, on a temporary basis, to modify its forecasts for the third and fourth quarters, and through them, those for subsequent years. However, when the third quarter's expenditure figures are eventually published, all of the "temporary" data relating to that quarter is discarded.

The procedure means, in effect, that the model is being supplied with new data, and might therefore be revising its forecasts, on a weekly basis. It is thought to be a valuable technique not only because it makes use of the latest economic information, but also because the "crawling-peg" aspect of its forecasts enables the rapid identification of those areas of demand which are undergoing significant changes, and which might, therefore, be subject to pressures which the model had not anticipated.

The third aspect of the model which differentiates it from most others is the degree to which it incorporates monetary variables. The research in this area has not reached any very firm conclusions, and yet the balance of probabilities points to the fact that, especially in the recent past, the addition of monetary variables adds increased overall accuracy to the model's forecasts. While it is not possible to endorse fully the views of what might be regarded as the more extremist of the monetary economists, it does nevertheless seem that certain monetary magnitudes have a significant effect on the movement of the U.K. economy.

It is considered that the explanation of the apparently increasing importance of monetary economies lies largely in the change that has overcome the authorities' official policies. In the early 1960's when the economy was controlled almost exclusively through variations in fiscal measures, monetary variables were found to respond to these adjustment according to certain well defined patterns. Indeed, in this period, the principal monetary magnitudes were found to react so consistently to changes in the fiscal environment that their incorporation into the model added no information that was not already supplied by the more traditional variables. In recent periods, however, the authorities have chosen to make use of both fiscal and monetary policies in order to control economic trends. But their use of monetary factors has disrupted the previously established patterns of behaviour and has meant that monetary variables do now provide additional information about the development of activity within the economy.

This third distinguishing characteristic of the model provides an indication of its essentially dynamic nature. As the environment with which the model is dealing changes, it is necessary that the structure of the model is adjusted to include the newly relevant factors. If the economy took on a static nature, one in which there was no growth either in absolute terms at the aggregate level or by one component relative to another it might be possible to complete the building of a model. But since such a situation is extremely unlikely ever to exist, model builders must continually examine the validity of the relationships that their model uses. Moreover even if the basic structure of a particular relationship persists through time, it is likely that its precise quantification will vary, and this itself requires that econometericians are constantly involved in research work. In addition they must continue to search for, and attempt to quantify, new relationships. This is particularly important in view of the additions to the coverage of official statistics that are being made available at the present time, and the implication is, therefore, that all models will be subject to sizeable modifications from time to time.

FORECASTS

After incorporating the adjustments to official policy introduced in the 1970 Budget, the model was used to provide forecasts of the movement of the economy in the remainder of this year. The following notes outline firstly the assumptions that were made about the future levels of some of the model's indirect variables, and secondly, the forecasts that were produced.

Indirect Variables

1. Apart from the changes to personal allowances, no major changes in rates of taxation occurred in the 1970 Budget, and it seemed reasonable to suppose therefore that the rates of taxation currently in operation would persist for the rest of the year.
2. Monetary policy formed an important part of the authorities' control of the economy in 1969 and it seemed likely that its importance would continue in 1970. However certain in problems arose when an attempt was made to present endogenous forecasts of monetary variables. In particular it became apparent that the authorities might encounter problems in trying to limit the growth of domestic credit to £900m at a time when the Bank rate was relatively low on an international basis and when inflation was relatively high. Nevertheless these problems were reconciled by assuming that any pressures arising from the simultaneous adoption of a 7 per cent Bank rate and a £900m expansion of credit would be absorbed in the area of free market rates of interest.

3. The U.K. economy is very sensitive to the international environment, and consequently assumptions about variables such as world trade and import prices are of crucial importance to the model. After looking at all the available data on the trends that were developing towards the end of 1969, it was considered that world trade might grow by 8 per cent in real terms and that import prices were likely to rise by 2¾ per cent.

On the basis of these principal assumptions, the model gives the following forecasts for 1970.

Summary of the model's 1970 forecasts.

	% Increase on 1969
Constant 1963 Prices	
Consumers' Expenditure	2.8
Public Authorities Current Expenditure	623.0
Gross Domestic Fixed Capital Formation	3.75
Value of Change in Stocks (£m)	450
Exports of Goods & Services	5.5
Imports of Goods & Services	5.0
Taxes on Expenditure less Subsidies	3.0
Gross Domestic Product	3.6
Current Prices	
U.K. Trading Profit	8.8
Wages & Salaries	10.0
Current Account Surplus (£m)	520

These forecasts suggest that the economy will experience a fairly high level of activity this year. Consumers' expenditure was very depressed in 1969 but under the stimulus of rapidly increasing personal incomes it is expected to advance strongly in 1970. Although our forecast of an increase of 2.8 per cent is somewhat below that expected by the authorities, it nevertheless represents the fastest rise since 1964. Investment is also likely to show a significant rate of growth. On the fixed capital formation side, a slight recovery in house-building taken together with a resumption in the upward trend of spending by the public sector, and a continuing increase in private corporate expenditure is expected to produce a growth of 3.75 per cent in investment at the aggregate level. Moreover on the stockbuilding side the model forecasts that after two years of very low growth, 1970 will see an increase of around £450m in 1963 prices. The forecasts of external trade represents a slowdown in the rate of improvement which has occurred since the middle of 1968. Nevertheless they suggest that the balance of payments will remain favourable, and in particular they imply a current account surplus of £520m. The aggregation of these estimates leads to an expected growth of GDP of 3.6 per cent. in real terms which is considered to be in line with the economy's potential growth and which should therefore halt the rising trend of unemployment.

The model's forecasts of corporate income suggests an increase of 8.8 per cent in trading profits arising in the U.K., but as a result of rather slower expansions of overseas income and non-trading revenue, the figure for aggregate corporate income represents an increase of only 7.6 per cent. When this forecast is lagged to reflect the delay in publishing results and after the normal accounting deductions have been made, the model predicts that a growth of earnings per share of around 7 per cent will occur over the next twelve months. Such an increase in earnings would reduce the markets' current PER of 14.7, given present price levels, to one of 13.7 by March, 1971.

CONCLUSION

Econometric models are still a relatively recent innovation in this country, but their forecasting performance has nevertheless been fairly encouraging. Although it is not certain that they will achieve the same success in a stock market environment that they have in the academic world, the systematic approach of models, their quantified analysis and projections, and their overall flexibility are considered to be precisely those qualities which will prove to be of value in making investment decisions.

12 Monetary Policy, Gilts and Equities

A. A. WALTERS

The article was published in The Investment Analyst *in December 1970. In this essay, Professor Walters examines the relationship between money and security prices. It had long been recognized that monetary policy had some effect on prices, but its precise influence was unclear. Beginning with his thoughts on Keynesian theory and gilt-edged securities, he introduces his own 'polar cases' to amplify the argument that nominal rates and gilt prices are partly explained by variations in the supply of money.*

With regard to equities, Professor Walters traces 'turning points' in the FT Index since 1955 and notes their coincidence with turning points in the quantity of money. However, although he offers the tentative conclusion that they are linked, he calls for more research on the subject.

Postscript: at one point, Professor Walters compares rates of inflation to 'rolling juggernauts – slow to start but very difficult to stop – as we shall all discover over the next few years or so'. And these words were written in 1970 . . .

Sir Alan Walters has been Vice-Chairman and Director of AIG Trading Group Inc. since 1991. Before that, he was Professor of Economics at Johns Hopkins University, Maryland. He has held academic posts at the University of Birmingham, Northwestern University, (Evanston, Illinois), LSE, MIT and Nuffield College, Oxford, and many posts as an economic advisor, including to Government bodies and to the World Bank. He is a Fellow of the Royal Economic Society, and has published extensively in the field of economics, econometrics and economic theory.

I

It has been long recognised that monetary policy has *some* influence on the prices of gilt-edged as well as of equities. The precise character of the influence is, however, much less clear. A casual glance at historical experience will show no obvious pattern of behaviour. "Laws" do not leap from the charts. No-one can naturally and easily adduce the lessons of long experience. One example will illustrate this point. It is common nowadays to associate high interest rates (or low gilt-edged prices) with high degrees of inflation; yet the statistics show that in the year 1946 gilt-edged were at a post-war high and inflation was proceeding at a frightening rate.

Although it would be charitable to believe that the apparently chaotic record of historical experience has led economists more intensively to explore the deductive or theoretical relationship between money and security prices, it would be untrue. Most economists—or perhaps one should say academic economists—are fascinated more by theoretical propositions about the cosmology of economics. Fitting interest rates into a grand design of the whole system is much more tempting—and we have all succumbed. But there is a difficulty. In order to make any progress with the grand model and interest rates, drastic simplifications had to be employed.

One of the grand designs which has provided the blue-print for public policy in the post-war years was that of John Maynard Keynes. Oddly enough, the thrust of Keynesian theory was designed to solve the interwar problem of depression and unemployment. In his model the price level was held constant—there was no inflation—and the main focus of interest was the quantity of output and the employment level. The price of gilt-edged appeared in this model, albeit in a very stylised form, in the choice which people make between holding their assets in the only two forms of wealth admitted in the model—money and long-dated gilt-edged.

An increase in the quantity of money in the hands of the public brought about by the authorities purchasing gilts will generate an increase in the price of gilt-edged and thus lower the interest rate. In order willingly to part with their bonds, holders must be attracted by a higher price. The simple provisional conclusion is therefore that in general an expansion of the stock of money will lead to higher gilt-edged and lower interest rates. Thus an expansionary monetary policy would raise the price of gilt-edged and a monetary squeeze would depress gilts. There was also a special twist provided by Kenynes—the so-called "liquidity trap". This suggested that when there was a lot of money in the system and the interest rates were very low, you could not get them down even further by expanding the money supply. People just simply would not believe that the price of gilts could go any higher so they would be prepared to sell at a minute rise in price. So the final conclusion of Keynesian theory is that the price of gilts is positively related to the quantity of money—except that there is an upper limit to the gilt price.

So far as it goes this is broadly agreed. But it does not go very far. For one might say what do the people do with the money the authorities have put into their hands by the authorities' purchase of gilt-edged? Unless they are locked in a "liquidity trap", they will not just leave it in the form of cash. The interest rate has gone down and so investment, hitherto unprofitable, will now become worthwhile. The expansion of spending, with Keynes' assumption of plentiful unemployed resources, will be achieved without disturbing the price level.

With full employment and virtually no unused capacity, however, such a result cannot occur. Prices must be affected sooner or later. And varying prices does produce different results. We must now distinguish between the *real* interest rate (*rr*) and the *nominal* interest rate (*nr*). The *nominal* interest rate measures the rate of return in terms of £ sterling counted as the same units at whatever date they occur (a 1965 pound is the same as a 1970 pound). Thus a bond costing £100 today and yielding $9 per annum in perpetuity has a nominal rate of 9 per cent. Now suppose that the price level increases in perpetuity by a rate of 1 per cent per annum. By our convention of counting £s as the same, whatever the date, the nominal rate is not affected. The real rate, however, is. Each year we must, as it were, put aside £1's worth of goods in order to maintain the same real value in the £100. The real rate is therefore approximately (£9 minus £1) per £100. Thus we have the general approximate rule

$$nr = rr + \dot{p}$$

where $\dot{p}$ is the percentage change in prices experienced in perpetuity.[1] Or putting it in the usual form:

$$rr = nr - \dot{p},$$

i.e., Real rate = nominal rate − percentage change in prices.

The nominal rate is observed on the market at any moment of time. The future price change $\dot{p}$, however, is not observed and cannot be observed *ex ante*. All one can do is enter the price change that is *expected* to occur, which we shall write as $\dot{p}^e$. Such a concept is in the mind, a psychology rather than a statistic. But there is no way out; we must say how people formulate their expectations if we are to have any hope of shedding light in these dark corners.

Two polar cases can be first distinguished. First there is the situation when the price level is *expected by everyone to remain unchanged*. Then, in spite of the fact that it has actually changed as a consequence of monetary policy, people do not incorporate this lesson of experience into their expectations. Wherever the price level happens to be, there it is expected to remain. We call this the *static expectations* case. The second polar case is when people predict with perfection the future course of prices: this case we might call the *perfect expectations case*. Then expected prices are the realised prices. Probably most people would be inclined to choose a middle ground between these poles and argue that price expectations are formed from past experience of price changes. And there are many standard forms that enable us to project past experience into expectations of the future.

Thus we have $\qquad\qquad rr = nr - \dot{p}^e.$

A. Polar cases:
   (1) Static expectations $\quad rr = nr$ since $\dot{p}^e = 0$
   (2) Perfect expectations $\quad rr = nr - \dot{p}$ since $\dot{p}^e = p$
B. Past experience case: $\quad rr = nr - f(\dot{p}\text{'s in past})$

(where by $f(\dot{p}\text{'s in past})$ we mean that we form an expectation on the basis of experience).

There is, of course, no a *priori* way in which we can choose between these hypotheses; the data must decide.

Broadly speaking, the following general tendencies have been observed in the data. First, during the inter-war years and immediate post-war years, people were very sluggish in adjusting the expectations to recent experience (*i.e.*, they approximated to polar case (1) the static expectations). In recent years the adjustment has been much more rapid—perhaps even with some "over-shooting". This may be associated with what it is now fashionable to call the "inflation psychology".

Now let us refer back to the effects on monetary policy on gilt prices and let us attempt to put this real-nominal-price effect into its context. Clearly an increase in the quantity of money will have an *impact effect* and will increase the price of gilts, reducing the nominal rate. All this is along good Keynesian lines (unless we are caught in the "liquidity trap"—but we can safely forget this for the post-war period). Some of us no doubt will be content to wait until the price level does start rising rapidly before we revise our expectations of future price increases. But increases of the money stock will themselves immediately generate expectations about future inflation allowing for suitable lags in the effects; all of us know about the elements of the quantity theory of money. Over a certain time span the $\dot{p}^e$ will increase and consequently the nominal rate will increase, so the price of gilts will fall. I suspect that this time span, once many years, is now rather short, but still a matter of years rather than months.

This pattern of behaviour fits in well with what we know about the effects of monetary policy. A cut back in the rate of growth of the money supply has its first effect some nine months later on the rate of growth of real income. Only much later—perhaps 18 months or two years later—does it affect the rate of inflation.[2] The rates of inflation are like rolling juggernauts—slow to start but very difficult to stop as we shall all discover over the next

---

[1] Note that it is approximate because strictly we should include an interaction term $\dot{p}rr$ which measures the interest that would be earned on the price adjustment to the nominal amount. But it is usually small except under conditions of hyperinflation.

[2] See my *Money in Boom and Slump*, 2nd edition, pp. 54, 55, I.E.A. 1970.

four years or so. But these inflation rates do determine the general long term level of the nominal rates over the years. The short-term oscillations of nominal rates and the prices of gilt-edged are to be partly explained in terms of the behaviour of the authorities in increasing or decreasing the supply of money.

II

Now what about the equity market? The essential difference between an equity and a gilt-edged is that the latter entitles one to a fixed money sum in perpetuity (as with consols) whereas an equity is a title to a share of the increase in the value of the assets of a firm. Usually it is thought that the firm's assets are real capital and are not denominated in monetary terms. However, it is clear that the net assets attributable to equity holders may include either sizeable quantities of cash or assets denominated in nominal terms. At the other extreme the financial structure of the firm may be highly geared with large debenture liabilities, a small amount of cash and large holdings of real assets. The effect of an increase in the expected rate of change of prices will have different effects according to the financial structure of the firm. And unlike gilt-edged the financial structure of the firm can in part be adjusted to expectations about future price inflation. Thus one would expect that the inflationary expectations would cause a switch from gilts to equities—driving up the price of the latter at the expense of the former.

Broadly, this has occurred in the statistics. The reversal of the yield gap occurs in the period of inflation so that, for example, at present gilts are about 8 to 10 per cent whereas the earnings yield of equities is in the region of 4 to 5 per cent. The difference gives a very rough measure (for reasons mentioned above) of the expected rate of inflation.

The secular growth of the price of equities is clearly due to a number of factors. The basic increase in productivity of assets in the corporate sector accounts for much of the *real* growth. But also the *nominal* growth of market valuations reflects the secular trend of inflation, which is in turn generated by the increase in the supply of money. It is clear, however, that the secular upward trend of the F.T. index contrasts with the secular downward trend of the price of gilt-edged from 1946 to 1970. Of course this is not the whole of the story of the determinants of the price of equities; many other factors, such as changes in the law, in the organisation of financial institutions, etc., must be adduced to give a proper account. One may well believe, however, that the broad movements are mainly a function of the general price level and productivity.

Nevertheless, the main interesting effect of monetary policy can be observed in its impact effect. It is remarkable that each of the turning points in the F.T. index is associated fairly closely with a turning point in the quantity of money. Consider the evidence from 1950 onwards as shown in the table opposite.

I have tried to identify the turning points visually from graphs of the F.T. Index and my own statistics of the money stock. This is by no means an exact science. Judgement is used and one may therefore introduce bias. It seems clear to me, however, that there is a re-markable correspondence between turning points in the two series. The turning points are more or less contemporaneous. The only case where there was a marked divergence was in 1956–58; and one may adduce special reasons for that.

A second feature is that the extent of the movement in the money stock and the size of the change in the F.T. index seem to be broadly correlated. For example, during the Butler monetary squeeze of 1955/56, the decline in the money stock was sharp and prolonged. The F.T. index reflects this. One would need to do more research on the nature of the series in order to determine precisely the relationships between the series. (It seems to be a useful task for a scholar seeking a subject.)

Turning points.

	Money	*F.T. Index*
Early 1951	Upper	
Mid-1951		Upper
Early 1952	Lower	
Mid-1952		Lower
Early 1955	Upper	
Mid-1955 or late		Upper
Mid-1956 or late 1956	Lower	
Early 1958		Lower
Early 1960	Upper	Upper
Early 1962	Lower	
Mid-1962		Lower
1964–65	(Upper one ill defined)	
Late 1966 or early 1967	Lower	Lower
Late 1968 or early 1969	Upper	Upper

One issue of considerable importance is that of causation. The debate on causation goes on at length in monetary economics. The usual concern is whether an increase in the supply of money causes income to rise or whether the rise in the supply of money is a passive reaction of the authorities in supplying the needs of the public for future planned spending.

The coincidence of turning points gives no clue on causation. But it seems clear to me that no-one can substantiate an argument that the equity market *determines* the quantity of money. In the typical "passive authority" case this would require that transactors *reduce* their demand for money as the equity market turns down. This is, of course, diametrically the opposite of everyone's experience. When there is a monetary squeeze and the equity market turns sour, the public is quite desperate for liquidity and tries to get as much money as they can. This is quite inconsistent with the view of a passive authority supplying money in response to demand.

Thus it seems that either the decline in the money stock is autonomous and actually *causes* the turn down (or up) in the equity market, *or* that both the turning points in *both* the equity market and the money stock are the consequence of some third force. It is difficult to choose between the two alternative hypotheses unless one specifies the third force variables and how they interact with the system.

My predilection is to believe that movements in the money stock are the *cause* of the oscillations in the equity market. But it must be admitted that sufficient properly documented evidence has not yet been produced to establish such a claim. One needs to specify *how* the monetary oscillations affect the stock market and to trace the linkages. Such a research programme seems worth exploring.

13 The Trustees' Meeting – A City Daydream

J. M. BREW

This article was published in The Investment Analyst *in December 1970. John Brew writes: In 1970, when 'The Trustees' Meeting was published, many people believed (and some died in the belief) that the measurement of investment performance was rapidly making the transition from an art to a science. All that was needed was that the investment world should be educated in the new techniques and that certain vested interests should be overcome. My article was intended as a light-hearted statement that life was not that easy. In fact it was taken very seriously, and has even appeared in university syllabuses!*

John Brew is a mathematician by training, and, for most of his career, was involved in the mathematics of investment. He joined the stockbrokers Grieveson Grant in 1953, and was managing Partner at the time of the amalgamation with Kleinwort Benson, having spent most of his time in the Gilt Edged Department. He has published papers on a variety of subjects from yield curves to traded options. He was Chairman of the Society of Investment Analysts 1971–73.

"Well", said the Chairman, "you have all had a few days to consider the figures of our pension fund's investment performance. Before handing over to the Secretary who will explain them in detail I must thank him for his foresight in instituting a scheme which makes performance so easy to assess. I hear at the club that some other funds have been having a good deal of trouble in this area. What it comes down to is that they don't really know whether their pension funds have been invested well or badly. I am confident that in our case the question has been made unusually straightforward and we shall be able to reach a decision fairly quickly".

Before seeing the Secretary's comments on the situation the reader should be told the story so far. Some time ago this pension fund decided to divide its equity portfolio into six equal parts and to entrust their management to six organisations which had offered investment management services. The Trustees presciently took the view that ordinary share prices would probably drift down during the period and accordingly made arrangements to put all their new money into property. In order that there should be no ambiguity about the investment performance the powers of management were restricted to investment in shares which were constituents of the F.T.A. All-Share Index with, of course, permission to hold cash and reinvest the dividend income. It was further stipulated that investment should be conducted within the normal bounds of prudence. The Trustees did not know quite what that meant, but it seemed the right sort of thing to say. So the reader will agree that the problem could hardly be simpler. Each management was subject to the same constraints and each portfolio could accurately be compared with the Index. The specific reason for this meeting was the fact that more money was now available for equity investment. Decisions were needed on the allocation of this new money and also, perhaps, on the re-allocation of the management of existing portfolios.

The first table produced by the Secretary showed the result of quarterly valuations between the starting date, 29 June 1968, and 2 October 1970, all expressed as a percentage of the starting value. The Secretary took the trouble to estimate what the periodic results would have been if the valuations had been exactly in line with the F.T.A. Index and income from the Index constituents had been reinvested as it was received. This is Table 1.

TABLE 1. Quarterly valuation totals allowing for reinvested income.

Valuation date	F.T.A. Index	Fund A	Fund B	Fund C	Fund D	Fund E	Fund F
29.6.68	100	100	100	100	100	100	100
4.10.68	107.17	135.13	112.10	104.50	115.20	107.30	93.10
3.1.69	114.89	142.04	127.91	109.73	122.23	115.24	101.12
3.4.69	108.83	130.86	117.68	105.89	116.61	110.17	97.90
4.7.69	95.70	111.36	95.32	98.48	89.79	97.17	87.13
3.10.69	94.86	107.79	95.32	97.79	98.14	96.68	87.13
2.1.70	101.65	113.50	104.85	103.66	107.95	103.84	94.20
3.4.70	99.49	108.66	102.23	102.11	101.47	101.97	94.20
3.7.70	88.75	95.62	85.87	95.98	86.25	91.26	88.29
2.10.70	98.83	105.56	103.04	103.66	103.33	102.21	101.65

Effective total quarterly rate of return as calculated by the Secretary	–0.131%		+0.603%	+0.333%	+0.400%	+0.365%	+0.243+	+0.182%
Trend rate of quarterly return as calculated by the Economic Adviser	–1.420%		–2.237%	–1.839%	–0.425%	–1.685%	–1.044%	–0.420%

"Well, Sir, fortunately the figures are sufficiently clear-cut to speak for themselves", the Secretary began, "but perhaps I could be allowed to elaborate very briefly. The first thing to notice is that, even allowing for reinvested income the F.T.A. Index showed a negative rate of return over the period, a rate of minus .131 per cent, per quarter to be exact. We should have been much better off to sell out completely and put the proceeds out on loan. So to some extent we can congratulate ourselves on the decision to channel our new money elsewhere during the period. I think most of us believe that the future for equities is now a little more rosy and, with new money to invest, it seems to me that we should take this opportunity of reviewing the performance of our managers. You will see that they all achieved a positive rate of return, and within the brief we gave them it was very satisfactory that they all beat the Index by a significant amount. I have designated the managements by letters, and my recommendation is that we should give all the new money to the one at the top of my league table, namely A".

The Chairman asked for comments and the first one to speak was the Economic Adviser. His economic advice had not been conspicuously successful in the immediate past and he was not in a mood to let anyone get away with praise too easily. "I should like to know why you have given us all these intermediate valuation results if the end figure is the only one that matters", he said. "I thought I ought to keep an eye on what was going on" replied the Secretary, "and having arranged for quarterly valuations I thought the Trustees would be interested to see the full result. But you are quite right that my recommendation is based on the last valuation".

"That is very interesting", said the Economic Adviser, "because I have been looking at the intermediate figures and I should like to ask you if there is any sort of intermediate fluctuation which might have made you change your mind". "I think I see your point" replied the Secretary, "but I am bound to say that it seems to me to be a trifle academic. After all there is no getting away from the fact that A has done a good deal better with our money than any of the others".

But the Economic Adviser was not quite finished. "If you want my specific recommendation it is that we should give the new money to those who are likely to do the best with it in the future rather than give it to those who have done best in the past. Your motive for the study of performance seems to be to reward those who have made the most money for us, on the basis that these will do the best for us in future. I think we should study your performance tables much more carefully."

Having made this suggestion the Economic Adviser produced Table 2 which shows the performance of each fund each quarter allowing for both capital and income.

TABLE 2. Quarterly rates of return allowing for both capital changes and income.

Quarter	F.T.A. Index	Fund A	Fund B	Fund C	Fund D	Fund E	Fund F
1	+ 7.17%	+35.13%	+12.1%	+4.50%	+15.20%	+ 7.30%	– 6.90%
2	+ 7.20%	+ 5.11%	+14.1%	+5.00%	+ 6.10%	+ 7.40%	+ 8.61%
3	– 5.27%	– 7.87%	– 8.00%	–3.50%	– 4.60%	– 4.40%	– 3.18%
4	–12.07%	–14.90%	–19.00%	–7.00%	–23.00%	–11.80%	–11.00%
5	– 0.87%	– 3.21%	NIL	–0.70%	+ 9.30%	– 0.50%	NIL
6	+ 7.15%	+ 5.30%	+10.00%	+6.00%	+10.00%	+ 7.40%	+ 8.12%
7	– 2.12%	– 4.26%	– 2.50%	–1.50%	– 6.00%	– 1.80%	NIL
8	–11.80%	–12.00%	–16.00%	–6.00%	–15.00%	–10.50%	– 6.27%
9	+11.36%	+10.40%	+20.00%	+8.00%	+19.80%	+12.00%	+15.13%
Arithmetic Mean	+0.194%	+1.52%	+1.19%	+0.53%	+1.31%	+0.57%	+0.50%

"Is it so obvious now", he said "that A is such a good manager? He started off like a shot from a gun and was miles ahead of the field at the end of the first quarter. After that he has done noticeably worse than the Index every single time. Contrast this with F who started very badly and has done outstandingly well since. Would you stake any money on A beating F between now and next year, because I certainly wouldn't? My impression is that F is much the better horse but that the finish came a furlong too soon for him. In fact I think we should seriously consider dropping A altogether. He is easily bottom of my league table".

The proposition being put by the Economic Adviser was that F, the management which had put up easily the worst end-to-end performance of all the six, was the one likely to do best in the future. He had some figures to prove it too. He had applied regression methods to the valuation figures (or, to be more accurate, the logarithm of the valuation totals) and derived a trend line for each management which can be used to estimate the rate of total return each is likely to achieve in future. The result is shown in the last line of Table 1. This new method of assessment turns the ranking order just about completely upside down and shows that only three managements have a trend rate better than the Index. There are other ways of fitting a trend line but the results would not differ substantially. But if the Economic Adviser had been allowed to fit a second degree curve the trend would have been even more strongly in favour of F. His second favourite was C.

At this stage the Finance Director introduced the question of variability and risk which became the subject of a somewhat lengthy argument. It is evident from the tables that some managements produced results which were much more variable than others. But it is not obvious how we should assess variability. Should one consider the periodic valuation totals, or the totals relative to the Index? Perhaps we should consider the variability of the quarterly rates of return, or, probably best of all, the difference between the actual rates of return and those achieved on the Index. The Chairman very much liked E on these grounds, but nobody quite knew how much the better performance should be required or expected before one is justified in pursuing a more risky policy. Still it was evident that E, though he produced rather unexciting results, did so in a way which gave confidence that he would rarely produce a bad performance and would nearly always be above average.

"But there is another, and much better, way of looking at it" said the Finance Director. "Ever since the Chairman and I went to talk to them about the company I have subscribed to the Journal of The Society of Investment Analysts. I read an article in the December 1968 issue by Taylor and Russell which explained what I think is the correct approach. This article applied an idea of an American called Jack Treynor to the analysis of U.K. Unit Trusts. The idea is that some managements consistently have portfolios which both go up more and down more than the Index. Others have portfolios which go up less and down less. By examination of Table 2 you can see roughly what I mean. Fund C moved the same way as the Index each quarter but its movement was always a good deal less pronounced. By contrast, Fund B was more volatile than the Index in both directions. The problem is easily analysed statistically by making a regression of each fund's quarterly rate of total return on the Index return". The results are shown in Table 3, which shows the equation of the regression line for each management. The variable x represents the performance of the Index expressed as a total return and the variable y represents the performance of the management under analysis. The gradient of the line for A is 1.39 which means that a 1 per cent increase in the Index tended in the past to be accompanied by a 1.39 per cent increase in the portfolio managed by A. Management C, on the other hand only showed a 0.645 per cent increase in the same circumstances. This line is called the "characteristic line" and there is some evidence that its slope is relatively stable in time".

TABLE 3. Regression equations for each management.

x = Quarterly Return on F.T.A. Index
y = Quarterly Return on the Fund

		Correlation
Fund A	$y = 1.25 + 1.39\,x$	$r^2 = 0.782$
Fund B	$y = 0.88 + 1.61\,x$	$r^2 = 0.996$
Fund C	$y = 0.41 + 0.65\,x$	$r^2 = 0.994$
Fund D	$y = 1.00 + 1.58\,x$	$r^2 = 0.939$
Fund E	$y = 0.38 + 0.99\,x$	$r^2 = 0.999$
Fund F	$y = 0.35 + 0.79\,x$	$r^2 = 0.789$

The Finance Director contended that the choice lay squarely between B and D because these managements had the steepest slopes to their characteristic lines and would therefore perform better in the rising market which the Trustees had agreed was likely to occur. He had a marginal preference for D because though its line was not quite so steep it intersected the vertical axis at a slightly higher point—which is supposed to reflect the amount by which the fund would beat the Index given a nil rate of return on the Index. But the Economic Adviser pointed out that the lines intersected at a point given by an Index return of 4 per cent which was surely less than one could expect in a normal year. The Finance Director then agreed that B was slightly preferable.

The Chairman was a bit dazed by now, but he felt obliged to put in another word for E. "I just don't believe it", he said. "You chaps are being much too clever about it all. Look at E's performance. He beat the Index by a perceptible amount every single time which is more than any of the others did. My second choice would be F who beat it eight times out of nine".

So there we have it. The Secretary chose A. The Economic Adviser chose C and F. The Finance Director chose B and D, and the Chairman chose E and F. About a hundred years ago Mr. Punch summed it up aptly when he said "You pays your money and you takes your choice".

Postscript

In real life the figures will never be as conveniently clearcut as those in the tables. But the reader will have noticed one respect in which this daydream is realistic. At the time of the meeting there was only one thing on which the trustees were in agreement—that the equity market was likely to rise. At the time of going to press the index is about 10% lower. But given the fact that they agreed to be bullish it would have been right to prefer B and D whatever Mr. Punch said. If you are going to make quarterly valuations you surely ought to use them.

We can all agree, though, that the matter is not quite so simple as the Secretary supposed.

14 The Role of the Institutions in the U.K. Ordinary Share Market

J. H. C. LEACH

This article was published in The Investment Analyst *in December 1971. The article, which followed two earlier ones examining 'The Weight of New Money', was written when both pension funds and unit trusts were, if not in their infancy, by no means the hugely influential forces that they have subsequently become; my suggestion that unit trusts would soon become as important as investment trusts was not far off the mark, though I did not guess the future explosive growth of pension funds. One may note that the level of equity turnover then, in both absolute and relative terms, was vastly smaller than it has since become.*

Colin Leach, FIIMR, whose City career began in 1957, remains active in the Square Mile (and Switzerland) as a Director of several investment firms. His Professorship relates to work on (mainly) Ancient Greek, but he has written and reviewed extensively on financial topics; and in the 1970s, he was Managing Director of ARIEL, the automated stock trading system, set up by the Accepting Houses, which in many ways anticipated current screen trading methods. As Editor, again in the 1970s, of The Investment Analyst *he regarded one of his main tasks as being to raise the overall standard of published work towards US levels. From 1965 to 1972, he was at Schroeder Wagg.*

On two previous occasions in this Journal (October, 1967 and December, 1969) I have commented upon the influence wielded on the U.K. equity market by institutional new money (making due allowance for new issues, take-overs, and so on). Readers will be relieved to learn that I do not wish here to rehash the arguments (nor, for that matter, should I wish to modify them) which I have already put forward; rather, I hope to set out on a broader canvas the present situation of the part played by the institutions in the equity market, and to answer such questions as: what proportion of U.K. ordinary shares is owned by the major types of institution? How rapidly is that proportion increasing? What percentage of dealing in equities (both buying and selling) is carried out by the institutions? That we can approach answers to these questions is attributable to a steady improvement in the available statistics.

1. WHAT PROPORTION OF ORDINARY SHARES IS NOW OWNED BY INSTITUTIONS?

At end-December, 1970, the market value, according to Stock Exchange statistics, of the quoted equity capital of "U.K. Registered and Managed Companies" was £32,498 million; this total excludes investment and unit trusts, and thus avoids double counting. At the same date, the value (known or estimated) of ordinary shares held by the main categories of institution was as follows:–

TABLE 1.

Category	Market value of U.K. equities	As % of all U.K. equities (as defined above)
	£ million	
Insurance Companies	5,200 (est)	16·0
Pension Funds	2,830 (est)	8·7
Investment trusts	2,462	7·6
Unit Trusts	1,034	3·2
	11,526	35·5

Figures for Insurance Companies, as given in *Financial Statistics*, are still for book values (£3,645 million at end-1970); but enough information appears in the Reports of individual companies to enable a hopefully fairly accurate estimation of the market values to be made. In the case of Pension Funds it has only been necessary to make adjustments for changes in market values in 1970, and this figure should also approximate quite closely to the truth.

The shift towards the institutions has (not surprisingly) been continuing inexorably. J. Revell estimated that, at the end of 1963, institutions held 25 per cent. of quoted U.K. equities; and I calculated that this percentage had risen to a third by end-1967[1]. Perhaps especial interest lies in the expansion in recent years of the unit trust movement (which to be sure, has doubtless been financed to some extent by individuals' sales of ordinary shares), and the figures can usefully be commented upon separately. At the end of 1963, there were some 70 trusts, with total assets of £371 million; and by the end of 1968—a high point in some ways—there were 181 trusts, with total assets of £1,482 million of which over £1,140 million was in U.K. equities. The rapid expansion comes out clearly in the table:

TABLE 2.

Year	No. of Trusts	Net Sales of Units	Total Funds	U.K. Equities	(As % of all U.K. Equities)
		£m.	£m.	£m.	
1965	121	59	522	420	(1·7)
1966	138	105	582	453	(2·0)
1967	156	84	854	664	(2·3)
1968	181	258	1,482	1,142	(2·8)
1969	206	186	1,412	1,095	(3·2)
1970	221	98	1,398	1,034	(3·2)

The influence of the generally poor markets of 1969 and 1970 is also apparent, and it is note-worthy that in 1970, for the first time in a long period, the unit trust movement did not increase its "market share". Equally, when one considers the U.S. experience of mutual fund expansion in the 1960s in conjunction with the low percentage—only just over 3 per cent—of U.K. equities now held by unit trusts, the scope for expansion is clearly very considerable. It is not within the scope of this note to discuss whether, or in what ways, this

[1] See note by author in Financial Analysts Journal (July–August 1969).

likely growth—which will have to be accompanied by a substantial and sustained marketing effort—will benefit the investing public; but it certainly seems likely that unit trusts will, during the 1970s, become a really significant factor in the market—quite possibly as important as the investment trusts are at present.

2. THE BUYING POWER OF THE INSTITUTIONS

My earlier notes on "The Weight of New Money" have gone into this subject in more depth than is necessary here. The net equity acquisitions of the institutions, which had reached the peak level of £797 million in 1968, were at lower (but still high) levels in 1969 and 1970:–

TABLE 3.

Type	1969	£ million	1970
Insurance Coy's	148		262
Pension Funds	219		391
Investment Trusts	–29		–29
Unit Trusts	132		48
Total net equity purchases	470		672

These totals mean that, in the five years from 1966 to 1970, the institutions made net purchases of no less than £2,862 million of U.K. equities—an average of £572 million per annum. Over the same period, new issues of ordinary shares came to only £895 million, or say £180 million per annum; and we must assume that the balance was made up by sales from the personal sector. Net disposals of "company securities" by the personal sector over the five year period came to £2,720 million, or £544 million per annum; but not all of this sum, of course, will have been represented by quoted U.K. ordinary shares.

3. WHAT PERCENTAGE OF DEALING IN EQUITIES IS INSTITUTIONAL?

The Stock Exchange provides figures for equity turnover in London (figures for elsewhere are also available), while *Financial Statistics*, in addition to the net totals for investment, gives separate institutional figures for purchases and sales. Hence we may derive the following table:–

TABLE 4.

	1969	£ million	1970
Total turnover in equities (a)	8,713		8,813
Institutional turnover (b)	3,248		3,414
(b) as % of (a)	37·3		38·7[1]

We may further look at these figures by purchases and sales, as under:–

TABLE 5.

	1969		£ million	1970	
	Purchases	Sales		Purchases	Sales
Total equity turnover (a)	4,356	4,356		4,406	4,406
Institutional turnover (b)	1,860	1,388		2,044	1,370
(b) as % of (a)	42·7	31·8		46·4	31·1

[1] It will be appreciated that this assumes that all institutional dealing goes through the stock market; a true figure would be slightly—but only slightly—lower.

Given the nature of institutional money, it is hardly surprising that it accounts for a higher percentage of purchases than sales; whether the figures are regarded as high or low in themselves will depend on individuals' subjective reactions. Some indication of the relative willingness of institutions to trade—by which I mean readiness to sell securities as well as to buy them—appears in the following table, where the lower the value; the greater the proportion of sales to purchases, and vice versa:–

TABLE 6.

Ratio of purchases to sales

	1969	1970
Insurance Companies	1·40	1·75
Pension Funds	1·63	2·19
Investment Trusts	0·92	0·91
Unit Trusts	1·42	1·18

The "minus" ratio of investment trusts of course reflects their lack of new money, while the low ratio of unit trusts in 1970 has a more or less similar cause. It could be argued that the relatively higher values for pension funds are proof of their basically "buy to hold" approach; by contrast, the ratios for insurance companies perhaps suggest a rather more active policy than is sometimes associated with them; in 1969 their ratio was actually a trifle lower than that of the unit trusts, which as a class are usually thought of as pretty active investors; as is demonstrated more adequately below.

Moreover, the available data, by giving separate figures for sales, allow us to estimate what proportion of their equity portfolios the various types of institution turn over in a year. Taking the two years, 1969 and 1970, together, in order to produce a reasonable average (not that the variances are great), the following table can be produced:–

TABLE 7.

Institution	Average equity sales, 1969/70 £m.	Sales as % of total equities (as at end 1970)
Insurance companies	361	7·0 (est)
Pension Funds	332	11·7
Investment Trusts	341	13·9
Unit Trusts	339	32·8

Few, perhaps, will be surprised by the progression revealed above; but in absolute terms the turnover of the unit trusts' equity portfolios seems unexpectedly—one might even say unhealthily—high. If so high a percentage were to become the rule, the unit trusts—or some of them—would come to resemble dealing companies rather than the long term investment vehicles which they are normally represented and marketed as being.

It has been the unambitious aim of this note to set out to quantify some aspects of the institutional role in our equity market; conclusions are, perhaps, best left to others to make. That role is important, and is increasingly so (though not, of course, all-important); and the interest of the topic is shown by its choice as a subject for discussion at the 1972 Congress of the European Federation of Financial Analysts' Societies. It will be interesting to compare our experience with that seen in the various European countries; the U.S.A. situation (as one would expect) is adequately documented.[3]

---

[3] Unless otherwise stated, the statistical source used in this note is *Financial Statistics*; as its figures can and do vary from month to month, I add that I was using the edition for August 1971.

15 What Are Earnings, Anyway?

J. N. LITTLEWOOD

This article was published in The Investment Analyst *in June 1973. It was written to expose some of the flaws in the market's almost total dependence on the PE ratio and consequent neglect of dividend yield.*

At the time when the article was written, John Littlewood was a partner in the stockbrokers, Read, Hurst-Brown. In 1975, the firm merged into Rowe & Pitman, which in turn merged in 1985 to form S.G. Warburg Group, of which he was a director and member of the Chairman's Committee.

After retiring in 1991, he began a long-planned project to write a history of the post-war London stock market. The Stock Market: 50 Years of Capitalism at Work *was published by Financial Times Pitman in November 1998.*

Many recent members might find it difficult to believe that in the early days of the Society between 1955 and 1960, an adjusted record of earnings or earned per cent was simply not available. An adjusted ten year record in an annual report was a rarity and the card services then provided by Moodies and Extel only gave a ten year record of earned per cent without any adjustments for scrip and rights issues. Working out adjustments factors to produce a proper ten year record of earnings and dividend from published figures was really quite advanced research in those days, particularly as there seemed to be more scrip and rights issues in the fifties. "Let's look at the Stores this week" presented a challenge to the enquiring analyst who might have had an idea that Marks & Spencer had been growing faster than G.U.S. but did not actually have any information to prove it. We spent much more time finding out about the past and taking it up to the present and the growth of the previous five years was somehow assumed to be the basis for future growth. Now the analyst spends his time looking from the present to the future with masses of information about the past to hand. Indeed, it often seems that the role of the analyst has been narrowed right down to answering one question, "What are the prospective earnings?"

Until 1965 analysts talked of earned per cent and earnings yields, although sometimes the reciprocal of the earnings yields was used and called a p/e ratio. This figure was not very meaningful as the earned per cent was a hypothetical figure that did not appear in the accounts. Companies paid income tax at the standard rate, and profits tax, both levied on the pre-tax profits. The earned per cent was calculated by grossing up the net profit after tax, at the rate of income tax only, producing a gross figure that was directly related to the gross dividend. This was the traditional earnings figure showing what the dividend would be if all available earnings were distributed, rather than the concept today which thinks in terms of a sum of money which the Company has actually earned after tax. In 1965 the introduction of corporation tax enabled analysts to use the transatlantic concept of earnings per share and p/e ratios, which were both adopted with alacrity. The first year or so witnessed an immediate sifting and widening of p/e ratios on a scale that was never contemplated when earnings yields were the fashion. Gradually earnings assumed an increasing importance and, together with p/e ratios, became the key to share prices.

Dividend yields were increasingly disregarded and drawing attention to the vulnerability of an earnings yield of 2½ per cent was very old-fashioned compared with pointing out the exciting prospects of growth suggested by a p/e of 40.

Earnings and p/e ratios have come to achieve a dominance which is extraordinary, considering that they are based on a single figure in the accounts which is residual, imperfect and easily capable of manipulation. It is subject to wide interpretation, but comparisons are drawn between a p/e of 15.1 or 15.6 or something with a precision that is absurd when compared with the imprecision of the "e". For a typical range of companies earnings might amount to between 5–10 per cent of turnover. In most cases it is a residual figure that could easily be made higher or lower, and in some cases significantly so, requiring only modest adjustments to stocks or depreciation, or a different treatment of various cost items. Accounting practice could enable two identical companies to produce quite different streams of earnings.

Nevertheless, earnings have become the arbiter of share prices. For example, in 1972 Lex reviewed several hundred company results, mentioning earnings in almost every case, but only referring to a yield perhaps once every three months. I wonder whether Lex believes he is reflecting a market where yield has no importance whatsoever; or trying to lead the market into believing yield has no importance. What is certain is that a far larger proportion of investment decisions are influenced by yield than would be suggested by listening to much recent City comment.

The use of p/e ratios has always depended on the availability of an earnings figure which is simple and acceptable. Many companies in fact produce figures that lack credibility and are controversial. They might exclude launching costs; research and development; or pension contributions. They might include once and for all windfall profits; stock profits; profits on sale of assets; and, in particular, the "capital gains" which are so difficult to interpret because they fall into the grey area where capital and income become confused. Capital gains often appear incapable of being repeated in the accounts with any regularity and to that extent one might argue that they deserve a p/e ratio of little more than 1. This is because they add to asset value and as capital should not then be capitalised by inclusion in earnings.

That is too strict an interpretation, but it illustrates for example how difficult it would be to make use of the true earnings figures of a discount house where "profit" (or "loss") is made up significantly of "capital" and where fluctuations are really violent. Similarly, the assessment of the value of bank profits is confused by the inclusion of capital gains arising from investment in giltedged securities.

Some of the quasi-financial Institutions that are so well known today seem to want the best of both worlds. They like to push up asset values and at the same time regard the building process that adds to the assets as trading profit, to be capitalised on a handsome multiple. Many of these companies often bring capital gains into earnings, perhaps to make the record look more normal, and one such company last year went a stage further and even brought *unrealised* capital gains into earnings, with these forming almost a fifth of the total. When investment trusts or insurance companies, who invest money just as much as anybody else, make significant capital gains, they normally carry them straight to the balance sheet to be reflected in increased asset values, or to Inner Reserves where they do not appear at all, and they are not included in the profit and loss account.

The whole concept of earnings is becoming increasingly confused and the Institute of Chartered Accountants, by seeking to improve standards with their admirable programme of accounting reforms, is showing just how imprecise and subjective is the calculation of earnings. The Accountants started by requiring the consolidation of the attributable earnings of associated companies, which are now brought into the calculation of earnings, and hence p/e ratios. This was followed by Accounting for Extraordinary Items, a measure to eliminate the inconsistencies of reserve accounting, which adds another rung to the profit and loss account—but earnings before extraordinary items or after? Another accounting standard requires companies to state earnings per share on the face of the Profit and Loss Account, but also requires that an alternative figure be given for the dilution arising from the issue of a convertible. The recent Exposure Draft, Stocks and Works-in-Progress, will in due course become an accounting standard and this draws attention to the difficulty of quantifying profit on long-term contracts which stretch over and beyond an accounting period. Nevertheless, construction companies and, less obviously, composite insurance companies are expected to provide a single figure to form the earnings per share, however discretionary it may be.

We now face further complication with the new tax system. Earnings no longer show both the amount of profit generated after tax and at the same time the maximum dividend payable should profits be fully distributed. This is a step backwards, with the two legitimate concepts now producing different answers, but even the consensus that the actual figure after tax should form the basis of earnings for p/e ratios is fragmented by controversy between the net and nil distribution methods which has already been widely discussed.

It is easy to foresee another complication. The Institute of Chartered Accountants is recommending that supplementary accounts be produced to show the effect of inflation on the conventional historical cost accounts. This will produce yet another alternative figure for earnings which we can use if we like—fully diluted, of course.

It is then all very well to talk of earnings and p/e ratios, but the question does arise of which earnings. Do you ignore extraordinary items? The once and for all writing-off that some companies charge to reserves but more prudent companies might charge to profit over a period of years? Do you dilute for a convertible that need not be converted until 1990? What about the associated company earnings which are accepted happily as a credit, although often clearly out of control of the parent, but sometimes conveniently ignored when they are associated losses?

For the last five years earnings and p/e ratios have dominated the picture to the exclusion of other criteria for share valuation, but it is tempting to ask whether their ready acceptance is justified and whether we do not over-estimate the validity of a single figure. We have seen the uncertainty of earnings and how qualitative judgement is required. The market exercises this judgement by the assessment it gives to the value of earnings, but the earnings figure is often accepted quite uncritically. On occasions a company in its latest Accounts will change last year's earnings to a lower figure, explaining with a casual air that last year was a mistake. The fact that the share price may have been overstated for a whole year seems to be neither here nor there.

Certainly, p/e ratios have obvious advantages. They are convenient when they show both the actual profit earned and the apparent maximum dividend potential, although in this situation the actual dividend and the dividend cover become less relevant. They are precise in calculation, if not in content, and a range of p/e ratios is a useful tool for comparing shares, sectors or markets as a whole. They suit the essentially short term character of so much investment today and with quarterly earnings often available, analysts have the continuous opportunity to revise earnings estimates and change the multiples appropriate to these earnings, which is done with a degree of apparent sophistication that is sometimes neurotic. It must certainly bewilder the companies producing the statements who know perfectly well that profits are up only 12½ per cent this quarter compared with 14 per cent last quarter, either as a result of the normal swings and roundabouts of business, or perhaps for a reason which would look trivial in print.

Our market could still be even further influenced by earnings. In the U.K. we accept the established fact of the p/e ratio on historic earnings, and we then consider prospective earnings and prospective multiples. In the United States historic earnings are strictly history, and the prospective earnings for the current year and for the year after seem to be what the market is about; and so as each quarterly statement comes along, we have the endless process of revised, revised, revised prospective earnings for this year and next.

Earnings forecasts are another subject. At an Analyst's meeting last year, a Company Chairman when asked why he had not given a profit forecast at the time of a recent rights issue, replied "because I am not out of my mind". It has been said cynically that if you put down this year's earnings for next, you will be right more often than if you attempted a series of forecasts, but this is about as helpful a comment as claiming that you could beat any football pools tipster each week just by putting down a home win for every match. Nevertheless, there is an abundance of guess work and crude assumption in many earnings forecasts. That these then form the basis for precise calculation of p/e ratios and hence share prices would be regarded as disturbing in other disciplines.

They also lead to the unhealthy habit of analysts producing competitive forecasts, as it is easy to attract attention when "my earnings are higher than yours" rather than going along with the consensus of opinion. Equally, companies become conscious of the importance of earnings to their share price and, as is well known, there are many ways in which a company can influence disclosed earnings to a pattern which might suit its convenience at the time, but will one day come unstuck.

Whether the importance of earnings will diminish is an interesting question. The new imputation tax system has caused immediate strain and might be restoring attention to the value of the dividend and the dividend yield. Here at least are facts that cannot be altered by interpretation. We are taught classically that the value of a share price is the present value of the future stream of dividends, and not the future stream of earnings. It is said in their favour that earnings provide the best guide to future dividends, but I suggest that the basic relationship between earnings and dividends has been distorted by the concentration on earnings and the neglect of dividends. Earnings are supposed to be the profits that are available for distribution, and the dividend is the part of those profits that the company is either able or willing to distribute. If however earnings are the name of the game, then anything goes to inflate or fuel the figure and there need no longer be either the intention or the capability to regard them as distributable as dividend. Where doubtful items are included we must cast doubt on the quality of the earnings, but this cannot be quantified. The analyst must therefore look beyond the earnings, and assess their *dividend paying capacity*.

This becomes a matter of judgement as to the quality of the earnings, and here the market has shown itself to be extremely sophisticated. Thus we see the highest multiple of all for property shares where the benefits of inflation are clear to see, but more particularly property companies produce earnings of unorthodox content, with interest charges relating to developments being capitalised, not for the purpose of making the earnings look higher but for the very real purpose of actually paying higher dividends. Conversely the engineering company with heavy capital requirements and long term contracts is recognised as being vulnerable to inflation and subject to heavy demand on its profits for working capital rather than distribution. The earnings of a life company are recognised for the stability of their growth, whereas the cycles of the textile industry are reflected in low ratings. Brewery companies and stores companies do not face heavy capital demands and their business is stable and controlled. As a result their growth is consistent, their dividend paying capacity is high, and they are well rated. Conversely a cement or a chemical company has heavy capital requirements and must use interest-free retained earnings for reinvestment, having therefore a low dividend paying capacity. Such shares do well when increased dividends can be anticipated on the back of a cyclical recovery or a profits surge, as this will produce earnings genuinely surplus to the needs of capital investment and available for increasing the dividend, but these shares are not generally well rated.

There used to be a certain mystique associated with a well covered dividend, but when combined with a low rating this suggests an awareness by the market that the dividend paying capacity of the company is limited. In this category could be included bank shares where profits have to be retained to expand the capital base; and companies with large overseas interests where remittance of all the earnings to pay dividends is impossible. It will be interesting to see which companies with well covered dividends can afford to relax dividend policy as encouraged by the new tax system.

Qualitative judgement will recognise in a high rating that management of a particular company can often be exceptional and will produce a faster growth of earnings and dividend. It will be recognised that at first young industries grow fast and generate very real profits, but that old industries die or have to be subsidised. Judgement of fundamentals tell us one industry is about to prosper but another is to languish. All these situations have strong implications for earnings, but these implications have also to express themselves in the clear ability to pay dividends.

It is interesting that now we are faced with the possibility of dividend control for some time, there has been a return to awareness of the dividend yield. I am suggesting in this article that in the last five years earnings and p/e ratios have been given too much importance and publicity. I have tried to show that whilst we pay tribute to earnings, the market in its wisdom takes good note of their quality, stability, credibility and, in particular, dividend paying capacity. The investment community seems to have been spending much time and money trying to prove that investment is a science and not an art, and earnings and p/e ratios have very much suited what is for many investors a numbers game. Earnings are of interest, but a historic p/e of 16 and prospective p/e 12 mainly tells me that profits might rise by one-third. I would like to know how that p/e compares with the Company's recent rating and with the market averages, but I would like to know exactly the same about the yield, both actual and prospective, and again relative to the market averages. I would like to know about the asset value which might put the price into perspective, and financially I would like to know whether there is anything unusual or unorthodox about any of the items in the profit and loss account and the balance sheet. All these are important factors which contribute to the making of the share price and none should be used in isolation. However, earnings appear to hold the stage. When buying earnings there is a strong implication that a company can quite freely retain them or distribute them, although the tax system has usually encouraged retention. There is further the assumption that if a company retains profits, they will be put to better use in the business than by being paid out to shareholders. Too often this is not the case—some companies get fat, others diversify and far too many could not survive at all without these interest-free retentions. Earnings are all very well but let us not forget the ability or willingness of a company to pay a dividend and let us see the only real return the shareholder receives.

16 Should Investors Be Responsible?

S. MASON

This article was published in The Investment Analyst *in December 1973. It was written at a time when the question of the social responsibility of companies was beginning to enter serious discussion, particularly in the USA. The purpose of the article was to explore some of the key issues in the discussion, notably as they affected the behaviour of institutional investors in UK companies.*

Sandra Mason is an economist who worked first for a leading merchant bank in the City and then as senior research officer at the London Business School. She was also senior economic consultant to Environmental Resources Limited, a company involved in projects on environmental impact, assessment and management. Since 1972, she has been a principal of Leisure Consultants, an independent research firm that she set up with Bill Martin to provide a specialist source of research on leisure, tourism and sport. She has written and lectured extensively on trends in leisure and their implications.

1. INTRODUCTION

There has recently been much discussion about the responsibilities of companies and their directors in modern society. Included in this discussion has been a reconsideration of the relationship between shareholders and the companies in which they invest. The White Paper on Company Law[1] contains several sections on both subjects under the general heading of "Wider Considerations" to be discussed in relation to future legislation. The report of the Company Affairs Committee of the C.B.I. (the Watkinson Committee)[2] covers this area in considerable depth and there have been several other reports recently on the question of corporate responsibility generally, notably John Humble's "Social Responsibility Audit"[3] and "Towards a Code of Business Ethics" published by the Christian Association of Business Ethics[4]. On a slightly different but closely related issue, there has been the so-called "Governor's Initiative", the steps taken by the previous Governor of the Bank of England, Lord O'Brien, to encourage more action by institutional investors to promote industrial efficiency; this initiative has resulted in the setting up of the new Institutional Shareholders' Committee with participation from the Insurance, Pension Fund and Investment and Unit Trust Associations[5].

Although much has been written and said on this question of responsibility, many of the viewpoints expressed are conflicting ones, at variance with each other and with the normal practice of investors. In addition, in the U.K. the comment that relates to investor responsibilities has come almost entirely from outside the investment industry. One of the aims of this article is to stimulate more discussion on the subject within investing institutions. The other aim has been to try to clarify the currently rather confused situation by setting out the main alternative stances that investors can take on the question of responsibility and considering some of their implications. As a background to this, current practices among investors in the U.K. and the U.S. and some of the key factors likely to affect future developments in this area have been briefly examined.

2. WHAT KIND OF RESPONSIBILITY?

Before looking at the current situation in more detail, it is important to be clear about what people mean by the responsibilities of investors. There is a tendency to talk rather loosely about subjects like social responsibility, and about action by investors, without delineating what is implied by these terms. Since there is often little agreement about definitions in this area the discussion tends to become rather woolly.

In practice three main types of issue run through the discussion. They are raised here in the form of questions; some possible answers are considered in sections 4 and 5 below.

(a) Responsibilities to Whom for What?

In law, the directors of a company are responsible solely to the shareholders or members (present and future) for their actions in operating the company. One of the key issues in discussions about responsibilities is how far directors can or should consider themselves responsible not only to shareholders but also to other interested parties such as workers, customers, suppliers and the public in general. In addition, are these different interests in conflict and if so is there a need to alter the formal structure of corporate responsibilities to allow for this fact?

Closely related to this question is the issue of economic versus social or public responsibility. Should the directors and shareholders of a company see their objective solely in terms of economic efficiency, often more narrowly interpreted as maximum return on equity for a given level of risk? Or should they include in their aims social goals relating to working conditions, the state of the environment and the like and how far do such social goals clash with economic and financial aims? Furthermore should investors put pressure on companies to attain social aims and will this damage their prospective economic gain as a result?

(b) What Kind of Action Should Responsible Investors Take?

Again in law, shareholders are given a number of important rights, notably the appointment of directors, which give them in theory effective control over the company in which they invest. Another of the major aspects of the debate on responsibility relates to how far and in what way investors should exercise these rights. Should they actively involve themselves in a company's affairs by action at meetings, by behind-scenes pressures or by use of publicity? Or should they act through the market by selling shares (or not buying them)? Critical to these questions is the effectiveness of different courses of action; for example how responsive are companies to share price movements alone and will public action be counter-effective in terms of management response?

(c) How Progressive Should the Responsible Investor Be?

Even if the investor has reached a view on the nature of the responsibilities that should be taken by companies and on the best course of action available to him as an investor, there remains an area of controversy relating to how forward looking investors should be; how far should any one act ahead of the general crowd of other investors, should he lead or follow the trend? Two issues are involved here. Is action as an investor the correct or best way to pursue economic or social aims or are more direct forms of political pressure for legislative or social changes either preferable or more effective? And secondly, in the case of institutional investors, who have responsibilities to other people affected by the outcome of investment action, how far should such institutions move ahead of the behaviour acceptable to all involved in their business such as employees, policyholders, unit holders or shareholders?

3. HOW INVESTORS BEHAVE IN PRACTICE

(a) The Tradition of Inactivity

The split between ownership and control of public companies, between management and shareholders, has been much discussed. Behind this development lie, *inter alia*, the growth in the scale of business, the increasing institutionalisation of shareholdings and the existence of an active secondary market in equities. Shareholders in most public companies have effectively handed over control to directors and management, with an implicit assumption that this control will be exercised in such a way as to meet shareholders' needs. Even if shareholders disagree with corporate policy, the most common action has been to dispose of holdings (or not to purchase the shares) rather than any more formal or informal intervention. Only when forced to act over disagreements among directors or in disputed takeovers, has formal action normally been taken.

In recent years it has also become conventional to assume that shareholders' needs will be best satisfied by maximising the return on investors' capital (or the value of the company) for the given level of risk assumed. There has also been a tendency to assume that this objective will be beneficial to all concerned since it is presumed to be equivalent to the aim of maximising the economic efficiency of the operation, that is obtaining the greatest possible added value from the scarce resources being employed. This presumption is normally justified on grounds of economic theory, which suggests that if the company is operating efficiently in competitive markets (with the aim of profit maximisation) not only shareholders but all other interested parties will tend to be in an optimal situation.

(b) Changing Attitudes

Latterly some of the assumptions underlying these conventional attitudes and patterns of behaviour have been questioned. First of all, through obvious inadequacies in the competitive system, companies do not always achieve the degree of efficiency considered to be desirable. Although official action has been taken with the aim of improving the competitive environment, investors have also been under pressure to exercise their rights and responsibilities to the end of improving corporate efficiency. Pressure has come partly from official sources as in the Governor's Initiative; in addition it arises directly from the increasing emphasis placed on performance in investment management, coupled with the problems of marketability of holdings in a large portfolio.

To date the effect of this type of pressure in increasing the active use of investor responsibility has been limited. In practice performance needs have stimulated increased market activity among many investors, but little formal action. Some of the large institutions, notably the Prudential, have taken a more active role in prodding management[6], but the emphasis has been on informal, behind-the-scenes activity. As the Bank of England statement in June puts it: "The Institutional Shareholders' Committee is very conscious that the co-operation of company managements will depend on the absence of publicity and no public statements will therefore be made about any of the activity of the case committees"[5]. And generally speaking the major investors have been reluctant to move at all rapidly in the direction of active responsibility. The main reasons normally given for this reluctance are two: lack of the expertise and resources required to get involved in management and fear of being considered over-mighty citizens usurping powers that society does not wish institutional investors to have.

Secondly, in the last few years, it has increasingly been suggested that both companies and investors should take on wider responsibilities than those implied by narrow economic aims. There has been both legislation and official statements of intent in relation to such matters as consumer rights and fair trading practices, questions of pollution and environmental quality (including acceptance of "polluter must pay" principle) and employee rights and participation. Pressure has also come from the political parties and from the general public via the media, and industry has tended to respond in a fairly positive manner; this is particularly true of the directors and managers of large scale businesses though doubtless not all industrialists would fully support the wide ranging responsibilities set down by the Watkinson Committee.

These calls for wider corporate responsibility have arisen partly as a reaction to the greater stress being placed, at the same time, on the need to improve economic efficiency and to maximise the return to shareholders. It has been suggested that this emphasis on efficiency has led to a neglect of wider responsibilities, that were always implicit in the business code, in the interest of maximising short term returns. This question is discussed further in section 4a. Whatever the correct view, an implicit challenge to the investor's position is involved; so far investors have been relatively slow to respond to this threat.

The setting up of the Take Over Panel represents an attempt to deal with the more narrowly financial abuses where there appears to be some consensus of view about what are correct and acceptable practices. Action has also been taken by institutional investors in such key issues as the Distillers' thalidomide affair.[7] But, very largely, socially responsible action by investors has been limited to action by the religious and charitable bodies who have always maintained a degree of social policy towards investment. Both the Church of England and the Society of Friends have made comments on the social aspects of their investment policy. More recently they have been joined by the pressure groups, such as the Haslemere Group and Counter Information Services, who have chosen to use shareholders' meetings and other types of action to achieve, at the least, publicity, both for their aims and for the corporate practices they consider undesirable. Certain institutional investors have expressed views supporting the call for wider corporate responsibility[8] and it is interesting that the Watkinson Committee with 19 members contained seven City representatives. It is not however known whether the institutions concerned have taken any informal steps to further their aims.

(c) Contrasts with the United States

As might be expected, in the United States the issue of corporate and investor responsibility has been explored both more vocally and more actively. There have also been some interesting differences in approach. In particular, recent discussion in the U.S. has centred more on the question of how wide the responsibilities of companies and investors should be and on what is the correct action to achieve these ends. This contrasts with the U.K. situation where the question of whether investors should exercise active responsibility to achieve more narrow economic aims is also a live issue. It probably reflects the fact that the U.S. discussion on responsibilities is more developed than in this country and also the different legal set-up where shareholder action through the Courts is both easier and more frequent. Another interesting difference is in the role of the authorities; in the U.K. the Government has been taking a lead in the discussion on active and wider responsibilities as well as introducing legislation on standards of behaviour, whereas the U.S. Government appears to have stayed more aloof from the responsibility question relying on legislative standards and competition policies. Again the contrasting regulatory systems, particularly the existence of the U.S. SEC, may be partly the cause.

The nature of the action taken by investors in the U.S. and the main views on the issues involved have recently been summarised in a report made to the Ford Foundation.[9] In many ways the action represents a more advanced form of what has occurred over here. Pressure groups have made widespread use of the publicity to be gained from action at shareholder meetings; they have been more active than in the U.K. in pursuing their policies and in putting up special resolutions to shareholders. Institutions have been more willing to make public use of their powers through disclosure of voting policies and open letters to companies. Special mutual funds have been set up with the explicit aim of investing in socially responsible companies and independent reporting on the social behaviour of companies has been more widely developed than in the U.K.

Among the U.S. institutions that have taken the social responsibility question very seriously have been the Universities who have come under attack from students and certain members of faculty for not taking a more active stance on this issue. Such attacks have led to several detailed studies of the question of investor responsibility, notably those carried out at Yale[10], Harvard[11] and MIT[12]. While all the reports differ in their detailed recommendations, they concur broadly in the view that investors cannot avoid taking some responsibility for the non-economic influence of the companies in which they invest and that to be really effective such responsibility needs to be exercised actively in the sense of trying to influence the company rather than passively by sales of the stock in question. Other U.S. comment has endorsed this view[13]. So far there has been no U.K. parallel to this kind of intensive study of the investor's problem by institutional investors.

4. RESPONSIBILITY IN THE FUTURE

It is evident that investors in both the U.K. and the U.S. are still far from unanimous about what if any should be their responsibility toward the companies in which they hold shares. It is equally clear that the general view of what both corporate and investor responsibilities involve is changing and that there is a considerable weight of official and influential private opinion behind this move. The precise direction of the change is still difficult to ascertain but there are a number of reasons for thinking that investors need to take these issues seriously. The reasons relate to the factors underlying the call for more responsibility and the way in which these factors can be expected to develop.

(a) The Changing Social Contract

Some of the most violent arguments about corporate responsibility relate to the question of economic versus social responsibilities; should a company see itself with any responsibility other than maximum efficiency in the production of goods and services? In a certain sense, from a practical viewpoint, this is a non-argument. As the Watkinson Committee puts it: "The company (is) an artificial creation of the law owing its existence to the will of the community"[2]. It has to operate within not only the legislative but the social contracts that are laid on it. Whether or not this is theoretically desirable may be disputed. But in practice companies have always had to accept implicitly certain codes of behaviour and corporate good practice as constraints on their profit maximising aims. The problem has been that agreement on the ingredients of these codes has been breaking down. Views are changing on what is socially acceptable practice and no obvious consensus has yet developed. At the same time the growth of companies has inevitably given them a more pervasive influence on society; it has also tended to make them less immediately susceptible to unwritten controls.

Hence the key question is not so much whether companies should take account of their influence on employees, customers and the rest of society; clearly they cannot avoid doing so. The practical issue is really how their activities in these areas as well as in the economic sphere should be controlled and directed. Can directors and shareholders be left to maximise profits on invested capital within a given social and legislative framework or should some alternative approach be adopted to enable changing economic and social goals to be attained?

(b) Who Should Exercise Control?

Different people and different groups will have their own individual views of what should be done to improve the society in which they live. Sometimes a degrees of consensus is established and, in a competitive world, the market system will help to balance out individual differences. As discussed, such consensuses and market pressures will influence the way in which companies behave. But, in practice, corporate actions are also strongly influenced by whoever controls their activities and the particular aims of this group. Traditionally this control has been given to shareholders as those responsible for bringing the company into existence and bearing the risk of its possible failure. Over the years, this responsibility has been taken over by default by directors and management. Galbraith has suggested that underlying this shift has been a move in the power balance within society reflecting the relative importance of different types of resources[14]. In the U.S., power has recently shifted further, moving more into the hands of the consumer movement and the same may be happening here to a lesser degree.

More important, however, from the investor's point of view is the growth in power of employees. It can be no coincidence that the call for more social responsibility by companies has come at the same time as increased strike activity, inflationary problems and attempts to devise prices and incomes policies, and calls both for more employee participation in management and for widespread nationalisation. All these reflect the shifting power balance in the U.K. towards labour as the scarce resource in the economy. The willingness of companies to take the call for social responsibility seriously indicates their implicit recognition of the changing situation. So far the shift in power has not been accompanied by serious calls for formal revisions in company structure (other than nationalisation); but, in the longer term, this could well develop, especially given the limited extent to which investors choose at present to exercise the rights that they have.

(c) Do the Different Interests Conflict?

Even if the balance of power shifts away from the investor, either formally by the removal of some of the present rights over companies or informally through a greater recognition of other interests in business, does this matter? Will the investor necessarily be harmed either materially or socially by any such trend?

To answer this question it is necessary to return to the economic assumptions underlying the traditional inactivity of shareholders and the questioning of these assumptions that was mentioned earlier. In the competitive world of theoretical economics, where all markets are perfect, all tastes are fully reflected in market prices, and there are no dominant buyers or sellers, the business objective of maximising profits will tend to ensure that all participants in the economic process, be they shareholders, employees or customers, are in an optimal situation. In addition in a position of stable equilibrium companies will make no profits in an economic sense, that is no surplus over and above a market return on capital commensurate with the risk taken.

In practice the world is, of course, not quite like this. There are three particular differences which have special relevance to the question of conflicting interests. All three relate in one way or another to the ability of business to exploit those involved in or affected by it.

First there is the ability of business to exploit its physical or social environment. As is nowadays widely recognised economic costs and social costs can differ and profit maximisation alone will not ensure that social costs are met. Pollution may be a highly profitable activity. Hence from a social point of view, the balance of interests achieved by straight profit maximisation may be undesirable. The classic approach to this problem has been to try to bring social costs into account by taxation or legislation. But in practice such an approach may not always be as effective as is desired, and direct public pressure for industry to take positive responsibility for its environmental impact may also be used. Whatever the method, the effect of bringing social costs into account is likely to be a lessening of private economic return and so of the monetary return to investors. Whether the latter are in fact worse off or not depends on the extent to which they personally benefit from and/or support the move to include social costs, and, if they do not do so, whether there are alternative investments to which they can switch with no loss of return[15].

Secondly, there is the form of exploitation due to monopoly power of various kinds. This leads to the breakdown of the market system's ability to ensure that all tastes are satisfied; employees or consumers have to accept conditions of work or products that are not exactly to their choice. In this situation the investor's interest in maximum return on capital obviously need not coincide with those of the other participants in business. A shift in power towards the other groups is likely to be damaging to his interests, unless again he believes that such a shift is socially desirable or he benefits from it in other ways.

The third area of exploitation relates to the distinction between short term and long term profitability. In theory short term profit maximisation will lead in the long term to an optimal situation through the operation of the market and the entry and exit of business in industries of differing profitability. In practice the long term may never come in the sense that in a dynamic world it is possible for a company and its shareholders to be continually in a position of exploiting short term opportunities without consideration of the long term viability of the enterprise. In this situation employees, customers and suppliers may be exploited in a manner that is socially unacceptable and this is the argument raised against both the so-called asset stripper and certain conglomerates. Thus, to the extent that investors become increasingly concerned with short term performance, their interests can diverge from those of other parties involved in business. They will also tend to produce a bias in the capital market favouring the short term profit maximisers in industry.

(d) A New Corporate Structure?

If investors' interests do indeed at times conflict with those of employees, customers or society in general, how is this conflict likely to be resolved? All the evidence suggests that this resolution is unlikely to be in the investor's favour, at least if this is narrowly interpreted as maximising return on invested capital. There appears to be widespread acceptance that some of the benefits of increased economic efficiency should be taken in non-monetary form such as more leisure, a better environment and improved working conditions; meanwhile, in the sharing of the economic cake, the power of interests other than shareholders is increasingly being recognised. So far both official and industrial comment implies action within the existing corporate structure, leaving shareholders with their existing rights but both urging and requiring companies to take more note in their decisions of wider responsibilities. Paradoxically shareholders are also being urged to use their powers to this end as well as for more narrow economic aims. But other groups call for more radical solutions, of which nationalisation is only one. Whether these alternatives will be realised remains doubtful but it is clear that investors should take seriously the threat being posed to their aims and powers.

5. WHAT SHOULD THE INVESTOR DO?

(a) Responsibility is a Fact of Life

In a very fundamental sense the investor cannot avoid being responsible. The acquisition of a shareholding automatically brings with it an involvement with the company concerned and certain rights and duties relating to that company. Whether or not the investor actively exercises his rights, he is responsible; the choice not to vote or otherwise exercise influence does not remove responsibility, it simply delegates powers to directors and implies acceptance of their priorities in the running of the company.

By the same token the investor cannot avoid making a decision about the balance between economic and social goals or between short term and long term profitability. In the same way as someone looking for a job has to balance the monetary reward against other advantages or disadvantages, the investor has to balance the aim of maximising his return on capital against whatever may be his social objectives. If he chooses to concentrate solely on economic return, this may be for a variety of reasons. He may give social objectives very low priority or he may feel that they are better achieved through other types of action, for example, in the political field. Whatever the precise cause, in so far as he puts his money into a company on the grounds of maximising his return and does not actively exercise the rights given to him he is implicitly accepting the particular balance between economic and social objectives chosen by the directors of the company.

Whether the investor is an individual acting on his own behalf or an institutional manager responsible for the money of others, these are the facts of investing life. But the institutional manager's position is complicated by the fact that he cannot make his judgement about how responsibilities are to be exercised on the basis of his own views of what is desirable; he has to take account of the views of others interested in the outcome of his decisions. These include not only the ultimate owners of the capital, the policyholders, share-holders or unit holders but also his fellow employees whose livelihood may be influenced by investment results and who anyhow will be affected by the image associated with the institution's investment policies.

In many ways the position of the institutional manager is very similar to that of the directors of the company. He has certain prime legal responsibilities but he also operates within a social framework and has to balance various conflicting demands made upon him. Even his prime responsibilities involve a certain unwritten code of behaviour. Just as shareholders delegating powers to directors assume a certain type of business practice acceptable to them, so unit or policy holders assume investment practices and aims that are in accordance with their beliefs. In both cases the problem is what to do when standards of behaviour are changing. How is the investment manager to know whether his particular constituency wishes him, for example, to exercise more active economic and social responsibility?

In practice there are three alternatives open to him. He can continue to maximise return as he has done in the past, ignoring the question of responsibility. He then risks the danger that his existing or potential clients will become dissatisfied and will move to other more responsible institutions. He can take the middle road, moving with the crowd if that moves in a more actively responsible direction. This avoids some of the danger of dissatisfied clients but equally makes it unlikely that he will gain clients from any new trends developing in this area. Or he can be in the van of the action, which both risks disturbing existing clients and has the danger of backing the wrong trend, but obviously offers big opportunities to those who take the right decision. The choice between these alternatives will depend on the views of the individual institutions, on the ease with which it is possible to gauge clients' views and the extent to which there are long term unwritten contracts which need to be respected.

(b) The Alternatives and Their Risks

In a sense the above discussion answers the question of what the investor should do about responsibility. The individual investor cannot avoid responsibility, he must make choices even if he does so in a negative manner. The institutional manager has also to choose, but must take account both of his responsibilities to his clients and others and of the implications of his choice for the development of his business.

But the different alternative choices open to the investor each have their own risks and for a rational choice to be made it is essential to be clear about what these risks are. And though strictly speaking the institutional manager need only be concerned with the outcome of other people's choice, it can be argued that his management responsibilities involve both consideration and assessment of these risks and explanation of them to his clients. Although the alternative courses of action are many, representing a continuum from nil responsibility to highly active pressures for social as well as economic ends, they can be characterised by four stages in this continuum; support for each of these can be found in the investment field today.

School (1): Maximum Short Term Performance   This school is characterised by the "go-go" fund manager to whom the sole objective of himself and his clients is to maximise short period return. To him, selling is a much more efficient way of achieving economic aims than action at meetings and social objectives are seen as irrelevant from an investment point of view, though he may take them very seriously in other aspects of his life.

He runs two main risks in taking this standpoint. The first is that he will tend to want to invest in companies who do not bear social costs; he is thus betting on his own ability to get out of a share before that company's prospects are affected by its anti-social behaviour. If social pressures grow stronger the risks relating to this type of policy will increase. He will also tend to lack the skills required to assess the effect of social behaviour on the company's performance. Secondly, his emphasis on the short term and unwillingness to exercise his rights as a shareholder may have political consequences. If a general consensus develops in favour of more social responsibility and long term profit maximisation, his behaviour may enhance pressure for the removal of shareholder rights and for legislative action to ensure responsible or acceptable behaviour by shareholders.

School (2): The Long Term Investor   Here the archetype is the traditional life assurance or pension fund manager conscious of the length of life of his obligations and the need to ensure that the fund maximises return over the long as well as the short period; he is thus unwilling to take some of the economic risks involved in full short period maximisation. If the climate of opinion is moving towards wider corporate responsibilities he will have to take account of the social behaviour by the companies in which he invests, if he is to achieve his target return. But he still believes that the most effective way of achieving his aims, both economic and social, is through the market system by selling shares rather than by active intervention.

His unwillingness to exercise the rights given to him as a shareholder mean that he risks losing these entirely though he will not add so much to the pressure for this as does the investor of the previous school. He also runs the danger that he will not be able to assess correctly the speed of social change and that he will misjudge its effect on any company's prospects. Furthermore, his adherence to the market system of influence presupposes that this system will be efficient in achieving his ends. In the current situation, where companies rely less and less on the equity market for their finance and seem not to be greatly responsive to changes generally in the cost of capital, he risks not making the impact on companies that he would like to have.

School (3): Reluctant Responsibility   The more forward looking of the institutional investors probably come into this category today. Basically the view of regular day-to-day investment is similar to that of the long term investor. But there is an awareness that there are certain situations where the market system may not be effective and which require a more active response. Action would only be taken reluctantly, reflecting fears of being thought to be throwing one's weight about, and would probably follow considerable outside pressure from the media and elsewhere. Responsibilities would only be actively exercised where it was clear that there was a broad consensus, or at least a majority, in favour of the aims being pursued.

Here again there is a risk that the position of public opinion will be misjudged, that there will be criticism, possibly leading to legislative action, either of too active a policy or of dragging the feet. In addition the action taken, public or private, could damage the investment prospects of the company concerned which may not be in accord with the wishes of the ultimate investor.

School (4): The Activist   The investor who is an activist is typified by the crusader, the pressure group or its members using the existing corporate structure and shareholder rights to achieve their desired aims. These aims need not necessarily be those of wider corporate social responsibility though in today's social climate they are likely to be. They include those who wish to see industry actively provoked to be more efficient in meeting its basic economic objectives.

This group of investors deliberately takes the risk of non-conformism, of being criticised for pursuing goals that are not now shared and maybe never will be shared by the majority. If the aims being pursued are social ones there is an even greater risk than in the previous situation of monetary gains being lessened by the action. For the institutional investor there are serious dangers of disrupting the unwritten contracts on which much of the business done is based; unless of course the institution explicitly includes its aims in its business prospectus like the socially oriented mutual funds in the U.S. Furthermore by making active use of the rights given to shareholders such investors risk a reaction against shareholder powers and possible legislation to remove them.

6. RESPONSIBILITY AND THE ANALYST

The choice between these various alternatives lies with the investor. He and his manager have to decide which risks they will take and which they will not; it is an "investment decision in the face of uncertainty", like most other decisions in life. The position selected will reflect among other things the clarity with which they see their goals and their personal balance between material gain and social progress. Most U.K. investors are probably today in schools 1 or 2; the trend may well be for them to move gradually into school 3.

Whatever the position ultimately selected, both the assessment of the risks involved and the practical operation of the chosen policy would be greatly assisted by improvements in the information made available to investors and the accounting and analytical techniques used to assess this.

Many of the problems associated with investor responsibility would be removed if more information were made more widely available on a greater number of aspects of company activities. Investors would be better placed to assess the consequences of social trends for companies and to understand the way in which companies really derive their earning power. In a similar way, more information needs to be made available by institutional investors about the investment policy followed and the results of this. At present it is virtually impossible for the individual investor to make a rational choice of an institution with investment aims that reflect his own particular needs.

More information inevitably puts an increasing burden on the analyst who has to interpret it. This will be particularly so with regard to the information that relates to aspects of a company's business that have not normally been quantified such as employment policies, community action and the like. It is the responsibility of the analyst together with the accountant to develop means of handling these areas within the framework of the investment decision, to explore ways of quantifying the impact of action in such fields so that different companies can be readily compared. Important developments are already taking place in the area of human asset accounting and other avenues are being explored. By developing his skill in these areas the analyst can do much to assist his particular organisation to take more efficient decisions. By so doing he will also assist the capital market to reflect more correctly the economic and social framework within which it operates, thus ensuring that it survives as an effective instrument for society.

REFERENCES

[1] White paper on *Company Law Reform.* Cmnd 5391, HMSO, July 1973.

[2] *The Responsibilities of the British Public Company.* Final Report of the Company Affairs Committee, CBI, September 1973.

[3] John Humble. *Social Responsibility Audit. A management tool for survival.* Foundation for Business Responsibilities, 1973.

[4] *Towards a Code of Business Ethics.* A consultative document compiled by Simon Webley. The Christian Association of Business Executives, 1972.

[5] See Bank of England Quarterly Bulletin, March and June 1973.

[6] See the Prudential Annual Report for 1970, 71, and 72.

[7] *Financial Times,* 6th January, 1973. See also *Financial Times,* 23rd February, 1973 and *Legal & General Gazette,* February 1973, for a statement of one institution's policy.

[8] For example Commercial Union in their Annual Report for 1972 and Mr. Jim Slater in an interview in *Investor's Review* commented on in the *Financial Times,* 11th January, 1973.

[9] B. Longstreth and H. D. Rosenbloom. *Corporate Social Responsibility and the Institutional Investor.* A report to the Ford Foundation, Praeger, 1973.

[10] See J. G. Simon, C. W. Powers and J. P. Gunnerman. *The Ethical Investor. Universities and Corporate Responsibility.* Yale University Press, 1972.

[11] *University Relations with Corporate Enterprise.* Harvard University Committee Report.

[12] *University Investing and Corporate Responsibility.* (See also E. H. Bowman in[14] below.)

[13] For example, B. G. Malkiel and R. E. Quandt. *Moral Issues in Investment Policy.* Harvard Business Review, March-April 1971, and[15] below.

[14] J. K. Galbraith. *The New Industrial State.* Houghton Mifflin Co., 1967. (Quoted in E. H. Bowman. *Corporate Social Responsibility and the Investor.* European Institute for Advanced Studies in Management Working Paper, 72–37, November 1972.)

[15] For a detailed discussion of the investor's position in such circumstances see H. C. Wallick and J. T. McGowan. *Stockholder's Interest and the Corporation's Role in Social Policy* in W. J. Baumol *et al. A New Rationale for Corporate Social Policy.* Committee for Economic Development, 1970.

17 Investment Pricing in the North Sea

P. H. RICHARDS

This article was published in The Investment Analyst *in May 1977, when the North Sea oil and gas search was in full swing. A series of successful oil discoveries had ensured that the UK was well on the way to becoming an oil exporter and independent of Middle East oil supplies. Probably the biggest disappointment for motorists was the hope of cheap petrol. This was dismissed even then, despite oil being found so close to shore.*

Paul Richards was an Exhibitioner in Natural Sciences at Cambridge University, where he subsequently read Mathematics. He did a masters degree in business administration at the London Business School, since when he has pursued a career in corporate finance in the City. He succeeded Colin Leach as the Editor of The Investment Analyst, *and has been a member of the Council of the Institute of Investment Management and Research. He lectures on the MBA and MSc programmes at City University Business School.*

When an issuing house brings a new company to the stock market it is faced with a major problem—how to price the shares on offer. The potential purchasers will also have to decide whether or not to apply for some shares. In other words they must decide if the offer price is low or high. More often than not, this is not a real obstacle. It is likely that there will be similar companies already quoted on The Stock Exchange and the ratings of these companies will give an excellent indication to a suitable price for the new issue. The issuing house will also make due allowance for differences in quality of management and other such factors before arriving at a final price.

The problem of pricing an investment is not confined to new equity issues. Private companies often have to be valued for acquisition or financing purposes. Likewise institutional investors undertake a certain amount of investment in unquoted companies and have to make a judgement as to the appropriate price at which an investment would be attractive. In these instances the method outlined above would suffice.

However there are cases where no comparable quoted company or stock exists. This is particularly true for new industries created through technical innovation. The North Sea is an excellent example of this. Nowhere else in the world is oil being recovered from such depth of water (500 ft) or in such weather conditions. In addition, there has been the uncertainty surrounding the oil price, fears about North Sea taxation and, perhaps the biggest bogey of all, participation. All these factors have produced a very high risk environment in which investment decisions have had to be taken.

This was the climate in which the oil industry began discussions with the Government in late 1974 on the structure and implementation of an oil taxation system. Then, the oil companies were pressing for (and justifying) a minimum after-tax rate of return of about 25% p.a. This required rate of return was a subjective assessment or "gut feeling" based on world wide industry experience set in the particular context of the North Sea. Given that this figure of 25% p.a. was a little on the high side as part of the industry's negotiating stance, the following table shows that the companies have been quite successful in achieving profitable rates of return.

Field Name	DCF Rate of Return
Argyll	92% p.a.
Piper	55% p.a.
Thistle	33% p.a.
Ninian	21% p.a.

These four fields can be considered representative since all the oil fields currently being developed have a DCF rate of return lying somewhere in the above range. In fact the majority of commercial fields have a return of between 20% p.a. and 35% p.a.

As a measure of profitability DCF rates have some attractions and some shortcomings and it is worth recalling exactly how they are determined. A profitability analysis is undertaken to determine if an oil find is commercial. This analysis will involve estimating the costs of production facilities, operating costs, likely production levels, sales proceeds, incidence of tax and so on. Once these estimates have been prepared a cash flow forecast will be made and would look something like:–

	1975	1976	1977	1978	1979	
Cash Flow ($m)	−300	−400	−200	+50	+500	...
Discount Factor	1	$1h(1.1)$	$1/(1.1)^2$	$1h(1.1)^3$	$1h(1.1)^4$	...
Net Present Value ($m)	−300	−364	−165	+38	+342	...

Each cash flow is discounted, in the above example, at the rate of 10% p.a. This determines the net present value (NPV) of each flow: these are then aggregated to get a total NPV. The DCF rate (or internal rate of return) is that discount rate which when applied to the cash flows produces an NPV of zero. In other words if the DCF rate is 15% p.a. then that implies that for every dollar invested a return of 15% (averaged over the life of the field) will be earned in each year.

The above table of rates illustrates how the oil taxation system fails to even out the rates of return. The Argyll field is very low in capital costs as it employs a converted drilling rig as a production platform in conjunction with a tanker loading system. The rate of return is therefore very high. In contrast, the Ninian field is very capital intensive requiring two (and possibly three) fixed production platforms and a very long pipeline. The total cost is more than ten times that of Argyll.

These rates of return are based purely on likely costs and can in no sense be described as market rates of return. A market rate of return would be the rate determined by the price in the sale of a field between a willing buyer and seller. Consider the Thistle field. Before development work began the DCF rate was calculated to be 33% p.a. But no member of the Thistle consortium would have dreamt of presenting their share of this investment opportunity to someone else without some kind of payment. If a third party were to acquire a share in Thistle then they would have to first purchase the share and then pay for the capital expenditure. This would therefore reduce the DCF rate to a level which can be described as a market rate.

At this point in time many of the uncertainties surrounding the North Sea industry have been substantially resolved. Indeed, there are now a number of yardsticks available from which market rates of return for North Sea investments can be derived.

These are:–

(i) Bank and equity financings,
(ii) Private sales of parts of fields,
(iii) Quoted companies having oil field investments.

This article examines transactions in each of the above categories to determine market rates of return.

(i) BANK AND EQUITY FINANCINGS

There have been a number of large financings announced for North Sea development, some of which are suitable for use in the analysis.

The first large scale bank financing for the North Sea was the £360m Forties field financing arranged in 1972. Although heralded at the time as a "project financing" the credit risk is not that of the project alone. By means of a series of forward sales and purchase agreements the parent company, B.P., guaranteed to get the oil out only if the oil was there. In other words, the banks were taking the risk that either there was insufficient oil (and at $2 per barrel the loan was five times covered) or if there was sufficient oil then B.P.'s balance sheet would be covering the risk of failure to extract the oil. The only difference between the risk in this case and that attaching to any loan to B.P. proper is the additional risk associated with the amount of oil in place. The pricing of this loan therefore does not take account of the technological risk inherent in a novel and unproven production system or of any other risks peculiar to North Sea development.

More recently I.C.I. has completed a syndication of a bank loan to finance its share of Ninian while Occidental has arranged two loans through the International Energy Bank for North Sea development. But, like B.P.-Forties these were loans to the general corporate coffers of I.C.I. and Occidental. Although the funds are to be invested in the North Sea, the pricing of these loans can only indicate the relative creditworthiness of each of the borrowers. It is therefore important to distinguish between loans direct to a company (e.g. B.P.) and loans direct to an oil field. The following are what might be called true project financings. They are "true" in the sense that the lenders look only to the cash flow generated by the field for repayment.

Oct. 1974	Thomson	Piper Field	$100m
April 1975	Tricentrol	Thistle Field	£38.3m
Feb. 1976	Thomson	Claymore Field	$100m
Feb. 1976	LASMO/SCOT	Ninian Field	£75.8m
May 1976	Ranger	Ninian Field	$120m

The basic feature of all of these packages is that the borrower is usually a company with a single asset, namely a share in a licence covering a proven commercial oil field. The amount lent is usually only a proportion of the total capital commitment and repayment is to be effected out of cash flow generated. The lenders are bearing the full risk that the project is successful and accordingly are being compensated with interest and an "equity kicker" in the shape of an overriding royalty. Like the Government royalty, the overriding royalty is levied on sales proceeds and provides the lenders with a participation in the profits of the project. This type of package can be regarded as a hybrid of debt and equity financing instruments. The cost of this type of financing will provide an indication of what the financial markets require as an acceptable rate of return on this type of investment.

Calculation of the financing cost is relatively straightforward. A cash flow is first prepared setting out loan drawings, interest charges, repayment of principal and payments of overriding royalties. This series of flows is then discounted to determine the DCF rate of return. This is the return the lenders earn on their investment and likewise represents the cost to the borrower of using such finance.

A word must be said about tax. The above quoted rates of return are calculated after deduction of corporation tax. What is now being compared is a direct investment in a company owning an oil field with an investment in one of the project financings. In the case of the company, the return on the investment in that company shall be taken to be the after-tax rate of return the company itself earns, while in the case of the investment in the project financing package, the return will be taken to be the gross income generated by the financing instruments. In this way all problems relating to the taxation status of the investor will be avoided and like will be compared with like.

The results of this analysis are summarised as follows:–

Financing	Field/Overriding Royalty Rate	Assumed Interest Rate	DCF Rate of Return	Cover
Thomson	Piper; 2½% gross (on first 642mbbl)	9% p.a.	15.9% p.a.	39.4%
Tricentrol	Thistle; Minimum 5% gross	12% p.a.	18.1% p.a.	64.2%
Thomson	Claymore; 3% gross on Claymore plus 2½% gross on Piper (after first 642mbbl)	9% p.a.	14.4% p.a.	26.0%
LASMO/SCOT	Ninian; 8.75% on income net of Govt. royalties and operating costs	14% p.a.	16.8% p.a.	90.6%
Ranger	Ninian; 9% gross	9% p.a.	15.8% p.a.	87.9%

A number of points arise from this table.

(1) No two oil fields are identical. Production profiles, flow rates, type of oil, nature of offtake, are all peculiar to each individual field. In this analysis no allowance is made for such differences and although not an unreasonable assumption, this will introduce some distortion in the results.

(2) Except where otherwise stated (i.e. LASMO/SCOT) the overriding royalty is charged on the gross sales proceeds. In such cases these payments appear to be treated as financing charges and are allowed as a deduction against corporation tax. However in the case of LASMO/SCOT, where the overriding royalty is levied on the sales proceeds after deduction of Government royalty and operating costs, the payments are treated as a distribution of profit and not allowed as a deduction against corporation tax. It would therefore seem to be crucial where exactly the royalty is levied in order to minimise corporation tax.

(3) The actual level of the overriding royalty is not a true guide to the total cost of the financing. (Compare the two Thomson packages.) The reason for this is simply that a royalty of 2½% on 642mbbl is worth more than a royalty of 3% or even 4% on 350 mbbl.

(4) The interest rate in the LASMO/SCOT issue is fixed at 14% p.a. while in each other case interest is charged on a floating rate basis. For calculation purposes a fixed rate has had to be used with obvious consequences for the accuracy of the analysis. This raises one further point, the currency of the loans: two are sterling denominated, the others in dollars. Unless the Government interferes in the domestic U.K. market, North Sea oil prices will be linked to the international dollar price. Hence the future movement of the £/$ exchange rate could affect the return on the sterling-based

financings. Likely exchange rate movements are to some extent mitigated by the interest rate differential.

(5) No allowance is made for the different timing of each transaction. Market rates of return do not remain constant over time as the F.T. index demonstrates daily. In the above table the Thomson-Piper package, which was negotiated prior to the construction of the oil taxation system, is compared with the Thomson-Clay-more package which was completed after all the major uncertainties had been resolved. Hence the Thomson-Piper deal is likely to be above average in terms of cost. In fact this timing factor affects all the calculations. For instance the LASMO/SCOT package has a stock market quotation and although the calculation was based on the issue price, the price has moved since the issue date.

Cover Ratio

The final column in the table details the cover ratios* of each package. The cover ratio is a measure of risk and is designed to take account of the situation where 2 equal amounts of funds are made available to 2 fields one of which has double the reserves of the other. Clearly the loan to the field with the larger reserves is less risky since it will be less vulnerable to changes in the oil price or damage to the production equipment and so on. The cover ratio measures this risk by comparing the amount of funds at risk with the value of the expected net cash flow. In effect the cash flow is the security for the Loan. There is an obvious analogy with a house mortgage. A building society will usually grant a mortgage up to say 90% of the house value (i.e. the value of the security). This percentage, which is equivalent to the above cover ratio, is a measure of the riskiness of the society's investment.

Here, the value of the security (i.e. the cash flow) is affected by the timing of the flows and so it is necessary to discount each cash flow.

$$\text{Cover Ratio} = \frac{\text{NPV of funds at risk}}{\text{NPV of net cash flow pledged to repay outstanding finance}} \times 100\%$$

The discount rate used to calculate the NPV is 20% p.a. The aptness of this rate will emerge during the rest of the analysis but as this rate remains constant for each calculation, any error in the choice of rate should not affect the relative values of the cover ratios.

Using this definition, the higher the ratio the riskier is the loan. The cover ratios are illustrated graphically on the next page. However, it is interesting to note that the rates of return all lie in the band 14% p.a. to 19% p.a.

It is not unreasonable to conclude that a market rate of return on a direct investment in a field (and this certainly applies to the fields financed by the above schemes) must be in excess of the highest rate of return generated by the above schemes. The reason for this is that if an investor were presented with the choice of investing in one of the above financing packages and investing directly in a field, both of which generated the same return, then he would most likely choose the financing package because the risk would be less. The finance package would allow the investors first pick at the cash flow until they were repaid. So, if there were a shortfall in production, the investors in the package might still be repaid but the direct investment in the field would show a reduced rate of return. This is exactly analogous to the difference between debt and equity where returns on equity are greater than returns on debt.

---

* A concept first developed in an article entitled "North Sea Oil—The Effect of Government Policy" by R. M. Goodfellow and P. H. Richards and published in the April 1976 edition of the London Business School Journal.

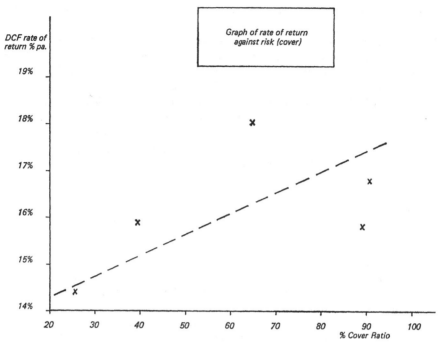

The dotted line is the type of relationship which is suggested by Capital Asset Pricing theory (see conclusion for reference) where rates of return increase as risk increases. Here the dotted line is a tentative fit for the relationship suggested by the five observations.

(ii) PRIVATE SALES OF PARTS OF FIELDS

Given the large sums involved, the heavy capital expenditure and few willing sellers, it is not surprising that no market has developed in the sale of parts of oil fields. Quite recently, all the partners in the Brae field have been either taken-over or have negotiated farm-out agreements—giving up part of their equity in return for an undertaking to finance their remaining share. This is something which could develop into a trend. Brae was really the first commercial find made by a consortium comprising minor oil companies only. Unfortunately little information is publicly available on the Brae field and these transactions are of little help in determining market rates of return. Nevertheless the following changes in licence ownership can be helpful.

Jan. 1975 United Canso sells 18.2% of Thistle to Deminex for $57m
April 1975 Union Pacific sells 20.5% of Thistle to Deminex for $72.8m
March 1976 Burmah sells 21% of Ninian to B.N.O.C. for £83m
July 1976 Burmah sells 11.25% of Thistle to B.N.O.C. for £87m.

Once again we can construct a cash flow for each of these transactions and hence determine an implied DCF rate of return.

	Implied DCF rate of return
Deminex buys 18.2% of Thistle	22.3% p.a.
Deminex buys 20.5% of Thistle	22.3% p.a.
B.N.O.C. buys 21.0% of Ninian	13.0% p.a.
B.N.O.C. buys 11.25% of Thistle	12.0% p.a.

The return on the Deminex transactions looks about right given the conclusion from the previous section, but the two B.N.O.C. transactions suggest that Burmah got very good prices. The B.N.O.C./Thistle transaction did involve some other assets so the above figure is probably artificially low.

Nevertheless the unavoidable inference is that B.N.O.C. could earn a higher rate of return simply by buying some of the quoted securities issued by LASMO and SCOT instead of buying up Burmah's assets.

(iii) QUOTED COMPANIES HAVING OIL FIELD INVESTMENTS

A quoted company is the most obvious place to look for market rates of return. Unfortunately no quoted company with an oil field as its only asset yet exists. (Siebens Oil (U.K.) is probably an exception but its asset is an interest in the Brae field about which little is known.) The procedure is to calculate the stock market capitalisation of a company with an oil field interest and then to deduct from this estimates of the market capitalisations of each component part of the company other than the oil field interest. This should leave a net sum which can be ascribed to the oil field as its market capitalisation.

This type of analysis is very difficult to apply to the majority of oil companies being so large and whose worldwise operations dwarf their North Sea activities. The errors in such a calculation are unlikely to be small.

Nevertheless there are two examples of non-oil companies taking participations in exploration consortia, finding oil and as a result experiencing a marked change in each of their fortunes.

Thomson Organisation

Market Capitalisation 43m shares at 296p	=	£127.3m
less value of non-oil interests:—		
earnings for year ending Dec. 1975 = 7.85p (all non-oil)		
based on a price earnings ratio of 7 for		
newspaper activities, this gives a value of 43m × 7.85p. × 7 =		£23.6m
implied capitalisation of oil interests	=	£103.7m

Associated Newspapers

Market Capitalisation 30.4m shares at 104p	=	£31.6m
less value of non-oil interests, 30.4m × 11p. × 6½	=	£21.7m
implied capitalisation of oil interests	=	£9.9m

These capitalisations can be regarded as a proxy for a sales price and rates of return can be calculated as before.

	DCF rate of return
Thomson Organisation (Piper and Claymore fields)	32% p.a.
Associated Newspapers (Argyll field)	50% p.a.

At first glance it would appear that Associated Newspaper Group (A.N.G.) is earning an above average rate of return and that therefore the A.N.G. shares are undervalued. This argument applies a fortiori when it is remembered that A.N.G.'s oil assets are not confined to Argyll alone. There are participations in the Bruce and Crawford fields. Although both these fields have yet to be established as commercial, they must have a positive value.

Hence this would decrease that part of A.N.G.'s market capitalisation attributable to Argyll and so put up the rate of return.

However before rushing out to buy shares in A.N.G. it is worth noting that this calculation is very sensitive to error. An increase in share price of 7p (to 111p) would increase the market capitalisation of the oil interests and so reduce the DCF rate of return to 25%. Given transaction costs there is little opportunity to make a profit.

The Thomson rate of return, 32% p.a., obviously takes account of the fact that both fields (Piper and Claymore) are externally financed by a non-recourse debt instrument. This is equivalent to gearing up and so the return on the equity is expected to be greater than the return on a direct investment in the fields. This level of return can be regarded as an upper limit for a market rate of return. In fact if it is assumed that the two Thomson finance packages were provided by the owners of the equity in Thomson Organisation then it is possible to calculate a return which would represent the total return Thomson earns on both fields. This is calculated to be 24% p.a. As expected this rate lies between the rates on the financing packages which are relatively low risk and the rate on the quoted Thomson equity which being highly geared in accordingly high risk. This figure yields the following risk/return classification.

	DCF return	Risk level
Thomson-Piper package	15.9% p.a.	low
Thomson-Claymore package	14.4% p.a.	low
Market Capitalisation	32.0% p.a.	high
Hypothetical investment comprising both packages plus the Thomson equity	24.0% p.a.	medium

CONCLUSION

Given that the analysis is not based on a large bank of data, it would be wrong to arrive at anything but tentative conclusions. Nevertheless, with the exception of the two B.N.O.C./ Burmah deals, it is clear that each item of data is consistent with the following classification:—

Category of Investment	DCF return	Risk level
Non-recourse field financing:	14%–18% p.a.	low
Direct field investment:	22%–24% p.a.	medium
Investment in the equity of a field which is financed on a non-recourse basis:	about 32% p.a.	high

This classification is compatible with Capital Asset Pricing theory* which suggests that expected rates of return increase with risk.

18 The U.K. Stockmarket and the Efficient Market Model: A Review

A. W. HENFREY, B. ALBRECHT AND P. H. RICHARDS

This article appeared in The Investment Analyst *in September 1977. Dr Henfrey writes: by the early 1970s, it was apparent that emerging capital market theory, which was little understood in the City at that time, would start to impinge on the very traditional ways of managing money that prevailed. This naturally appealed to a newly qualified scientist trained in a quantitative discipline – a very rare type in the City 30 years ago. Describing these emerging trends in non-mathematical terms for a skeptical audience and what they might mean for money management and stockbrokers' commissions proved a rewarding task. Even with the benefit of hindsight, I'm not sure I'd really want to change very much in what we wrote.*

Dr Henfrey, who holds a doctorate in solid state chemistry from Oxford University, began his career in the City in 1970 as an analyst in Hill Samuel's Investment Division. He relocated to Houston, Texas in 1977, where for 14 years he was a partner of Simmons & Company International, an investment banking firm specializing in oil- and gas-related transactions. It was during this period that he became actively involved in the management of corporate turnrounds and recovery situations. He returned to Britain in late 1990, since when he has continued to pursue his activities in the corporate turnround area. He has served on the boards of a number of public and private companies on both sides of the Atlantic. He is currently a director of both Postern Fund Management and Postern Executive Group, where he specializes in the management and funding of private equity-funded turnrounds. He is a Chartered Financial Analyst, an Associate of IIMR, served as President of the Houston Society of Financial Analysts in 1986/87 and is a Fellow of St Catherine's College, Oxford.

At the time of writing in 1977, Bruce Albrecht was an investment analyst at W.I. Carr. Presently Bruce is Chief Investment Officer at Rothschild Asset Management in London. In the intervening period, Bruce spent ten years with Banque Pictet, where he was Chief Investment Officer in London, and nine years in Abu Dhabi in the Middle East at the Abu Dhabi Investment Authority, where he was the manager of the European portfolios and a member of the government's asset allocation committee. Although many of the comments in the paper are readily accepted now, the conclusions did not endear Bruce to his then employer.

Paul Richards – see Chapter 17 for biographical details.

ACKNOWLEDGEMENTS

We are grateful to the many people who have allowed us access to unpublished work who are referred to in the text of the review. Particular thanks are due to Michael Firth (University of Stirling), Dr. Jack

Broyles (London Graduate School of Business Studies), and Charles Ward (City of London Polytechnic) for reading through the review in draft form and for making many helpful suggestions. Any errors that remain are, of course, our own.

One of us (AWH) would particularly like to thank the staffs of the libraries of the London Graduate School of Business Studies, the City of Houston and Rice University, Houston for their patient assistance and also Matthew R. Simmons, President of Simmons & Co., Houston, for the provision of the stimulating environment in which a significant part of this review was written.

This article reviews the present state of understanding of the validity of the efficient market model within the context of the U.K. stockmarket. In the United States the model has attracted much attention in both the academic and financial communities but in Britain the debate has been one of largely academic significance. What is imperfectly perceived is the extent to which the model has gained acceptance amongst American asset managers and the implications it has for many aspects of the American securities industry. There is a growing body of empirical work relating to the applicability of the model to the U.K. stockmarket, of the possible implications of which investment analysis in Britain should be aware.

1. THE U.S. BACKGROUND

The U.S. securities industry has gone through momentous changes in recent years. The introduction of negotiated commission schedules, the steady erosion of the quasi-monopoly of The New York Stock Exchange, the introduction of trading in listed options and the concept of the "prudent man" formulated in the 1974 Employee Retirement Income Security Act (ERISA) have all had far reaching effects accentuated by an extensive range of SEC rulings[1]. The impetus behind many of these institutional changes has been a single empirical observation. Asset managers in the United States have not been able to deliver to their clients the superior performance they promised. Many of their traumas follow directly from the fact that whilst there is an overwhelming body of evidence that shows that U.S. stockmarkets are highly competitive and efficient in pricing securities, most of the participants in the market place have either been unaware of this fact or unwilling to accept it.

At the same time, there has emerged a greater understanding of the concept of investment risk and of the role of chance as they relate to investment performance, and also of the extent to which high levels of fixed brokerage charges and other management expenses have been channelled into activities such as investment research for which there could be no economic justification in terms of improved investment performance given the competitive nature of the market. Indeed the wheel has come around full circle to the extent that a major growth concept in the U.S. securities industry is the "index fund" which aims to do no more than match the performance of the widely based indices of stockmarket performance by pursuing a passive buy/hold investment policy and minimising expenses. Given the competitive nature of the U.S. securities markets there are sound theoretical reasons for pursuing such an investment policy[2] which at the same time is estimated to result in management fees and transaction expenses that on average are less than a quarter of those for traditional funds[3], and index funds have been able to negotiate particularly large commission discounts. It has been estimated that by the end of 1977 $5 billion of trust funds in the U.S. will be managed in this way[3]. This of course raises the question of what might happen if everyone pursued such a policy, but discussion of this point is left to a later section.

2. THE U.K. BACKGROUND

The findings of U.S. research studies cannot be automatically extrapolated to U.K. stockmarkets, for the structure and institutions of the U.K. securities industry are very different from those in the United States. Nevertheless there is a growing body of academic research in the U.K., much of it as yet unpublished, which is throwing extensive new light on the applicability of the model to U.K. stockmarkets[4].

By comparison with the U.S. the volume of this research is still small. There are many areas of the stockmarket where the applicability of the model has yet to be tested; there are others where the results are conflicting and there are many uncertainties in some of this work owing to the availability and quality of the underlying share price data. Nevertheless a picture is beginning to emerge and we believe that the present moment is an opportune one to review the model within the context of the U.K. stockmarket and to discuss its implications for asset management and investment analysis in the U.K.

It would be premature to conclude that the efficient market model is as applicable in the U.K. as it appears to be in the U.S. but the evidence to date does suggest that its validity is much more widespread than many might suspect or be willing to accept.

The conclusion to be drawn from this is not that fund managers and analysts should shut up shop. In the first place the possible validity of the model does not imply that no investment research should be carried out. A certain volume of research is necessary to keep the market efficient but there comes a point beyond which the incremental gain in investment performance is more than offset by dealing expenses and the costs of conducting conventional research. The available evidence suggests that given a high level of transaction costs this point is below the current level of research activity but by exactly how much is difficult to answer precisely.* In addition the existence of an efficient market can be used by analysts and managers as a starting point for research activities but this means that their work will be very different from that which they have traditionally carried out.

The sooner we understand the implications of the empirical research and the impact negotiated commissions have had in the U.S. on investment research then the better equipped our profession will be for the changes that may eventually materialize in Britain.

Anyone reading Chris Welles' account of the recent troubles of the New York Stock Exchange[1] must be struck by the similarities between the symptoms of the malaise in New York and what many people in London already feel intuitively about the state of the U.K. securities industry. Are institutional investors, for example, really satisfied with the value for money they receive in terms of a superior investment performance when they pay current commission schedules to support investment research?

We start by discussing the many misunder-standings about the model and its implications. Next we review the growing body of evidence concerning its validity in the U.K. stockmarket. Finally we discuss the implications for fund managers, analysts and brokers, and suggest the ways in which their activities and ideas should be going in light of this evidence. Throughout we have been aware that it is not our task simply to review what has been done in the U.S. as that has been done more than adequately elsewhere[6]. Our hope has been that this review will trigger off a continuing debate about the future of our profession.

3. THE EFFICIENT MARKET MODEL

In its broadest terms the model states that:

New information is widely, quickly and cheaply available to investors, that this information includes what is knowable and relevant for judging securities and that this is rapidly reflected in securities prices[7].

---

* This question as it relates to the American stockmarket is discussed in detail by Boudreaux[5].

This general statement of the model is unprovable in a direct way. To verify its applicability, therefore, a variety of empirical tests have been devised to see whether stock price and portfolio behaviour under specified test conditions have been in line with its implications.

In defining "efficient" within the context of this review a distinction should be made between "efficient" as a description of a market in which share prices are set in a competitive environment and a broader definition which implies in a macroeconomics sense that share prices are established at "economically" correct levels which optimise capital allocation within the economy as a whole rather than simply within the quoted sector.

The former type of efficiency might be described as "fair game" efficiency but the fact that share prices may be set in a competitive market does not necessarily imply that the broader definition of efficiency is valid. At any one time there may be gross systematic biases operating against the market which may change as a function of time but such biases are not inconsistent with a "fair game" market.

The broader definition of efficiency takes one into highly controversial territory which has expanded enormously as a result of the pronounced volatility of stockmarkets in recent years. Whether stockmarkets have optimised capital allocation in an "efficient" way is a much more difficult question to answer and is clearly beyond the scope of this short review.

It is the narrower definition of efficiency that has been the prime target for capital market research in the past decade and this review is concerned solely with whether U.K. stock prices are set in a competitive environment in such a way that it is a "fair game" for participants and, if this is the case, what the implications for asset managers and analysts might be. Efficiency within the context of this review should therefore be taken as referring to a "fair game" market.

It has been found convenient in this work to subdivide the model into three separate forms:

(1) The *Weak Form* of the model which states that current prices fully reflect what is knowable from the study of historical share price patterns; that is share price behaviour conforms to a random walk.

(2) The *Semi-strong From* of the model which states that current prices fully reflect all *public* information about the company.

(3) The *Strong Form* of the model which states that share prices reflect not only what is publicly known about the security *but also what is knowable*; that is the activities of analysts and others make it impossible for investors who pay transaction expenses to achieve a consistently superior risk adjusted investment performance. This incidentally is much the most controversial form of the model.

As Fama has pointed out[7] it is unlikely that the model is entirely true especially in the strong form and empirical evidence on both sides of the Atlantic suggests this to be the case. The real importance of the model is whether it is sufficiently valid as to provide a practical framework for studying the behaviour of securities prices. The evidence in the U.S. and, we believe, in the U.K. suggests this to be the case.

There most certainly are divergences in the behaviour of stock prices from the predictions of the model in both the U.K. and the U.S. but these divergences have frequently been found not to be great and it is questionable whether advantage can be derived from many of them once transaction expenses have been taken into account. There is also the question of who is able to take advantage of such opportunities. This latter consideration has led to the further division of the concept of efficiency into "external" and "internal" efficiency[8].

The type of "fair game" efficiency we have discussed so far might also be described as "external" efficiency since:

"A market in which prices fully reflect available information is only a fair game in the sense that those who are outside the market making process are faced with a common set of rules and cannot be expected to outperform each other by trading solely on existing information. These rules can however be most unfair"[8].

The fair game definition of efficiency is in fact consistent with a number of types of market structure including some very inefficient ones such as a monopoly which can discourage the efficient allocation of resources even if the game remains "fair" or externally efficient from the point of view of those who pay transaction expenses. Internal efficiency is best described as an indication of whether transaction expenses are so high as to discourage dealing by outsiders who keep the market externally efficient and whether those who do not have to bear transaction expenses make excessive profits.

This is an area which in the United Kingdom has attracted almost no attention from academics, largely owing to an almost complete absence of published data concerning market markers' turnover, stock positions and profitability. In the United States the classic work of Niederhoffer and Osborne[9] on the profitability of market makers showed that those who do not bear commission expenses can and do achieve superior risk-adjusted investment returns at the expense of those that do. Similar work by Galai on CBOE transactions draws parallel conclusions[10].

However, these profits represent the price investors must pay to keep a market in being. One avenue of research in the United States is to ask whether this price is justified and whether the same result could be achieved at lower levels of "insider" profit. Large amounts of commission earned have undoubtedly gone into superfluous investment research, for example, but the question that has not really been satisfactorily answered yet is exactly how much of this research could be sacrificed without a significant loss of efficiency and the benefits of lower transaction expenses passed on to clients. An extension of this line of thinking in the U.S. has been to ask whether the superior risk-adjusted profits that can be realised by non-commission payers has been reflected in the price of New York Stock Exchange seats[11].

4. SOME COMMON MISCONCEPTIONS

One of the most commonly held misconceptions is that the efficient market model is precisely the same thing as the "random walk" model which simply states that successive price changes are independent of each other or, in statistical terms, that there is no serial correlation between such price changes. In practical investment terms the corollary of the random walk is the weak form of the efficient market model as stated above which we have indicated is but a special case of the model.

As we shall see in the next section most of the studies which have investigated the independence of successive share price changes have found that there is a degree of serial correlation between successive price changes which appears to violate the random walk model. However, the existence of such serial correlation does not necessarily invalidate the efficient market model. The degree of serial correlation found in many of these studies has often been so small that it has not been possible, once transaction expenses have been taken into account, to deal profitably against the trading rules such correlations appear to have given rise to. Only if it were possible to deal consistently at a profit would the efficient market model be invalidated.

In purely statistical terms the pure "random walk" theory implies that the entire *distribution* of tomorrow's stock prices is known. In a pure random walk share price returns would follow what is known as a lognormal distribution and this distribution would be stationary through time. All the efficient market model implies is that the current price of a share is the best estimate of today's price given today's state of knowledge and it says nothing about the possible distribution of prices around this estimate or about the stationarity of this distribution.

An efficient market, for example, is not inconsistent with a market in which there is a long term upward trend since in such an efficient market investor expectations will already have discounted this trend in arriving at today's price. The effect of an underlying upward trend is to make it more probable that a share price will rise rather than fall and this is not even inconsistent with a lognormal distribution of share price returns.

There has therefore been a tendency to dismiss the applicability of the efficient market model because certain studies of share price behaviour, which we shall review in the next section, suggest that there are departures from randomness (albeit small). In fact it is quite surprising that the apparent degree of randomness found in most of these studies has been as high as it is and the existence of some degree of serial correlation should not be taken as being inconsistent with the efficient market model.

A second commonly held misconception is that the efficient market model states that it is impossible to beat the market. Some people obviously do beat the market and this is also not inconsistent with an efficient market. What the model casts doubt upon is whether this superior performance can be achieved consistently and whether it can be ascribed to superior investment information. In a completely efficient market the determinants of portfolio performance relative to the market will still depend on:

(1) The level of investment risk assumed by a portfolio. The question few investment managers ever ask themselves or indeed know how to ask themselves in a quantitative manner is whether the possibilities for superior performance are offset by the disadvantages of a higher level of investment risk.

It is not the purpose of this paper to review the various methods of measuring risk and some of the conceptual problems involved. This has been done elsewhere[12]. But it is critically important to realise that any objective comparison of fund performance must adjust for the possibility of differing risk levels. Much of the literature over the past 10 years or so has been dominated by the definition that risk is the variance of the distribution of share price or portfolio returns and the results we discuss in this review have largely utilised this, or closely related, definitions of risk.

(2) Chance—the possibility that a superior investment performance can be realised purely by chance is also not inconsistent with the efficient market model. The role of chance can be illustrated by the conventional wisdom that small funds do better than big ones. In fact the evidence suggests small funds as a group do about as well as large funds[13] but since many small funds are less well-diversified luck plays a greater role in the performance they are able to achieve.

(3) The level of transaction and management expenses paid by the portfolio. There would appear to be an insufficient awareness amongst many investment practitioners of the implications of much recent theoretical and empirical portfolio research on this particular aspect of investment performance.

The conventional and probably representative view of the value of investment research and the possibilities of superior stock selection is well illustrated by a recent paper[14] on "A Fund Manager's View of Stockbrokers' Research" which concentrated entirely on how fundamental research could be made "better" and which made not one single mention of the word "risk" or of how it could be measured or of how securities could be selected in such a way as to balance a fund's objectives against the potential and measurable risks. As we shall discuss in a later section, this looks to be one of the primary avenues for future investment research.

A failure to distinguish between these reasons for better relative performance and the influence of supposedly superior investment information is also a common source of confusion not only amongst press commentators but also amongst advertising agents retained by fund management groups[15].

5. EMPIRICAL RESULTS—TESTS OF MARKET EFFICIENCY IN THE U.K. STOCKMARKET

(i) The Weak Form or Random Walk

There has in fact been a considerable volume of work in Britain over the past twenty years in this area which in part reflects that it is only in recent years that the theoretical framework for the other two forms of market efficiency has been developed and the appropriate tests devised.

Tests of the weak form have fallen into two broad categories. One group of tests has set out to "prove" the hypothesis by studying the degree of statistical independence of share price differences, or more frequently, of differences in stock prices indices, whilst the second group has consisted of testing trading rules which purport to beat a random selection of securities. Tests in the U.K. have tended to fall into the first category.

Tests of the random walk have been a matter of controversy since the celebrated paper of Kendall in 1953[16] who tested for serial dependence in weekly movements of sector indices over a 10 year period. He concluded that:

"Such serial correlation as is present in these series is so weak as to dispose at once of any possibility of being able to use them for prediction."

Subsequent statistical work by Brealey[17] and Cunningham[18] on U.K. stockmarket indices has largely corroborated Kendall's findings in that although these studies have found some serial dependence (i.e. non-randomness) in share price returns the departures from randomness have tended to be small. The work of Brealey is of particular interest since he was able to throw light on the non-stationarity of share price returns through time.

A major drawback of these studies, however, is that they analysed the movements of *indices* rather than of individual share prices and in consequence they incorporate potentially serious statistical weaknesses. Working[19] has shown that if instead of instantaneous prices averages or indices are used to test for serial correlation, then spurious correlations not present in the instantaneous price series may be introduced. This arises from the fact that indices are not necessarily constructed from prices prevailing at precisely the same times and the behaviour of indices can also conceal the frequency of "no change" observations in the individual share price series. In this regard it is interesting to note that Kendall observed that serial correlation was more noticeable in the market index than in individual sector indices.

One of the first studies on individual share price changes in the U.K. market was published by Kemp and Reid in 1971[20] who used a variety of statistical tests that did not make "unnecessary assumptions about the underlying distribution of price changes". These researchers found that significantly non-random price changes existed in 80% of their sample, a figure that was reduced to 50% once "no change" data was removed from the price series. They therefore concluded that:

"Our results strongly support the view that the random walk hypothesis has been over-generalised."

However, the data they used was based on closing prices which are not necessarily indicative of prices at which one might actually deal. These researchers also gave no clear indication of the size of the departures from randomness and they took no account of transaction expenses. Their work did not therefore answer the question of whether it would actually be possible to use this non-randomness profitably and consistently. In consequence, although their main conclusion regarding the random walk hypothesis is correct so far as it goes, their results cannot be taken as invalidating the efficient market model.

A recent paper by Benjamin and Girmes (1975)[21] on the movements of 543 U.K. stocks is probably one of the most thorough and utilised a number of statistical techniques to test for the independence of share price movements. They found in practice that approximately 20% of prices did not vary according to a random walk; that around 30% behaved like a genuine random walk whichever test was utilised whereas the rest were inconclusive, showing conflicting results depending on which statistical test was utilised. As expected the non-random walk results tended to occur in the case of the small unmarketable securities (their sample included preference shares) whereas share prices of large marketable companies appeared to follow a random walk whichever test was applied. One important question not discussed in this work was "non-trading" effects since latest prices do not necessarily represent the prices one could actually deal at. As Kemp and Reid[20] have shown the inclusion of "no change" data has a significant effect on the tests of randomness.

Non-trading effects appear to be much more serious in studies of London stock price movements than they are on the New York Market. Data quality is a factor that should be continually borne in mind when considering British work for it is only recently that computerised data banks with the appropriate identification of "non-trading" days have become available. Although many of the results do tend to show evidence of non-randomness the question remains of whether it would actually be possible to deal against such apparent non-randomness and to realise sufficient profits to justify the transaction expenses.

More recently, however, there has been a growing concern over the validity of the statistical tests used in much of this work since they have been based on the assumption that the distribution of share price returns (as opposed to share price changes) have been normally distributed and that such distributions have been stationary through time. These assumptions simplify the mathematical manipulations very considerably and also mean that the distribution of historic rates of return can be used to determine the distribution of future rates. However, empirical tests[17] have shown that share price returns show a much higher than expected number of observations with large values and that the variance of such a distribution may be non-finite, which may invalidate standard statistical tests of non-randomness. The differences appear in practice to be quite small but may be sufficiently large to explain the apparent non-randomness shown in many of the serial correlation tests. There is still no real solution to this problem which is likely to be an area of intensive theoretical investigation.

Tests falling into the second category, i.e. the so-called "trading rules", have been much more extensive in the United States than in Britain. The classic work in this category has been that of Jensen and Bennington[22] who showed that the realisation of a superior investment performance on the basis of relative strength patterns could not be sustained once transaction expenses had been taken into account.

In the U.K. Dryden[23] has examined a number of filter systems which work by triggering buy or sell decisions when a change in the share price or index of X%—the filter size— occurs. Using a range of filter sizes Dryden compared the results of this approach using U.K. share price *indices* with a simple "buy/hold" policy. Dryden did find a small degree of dependence in successive changes in the indices but it is apparent from his results that transaction costs would in practice more than swallow any superior profits that the filter system appeared to give rise to.

More recently Girmes and Damant[24] have attempted to identify "head and shoulder" formations from charts of relative prices over the period 1969–1973 for 484 stocks and to test the profitability of trading on these patterns.

Their preliminary work suggested a "significant" number of head and shoulder tops in share price series by comparison with a simulated price series and their trading rule was accompanied by a "significant" degree of success with the subsequent average decline in share price following the tracing out of a head and shoulder pattern more than compensating for dealing expenses incurred in trading on these chart patterns. At first sight these results appear to represent a serious challenge to the validity of the efficient market model. However, no risk adjustments were made in assessing the returns that were derived from application of the trading rule and, furthermore, the trading rule was derived from and tested on ex-post data. An extension of this work to see whether ex-ante projections using the trading rule would be accompanied by a similar degree of success would constitute a much more valid test of the efficient market model.

This is certainly an area where more U.K. work can be expected and it would be a major step forward if more chartists in the U.K. were prepared to submit the profitability of their recommendations to rigorous statistical testing in the way that Girmes and Damant have done.

The apparent absence of totally objective tests of the performance of professional chartists' recommendations is a major gap in the empirical investigations that have been carried out. One further uncertainty is how many chartists actually rely on chart formations alone in forming their recommendations without regard either consciously or subconsciously for the prevailing macroeconomic circumstances or other background information relating to the security. Academic tests by and large have not taken into account the possibility that the value of chart data in isolation may have no relationship to its value in combination with other data.

However, the discovery of non-randomness in much of the recent statistical work is less startling, and from a practical point of view much less significant, in its implications than it might have been some years ago. There is now a greater theoretical understanding of the nature of the efficient market model and of its compatibility with a degree of non-randomness. Indeed, looking at the results retrospectively it is surprising that so many of the statistical tests have in fact so closely approximated randomness.

(ii) Tests of the Semi-Strong Form of the Efficient Market Model

The semi-strong form of the model postulates that the current price of a security reflects all public information about that company and that any new information is reflected unbiasedly in the share price and is therefore instantaneously discounted. If there is any over or under adjustment to this information then it is randomly distributed. Once again it is unlikely that this state of affairs is strictly true. The real question is whether this is sufficiently close to reality to represent a useful description of share price behaviour.

The *principle* behind empirical testing of this form of the model has been to observe the *risk adjusted* returns of share prices prior and subsequent to specific kinds of information generating events to see whether abnormal returns could be realized upon the release of the information. The trail-blazing work on this subject was that of Fama, Fisher, Jensen and Roll (1968)[25] in a paper on the adjustment of share prices to new fundamental information implied by large stock splits and the methodology used in this work has been a model for subsequent research on both sides of the Atlantic.

Their work showed that by the time the stock split was announced the market had fully discounted the fundamental information implicit in the stock split. There is a large volume of subsequent work based on this methodology in the United States but only recently has similar work been carried out in Britain, associated mainly with Michael Firth of the University of Stirling and Dr. Jack Broyles and Julian Franks of the London Business

School. A major step forward has been the availability of data banks, especially data banks which identify non-trading effects.

Firth, for example, has repeated the work of Fama et al. on U.K. stock splits[26a] and has also investigated the extent to which the market discounts the public announcement of 10% holdings in companies[26b]. In both cases Firth found that the share price adjustments to this new information were completed in a very short period of time and that it was not possible to profit from the information once it had been released. Marsh[27] has also shown that the behaviour of U.K. stock prices at the time of rights issues is entirely consistent with the semi-strong form of the efficient market model.

An interesting consequence of this research relates to the current debate in Britain and the United States on accounting standards[27]. There is a major body of research in the United States which has looked at whether share prices adjust to significant accounting changes such as those in reported earnings which result from changes from FIFO to LIFO or from straight-line to accelerated depreciation. However, unless they have an economic impact on the value of the firm, for example by influencing the tax charge, they should in an efficient market have little effect on share prices while those accounting changes which do convey fundamental information affecting the economic value should have been fully discounted by investors by the time they are announced. Most researchers have found that the market is efficient in this respect and that investors are not fooled by changes in accounting practice[28].

There is not a comparable volume of research work in the U.K. but in a study entitled "Evidence of the Impact of Inflation Accounting on Share Prices" Morris[29] did find that the inflation adjusted earnings of U.K. companies had been discounted by the market and an empirical observation of the U.K. stockmarket in 1974–1975 suggests that the market may have been a better discounter of the true status of corporate finances than published financial statements. This debate is particularly relevant in any discussion concerning the introduction of current cost accounting for there is sufficient evidence concerning the efficiency of the U.K. stockmarket to make it likely that the market has already discounted these figures. Some opponents of current cost accounting, however, have based their arguments on the ground that many stocks would be selling on unsustainably high earnings multiples once current cost earnings per share figures were released and that shares would react downwards once such information was released.

Particularly interesting and elegant work to test the applicability of the semi-strong form of the model in Britain has related to takeovers as a specific information generating event. Both the major pieces of work which we discuss shortly have provided evidence of inefficiencies but more research needs to be done to determine the nature of these inefficiencies, who profits from them and whether anyone who is not in possession of truly inside information can also profit from them.

In still unpublished work, Franks, Broyles and Hecht[30] tested the efficient market model on brewery and distillery mergers in the U.K. between 1955 and 1972 and in a particularly elegant piece of work which allowed for non-trading effects, overlapping mergers and the influence of pre-existing published holdings in companies to be acquired they found that on average the market began to anticipate a merger at least three months prior to the announcement date. Over this period abnormal share price returns averaged 27%. The presence of abnormal gains prior to the public announcement of the takeover does not necessarily imply market inefficiency. In the first place the sample contained only those mergers we later knew to be successful and so there is no way one could devise a profitable trading rule from these results whose existence would violate the efficient market model. Once the merger announcement was made there were limited opportunities for abnormal returns and what apparent gains there were would be readily swallowed by transaction expenses. Their work showed that stock price behaviour both prior to and subsequent to the bid announcement was consistent with the semi-strong form of the efficient market model and that market prices fully reflected relevant information. They also concluded from their work that the economic gains from the takeover were correctly anticipated by the market movement at the time of the takeover announcement and that most, if not all, of these gains accrued to the shareholders of the company being acquired at the time of the takeover.

A similar programme of research has been pursued by Firth in work on U.K. takeovers in 1973 and 1974 again using the methodology of Fama et al.[31] Prior to bids Firth also found abnormal increases in the share prices of target companies which he suggested might imply information leaks. If such leaks were confined to a small number of investors this would represent a major inefficiency but Firth's work was unable to distinguish this source of inefficiency from the possibility that the company making the acquisition was active in the market prior to the bid.

After the bid announcement, however, Firth found that share price performance was much in line with the predictions of the efficient market model. The market was able to anticipate revised and counterbids and also that the value of equity consideration bids would fall over a period of time. Firth also examined in detail the profitability of a variety of trading rules and concluded that apart from two minor exceptions there were on average no opportunities for superior profits.

Studies of this kind in the U.K. are still incomplete and there are many areas of the market and types of information generating event that remain untested but from the evidence so far the semi-strong form appears to represent a surprisingly good description of U.K. stockmarket behaviour. The observed abnormal returns may be derived from insider trading but in any case they are frequently so small as to be swallowed by transaction expenses.

There is now a relatively large body of work in the United States which looks at such inefficiencies but as yet little in the U.K. An interesting, but as yet unpublished, piece of work on one particular type of inefficiency in the U.K. stock-market has recently been carried out by Fox at Warwick University[32] in work on traditional "over the counter" options markets. In an investigation on the relationship between the prices of put and call options which should, in theory, be related to the riskless interest rate, Fox found that before transaction costs the market was highly inefficient (frequently implying negative interest rates!) but that after "heavy" transaction costs the profit opportunities implied by such inefficiencies largely (but by no means entirely) disappeared.

That this relatively little used backwater of the securities market should harbour such major inefficiencies is not altogether surprising and certainly should not be taken as invalidating the applicability of the model in more active and competitive parts of the stockmarket.

Opportunities for true insider trading are furthermore likely to be reduced by prospective changes in U.K. criminal law. Even without a change in the law, however, the question arises of whether any one investor has access to a continuing source of inside information sufficient to constitute a *consistent* source of superior profit. As we shall see in the next section there is no evidence that institutional investors have consistent access to such inside information which they utilise for profit in their investment activities. There may of course be others who do so but who do not choose to publicise their results!

One interesting category of potential investor with consistent access to what could be considered "inside" information is the newspaper share "tipster"—the consistent source of possible inside information in this case being advance knowledge by the "tipster" of the publication of his recommendations. Firth[33] has investigated this possibility in some detail by studying the portfolio recommendations of several well-known press commentators and seeing whether they constituted profitable trading opportunities.

He discovered that investors following these recommendations usually found that by the next day the price of the shares had been marked up to a level which often took all the upside potential of the share. The investor had usually bought a correctly priced security with no expectation of a future price rise. This was particularly true in the latter part of the period studied by Firth when jobbers had learnt from experience the extent to which such recommendations should be discounted. In other words the information content of newspaper recommendations appeared to be fully incorporated in share prices almost immediately, a conclusion in line with the semi-strong form of the efficient market model.

It might be added that Firth found no evidence that the newspaper commentators he studied derived profit for themselves by trading prior to publication. He simply suggested that a potential source of superior profits existed.

One important area where almost no work has yet been done in the U.K. is on the effect of taxation on market efficiency. Profitable opportunities that would appear to exist in a tax-free world may be negated by tax considerations and are likely to be dependent upon the particular tax status of the investor. Unexpected changes in dividend payout policies by companies, for example, can result in sharp fluctuations in share price since different categories of shareholder, having different investment objectives, may be tempted to switch into or out of other securities and this decision may be heavily influenced by tax considerations.

(iii) Tests of the Strong Form of the Efficient Market Model

The strong form of the model states that not only is public information fully reflected in stock prices but that all *knowable* information is incorporated as well through the activities of competing analysts and investors. It represents much the most controversial of the three forms since it challenges in a direct manner claims by professional investors and analysts that they can beat the market on the basis of superior stock selection after allowance for the predetermined levels of risk in their portfolios. The basis of testing this form of the model is to start by asking who has access to "superior" information and whether there is evidence that they can use it to realise superior investment returns. One obvious category of investor who might be presumed to have access to such information is obviously the institutional investor able to command the services of top financial analysts. Unit trusts and mutual funds have been closely studied both in the U.S. and the U.K. since not only are they an obvious category of institutional investor but they also have a long record of public disclosure of investment performance. The existence of any significant successful fund would imply that its managers had special access to information or exceptional skills and therefore such results would be contrary to the strong form of the model. More recently there has been in the U.K. a more scientific appraisal of pension fund performance and again the results of this research are throwing considerable light on the validity of this form of the model within the context of the U.K. stockmarket. It is fair to say, however, that these results are highly conflicting.

The first methodical testing of the strong form in the U.S. was the classic work of Jensen in the 1960's which showed that mutual funds did not consistently outperform a randomly selected portfolio of comparable risk and that after transaction expenses the performance of the majority was noticeably poorer[34]. Subsequent work has in large measure confirmed the validity of these results. What is less widely appreciated is the extent to which similar studies, some of which are still unpublished, have been carried out on U.K. unit trusts.

The results have been conflicting for reasons we shall discuss in a moment but it is an area of continuing and intense academic research and from most of these results it is possible to draw some broad conclusions regarding the performance of U.K. unit trusts.

The first published study on British unit trusts was that of Brisoe, Samuels and Smythe as long ago as 1969[35] who looked at the performance of 14 unit trusts over the period 1953–1963 and concluded that the U.K. investor behaved as if risk was not a significant factor and that the efficient market model was invalid—at least in its strong form. No details about the sample of unit trusts were given and the results were based entirely on ex-post data. Market efficiency, however, does not imply that ex-ante expectations necessarily equal ex-post investment returns; it is possible with hindsight to show that most securities or funds have been "mispriced". However, this involves information not available at the time. Market efficiency only requires that *currently* available information be fully reflected in the price.

One important distinction between U.S. mutual funds and U.K. unit trusts is that British unit trusts frequently invest in foreign stocks and therefore have an exposure not only to market risks but also to exchange rate fluctuations. The use of the FT Actuaries Index or 30 Share Index as the surrogate for the market when measuring the degree of market or systematic risk of British unit trusts would not seem to be an entirely appropriate procedure when one is attempting to test the efficiency of the U.K. market. In the United States mutual funds are virtually exclusively invested in U.S. stocks and therefore the use of the broadly based American stock price indices as the market surrogate is likely to be more valid.

More recently conclusions similar to those of Briscoe et al. have been arrived at by Moles and Taylor[36] in work at the City University who concluded that the average unit trust managed a return of a little over 1% per annum above a naive buy/hold strategy. Moles and Taylor studied 86 U.K. unit trusts over the period 1966–1975. They found that there was no relationship between beta and the different categories of fund although, one should point out, there is no evidence that growth funds for example are, a priori, necessarily run as high risk funds by unit trust managers. They also found that there was no correlation between the unit trust betas during the 1966–1970 period and the corresponding fund betas between 1971 and 1975, and that betas during the first period were not a particularly successful guide to investment performance during the subsequent time period. One suspects however that the performance results between 1971 and 1975 were heavily influenced by the wide fluctuations in the cash content of portfolios especially during 1974 and 1975 and which they were not able to account for adequately in their seemingly small number of time periods. This being so the exact significance that can be attached to the main conclusion of Moles and Taylor, viz.

"Beta (or systematic risk) gave a poor showing, appearing totally unstructured and apparently completely random in its behaviour"

is open to considerable question.

We would however agree with another of their conclusions that:

"One must be wary of a blind application of modern investment techniques without a proper analysis of their validity."

A number of matters arise out of this work, notably whether unit trust investors are aware of the extent to which performance may be simply a matter of cash management and not stock selection. It might be advanced that the performance of unit trusts in 1974 was strongly indicative of the fact that they *could* beat the market on the basis of superior judgment but this must be balanced against the fact that in the subsequent two years unit trusts in general underperformed the market[37]. Such observations therefore do not necessarily invalidate the efficient market model.

Whilst not disputing the methodology and statistical conclusions of Moles and Taylor there is in fact no way of distinguishing whether the excess returns they observed arise from currency effects or from superior stock selection, and therefore their results cannot be used as a completely valid test from which conclusions about the efficiency of the U.K. stock-market can be drawn. Although they tried to segregate specialist trusts in their sample, most unit trusts in fact contain some foreign holdings. We would want to have considerably more information regarding the exact composition of their sample of trusts before we would be as emphatic as they seemed to be in drawing conclusions about the inapplicability of the efficient market model in U.K. stockmarkets.

The influence of exchange rate fluctuations on unit trust performance is not a subject that has received any rigorous investigation but the "one way" market in sterling is not one of which individual U.K. residents have normally been able to take full advantage of because of exchange control regulations and the existence of the dollar premium. It is not altogether surprising therefore that the possibility of superior performance by comparison with a totally U.K. investment strategy arises in the case of funds who have had opportunities to alleviate some of these barriers or who were able to buy and subsequently hold overseas investments prior to the existence of many of the barriers and the remorseless decline in the exchange rate. This, it should be noted, is an important rationale for such trusts—to provide opportunities for investors not normally open to them as individuals—as opposed to an ability to make superior stock selection which the evidence does not in general support.

The results of Moles, however, are in direct contrast to two other recent unpublished papers by Firth[38] and Ward and Saunders[39] on the risk-adjusted performance of U.K. unit trusts over the period 1965–1975.

In Firth's sample trusts which specialised in investing in foreign stocks were excluded and this is an important distinction compared to the results of Moles. Firth found that over this period, which included 1974 and 1975, unit trusts on average earned 1.34% less per year than they should have done given their level of market risk. Only 7 unit trusts showed a better performance than the market given the level of risk while 65 were poorer—a much higher proportion than could simply be explained by chance. The proportion was also significantly higher than that found by Jensen in his work on U.S. mutual funds[34] and this may be related to the observation of Corner and Burton[40] who found that U.K. unit trust management expenses were considerably higher than those of U.S. mutual funds. In addition the performance figures may reflect the effect of high U.K. transaction expenses and strongly *suggest* that in the context of an efficient market benefits might accrue to U.K. unit holders in terms of risk adjusted performance if commissions were negotiated, since the research which their commissions go to support does not appear to have generated superior returns. There was no evidence from Firth's study that the size of a unit trust, or the relative number of investment holdings and unit holders had any significance for performance. Firth was quite emphatic in his conclusion that:

"The results of this paper have indicated that on average managers of unit trusts in the U.K. have not been able to forecast share prices accurately enough to outperform a simple buy and hold policy. Additionally there was no statistically significant evidence of any individual unit trust having superior performance; there was, however, evidence of statistically significant inferior performance. These results held even when management expenses were added back."

Another significant finding of Firth, which parallels that found by other researchers, is that the risk coefficient (or beta) of U.K. unit trusts is invariably less than one. In Firth's sample the highest figure was only 0.921 and this is in marked contrast to the U.S. where mutual funds frequently have risk coefficients in excess of 1. Once again, these results are strongly suggestive of a high cash content in U.K. unit trust portfolios. According to Firth:

"There did not appear to be any U.K. unit trusts (in the period covered) which offered the opportunity of a systematically more risky investment than investing in the market portfolio."

In an independent piece of work Ward and Saunders studied 49 unit trusts and calculated levels of systematic or market risk over the period 1964 to 1972. This risk data was then tested against the performance of unit trusts in 1973 and 1974. Results for 1973 were very much in line with the expectations of the efficient market model but once again the results for 1974 were heavily influenced by the strong cash emphasis of portfolios which meant that the risk levels calculated over the period 1964 to 1972 were not a significant measure of risk during 1974. Their conclusions were very similar to those of Firth:

"No unit trust achieved a significantly superior rate of return over the period whilst nearly a quarter (21%) of the sample performed significantly worse than expected."

They also concluded:

"If Unit Trust managers maintained the levels of risk (beta) then investors might reasonably use Unit Trusts as a mechanism for buying into an efficiently diversified portfolio. If, as we found during 1973 and 1974, the risk characteristics were changing, then the 'usefulness' of the Trusts would be diminished unless of course managers have a more accurate forecasting ability than the market price makers. In the light of the 1964–1972 empirical results this view appears insupportable."

More highly significant, but as yet only partly published, work is that of Bacon and Woodrow, a leading firm of consulting actuaries. In their annual survey of performance of pension funds for 1975[41] which looked at the performance of some 100 pension funds—some going back to 1970 and ranging in size from £270,000 to £270,000,000—they concluded after studying six years of U.K. equity performance that:

"We have not found any significant differences in performance between small, medium and large funds. Neither have we found any significant differences between the performance of various types of manager and it is clear that no one manager in our measurement of investment performance service has managed to stay constantly ahead of his rivals."

Additional but unpublished statistical tests by Bacon and Woodrow have lead to the further conclusion that, "there is no evidence to reject the hypothesis that all funds do equally well in the U.K. equity markets."[42] On the ability to "time" the market, Bacon and Woodrow concluded that:

"No managers have been able to consistently and correctly switch their strategy between being heavy in equities in good equity years and light in equities in bad years."

Holbrook, a leading consulting actuary, in a paper that provides an excellent review of performance measurement has also looked at the performances of U.K. pension funds over the past six years[43]. His preliminary findings are closely in line with those of Bacon and Woodrow and with the implications of the efficient market model. Among his significant conclusions were:

(1) There was no evidence that a fund's performance was affected by its size or rate of growth.
(2) It is questionable whether high levels of activity in the equity sector were justified by improved returns.
(3) Very few funds consistently achieved above—or below—average performance, either in the Main Fund as a whole or in the sectors.

(4) The results of the investigations give little grounds for belief that consistently good or bad performance is achieved in practice by more than a very small minority of funds.

The practical conclusions to be drawn from this were well summarised by Holbrook, "there may well be scope for improving returns on equity portfolios, either by reducing activities in diversified portfolios, or by reducing diversification and so increasing the chance of outperforming the market."

Such actuarial conclusions are therefore now reaching pension fund trustees, which raises the question of how long it will be before we see a fully-fledged U.K. "index fund" designed especially for U.K. pension funds for whom the only investment decision will then be as to what proportion of their assets to hold in the "index fund". The implications of this work for fund management organisations, brokers and analysts are obvious[44]. A large step has recently been made in this direction by Investment Research of Cambridge who are now providing an index matching service for institutional investors with many of the ideas discussed in this paper forming the basis for the investment strategy.

Such an investment strategy raises further questions, notably what might happen if everyone pursued such a policy. This leads to an apparent paradox, for what keeps the market efficient and makes it difficult to beat on any consistent basis is the presence of competing analysts and asset managers who believe they can do just that. What has yet to be answered with any degree of precision is how much research could be abandoned before the inefficiencies became so great as to make them worthwhile exploiting. Since index funds invest exclusively in the market leaders which compose the yardstick indices there is also the possibility of whether efficiency might become two-tier. Studies which suggest a high degree of efficiency have largely concerned the major stocks but as we have seen in our review of the U.K. market there is evidence of marked inefficiencies amongst the less marketable securities and neglected parts of the market such as put and call options. However, most institutional investors are confined for purely practical reasons to the larger more marketable securities and so these inefficiencies do not necessarily hold out substantial benefits. Ultimately though there must come a point at which major inefficiencies amongst even the smaller stocks would be worthwhile searching for and exploiting even by large investors and the market therefore contains an element of self-correction.

If it is so difficult to beat the naive buy/hold strategy on the basis of picking stocks, can one do so *consistently* by superior "market timing"? Apart from the observations described above there is little, if any, published work on this subject in Britain although it is an obvious area for future research. In the United States there have been a number of recent studies which suggest that beating the buy/hold strategy on the basis of market timing is a difficult task once transaction expenses are taken into account. In a recent paper Sharpe (1975)[45] using annual market returns over a period of thirty years investigated the question how much of the time one must be right about whether to be in cash or the market to beat a buy/hold policy. After transaction expenses were taken into account he concluded that one had to be right nearly four times out of five in the American market—a tall order for anyone! The test portfolio used by Sharpe was somewhat artificial in that it was reviewed only once a year and could only be fully liquid or fully invested, but the methodology can be extended to cover an indefinite number of reviews and combinations of assets. Farber has used Sharpe's methodology to test the efficiency of the Belgian market on the basis of monthly portfolio reviews and concluded that one had to be right nearly nine times out of ten to beat a buy-hold policy[46]. Farber in the same work also studied whether one could generate superior returns through international market timing. He looked at a portfolio consisting of ten different stock markets (including the U.K.) and at the beginning of each month constructed a portfolio by investing in the market which the manager thought would perform best over the following month, and compared the subsequent performance with the buy/hold policy for a portfolio consisting of the ten national markets, each market holding being weighted according to the capitalisation of the national market. After allowing for transaction expenses Farber concluded that if the investor were to beat a buy/hold strategy of the international market portfolio then the investor would have to be correct nearly four times out of ten in selecting the best performing market each month. Again, not an impossible target but an unlikely one to match.

Another area of research in the U.S. has been the investigation of whether it is possible through the study of macroeconomic time series to beat on a *consistent* basis the buy/hold strategy. Given the frequent claims of market commentators and others about the influence of such statistics on market behaviour this is clearly going to be a fascinating area of investigation. A taste of what might come is provided by recent work of Rozeff on the influence of published United States money supply statistics on U.S. stockmarkets[47]. Rozeff concluded that there were no superior opportunities to be gained from looking at money supply statistics, for the market in fact accurately discounted money supply statistics ahead of publication rather than reacting to them once they had been published.

A less complete study of the relationship between money supply and European equity markets (including the U.K.) has been carried out by Bird[48]. His conclusions were remarkably similar to those of Rozeff in the U.S. in that while there was in general a correlation between money supply and equity market movements, an equity market movement was more likely to lead a movement in money supply than the reverse. For only a quarter of the time did money supply movements precede equity market movements and even then the relationship was an unstable one which would have been useless for forecasting purposes. Similar results have been obtained by Saunders and Woodward[49].

The results of these tests on the profitability of market timing are consistent with the semi-strong form of the efficient market model.

6. INVESTMENT RESEARCH AND THE MARKET

The preceding review may seem to be incomplete but we do feel that the broad picture it paints is sufficiently valid to provide a useful guide to stock price behaviour. Can we relate this discussion to what many market participants will already feel intuitively? In the first place the professional is concerned not usually with the present economic situation or profitability but with future expectations and whether they are already "in the price". Market observers are continually concerned with what the market is going for on company results and rating their own estimates against those expected by the market. In saying this they are tacitly admitting that the market reflects the average anticipated result of a coming event.

Once information is publicly available investors try to purchase those securities which are expected to show strong growth and to dispose of the less attractive situations but by these actions the prices of securities which are expected to do well are bid up to a price which reflects *the average expectation* and vice versa. It is the action of competing decision takers that makes the market efficient, giving rise to the apparent paradox that what keeps a stockmarket efficient is the presence of competing investors who believe the market to be inefficient.

For a market to be inefficient there must be either a desire on the part of investors not to try to profit from knowledge or else an incomplete dispersion of that knowledge.

Amongst the assumptions of the efficient market model are that investors have the same time horizons and are risk averse with an interest in maximising their return subject to a given level of risk. These seem to be good approximations in equity markets but is not necessarily true elsewhere. In the gilt-edged market, for example, there is an overwhelming dominance by one participant, namely the Government Broker, who is not so much interested in maximising his return as in selling stock. There is evidence to suggest that unlike the equity market it *is* possible to make consistently superior returns in the giltedged market where, in addition, transaction expenses are low[50]. The same is probably true in commodity markets.

There are two ways in which information may not be commonly known and thus able to afford exceptional opportunities for gain for its discoverer. One is an ability to gain real "inside information", but tighter regulatory controls make it increasingly difficult to profit from this, at least on any significant scale. But can, in fact, such information be obtained on a *consistently* profit making basis? Plenty of money has been lost on so-called "hot tips". The second way in which information can be incompletely distributed is if unusual effort is required to gain and analyse new facts or insights. Many attempts have been made to show that very careful searching of company information coupled with extensive industry background knowledge can be used to produce abnormal profits but there is little hard evidence from the results of portfolio management that this information can be utilised for profit once the actual or opportunity costs of the search have been accounted for.

We then have a dilemma, for to maximise the probability of discovering such information an analyst should cover a large number of companies or sectors and yet to be able to recognise the full significance of new information the analyst must be a specialist. This is a dilemma continually faced by institutional and brokerage house research where an arbitrary trade-off point has to be established between wide coverage and specialisation. Perhaps this means that analysts should trend away from specialisation and the "reporting" type of research towards new ideas and insights based entirely upon publicly available information. As James Lorie has written:[51]

"Most security analysts are usually capable of knowing only what is generally known. The conventional scrutiny of public information and the conventional quest for private clues produces only conventional wisdoms and returns ... The first suggestion therefore is to abandon conventional security analysis. Its occasional triumphs are offset by its occasional disasters, and on average nothing valuable is realised ... If security analysis must be carried out, it should be done by fewer, more highly paid persons who seek their insights in unconventional ways."

In other words, exceptional ability at interpreting information that is equally available to others in the market rather than the search for new information.

Treynor[52] has pursued this line of thinking in drawing a distinction between investment ideas whose implications are obvious and consequently travel quickly and ideas that require lengthy reflection and exceptional judgement and which therefore travel slowly.

Systematic biases operating against share prices of the type we discussed in section one clearly fall into the second category, but inefficiencies resulting from this may not be inconsistent with an apparently "fair game" market since the majority of investors may have the *same* biases—the herd instinct. Although Treynor has argued that this is the basis of "long term" investing it can be countered by saying that research that tries to develop the second type of idea is impractical because most investors will lack the special expertise and therefore the market will not respond to this type of idea.

Returning to the "fair game" market and the existence of undiscounted new information it is probable in the light of the empirical evidence that there is a surprisingly small quantity of this undiscovered price-sensitive information in existence and there are numerous institutional and brokerage analysts searching for it. Each analyst should evaluate the chances of being the first to discover a useful piece of information in a larger dealable share a *significant* number of times.

With several analysts in each market sector, many of them high quality researchers, for any individual to identify a sufficient number of pieces of new information to justify the expense of the research there must be numerous pieces available. But if there are many such facts available, the ones that he does not discover will also affect the price in a fashion that he, not having discovered the information, will not be able to predict. In effect, the market will appear to him to move in an irrational or random fashion as it reacts to other people's findings. Conversely, if there are only a few pieces of information to be found the average analyst may have a poor chance of finding a large enough percentage of them to justify the cost of his investigation.

Finally, if despite the odds being heavily against it, one analyst has a good record in acquiring price-sensitive information, then other brokers or firms will perceive a possibly fruitful sector to investigate and competition will increase until the analyst's strong showing is diluted. This particular aspect of the impact of analysts' recommendations is discussed in detail by Firth in his work on the performance of investment recommendations by newspaper commentators[33].

This then leads us to the question of why so much research is done if the apparent gains are not great. In a world of fixed commission schedules the investor is paying for research regardless of whether he needs it or not. And other things being equal it is only natural that people prefer to have something to show for the commissions, i.e. research reports, even if the value of much of it is marginal from an investment performance standpoint. From a broker's view research material simply becomes advertising material[53].

One argument that might be introduced at this stage is that most academic tests of the value of conventional security analysis have investigated the value of the individual items of data or information generating events. It can be argued that the value of such data in isolation may have no relation at all to its value in combination with other available economic, financial and political data[54] which takes us immediately into the arena of Treynor's discussion[52]. Against this, however, must be set the fact that the available rigorous evidence on investment performance does not suggest that many classes of institutional investor who, a priori, might be thought to have a succinct broad spectrum of insights and information are able to use it to achieve consistently superior performance.

To an outsider it must appear strange that so many funds can underperform consistently for so many years. Are they receiving poor advice, are they making poor decisions or is good advice impossible to obtain?

Many of the results are clearly explained by the fact that many managers do not believe the market is or can be efficient and continue to act as though it were not. The same charge can be laid at the door of the analyst fruitlessly looking for the undervalued security amongst his sector coverage.

As a reference point the reader will be familiar with the typical broker's research comment which gives the prospects for a company or industry in great detail. Profits and dividends are forecast and an investment recommendation made. Often the analysis is of extremely high quality with the interpretation amongst the best available and where and the accuracy of brokers' profit forecasts is surprisingly high[55]. The outsider might conclude that the recommendation to buy companies which are on the upturn and sell those experiencing troubles seems sensible. But is it? In an efficient market probably everything in the broker's report is known by one investor or another who has already had the opportunity to deal in the shares. One may argue that at best no one else has "put it all together" but this does not matter in an efficient market. Each investor will act on the information he possesses so that the average expectation of all investors is reflected in the market price. It matters not if no one investor has the whole story because the price reflects the accumulation of all investors' actions and expectations.

It is ironic that the available evidence suggests that the most profitable strategy on average, certainly for the large investor, is one of "buy and hold" rather than active management, making only a strictly limited number of changes to the holdings to balance the risk and diversification of the portfolio to the level appropriate for the client. The extreme use of this policy is the index fund although even here there are practical considerations such as transaction expenses and reinvestment of dividends that make the perfect index fund an unobtainable objective[56]. This has obvious implications for stock market turnover and hence commissions.

Limited adjustments might also be made to reflect reappraisals of the longer term outlook for particular shares or sectors but such a strategy might well require very few managers indeed. Although most investment professionals assume it is investment analysts who have the most to fear from efficient markets it is equally the multitude of fund managers. American experience shows how easily and economically a fund can be diversified and balanced for risk considerations once the efficiency of the market is accepted. Not surprisingly one frequently hears professional fund managers' derogatory comments on academic research. Possibly their motive is simply self-preservation but in any event views have not radically changed since Lord Keynes wrote:

"Most of these persons are, in fact, largely concerned, not with making the most superior long-term forecasts of the probable yield of an investment over its whole life, but with foreseeing changes in the conventional basis of valuation a short time ahead of the general public. They are concerned, not with what an investment is really worth to a man who buys it 'for keeps', but with what the market will value it at, under the influence of mass psychology, three months or a year hence."[53]

We devote the final part of our review to a consideration of the role of the analyst in an efficient market or one sufficiently efficient for the model to represent a practical description of share price behaviour at least for the large investor. We have no magic formulae about how to outperform an efficient market. Rather we point out ways in which a fair game market might be used as a *starting point* by analysts and asset managers to improve and assess true portfolio performance, to quantify investment risk and to suggest novel lines of research into security price behaviour.

7. CONCLUSIONS

If future empirical results prove to be broadly in line with the evidence to date then it can only be in the best long term interests of analysts and asset managers to try to adapt to its implications. As we have suggested, many of the conflicts and pressures in the securities industry are readily explained by the fact that whilst the market is, broadly speaking, efficient the majority of participants in the market place are either unaware of this or are simply not prepared to accept it. As we have repeatedly stressed, however, much more work needs to be done before the degree of efficiency and the nature of any inefficiencies in U.K. stockmarkets can be defined with any degree of precision.

The sceptic might conclude that investment research and fund management activity are useless and that equity investment might just as well be concentrated in index funds. This would be wrong. What we can say is that investment research and asset management are going to be a different type of activity if it becomes generally perceived that the U.K. market is efficient.*

The pattern of change will not necessarily be the same as that in the U.S. since there are

---

* A critical discussion of the value of investment research is provided in the proceedings of a seminar organized by the American Institute of Chartered Financial Analysts and the Financial Analysts Research Foundation in 1974[58].

important institutional differences between the two markets and a much more practical approach to risk control in the U.S. since the formulation of the "prudent man" rule in the 1974 ERISA. There is the question of fully negotiated commissions which is having a profound effect on security analysis in the United States. If and/or when we follow suit on this score is a matter for legitimate debate but there can be no doubt that the distortions on the profession of conducting investment research resulting from fixed commission schedules are as applicable in the U.K. as they were in the United States prior to "May Day".

Much investment research *is* aimed at impressing the client rather than improving his investment performance and many brokerage houses themselves will freely admit this[6d]. This is not to decry the quality of the research or to say that it cannot be used for purposes other than that for which it was intended. If the market is efficient what we can say is that much research output cannot be justified in terms of the improved investment performance it was designed to produce. Because of fixed commission schedules no one really knows what a client is paying for research but given the difficulty of improving his performance by utilising it that price is probably too high. If this is true then it means that the future of investment research activities are difficult to plan on any quantitative basis and this is not, in our opinion, a sound long term basis for our profession.

If negotiated commissions ever do come to the U.K. we believe this will become strikingly obvious. As in the U.S. this will probably result in fewer but better analysts, with the emphasis perhaps on general ideas and portfolio counselling rather than on specialisation and reporting. Although specific events such as the next earnings announcement are quickly reflected in the share price, longer term trends and ideas by their very nature develop slowly and might therefore be capitalised upon by high quality analysts possessing unusual insights. It may be because of an increasing uneasiness of asset managers at their inability to outperform stockmarket indices *consistently* that some longer term inefficiencies in the market might open up. Managers are less and less likely to leave the herd and take a very different view from the conventional wisdom. Lord Keynes noted this phenomenon forty years ago:

"Worldly wisdom teaches that it is better for reputation to fail conventionally than to succeed unconventionally."

But rather than fight or ignore it we believe that the thoughtful analyst and asset manager can utilise the efficient market model as a basis for his activities. There will always be those who want to try to beat the market on the basis of chance and the assumption of a high degree of investment risk even though the odds may be stacked against them. By all means let them do so.

The evidence to date, however, suggests that asset managers should be spending much more time analysing quantitatively the range of risk preferences that they and their clients require and the ways in which funds can be designed to meet these objectives rather than trying to improve performance by picking stocks on the basis of traditional fundamental research.

It goes without saying that different funds have vastly different goals yet most investment research is not particular but rather for general consumption. Almost every piece of research on U.K. unit trusts for example has shown that almost no trust has a systematic risk level greater than that of the market. Is there a need for such a fund? There are similar types of question that require an answer, and at the research level portfolio counselling rather than traditional stock selection should be a far more important activity. How securities can be combined in a portfolio to meet specified risk/reward objectives and the simulation of portfolio performance under different market conditions could become the important

concerns of analysts in an efficient market environment. Are portfolios optimally diversified having regard to management expenses? Diversification has the effect of reducing the
level of risk in a portfolio attributable to the specific risk factors of individual securities but a
highly diversified portfolio can still nevertheless carry a high degree of *market* or *systematic*
risk. Procedures for measuring and adjusting risk levels and the degree of diversification in
a portfolio represent a fascinating and fruitful area for the analyst.

An added impetus to this type of work might be the start up of a secondary options
market in Europe along the lines of the CBOE, since such a market, if it were to prove in
practice as effcient as the CBOE now appears to be, would constitute a market in pure
investment risk and if used properly could be a means of fine-tuning portfolio risk levels
(both up and down) in a *prudent* and inexpensive manner that is simply not possible with
traditional-style option markets and their heavy transaction expenses.

A whole new and important area for research that is emerging in the U.S. is the study of
the fundamental factors in a company that effect its market risk factor (or beta)[59]. The
analyst will not be made redundant by these developments, only his analysis will be of a
very different type from the traditional idea of investment analysis and numerically much
more demanding. The growing accessibility of cheap data banks, which until recently has
been a major barrier to the extension of risk analaysis in the U.K., is now making this type
of work a practical reality for the first time. The techniques and theoretical understanding
such analytical concepts will require have been reviewed many times elsewhere[60]. What is
not yet fully perceived in Britain is the extent to which efficient market concepts have been
accepted not only in theory but also (often implicity) in practice in the U.S.[61]. No longer is
it simply an abstruse academic debate and given the growing body of evidence about the
effciency of the British stockmarket the analyst should at least be aware of what could
happen here.

The truly talented analyst will still remain much in demand but even he will be bound by
what the client demands and is prepared to pay for but he could also take the initiative and
in the meantime have a major educational role to play.

We end this article on an optimistic note for even in an efficient market there are, we
believe, great opportunities for the investment analyst who wishes to explore and utilise its
implications. We have no doubt whatsoever there are many in our profession in London
who will do so with great distinction.

BIBLIOGRAPHY

1. C. Welles, "*The Last Days of the Club*", Dutton 1975. This book was reviewed in The Investment
Analyst (April 1976), No. 44.

2. (a) A. F. Ehrbar, "*Index Funds—An Idea Whose Time is Coming*", Fortune, June 1976. (b) C.
Hill, "*Indexation vs. Analysis*". Financial Times, May 12th 1977, and March 17th, 1977.

3. The Wall Street Journal, March 17th, 1977. See also Ref. 44 below.

4. A good review is provided by Michael Firth in "*Share Prices and Mergers*", Saxon House 1976.

5. K. J. Boudreaux, "*Competitive Rates and Market Efficiency*", Financial Analysts Journal,
March/April 1975.

6.(a) J. H. Lorie and M. T. Hamilton, "*The Stock Market—Theories and Evidence*", Irwin 1973. (b)
J. H. Lorie and R. Brealey, "*Modern Developments in Investment Management*", Praeger, 1972. (c) E.
F. Fama, "*Efficient Capital Markets; A Review of Theory and Empirical Work*", Journal of Finance,
May 1970 (reproduced in (b) above). (d) B. G. Malkiel, "*A Random Walk Down Wall Street*", Norton
& Co. 1975. (e) M. C. Jensen, "*Tests of Capital Market Theory and Implications of the Evidence*",
Financial Analysts Research Foundation 1975. (f) There is an excellent review of the Efficient Market
Model and its implications for accounting standards in "*Tentative Conclusions on Objectives of
Financial Statements of Business Enterprises*", Financial Accounting Standards Board, December 1976.

7. E. F. Fama, Ref. 6 (c) above.

8. R. R. West, *"Two Kinds of Market Efficiency"*, Financial Analysts Journal, November/ December 1975".

9. V. Niederhoffer and M. F. M. Osborne, *"Market Making and Reversal on the Stock Exchange,* Journal of the American Statistical Association, December 1966.

10. D. Galai, *"Pricing of Options and the Efficiency of the Chicago Board Options Exchange"*, Ph.D. Dissertation, University of Chicago 1975.

11. G. W. Schwert, *"Stock Exchange Seats as Capital Assets"*, Journal of Financial Economics, January 1977.

12. Robert E. Machol and Eugene M. Lerner, *"Risk, Ruin and Investment Analysis"*, Journal of Financial and Quantative Analysis. V.1. 4 (1969) 473.

13. J. P. Gurney, *"Rank Correlation of Unit Trust Performance"*, The Investment Analyst (December 1976), No. 46.

14. T. Yeo, *"A Fund Manager's View of Stockbrokers' Research"*, Report of Commission on Practical Fund Management. 9th Congress European Federation of Financial Analysts Societies, May 1976.

15. See for example Financial Times, April 16th, 1977.

16. M. G. Kendall, *"The Analysis of Economic Time Series, Part 1; Prices"*, Journal of the Royal Statistical Society Vol. 96 (1) 1953.

17. R. A. Brealey, *"The Distribution and Independence of Successive Rates of Return from the British Equity Market"*, Journal of Business Finance 1970.

18. S. W. Cunningham, *"The Predictability of British Stock Market Prices"*, Applied Statistics, Vol. 22 1973.

19. H. Working, *"Note on the Correlation of First Differences of Averages in a Random Chain"*, Econometrica. Vol. 28 (1960) 916.

20. A. G. Kemp and G. C. Reid, *"The Random Walk Hypothesis and the Recent Behaviour of Equity Prices in Britain"*, Economica Vol. 38 (1971) 28.

21. D. H. Girmes and A. E. Benjamin, *"Random Walk Hypothesis for 543 Stocks and Shares Registered on the London Stock Exchange"*, Journal of Business Finance and Accounting, Spring 1975.

22. M. C. Jensen and G. A. Bennington, *"Random Walks and Technical Theories; Some Additional Evidence"*, Journal of Finance Vol. (25–2) 1970.

23. M. M. Dryden, *"A Statistical Study of U.K. Share Prices"*, Scottish Journal of Political Economy, November 1970.

24. D. H. Girmes and D. C. Damant, *"Charts and the Random Walk"*, The Investment Analyst No. 41, May 1975.

25. E. F. Fama, L. Fisher, M. C. Jensen and R. Roll, *"The Adjustment of Stock Prices to New Information"*, International Economic Review, February 1969 (reproduced in 6 (b)).

26(a) M. A. Firth, *"An Empirical Investigation of the Impact of the Announcement of Capitalisation issues on Share. Prices"*, Journal of Business Finance and Accounting, Spring 1977.

(b) M. A. Firth, *"The Information Content of Large Investment Holdings"*, Journal of Finance, December 1975.

27. P. Marsh, Ph.D. Dissertation, London Graduate School of Business Studies, 1977.

28. A good review of this work is provided by: I. R. C. Eggleton, S. H. Penman and J. R., Twombly, *"Accounting Changes and Stock Prices: An Examination of Selected and Uncontrolled Variables"*, Journal of Accounting Research, Spring 1976.

29. R. Morris, *"Evidence of the Impact of Inflation Accounting on Share Prices"*, Accounting and Business Research, Spring 1975.

30. J. R. Franks, J. E. Broyles and M. J. Hecht, *"An Industry Study of the Profitability of Mergers in the United Kingdom"*, to be published Journal of Finance, 1978.

31. See reference (4).

32. A. L. Fox, *"Put and Call Parity Theory and the London Share Option Market"*, Unpublished Paper (submitted to the Journal of Finance) 1976.

33. M. A. Firth, *"The Performance of Share Recommendations made by Investment Analysis and the Effects on Market Efficiency"*, Journal of Business Finance, Vol. 4, 1972.

34. M. C. Jensen, "*The Performance of Mutual Funds in the Period 1945–1964*", Journal of Finance Vol. 23, May 1968 (reproduced in 6 (b)).

35. G. Briscoe, J. M. Samuels and D. J. Smythe, "*The Treatment of Risk in the Stockmarket*", Journal of Finance Vol. 24, 1969.

36. P. Moles and B. Taylor, *Unit Trust Risk—Return Performance, 1966–1975*, The Investment Analyst (May 1977), No. 47.

37. Planned Savings, January 1977. See also Financial Times, 7th January, 1977.

38. M. A. Firth, "*The Investment Performance of Unit Trusts in the Period 1965–1975*", Unpublished Paper.

39. C. Ward and A. Saunders, "*U.K. Unit Trust Performance 1964–1974*", Journal of Business Finance and Accounting, Winter 1976.

40. D. C. Corner and H. Burton, "*Investment and Unit Trusts in Britain and America*", Elek 1968.

41. Bacon and Woodrow, Consulting Actuaries, "*Measurement of Investment Performance*", Report for 1975 and Retrospective Analysis.

42. *Ibid.*, Unpublished Paper.

43. J. P. Holbrook, "*Investment Performance of Pension Funds*", Journal of Institute of Actuaries, 1977.

44. See, for example, the prospectus of First Index Investment Trust where annual expenses are estimated at "2/10 of 1% of net assets".

45. W. F. Sharpe, "*Are Gains Likely from Market Timing?*", Financial Analysts Journal, March/April 1975.

46. A. L. Farber, "*National and International Market Timing Strategies*", Commission on Practical Fund Management, 9th Congress, European Federation of Financial Analysts Societies, May 1976.

47. M. S. Rozeff, "*The Money Supply and the Stock Market*", Financial Analysts Journal, September/ October 1975.

48. A. P. Bird, "*The Relationship Between Money Supply and Equity Markets*", Report of Commission on Fixed Interest Markets, 9th Congress, European Federation of Financial Analysts Societies, May 1976.

49. A. Saunders and R. S. Woodward, "*Money Supply and Share Prices; The Evidence for the U.K. in the Post-C.C.C. Period*", The Investment Analyst (December 1976), No. 46.

50. See Lex Column, Financial Times, 6th December 1976 and ref. (38).

51. J. H. Lorie, "*Four Cornerstones of a New Investment Policy*", Institutional Investor, November 1971.

52. J. L. Treynor, "*Long Term Investing*", Financial Analysts Journal, May/June 1976.

53. See for example, M. Braham, "*The Growing Impact of Stockbrokers' Research*", Money Management and Unit Holder, June 1972.

54. R. D. Riecke, "*The Efficient Market Hypothesis and the Value of Traditional Security Analysis*", Journal of Financial and Quantitative Analysis, November, 1975.

55. R. Morris and K. Bhaskar, "*The Accuracy of Brokers' Profit Forecasts*", University of Bristol, Department of Economics, 1975.

56. W. R. Good, R. Ferguson and J. Treynor, "*An Investor's Guide to the Index Fund Controversy*, Financial Analysts Journal, November/December 1976.

57. J. M. Keynes. The General Theory of Employment, Interest and Money. Chapter 12. Macmillan 1936.

58. The Financial Analysts Research Foundation, "*Is Financial Analysis Useless?*", The Proceedings of a Seminar on the Efficient Capital Market and Random Walk Hypotheses, 1975.

59. B. Rosenberg and J. Guy, "*Beta and Investment Fundamentals*", Financial Analysts Journal, May/June 1976.

60. See ref. 6 (a).

61 (a). "*Index Funds—an Idea Whose Time is Coming*", Fortune, June, 1976. (b) "*Wall Street Goes Slow*", Business Week, October 11th, 1976.

61 (a) = 2 (a).

Part III
The 1980s

19 The Wrongs of Rights

B. RILEY

This article was published in The Investment Analyst *in January 1980. By that year, there was clear evidence that many large companies performed poorly following rights issues. In fact, rights issues had become associated with declining profits and subnormal investment returns. But this had not always been the case, and Mr Riley's essay argues for greater disclosure by companies and more effective monitoring as the first steps towards rehabilitation.*

Barry Riley studied at Jesus College, Cambridge, from 1961 to 1964 for a degree in Natural Sciences (Part I) and Economics (Part II). He worked at the Investors' Chronicle *from 1964 to 1966 and then in the London City Office of the* Sheffield Morning Telegraph *before joining the* Financial Times *in 1967. At the* Financial Times, *Barry wrote on the Lex column throughout the 1970s and was Financial Editor from 1982 to 1987. He has written many features and survey articles for the* Financial Times *and for publications elsewhere, including the* Professional Investor. *From 1993 to 1997, he was a trustee of the Pearson Pension Plan, and has continued as a member of the Plan's investment committee.*

Signs of strain have developed in the process by which British companies raise new money from their shareholders through rights issues. Evidence has been accumulating that the shares of companies—at any rate, large companies—launching rights issues tend to perform badly over subsequent months and years. Extreme fluctuations have been evident in the rate at which capital has been raised: in the second half of 1975, for example, companies raised £730 million against only £270 million in the second half of 1976. There would be advantages for both sides if the process could be refined. Shareholders would be protected against the possibility that they could invest new capital in a company at an unjustifiably high share price, and suffer subsequent underperformance. Companies would find that the market continued to be open to them in difficult times when normally rights issues activity is choked off.

Evidence that rights issues are associated with poor share price performance has appeared only quite recently. Previously it has been thought that there was no tendency for rights issues to be linked to abnormal share price behaviour. Then in 1977 an unpublished PhD thesis produced by Dr. Paul Marsh of the London Business School suggested that over an extended period between 1962 and 1972 rights issues had been associated with abnormal capital gains. This study dealt with a large number of issues, many by small companies.

More recently, however, several analysts have focused their attention upon the issues by large companies. The Lex Column of the *Financial Times* pointed out in June 1979 that of the seven British companies which had raised £25 million or more between the beginning of 1978 and January 1979, none had outperformed the stock market as a whole in the sub-

The table shows the relative price movements since, and prior to, the rights issues.

Company	Ex-Rights Date	Relative Price Performance		
		A	B	C
Glaxo	16.06.75	+47.9	−29.5	−28.2
Royal Insurance	29.09.75	+17.5	−31.4	−26.1
Grand Metropolitan	10.10.75	−29.7	+28.8	+47.6
Eagle Star	19.12.75	−14.1	−20.7	−14.1
Plessey	22.12.75	−33.7	−2.5	−0.5
Lloyds Bank	06.02.76	−15.1	−16.0	+0.7
Standard & Chartered	02.03.76	−23.4	−17.5	+2.2
Lucas	11.05.76	+114.4	−13.1	−24.1
ICI	17.05.76	+24.3	−36.9	−31.6
Reed International	30.07.76	−24.6	−54.5	−28.2
National Westminister	30.07.76	−19.0	−2.2	+11.6
General Accident	12.10.76	−1.8	−14.1	−27.2
GKN	13.04.77	+7.0	−40.5	−23.8
Thomas Tilling	17.05.77	+12.9	+13.9	−4.1
Dunlop	24.05.77	+90.5	−51.9	−23.7
Bowater	25.05.77	−1.3	−33.2	−23.6

A: Two year period prior to ex-rights date
B: Ex-rights date to 14.6.79
C: One year after ex-rights date to 14.6.79
Source: Wood Mackenzie & Co.

sequent period. At about the same time a more comprehensive survey by stockbrokers Wood Mackenzie showed that of 16 major companies that launched rights issues of over £25 million between May 1975 and May 1977, only two achieved any relative share price strength between the ex rights date and the closing date of the analysis (June 14, 1979). Choosing the ex rights date as the basis for the study, rather than the date of announcement of the issue, removed the impact of immediate post-issue weakness, which in most cases would have made the overall performance still worse.

The reasons for this emerging bias are not entirely clear. It has been suggested by Dr. Marsh (*Financial Times*, June 15, 1979) that the underperformance by companies making large issues mainly reflects the poor performance, relative to small and medium sized companies, shown by large companies generally in the stock market in the past few years. Yet the sheer scale of the relative weakness makes this hard to accept, especially for the more recent cases quoted by the Lex Column.

If the bias in the performance of companies raising money through rights issues really exists, then it implies that there is an imperfection in the capital market. The efficient market hypothesis implies that when adequate information is in the possession of all participants in the market it is impossible for one participant to obtain an advantage over the others. It is not possible for a company, under these circumstances, to obtain new capital at an unduly low cost—that is, at an unduly high share price.

Yet the evidence suggests that in current conditions in the London stock market, shareholders have indeed been persuaded to subscribe for new shares at excessively high prices. This suggests that the market is not working efficiently because the managers of the company, or their financial advisers, are making use of inside information. This does not necessarily take the form of deliberate manipulation of the flow of facts about the company. But it is apparent that when finance directors and their merchant bank advisers are considering a call upon shareholders for funds they are dominated by consideration of "good timing".

What do they mean by "good timing?" According to the classical theory of the firm, which is reflected in U.K. Company law, companies are owned by their shareholders and are run in a way which will maximise their interests. If that is so, then it will be pointless for directors of a company to raise new capital from shareholders in a way that is favourable to the company but unfavourable to shareholders. It is possible that timing considerations may relate to the short term condition of the market; if the market is strong, the short term effects of a large capital raising exercise, and the cost of underwriting, will be minimised. But there is a strong suspicion that this is by no means the full explanation in most cases. There is a suspicion that managers do indeed try to obtain capital on advantageous terms, and they do this by selecting a moment at which they sense that the market—perhaps only temporarily—is setting too high a price on the company's shares. Many finance directors, in fact, believe that it is their job to do precisely this. They try to select a time when the stock market is cyclically high—implying that it is an unfavourable moment for shareholders to invest new money. They try to select periods when their own company's profits are performing strongly, because the rating in the stock market will be high. But shareholders would be better served by being offered an opportunity to subscribe for new shares when the market was low.

If the market mechanism is faulty, then the increasing inadequacy of rights issue documentation must have a lot to do with it. So-called rights issue "prospectuses" are distributed to the underwriters and the shareholders but contain little information that is not already published. Companies are increasingly reluctant to publish forecasts (though in partial compensation it has become usual to raise money only when up-to-date profits information is available). There is no attempt to provide a medium term perspective, with projections of future returns on capital from new investment and cash flow forecasts for the whole business. Rights issue prospectuses never give any adjustments for inflation, which means not just that the profit and dividend cover figures given may be misleading, but also that an illusory impression is being given of the growth of the business. It has become possible for many British companies to raise new capital supposedly to "sustain the growth of the business" when there may well have been no growth at all in real terms.

This is of fundamental importance because a shareholder asked to subscribe new capital needs to know how the company has been performing. He needs to know whether the capital is in fact needed to expand the structure of the business; or whether it is needed to support the business; or of overdistribution or of actual losses in real terms.

The theory of rights issues is that they provide a means whereby a company can grow at a faster rate than can be achieved on the basis of fixed investment financed only from retained profits and from such borrowings as can be supported within prudent gearing restrictions. Yet a great many of the right issues since 1975 have in fact fallen into the category of recapitalisation. Such "distress" rights issues may still be valid. Shareholders may still be willing to put fresh capital into their company to support their existing investment even though they know it to be losing money in real terms, and even though it may be unable to justify its level of distribution. But at the very least they will demand drastic management changes and a transformation of prospects. Inflation has provided the cloak whereby managements have all too often avoided this challenge.

Instead, finance directors have come to rely on a system which allows companies in good standing with the market to raise almost without question a sum of around 20 per cent of the market capitalisation—equivalent to the amount they can raise through a one-for-four issue at a discount of, say, 16 per cent. This system does offer an element of rough and ready justice, because highly rated companies can raise more, in proportion to their underlying assets, than lowly rated ones. But this facility has become abused, judging by the under-performance of so many issuers in the market.

The growing gulf between managers and shareholders has led to the appearance of that contradictory phenomenon, the "opportunist" rights issue. Companies raise new capital not because there is any identifiable current need, but because the money appears to be there in the market, especially in the investment institutions, and because it might become useful in some future hypothetical acquisition or credit squeeze. The "opportunist" rights issue is rarely indulged in by entrepreneurial companies in which the directors have large personal shareholdings.

How can the system be made more flexible? It is not just that the present system makes it too easy to raise new equity capital. It can also make it hard to raise enough money for a company's real needs. "Heavy" issues are difficult to arrange, and so the maximum raised through a single issue is related more to the market capitalisation than to the justifiable requirements of the company. Some companies have for this reason been forced to launch several successive issues, reaching their initial capital target only after several years.

What is required is the introduction of a system more akin to the medium term lending arrangements developed by banks, especially American banks. Specific project finance schemes have also become common. In such schemes returns on capital are projected in detail for some years ahead and are carefully monitored. In some cases, indeed, protective clauses may be triggered and special powers may thereby be conferred upon the bank.

Clearly, equity capital does not require the same degree of protection as bank money. Providers of risk capital have to rely for their ultimate security on their ability, through their voting power, to appoint or remove directors and to control their actions. However, it is not so clear why shareholders in practice are prepared to accept such inadequate disclosure of information. As the system exists, a subscription for new shares in a rights issue is not so much a rational investment decision as an act of blind faith in the company's management.

It is true that considerations of commercial prudence and confidentiality restrict the disclosure of information to shareholders of listed companies, compared to the amount of discussion which is common with bankers. There has to be a compromise here. Never-theless there is a need for detailed financial justification to be made of any call upon share-holders for funds. Prospectuses should include, for instance, an analysis of the existing real returns being achieved by the company, and medium term projections of the returns on planned new investment. In this way sufficient information can be made available to both sides and the market can be expected to work in an efficient manner, with a price being set on the new capital which cannot lead to a tendency towards either under-or over-performance by the share price in future.

There is a need for more precise yardsticks against which to judge the performance and progress of a company. During the years of dividend controls the apparent ability of a company to pay high and rising dividends became the principal attraction—the rights issue being an officially authorised route to higher payouts. But the legacy is a large group of industrial companies with very high yields which are inadequately covered. Strictly speak-ing the dividends should be cut—but having entered into a commitment to shareholders at the time of their rights issues the companies are reluctant to take such action. They may feel, moreover, that a dividend reduction would cut off their access to the market should another rights issue be seen as a possibility.

The way ahead lies in greater disclosure and more effective monitoring. This might be unattractive to many Boards of directors; indeed, close scrutiny by investors would rule out many proposed rights issues. But on the positive side, it might open the way to much more rapid expansion by companies which could put forward viable investment propositions on a scale greater than would fit in with conventional rights issues.

The recent association of rights issues with declining profit performance and subnormal investment returns has given rights issues something of a bad name. However, this does not appear to have been true in the past and need not be true in the future. If the issue techniques can be improved so that companies are only likely to use rights issues to finance profitable investment opportunities, the market will soon learn to react with more enthusiasm.

20 "The Wrongs of Rights" – A Reply

S. P. KEEF

When this article was published in The Investment Analyst *in July 1980, Steven Keef was a lecturer in the University of Aston Management Centre. His reply to Barry Riley suggests that no distinction can be made between the interests of the company and the interests of shareholders. In the early 1980s, Mr Keef left Aston to take up a teaching post in Wellington, New Zealand.*

The classical or perfect market approach to a rights issue shows that (1):

(i) the issue price is irrelevant;
(ii) the action taken by the shareholder, assuming he either accepts the new shares or sells the rights, does not affect his short term net wealth.

We can also show, using the scrip issue effect, that the share price per se, that is the cum-rights price at the time of the issue, is not a factor of any importance. Now, very few people would agree with the tenet that stock markets are absolutely equivalent to the economists' perfect market dream. So we have to accept that the valuation of companies, say proxied by the market capitalisation of their ordinary equity, will on occasions be temporarily over or under stated. The purpose of this paper is to illustrate that in the real world a shareholder facing a rights issue where the company's shares are not at a fair and true equilibrium does not entertain any greater risk than does a shareholder of a mirror company. We shall define the mirror company as one which is identical in every respect except the important fact that it is not carrying out a rights issue.

Let us examine two companies, see Table 1, quoted on a stock market with the benefit of hind-sight. Company A's shares are currently and temporarily overvalued and those of Company B are undervalued. If two investors were to invest a fixed sum of money each into the equity of one company, what would be the outcome when the share prices returned to their equilibrium or intrinsic values? Obviously, the shareholder of Company A would suffer a decrease in wealth and the converse would be true for the investor in Company B. It is fair, and patently obvious, to say that the shareholder in Company A has been disadvantaged. Of this there is no doubt, but surely this is a major risk inherent in equity ownership. Since it

TABLE 1.

COMPANY	STATUS OF SHARE PRICE RELATIVE TO INTRINSIC VALUE
A	Temporarily Overvalued
B	Temporarily Undervalued

is not germane to the argument being presented it is not proposed to discuss either the causes, or to whom the blame should be attributed, of the temporary deviation of the share price from its intrinsic or fundamental value.

Now let us assume that both Company A and Company B carried out a rights issue. Although unspecified let us presume that the two important parameters of the issue, namely the rights ratio, the issue price and consequently their product which determines the value of the cash raised, all fall within what can be termed generally accepted norms. Basically these assumptions mean that the only effect we are considering is that the shares deviate in price from their intrinsic value. Now, excluding actions that are a mixture of those to be stated, the three basic strategies open to the shareholder are:

(i) sell all his shares, that is existing shares and their rights;
(ii) accept the new shares allotted;
(iii) sell the rights attached to his existing shares.

For the sake of simplicity we shall assume that the shareholder has just been stimulated, by the announcement of the impending rights issue, to review his holding in the company concerned. If the shareholder perceives the shares to be overvalued then he will sell all his shares and put the cash so realised to other uses. This is the only strategy open to the reasonable, logical man who has confidence in his judgement. His methodology in determining the true value of the shares is of no interest to this particular study, although if true and correct would have tremendous implications in the real world. On the stock market where share prices may react upwards or downwards due to new information being available, say for example the announcement of the rights issue, we can argue that any such loss or gain associated with this new piece of information is again one of the inherent risks associated with share ownership.

If the shareholder perceives, at that time, the shares to be undervalued, then he will invest further monies in the equity of the company. The point to be discussed is whether this should be effected through the purchase of existing shares or by the rights allotted in the rights issue. Well, if we assume that the stock market operates in a near perfect manner in valuing the complementary value of a right and the ex-rights price then the difference is a matter of semantics. Except of course where transaction costs may show a marginal advantage. Research by MERRETT, HOWE & NEWBOULD (2) and BACON (3) has shown that the stock markets in the U.K. and U.S.A. respectively operate, using the ex-rights price as the criterion, in a manner which is not radically different from the perfect market approach. A critique of these two studies is, unfortunately, beyond the scope of this paper; nevertheless it is sufficient to say that they found a high degree of correlation between the theoretical and actual ex-rights prices and furthermore each study reported a mean error less than two per cent from the expected relationship. Thus in the real world, as would be expected where arbitrage acted on two almost identical securities, shareholders are financially indifferent to either buying new shares through the medium of rights, that is purchase sufficient rights to be able to subscribe for the new shares, or by purchasing existing shares ex-rights.

Now to further our argument let us introduce two shareholders whose financial constraints are presented in Table 2 and who besides being shareholders of Company B have come to the same belief through independent, yet unspecified techniques, that the shares of Company B are undervalued. Investor Y, who has more than sufficient cash available for investment can not only subscribe to the rights issue but can also invest as much money as he wishes into the equity of the company. If his share evaluation technique is correct then he has made a profit; if not then the loss is a manifestation of the risk inherent in attempting to determine how the body of the stock market values shares.

TABLE 2.

INVESTOR	FINANCIAL SITUATION
X	Devoid of Cash
Y	More than sufficient Cash Available

Now Investor X, who has no spare cash available for investment can neither participate in the new issue nor even increase his holding by buying existing shares. Assuming that he cannot benefit from an increase in his personal gearing by borrowing—if he could then he would be in a basically similar position to Investor Y—then he has no choice but to sell his rights. The question one must ask is, "Has he been disadvantaged, say compared to Investor Y?" Well, the answer is a mixture of "yes" and "no" and depends upon the interpretation of the word disadvantaged. It is obvious if we use the connotation related to equality of wealth that he is at a strong disadvantage in that he cannot fully back his judgement. However, this is a fact of life and of no concern to the argument of this paper. It is worth commenting however that since he can not invest further monies his risk is limited, particularly compared to Investor Y.

Having been forced to sell his rights leads one to question whether he will get a fair price for them. In a perfect market the answer would be in the affirmative and the balance of the empirical evidence, quoted earlier, suggests that in the real world the same conclusion will be reached. The small error, where the actual ex-rights price and consequently the value of a right, deviates from that predicted by theory, observed in the studies of MERRETT, HOWE & NEWBOULD and BACON can be explained, in part, by the natural Brownian volatility of the market reacting to the new information that is becoming available all of the time. So we must conclude that Investor X has been forced to sell his rights at a value based upon the temporarily depressed price. Being unable to participate in the rights issue, yet confident that the share prices are depressed temporarily his best strategy is to effect a null cash change operation. That is sell the rights and immediately re-invest the monies into existing shares at their ex-rights price. In this situation he has basically benefited from a scrip issue which most people would accept as being effectively neutral to the net wealth of the shareholder.

Having examined the logical strategy when the share prices deviate from their intrinsic value and discussed the situation of the shareholder we now need to explain what a rights issue really is. To all extents and purposes a rights issue can be considered to consist of part scrip issue and part new issue (4). It is not proposed to discuss the scrip issue effect except to state that any gain or loss so occasioned can normally be readily explained. Now the critical aspects of a new issue is the setting of the subscription price. Any error in this sphere will result in either an unwarranted loss or gain being made by either the buyer or seller. Even allowing for the customary ten to twenty per cent introductory discount the setting of the issue price will invariably be proved incorrect by the stable trading period that follows. But in a rights issue the basic new issue price, defined as the ex-rights price, is extremely well characterised and is set by the current supply and demand in the market. There will be volatility, no one would be so foolish as to deny this, but it is contended that the volatility, defined as the issue price and the market price in their respective environments, will be much more stable in a rights issue than in the customary Offer for Sale new issue. The fact that the share price is over or under valued compared to the imaginary intrinsic value is of subsidiary importance provided the status quo is maintained during the period of the issue. If powerful arbitrage pressures start to force down the share price towards its natural levels then problems can arise in a rights issue especially if a relatively low discount is offered. However, for the sake of simplicity we shall assume such pressures are absent. So a shareholder owning a pre-emptive right to participate in a right issue is in the same situation as another investor who is debating investing in the equity of the company under investigation. The potential investor has the two choices of buy or not buy (or sell) and these are basically the same alternatives facing the existing shareholder confronted by a rights issue.

Finally we would like to squash the myths related to the accepted adages that the best strategies for the company is to set a high issue price when the current share prices are at a peak (5); and thus incur what some authors (6) consider unnecessary underwriting expenses.

The logic of going back to the market when the company's current share price is high has a number of attractions, not least of all the fact that the high price represents a significant interest and confidence in the equity of the company. But one must question whether this aspect is of any importance. For those analysts who support the need to underwrite the rights issue we can suggest that such a mechanism must surely guarantee the success of the issue as far as the company is concerned. For the proponents of the opposing view that the best strategy is to set a relatively low issue price so as to make underwriting unnecessary since the rights will always have a positive value, we must come to the same conclusion. So whether or not the share price is at a peak would appear to be irrelevant. RILEY (7) discusses at some length the wrongs of rights issues and suggests:

"There is a suspicion that managers do indeed try to obtain capital on advantageous terms, and they do this by selecting a moment at which they sense that the market—perhaps only temporarily—is setting too high a price on the company's shares. Many finance directors, in fact, believe that it is their job to do precisely this. They try to select a time when the stock market is cyclically high—implying that it is an unfavourable moment for shareholders to invest new money. They try to select periods when their own company's profits are performing strongly, because the rating in the stock market will be high. But shareholders would be better served by being offered an opportunity to subscribe for new shares when the market was low."

Although RILEY is only expressing his suspicions on the attitude to rights issues he strongly infers that the financial directors are seeking to obtain new capital at an unduly low cost, that is due to an unduly high share price. And furthermore, he implies that this may be favourable to the company but unfavourable to the shareholder. The tenet implied in this extract is based on false logic. The cost of equity capital is not a static parameter, in an analogous fashion it can be considered somewhat similar to a clearing house bank's base rate. To say that it is advantageous to take out a variable rate bank loan when the base rate is low has little foundation. In this situation the borrower has to pay the going rate, set by the market; and the same considerations apply to the equity component of the weighted average cost of capital. The suggestion of an action being to the good of the company yet unfavourable to the shareholders is so preposterous as to need no further comment. In fairness to RILEY one must support the general conclusion, but not necessarily the logic used to arrive at such a view, that shareholders should not participate in rights issues when the shares are at their peak values. The basis for this conclusion must lie in the illogicality of purchasing any security when the price is at a cyclical maximum.

A recent questionnaire has shown that a high proportion of private shareholders are very poorly informed on the importance of the issue price in a rights issue (8). The survey of 150 shareholders of each of two public companies showed that over half of the 102 respondents truly believed that they were getting a bargain if, as is normally the case, the issue price is a rights issue was below the current market price of the shares. Furthermore, they supported the statement "the greater the discount the greater the bargain". The implications of this result are twofold. First, we cannot deny that such a naive shareholder is at some disadvantage compared to say an informed shareholder. However, this disadvantage does not lie in the area of short term financial loss but is more a matter of the implications of the strategies that they believe are best suited to their needs. Thus they may go to some lengths and expense to find the monies required for the new issue. It is in this area that their lack of knowledge may put them at a disadvantage to their informed, fellow investors. Second, the false premise of the shareholder has motivated him to participate in the new issue, but we must question whether or not he had paid a fair price for the new equity. Returning to the all important assumption that the perturbation, if any, is relatively stable during the subscription period, then we can argue that the shareholder has not been treated unfairly. He has increased his holding at the market price. Furthermore, we must consider whether such a shareholder falls into a different category to another investor who believes that the equity of a company is undervalued and then backs his judgement by becoming a shareholder.

The major logic used to justify a high issue price in a rights issue is the fact that it protects the shareholder (cf Investor X) who through his own unique circumstances is forced to sell his rights when the share price is currently depressed (9). This rationale is irrefutable but relies very heavily on the market temporarily taking a pessimistic view on the current share price compared to its intrinsic value. From a behavioural point of view one instinctively feels that any director worth his salt would quite naturally believe that the share price of his company was undervalued by the stock market. If the share price were overvalued then the contrary would be true, that is, it is in the best interests of the shareholder to set the issue price as low as possible; say the absolute lower limit under normal circumstances which is the nominal share value. The debate over the relative merits of the issue price compounded by the deviation of the share price from an intrinsic value hinges on what is the true effect of selling the rights. The Capital Gains Tax treatment of the proceeds obtained by selling rights gives the answer; it is a part disposal of the asset (10). The greater the dilution, that is the lower the rights ratio and the lower the issue price, then the greater the degree of part disposal. But in the case of the shares being over valued this is only part of the way towards the indicated strategy, namely if the shareholder believes this situation to pertain he should divest himself of all his holding in the company rather than just the segment implicated by the rights issue.

CONCLUDING REMARKS

In a perfect market nobody would deny that the parameters of a rights issue have any relevance whatsoever. As a corollary, the parameters of a rights issue are of paramount importance in an inefficient market. This paper has attempted to separate the inefficiency of the market into two discrete sections, namely the treatment of the dilution inherent in a rights issue and the possibility of a temporary, yet relatively stable for the period of the issue, perturbation of the share price from an intrinsic or fundamental norm. Whether these two aspects are mutually exclusive, as implied in the analysis presented in this paper, is a moot point.

Empirical evidence has shown that, on average, the inefficiency in the treatment of the ex-rights price is relatively small and this is supported by MARSH (11) when he stated:

"It seems fair, therefore, to conclude that our results do not furnish any very strong evidence of significant market inefficiencies associated with rights issues. Because of this, we cannot reject the hypothesis that the U.K. market is efficient with respect to rights issue announcements."

It is possible that the small deviations reported by the MERRETT, HOWE & NEWBOULD and BACON studies could in part be explained by random movement in share prices.

The fact that some time after the rights issue has been effected the market proves that the share price was at a maximum, a minimum or even a saddle point is the grist of investing in the equity of companies; the gains or losses to be made from such share price movements are the same whether or not a company is carrying out a rights issue.

REFERENCES

1. See for example: J. C. Van Horne, "Financial Management and Policy", Prentice Hall International 1975. J. F. Weston and E. F. Brigham, "Managerial Finance", Holt, Rinehart and Winston, British Edition 1979. J. M. Samuels and F. M. Wilkes, "Management of Company Finance", Nelson 1976, or any text book on business finance that discusses Rights Issues.

2. A. J. Merrett, M. Howe and G. D. Newbould, "Equity Issues and the London Capital Market", Longmans 1967.

3. P. W. Bacon, "The Subscription Price in Rights Offerings", *Financial Management*, Summer 1972, pages 59–64.

4. S. M. Keane, "The Significance of the Issue Price in Rights Issues", *Journal of Business Finance*, Volume 4, No. 3, pages 40–45.

5. B. Riley, "The Wrongs of Rights", *The Investment Analyst*, Volume 55, January 1980, pages 4–6.

6. Merrett, Howe and Newbould, op cit. and G. D. Newbould and P. E. H. Wells, "Underwriting of Rights Issues—A Theoretical Justification: A Reply", *Journal of Business Finance*, Volume 3, No. 4, pages 53.

7. Riley, op cit.

8. S. P. Keef, "The Importance of the Issue Price in a Rights Issue: A Survey of Shareholder's Beliefs", University of Aston Management Centre Working Paper Series (to be published).

9. Keane, op cit.

10. The Board of Inland Revenue, "Capital Gains Tax" (booklet CGT8) February 1973.

11. P. Marsh, "Equity Rights Issues and the Efficiency of the U.K. Stock Market", *Journal of Finance*, Volume 34, No. 4, pages 839–862, September 1979.

21 The Current and Future Role of Stockbrokers

G. J. J. DENNIS

This article appeared in The Investment Analyst *in October 1981, It is the text of a speech given at the Annual Conference of the National Association of Pensions Funds held in Birmingham from 7 to 10 May 1981.*

In 1986 the Big Bang revolutionised the London Stock Exchange. Five years earlier, George Dennis examined in considerable detail the outlook for UK stockbrokers. He forecast that radical changes would take place in their role and those changes would occur due to market pressures. Subsequent events have underlined the prescience of his comments.

George Dennis commenced his career in the investment area with the BP Pension Fund, after a spell with The Distillers Company and a period in South Africa with BP. He was a portfolio manager with BP for some years, and then joined Williams de Broe as Research Manager. He was appointed in 1972 as Investment Director of Postel Investment Management (now called Hermes). He served with Postel for 16 years, with responsibility for all securities investments. He was then appointed managing director of TSB Investment Management. Subsequent to that, he was Managing Director of the National Bank of Kuwait Investment Management. Currently, George Dennis is Chairman of the Housing Finance Corporation (where he was a founder member), Chairman of the Hill Samuel Property Unit Trust, and a non-executive director of Foreign and Colonial Emerging Markets Trust. He is also an adviser to pension funds, and is involved with a research company. He has been a member of the IIMR Committee since 1987.

The Stock Exchange is defending the two major supports of the present market structure i.e. minimum fixed commissions, and "single capacity"—the principle whereby members may act either as principals or agents in selling stock, but never officially as both. It is my view that, irrespective of the findings of the Court, radical changes will take place in the role of stockbrokers, with changes determined by intense market pressures. The findings of the Court will determine the rate of change—they are unlikely to influence the direction of change. The NAPF has canvassed its members on their attitude towards present commission structures and dual capacity, and the findings have been reported in the Press, the general consensus supporting unbundling, with the retention of a minimum scale of commission and greater flexibility in the area of dual capacity.

The NAPF did in fact conduct two studies on this subject. Both studies expressed some dissatisfaction with the current commission structure but it is interesting and important to know that most members are keen to see the retention of a minimum scale of commission but with some degree of unbundling. I think this is a very important point to bear in mind because it indicates that while most institutions see a need for a change, they are concerned at the rate of change and are anxious to ensure that there is both an orderly and a competitive market within which they as buyers and sellers can operate. I know that the Stock Exchange questioned the survey and in particular the brevity of the questionnaire, but nevertheless I think the results do reflect a realistic attitude on the part of institutional investors.

SERVICES PROVIDED BY STOCKBROKERS

In his recent book, Dundas Hamilton defined the functions of stockbrokers in the United Kingdom as follows. Initially, they make arrangements for the listing of the stock or shares of a company so that dealings can take place in the market. Secondly, they act as agents in the buying and selling of securities, since no outside investor can deal through the medium of the stock Exchange without using the services of a stockbroker. And finally, they act as advisers to their clients in the selection and administration of their investments. He then goes on to say that it is the last function, the service of the client, that turns stockbroking from being purely an industry into a profession.

We tend to think of brokers acting solely as agents in the buying and selling of securities. In actual fact, the range of services is extremely wide, covering dealings in securities, the provision of analytical advice on companies and industries, the provision of research services to the corporate sector, the provision of corporate advice, dealing in gold, kruggerand, and kaffirs, dealers in foreign shares and currencies, providers of measurement of performance services and risk analysis services, advisers on modern portfolio theory, introducers of new companies to the market, fund managers for both private and institutional clients, tax advisers for private clients, tax advisers for institutions, dealers in gilts, eurobonds, other foreign bonds, and other fixed interest investments, money dealers, advisers to local authorities, advisers to prospective mortgagees, property advisers, leasing specialists, advisers on hedging operations, advisers on company management, investment and unit trust managers, catalysts in the primary market, financial advisers to companies and foreign Governments, promoters of venture capital schemes, economic advisers, insurance broking etc. etc.

UNIFICATION

This extension in the role and functions of the stockbroker is in response to market forces. And the rate of change has been particularly fast in recent years. In 1968, there were Stock Exchanges in 21 of the major towns and cities, which had recently been linked into four main groups—London, Midland and Western, Northern and Scottish, together with about 100 firms in other provincial areas. In March 1973 these were unified into one Exchange, the Stock Exchange, which also included members of the Belfast Stock Exchange and of the two Southern Irish Exchanges in Dublin and Cork. This centralization, self-imposed by the stockbroking profession, has undoubtedly increased both the degree of professionalism and the rate of change of functions which we have seen in recent years. But of course, many of these services are charged separately. And this growth in the range of services provided by brokers has been in response to market forces, helped by the fixed commission structure which enabled many firms to stay in a financially healthy condition during the gestation period of breaking into new markets, when costs were of necessity high and revenue relatively low.

Of course, one should not forget that brokers often have their own money at risk although we should not forget the role played by limited partners and corporate membership. Given the high rates of marginal tax in recent years and the difficulty for private individuals to build up adequate capital to start new ventures, there is no doubt in my mind that the fixed commission structure has been an important factor in the ability of broking firms to adopt an aggressive stance and to expand into new markets in response to market factors. The lower rate of marginal tax introduced by the present Government should enable individuals to amass capital at a slightly greater rate but in my view not quickly enough to finance major thrusts into new markets. Sources of outside finance will continue therefore in my view to be essential.

Obviously, individual stockbroking firms provide only some of the services indicated and indeed there is considerable specialization by individual firms. In order to appreciate and understand the future role of stockbrokers, it is important to job backwards and to try to understand why they developed such diverse roles. It is also important to bear in mind that the Stock Exchange is part of the City which in turn is the major financial centre in the world. As such, it has been affected probably as much by changes in the international environment as changes on the domestic scene. Historically, U.K. stockbrokers have always had an international orientation. One has only to acquire an investment trust as a pension fund to see how active investors were in the late 19th century and the early part of this century in some very strange places in the world indeed. Some of the paper still surviving in these portfolios indicates how wide were the ramifications of London as a financial centre.

RECENT DEVELOPMENT

The Stock Exchange has always, rightly in my view, seen itself as a foreign exchange earner, and individual firms have often clung on in overseas markets, motivated often by national pride as opposed to the profit nature. Indeed, many firms, particularly those established in Europe, retained their offices there when commercial pragmatism indicated closure as the only realistic step. It seems to me that the development of stockbroking firms since the second world war to date has been determined by five main factors viz.

1. A growing need for specialist services;
2. greater competition;
3. U.K. Exchange Control;
4. changes in customer mix, with increasing dominance by the institutions; and
5. relatively low GNP growth in the U.K.

Let us examine these in greater detail, bearing in mind that they are inter-related. In the last 20 years, investors in general have become more sophisticated. This applies not only to the U.K. and foreign institutions, but also to the private investor who was forced to think more deeply about diversification of risk and tax efficient methods of saving. This growing sophistication presented interesting opportunities to the stockbroker, particularly in the fields of investment research, arbitrage dealing and institutional liaison. Companies were seeking more sophisticated advice in their corporate and treaty activities and were showing flexibility in going to those sources which could respond quickly to highly volatile movements in the environment. At the same time, there was grater competition in the City in general. The Bank of England has always shown extreme foresight in implementing appropriate measures to retain the City as a major financial centre with a highly competitive environment. The accompanying influx of foreign banks and other financial institutions to the City increased the competitive environment, but at the same time presented new opportunities for the aggressive stockbroker. At the same time, the total size of the domestic business cake in real terms as far as the brokers were concerned was not growing very much, and the result was seen in rationalization moves, greater efficiency and moves to bite at the international business cake. And in a curious way, U.K. Exchange Control regulations helped in this. Exchange Control made the grass in the field overseas that much greener, and the

Bank of England showed considerable flexibility in approving financing schemes for overseas investment which did not impair the U.K. reserves.

In fact, I would say that the Bank of England really went out of its way to encourage U.K. institutions to invest overseas, not only because it appreciated the need to diversify risk but also because overseas investment from London is an essential pre-requisite for the retention of London as a major financial centre. And as we all know, many strange and complicated financing instruments were developed to enable investors to go overseas including such things as back to back loans, swap deposits and some interesting off-shore vehicles. The result was that expertise in overseas investment, built up over many decades, was not dissipated, and many brokers opened offices overseas to sell primarily to both U.K. and foreign institutions. A great deal of talent in brokers' offices was however diverted from the U.K. market to dealing with the problems arising from Exchange Control regulations. Over this period, the institutions became more dominant, and by virtue of their size were demanding more specialist services—a situation which is likely to continue.

Finally, with growing emphasis on performance, the institutions in effect were encouraging brokers to look more widely afield for investments which would show a good relative return in sterling terms. The much higher growth rates in GNP in certain overseas markets compared with the U.K., coupled with diversification of risk objectives, encouraged U.K. institutions to take on the currency risks associated with overseas investment.

FUTURE DEVELOPMENTS

In terms of the environment in the future, there will be two dominant factors viz. far greater competition, and greater dominance by the institutions who will force a re-think as to the definition of the "market place". Competition indeed can take many forms. Stockbrokers themselves compete on the range of services they offer and often compete on price through soft services. Increasingly, however, they will meet further competition from other financial organizations who are offering competing services and a different range of investment instruments. Such competition will of course be in primary and secondary markets, both in the U.K. and overseas. It is noticeable that in the last year or so, foreign brokers and U.K. and foreign bankers have been offering a wider range of investment instruments to U.K. institutions. There is pressure on U.K. fund managers to perform and therefore greater flexibility by them in looking at this greater variety of new instruments. So while the stock market is still the main market for the institutions and is likely to remain so, one must be aware of the growing number of investment opportunities which by-pass the market. Such investment opportunities include leasing deals, mortgage paper, venture capital schemes, indexed paper, loan cum equity schemes of various sorts, equity deals of various sorts and of course, a large range of property deals. This therefore, is the environment facing the stockbroker, how will he react in this situation? At least one firm has taken the decision to leave the Stock Exchange in order to specialize in corporate financial advice and risk analysis services.

I do not believe that many firms will follow suit. For several years now there has been a move to increased specialization amongst stock brokers, and certainly, there seems every indication at the moment that firms will seek to find and consolidate their hold in a special area where they can see minimum competition and commercial viability.

Indeed, some stockbroking firms have been moving into the property area where demand appears to be almost insatiable and where the returns are attractive. Such a move also enables brokers to give strategic investment advice as to portfolio mix.

There are a number of areas where I think stockbrokers will concentrate their energies in order to ensure their viability in the future.

1. SPECIALIZATION

Inevitably, market pressures will encourage an increase in specialization. Some firms are already specializing in the provision of computer services and special avenues of research. There is a growing trend to provide research to industry. Other firms are expanding in the international sphere. The days when a broker could rely on performing a pure mechanistic middleman's role are inevitably over, and increasingly investors are objectively appraising the relative merits of brokers, particularly in the area of research. Most decisions in the investment area do involve a decision based upon value and factual premises, and those brokers who can develop their judgemental skills and establish a good track record in an appropriate area where investor interest is high will do well. And in this concept, I expect brokers to develop their overall financial skills, to become more DCF orientated, and to extend their innovative skills into new investment areas.

The abolition of Exchange Control Regulations will provide opportunities, particularly with newer markets opening up in the Far East and the Continent of America. An international financial market, characterized by volatile interest rates and volatile currency movements, will provide rich pickings for those firms that can establish proven expertise. But the environment will be highly competitive. Foreign brokers and bankers will become more aggressive in London, while other financial centres will be using various incentives and applying maximum pressure to attract business away from London. And we should not underestimate the ability of other major financial centres to compete with London. New York for example is endeavouring to attract far more insurance business and it seems to me almost inevitable that if they are even partially successful in that area then other peripheral services will develop there to the benefit of the financial community in that city. The French are likely to be particularly aggressive and even now their earnings from invisibles exceed U.K. invisible earnings.

Although this year will see a substantial increase in international investment business, the City Broking Fraternity has widely differing views on how big a share of the boom will come to its members. Quite a few brokers see a large volume of business turning to the Japanese market while others fear the growth of the foreign brokers based in London doing deals which by-pass the market place. Peter Wills of the Stock Exchange has already expressed concern at the obvious efforts of the French Government to reconstruct the Paris Stock Exchange and win European business away from London. He has criticised the over regulation in the London market. According to the Committee on Invisible Exports, overseas earnings of the U.Ks leading service industries are likely to grow by between 2% and 3% in money terms again this year, following a 2½ growth in 1980. After allowing for inflation the volume of services being sold abroad will decline, and even though the world invisibles market is generally depressed, Britain's share in the volume of business will decline again. This is not really a healthy scenario.

In this area of further skill specialization, there is likely to be less dependence on the skilled entrepreneur in a firm and greater emphasis on team development, implying a synthesizing of complementary skills, so that investment propositions are fully polished and packaged before they reach the investor. All too often at the moment direct investment propositions arrive from brokers badly presented and without concomitant tax questions and control procedures crystallized.

2. PRIMARY MARKET OPERATIONS

I see brokers having a growing role in the primary markets, covering not just the established market but the unlisted securities market, venture capital and increasingly direct investment deals. The Wilson Committee has been a useful catalyst in this respect. It concentrated attention on the importance of the Stock Exchange as a means of raising new money and it also turned attention to the subject of new investment media—even if we as investors were not too happy with the main new investment medium proposed. The Committee also emphasized small company investment. Now I believe that brokers will become more imaginative in the area of capital raising—indeed, I see this happening already, although one or two brokers I know are not too happy at the attitude of the Stock Exchange. However, it must be remembered that the Stock Exchange has to look after its reputation. Reputations are hard to earn but easy to lose and perhaps we as institutional investors should approve of the high standards laid down by the Stock Exchange.

It is to be expected that in this area, as institutions get closer to the companies in which they have investments, the broker and banker might be by-passed, particularly if property deals are involved. However, there will always be room for creative and imaginative thinking, and currently I am sure we are all agreed that there is room for innovation in the fund-raising area, not just in the U.K. but overseas as well.

Indeed, moves in this area could be accelerated by a resurgence of interest in fixed interest instruments following the fall in interest rates. And the fortunes of each institution here and for that matter each stockbroker are finally interwoven with what happens to U.K. Limited. We tend at times I think to forget this fact. It is important therefore that we play our part to increase productivity by encouraging an expansion of investment within British industry. And to achieve this I think we must not rely solely upon existing communication structures and existing investment instruments but do our utmost to ensure that communications between the City and industry are improved. And concomitant with this, to offer to industry a greater variety of investment instruments that can be dovetailed to meet the individual requirements of industrial companies. I often think that we have been slow to develop suitable investment instruments when I see the range of investment vehicles available in the U.S. market.

3. THE "IDENTITY" AREA

I define the identity area as the necessity for brokers to identify themselves with the policy objectives of their clients. Now why do I emphasize this? Simply, stockbrokers are not salesmen and should not consider themselves as salesmen. The word "salesman" does not do them justice and it debases the role which they do and should play. The stockbroker should regard himself as an equity or gilt adviser. On this definition, it follows that he cannot fulfil his role adequately unless he understands and identifies himself with the objectives of his client. With the growing dominance of the institutions, brokers who cannot identify themselves with clients objectives either expressed specifically or in general terms, will tend to lose out. And indeed, there is surprising variation in comprehension of this point by brokers at the moment.

Those brokers who manage institutional funds at the moment or have a special relationship of one sort or another with institutions are at a tremendous advantage in terms of getting further business. Currently, some 25 firms account for 80% of the turnover in equities. By my reckoning, the majority of these firms are quite substantial in fund management themselves or by other relationships identify very strongly with their institutional clients. In broad terms the service provided by these firms has underlying it a consistent set of hypotheses, the area and quality of service is tailored to institutions' requirements, and usually there is a total absence of any form of hard sell. Having made this eulogy, there is plenty of scope for improvement. Very few brokers in my experience ask questions about a pension funds' objectives, the risk/reward ratio sought, or criteria for direct investment.

How many managers have been asked by brokers for copies of their accounts and reports? Very few I suspect. I see institutions being far more objective in their analysis of services provided by individual brokers and allocating business in a way which reflects these weightings. Measurement of performance statistics are a hard task master and eventually will repercuss on those who recommend stocks. I know that many brokers at the moment often see themselves as tacticians concerned primarily with stock and sector selection in the equity market and tactical plays around the yeild curve in the gilt market. But an understanding of the strategy of their clients must improve the quality of service they provide and indeed will lead to a better utilisation of resources. And my comments apply equally to the private investor as to the institutional investor.

And I am not asking the stockbroker to do the fund manager's job. I am just indicating an area where some understanding of objectives is absolutely essential so that both parties can perform their roles more efficiently. I have never believed in any management situation that authority and responsibility should be divorced. I therefore, while believing that authority and responsibility should lie firmly with the fund manager for performance, believe that the stockbroker cannot perform his role adequately without some understanding of the strategy of his institutional clients.

4. NEW INSTRUMENTS

A very limited number of gilt brokers and even fewer equity brokers have devoted time and resources to extensive pure research work. Many institutional investors on the surface may express cynicism of such work, but if this industry is to progress in London we are all aware of the need for this sort of work to continue and for new tools to help with decision making. But alongside this, I see the development of new investment instruments. In the last year we have seen the appearance of many new instruments including drop lock-loans, drop-lock leases, indexed instruments, secured convertible debentures and so on. Pension funds are a natural for such innovations. We work to a long-term investment horizon, and provided that the DCF over a period is attractive, we do not usually need a regular income flow. We can therefore be highly flexible in our approach. There is always scope for the provision of special services of a support nature, such as accountancy services, risk analysis, fund measurement services and so on.

5. FUND MANAGEMENT

This is an area of controversy in some quarters but I for my part see no reason why a broker should not provide fund management services, using soft or hard dollars. In the ultimate, brokers in this area have to perform, and I am sure that most trustees are not so short-sighted as to put funds for management with a broker because of a saving on the management fee. From my own experience, the management fee is way down the list as a factor for consideration when appointing a fund manager. And I see an extension of the role of brokers in this area, covering not just pension fund management but also unit and investment trust management, and management of venture capital money for both private clients and companies, following the proposals in the Budget of 10th March. And there will always be scope for the specialist in the fund management field, with the pension fund manager having control of the rump of a fund's investments and the broker supplementing his skills by the provision of fund management in specialist areas.

Indeed, changes in the last two Budgets present a challenge to brokers to find suitable venture capital schemes for private and institutional clients. I would also anticipate brokers offering their services for fund management in specialized areas to overseas institutions who lack expertise in certain areas. In short, I see greater not lesser competition between brokers and merchant bankers in this area.

And indeed, competition in this area must be a good thing for the industry. I personally am somewhat frustrated when I am approached by a stockbroking firm for whom I have a high regard who is trying to sell us units in a vehicle to be run by a third party. Often I feel that the stockbroker could do a much better job than the third party but frequently it is not the policy of a stockbroking firm to manage funds in competition with some of their major clients. Indeed, I know that certain parties do discriminate against those stockbrokers who compete with them. I find this questionable and indeed rather sad. To my way of thinking, healthy competition is to be encouraged and speaking as an institutional manager, I know there are some things in specialized fields which we cannot do as well ourselves as outside bodies. I would be doing my own job rather badly if I was so arrogant as not to farm out money for management in those specialized areas.

6. FLEXIBILITY

Brokers will have to respond to a volatile environment, increased competition and a changing customer demand pattern for services by showing greater flexibility. It is perhaps a pity that the Stock Exchange is about to face the OFT inquiry over the next few years—a time when competition will intensify and the need for flexibility will be at a maximum. Being in the footlights of the OFT stage is likely to inhibit flexibility. Quick response to changes in market demand will be slowed down as brokers look over their shoulders to check the likely impact of any changes on their defence submission to the Office of Fair Trading. There is likely to be further rationalization within the stockbroking industry, partly for defensive reasons but also for aggressive reasons as brokers seek to provide a more comprehensive service to their clients, and acquire the ability to respond quickly to changes that take place anywhere in the market place. It can be argued that flexibility will be inhibited by the maintainance of the present commission structure and result in an unjustified degree of complacency. It is interesting to note that several brokers I have spoken to have argued that in any event in real terms commissions are unlikely to rise to keep pace with inflation. If anything, gilt commissions could fall. The fear of a substantial fall in volume on the Stock Exchange as in 74/75 is considerable incentive for brokers therefore to diversify into related areas. I will come back to the commission question later.

7. INTEGRATION BY COOPERATION

There is a greater awareness that in many areas the institutions have mutually interdependent interests with brokers. In some cases, institutions have sponsored, either through soft dollars or hard cash, research for the provision of special services, such as computer programming.In some instances, the client has a commercial contract with the broker, with both parties benefiting from the sale of any resulting end product. I see this type of cooperation growing dramatically, principally for two reasons:

(i)   the broker in some cases has not got the resources to take on by himself the risks involved in some areas of diversification. This risk can be shared by a suitable partner, often an institution with considerable financial resources, and enables a broker to raise his sights in terms of diversification; and

(ii) this form of cooperation is conducive to a marriage of skills. Some brokers have, over the years, formed close associations with insurance companies, pension funds, merchant banks and foreign banks, and other financial institutions. Such associations are likely to show greater meaning in the years to come, as opportunities are seized via cooperative ventures. There are some brokers who are not keen at all to develop such close relationships with institutions. The rules of the Stock Exchange indeed lay down very firm guidelines for such joint endeavours. However, I suspect that under the pressure of market forces these guidelines will be interpreted more flexibly or changed and those brokers reluctant to exploit opportunities in this joint manner will lose out.

8. DEALING

The whole dealing area is going through a period of rapid change. This has been brought about by the activities of foreign brokers and banks in London who have been extremely price competitive, executing contracts on a net basis in foreign deals, and absorbing part of the foreign exchange costs and other arbitrage costs in order to compete effectively with the London market. Institutions are under ever-increasing pressure to perform, and any savings on dealing costs must be beneficial to their overall return. I do not want to spend time on the controversial issue of the present commission structure, but is there any rule which says that a foreign institution, say a well financed U.S. or European market maker cannot make a market in U.K. blue chips, locating himself elsewhere in the E.E.C. if necessary and dealing in blocks directly with the institutions outside the Stock Exchange. And even if the Office of Fair Trading upholds the present commission structure, would such a verdict be acceptable in the E.E.C. under E.E.C. regulations. I suppose I really am asking the question "is the Stock Exchange being short-sighted in defending the existing rule book given that other Governments in the E.E.C. are anxious to make financial centres of their capitals"? I personally am concerned to see London remain the major financial centre in the E.E.C., and I have a great appreciation of the will and determination of other countries in the E.E.C. to compete. Until this issue is resolved, I see increased pressure by the institutions to obtain soft services. And I would like to emphasize one very important point. There is tremendous pressure on institutions to keep costs to a minimum and push up performance. This pressure is very considerable. So brokers must forgive us if we in turn pressurize them. Of course, we need a healthy and financially viable broking community, and we have to find a formula which ensures this while at the same time convincing investors that they are getting full value for money. Judging by the NAPF survey, the present arrangements are not seen as satisfactory in this respect. I have no easy answer to this, I do not believe there is an easy answer. Experience in the U.S. indicates that negotiated commissions cause substantial rationalization but the leading firms can and do adjust to a new environment. On the other hand, I would not like to see a repeat of the stresses and strains in the system which appeared in 74/75 when low volume threatened substantially the healthy competitive environment we have at the moment.

THE OPERATING ENVIRONMENT

I can foresee considerable changes taking place throughout the whole of the maturity spectrum of the yield curve, and short dated investments and long dated investments, whether they be equities or gilts, will be profoundly affected. The factor most likely to cause some volatility at the short end is the changes proposed in the monetary control system by the Bank of England. The Bank stated on 24th November 1980 that its intervention will place greater emphasis on open market operations and less on discount window lending; it also stated that it had been decided that these operations should continue to be conducted in the bill market rather than through the inter-bank market, and in large part through the existing intermediaries i.e. the London discount houses. Concomitant with this, it said that the reserve asset ratio would be abolished. This announcement was followed by a subsequent announcement in March 1981 in which the Bank stated that it is now placing greater emphasis in its money market management on operations in bills rather than in discount window lending. The emphasis on open market operations means that there will remain a need for bill markets of adequate size and depth to provide the paper in which the banks operations will be conducted. Also, the present list of eligible names will need to be extended. These changes in my view are quite profound and inevitably will repercuss on the stock market. In my view, they will mean greater volatility in short term interest rates, have repercussions on short dated gilts and other money market instruments, will repercuss on a variety of local authority short term money market instruments, and will inevitably affect the borrowing costs ultimately of brokers. While the Bank tends to ensure that there should be an adequate availability of funds to enable the giltedged market to continue to function efficiently, those jobbers having to borrow stock may find the cost somewhat higher than it would otherwise have been. In so far as there will be higher volatilty of interest rates than there would otherwise have been, certain equity sectors will be affected probably by a reassessment of their price earning ratios.

The indexed Government bond has in my view opened a Pandora's box. While it may repercuss on the measurement of performance of pension funds, the impact of this bond is likely to be very profound on the insurance industry. It does give a criterion for performance and those who have deferred pensions with insurance companies will naturally be expecting as a minimum return the level of return on this indexed bond. It is difficult at this point in time to say what the impact of this bond will be on long dated gilts and equities, but if more of this type of paper is issued there must inevitably be a reassessment of pension fund investment strategy and a rethink as to the relative merits of equities and bonds. This could mean some price readjustment.

And we must not forget the dangers of crowding out if further substantial amounts of indexed paper are issued.

COMPETITION

I have already mentioned increased competition which I expect to see from foreign banks and foreign brokers. I would also expect to see further changes in the Euro-dollar market with increased pressure from foreign centres to have a larger share of this business and concomitant with this an extension in the type of instruments available. We have already seen the drop-lock floater make some impact on Euro-dollar market. Further changes in my view are inevitable.

Increased volatility in foreign exchange markets is likely to be more pronounced and this could be accentuated by either political strife in a sensitive area of the world or a further hike in energy prices as the world moves out of recession.

As investment power becomes concentrated in fewer hands, users of money will seek increasingly to establish a dialogue with the providers of money and by-pass intermediaries. Indeed, this has already happened, specifically in the property area where financial institutions and industrial and service companies have negotiated directly sale and lease-back deals. It seems to me that intermediaries will have to react to this situation by ensuring that their expertise is first class and that they can provide an essential role in bringing the user and provider together. This may mean developing a further range of skills and in particular having a much more sophisticated corporate financial knowledge. Otherwise, it seems to me that stockbrokers must lose out in competition with the banks in this area. At the same time, it is almost inevitable that the institutions themselves will develop infrastructures capable of appraising such direct investment proposals. In short, the whole environment here will become extremely competitive.

I would also expect to see a demand develop in the very short term for different types of investment instruments. Industry is short of capital and while the institutions are most keen to be active in the primary markets they naturally have to ensure that investments here do meet with their investment criteria. Again, there is a bridge to be built between the providers of money and the users of money and those brokers who can design and construct this bridge efficiently and quickly will obviously do well.

But what about individual stockbroking firms. I still see tremendous heterogeneity within the stockbroking industry. There will always be room for the specialist but if we look at one individual firm, I think it is possible to highlight ten areas where I, if I was a broker, would be concerned in the light of the above.

1. I think inevitably the greater competitive environment which we will have in the coming years will put increased stress upon stockbrokers. (And, incidently, fund managers.) The stockbrokers will have to show greater adaptability and flexibility. (The incidence of heart disease and ulcers among stockbrokers is very high and inevitably will increase.)

2. I think that the earnings picture in the stockbroking industry will become more volatile than they are at the moment. I think many firms must try to diversify into areas where this volatility in earnings can be ironed out and where activities dovetail into each other both in terms of skills available and the income pattern from activities.

3. Against a more competitive environment, I see many firms trying to consumate defensive mergers and the less able firms going to the wall. This is inevitable and is purely a continuation of a pattern that we have seen in the last few years. Contrary to many forecasters, I believe that rationalisation and mergers will continue irrespective of the finding of the Restrictive Trade Practices Court.

4. I believe that the more enterprising stockbroking firms will seek liaisons of one sort or another with other institutions and will diversify into areas where their talents and the financial resources of institutions can be harnessed to provide sensible and meaningful diversification. This means that in fact that stockbrokers probably will be competing increasingly with the merchant banks and extending the range of financial services which they provide.

5. I believe that stockbrokers will continue to emphasize selectivity in their recruitment programme. The introduction of examinations has undoubtedly improved the status of the profession and I see these changes continuing. I did emphasize in my talk that there would be less emphasis upon the talented single entrepreneur and greater emphasis on team activity. This means that the stockbroking firm will consist increasingly of a mix of complementary skills aimed at one specific function in order to give the quality of service which institutions will be demanding in the future.

6. I see as inevitable the growth of specialist departments within stockbroking firms. The emphasis must be on professionalism and emphasis on professionalism in the performance of one specific function.

7. Overseas expansion: this is self explanatory but I do see firms devoting greater effort and resources to expansion of overseas markets with emphasis upon the Pacific Basin area and the U.S. I do not think that Europe will figure very high on the priority list for overseas expansion.

8. The internal structure of stockbroking firms: I think there must be increased emphasis upon rationalising internal structures so as to improve administrative procedures. This would cover such things as the establishment of policy objectives, internal organization, staffing, overall direction, internal co-ordination, reporting systems, budgetary control,

leadership and accountability. I think many firms pay too little attention to what are basic business administrative procedures. This will have to change if a firm is to remain competitive.

9. The mode of dealing with institutions: I think there must be a rethink both on the part of institutions and stockbrokers as to how they communicate and liaise. I think there must be far greater trust and a far better understanding by brokers of the strategy of institutions. Enough has been said on this already.

10. If brokers are to fulfil their natural role in the primary markets, I see a need for much better communications between brokers and industry. This would involve more travelling by both industry and people in the City, and possibly in the longer term the establishment of administrative and research offices in the provinces so that industrial clients can be better served, with the local office performing a bridge between industry and financial institutions, with the stockbroker being the essential catalyst.

MINIMUM COMMISSIONS AND DUAL CAPACITY

I have indicated that the environment within which stockbrokers operate is going to change dramatically in the near future. In particular, I have emphasized three major areas of change, viz. an increase in competition, a possible increase in the volatility of revenue from traditional stockbroking business, and the need to diversify, with increased emphasis on specialization. In short, this means that stockbrokers will have to adjust quite dramatically in a short period of time to dramatic changes in the environment.

This is going to present brokers with a great number of problems. Above all, the sort of changes I have indicated will require not inconsiderable financial resources, particularly when one looks at the cost of setting up overseas offices and establishing specialist areas of development. This may mean the infusion of external capital and possibly the development of new financial structures. And this is one reason why I personally do not favour dramatic change in commission structures in the very near future. Brokers should be given some time to adjust, and I think it is essential for institutional investors that there be adequate competition within the market place. We will have to pay for this. Now I do favour change in the longer term. As brokers diversify and go into new lines of territory, it seems to me that unbundling is essential. And indeed, we have had unbundling at the moment. There are many services which brokers perform which are charged separately, such as for example corporate financial work.

Having said this, however, I think that before customers of the Stock Exchange can pronounce objectively on this question of commissions, we need far more facts. We certainly need data on the break down of revenue and profits as between various activities. For example, to what extent if at all do we subsidise non-stockbroking activities of stockbrokers. And without this data I think it is difficult for us to understand the implications of a radical change in the commission structure, and the impact on the provision of services, such as research services and competition within the stockbroking community.

So yes, I do favour change, but change based upon objective analysis and less upon subjectivity. We have seen a great deal of emotional outbursts on this subject and I think the time has come for a much closer and detailed dialogue between the Stock Exchange and its major customers. If there is to be a monopoly of any sort it should be justified. At the moment, I detect little sympathy with the Stock Exchange on the subject of commissions and dual capacity. But I think we must bear in mind that if we want a service we have to pay for that service and payment should be based upon an objective analysis of available data. And to my mind we should ensure that things are organized in such a way that the efficient do make profits and in my view good profits. Any commission structure should reflect the risks involved in broking while at the same time not making life so cosy that competition is inhibited and rationalization of the industry does not take place.

In the final analysis, we will only get what we pay for. And it seems to me that the results of the survey conducted by the National Association of Pension Funds do reflect my view. There seems to be some acknowledgement that the present system may not be entirely satisfactory. On the other hand, people do want to ensure that brokers' remuneration is such that we do have viability in the system. In addition, I think the consensus view that there should be a minimum level of commission reflects the fact that we do not want to see such a degree of volatility in the earnings of brokers that, given the next downturn, many go out of business to the detriment of competition.

Having said that, I would once again like to emphasize the need for negotiations between consumers and the Stock Exchange in this area. The Chairman of the Stock Exchange is sympathetic to this but for various reasons is emphasizing the need to hasten slowly. It is unfortunate that this whole matter has been referred to the Office of Fair Trading at a time when the whole stockbroking community must change quite dramatically if it is to meet competition. The Office of Fair Trading situation could, as indicated earlier, inhibit change.

On the subject of dual capacity, I believe that in overseas markets we do have limited dual capacity at the moment. My own fund has raised this subject with the Stock Exchange and has tried to establish our own legal status when dealing with firms who are acting as both principals and agents when selling us stock. For example, we have been told by one firm that occasionally, in overseas transactions, they will make up our order as principals if they cannot get adequate stock as agents in the market place.

This has obvious legal significance for a pension fund. I am sure in my own mind that an increasing amount of business is being done outside the stock market because brokers are not currently flexible enough to operate as principals. This business is often executed by merchant banks who can perform the role of arbitrator between a buyer and seller of a big line of stocks or a portfolio of stocks on a negotiated commission basis. Since it is stock market prices which are being used, the losers in the situation must be the Stock Exchange itself. Again, I think a dialogue in this area is essential. I do not believe currently that there is adequate flexibility in the system and somehow we have to introduce adequate flexibility but at the same time ensure an efficient market place. The Stock Exchange has taken upon itself to define what is an efficient market place. I think it is time that we had a much fuller and wider discussion between the Stock Exchange and the users on this.

22 The UK Economy in the Declining Oil Years

G. DAVIES

This article was published in The Investment Analyst *in July 1984.*

Gavyn Davies graduated in economics from St John's College, Cambridge in 1972, followed by two years of research at Balliol College, Oxford. He joined the Policy Unit at 10 Downing Street as an Economist in 1974, and was an Economic Policy Adviser to the Prime Minister in the same organisation from 1976–79.

Since then, he has pursued a career as a City economist, first with Phillips and Drew (1979–81), then with Simon and Coates (1981–86). He joined Goldman Sachs International in April 1986 and became a Partner in November 1988. He is Chief International Economist, responsible for managing the global economics department, and is also Chairman of the Investment Research Department. He has been repeatedly ranked as the City's top UK, European or global economist in surveys of institutional investors over the past two decades. He was a member of HM Treasury's Independent Forecasting Panel, Economic Adviser to the House of Commons Select Committee on the Treasury and a Visiting Professor at the London School of Economics. In July 1998, he received an Honorary Doctor of Science (social sciences) from the University of Southampton. In 1999, he chaired a UK government inquiry into 'The Future Funding of the BBC'.

"Mr Lawson's blunt answer to the question what do we do when the oil runs out is: nothing."

Financial Times, 14 April 1984

Britain's production of North Sea oil is nearing a peak. In eight short years, oil production has risen from virtually nil to around 115 million tonnes a year, and the UK is now the sixth largest oil producer in the world. Oil is worth about £12bn a year to the balance of payments, 5% to the British gross domestic product (GDP) and over £9bn a year to government tax revenue. But these benefits will not last forever. After 1985, the focus of debate will shift away from considering how we *spend* the oil benefits, and will concentrate instead on how we *replace* them. Already, it is being suggested that the non-oil sectors of the economy have been so weakened by the post-1979 recession that they will be unable to replace the output of the declining North Sea fields unless urgent action is taken now.

The government naturally repudiates this view: indeed, the Chancellor sees it as another manifestation of "a national genius for gloom". While not quite going so far as to suggest that the drop in oil output will be a positive advantage, the government believes that it is nothing to get concerned about, and certainly nothing to warrant any change in economic strategy. In a characteristically buoyant analysis of Britain's future in the declining oil years (in a speech at Cambridge on 9 April 1984), Mr Lawson has spelt out his approach in some detail. The speech was divided into four parts: the likely speed of decline of oil production;

the effects of oil on the economy so far; the impact on the economy of declining oil output; and the correct policies for "re-entry". Each of these areas will be considered in turn.

WHAT SORT OF DECLINE?

The government's analysis is based on the belief that the UK experience on the oil down-slope need not be simply a mirror-image of what happened on the way up. Mr Lawson, for example, argues that the shock to the economy represented by the discovery and exploit-ation of oil reserves was exacerbated by three factors in particular: (i) the rapid pace of build-up in production; (ii) the fact that the build-up happened to coincide with a rise of 2½ times in the nominal price of oil from spring 1979 to the end of 1980; and (iii) the fact that it also coincided with a macro-economic stance which was strongly disinflationary. These factors, the Chancellor believes, increased the shock-effect of oil on the economy, but none of them is now expected to work in reverse. Oil production is expected to decline much less rapidly than it built up, no general collapse in real oil prices is expected, and the govern-ment's macro-economic policy stance is intended to be much more stable than it was after 1979. Hence the declining oil years will offer the UK a much more gentle opportunity to adjust to a new situation than did the 1976–81 period.

There is no doubt that this line of argument looks plausible, especially on the govern-ment's central estimates for the likely profile of oil production. These show output rising from 115m tonnes in 1983 to a probable peak in the range 110–130m tonnes in 1985. There-after, production is expected to fall back gradually, reaching 80–115m tonnes by 1988 and 40–90m tonnes in 1993/94. These projections are broadly in line with Simon and Coates' central projections, as Table 1 shows. But how much risk is attached to them?

Basically, there seems little doubt that there *exists* enough hydrocarbon in the North Sea to keep the UK self-sufficient in oil until at least the turn of the century. The Department of Energy has just released new estimates of total reserves, which are considerably higher than those published in 1983. (See Table 2.) The new figures show that total reserves in present discoveries (proven plus probable) amount to 1,950m tonnes, of which 572m tonnes had been produced up to the end of last year. This leaves only 1,378m tonnes still to be pro-duced, which translates into only 12 years of output at the present rate of extraction. (Since consumption is now running at around 72m tonnes, only a little over half the present rate of production, these reserves could ensure a period of self-sufficiency lasting over 20 years if all net exports were eliminated.) However, even these figures are based on proven plus probable reserves, and relate only to existing discoveries. Making allowance for possible reserves in existing discoveries, and for future discoveries in parts of the continental shelf not yet fully explored, it seems likely that a considerable addition to hydrocarbon reserves on top of the proven plus probable reserves will occur. The official range for *total* re-coverable reserves from the continental shelf is 1,980m tonnes to 5,850m tonnes, which translates into a further 17 to 51 years of production at present rates. Most of the increase in undiscovered reserves since last year's estimate has stemmed from a more complete seismic examination of geological characteristics in the North Sea area between 56°N and 62°N. The Energy Department rightly points out that these estimates should be regarded as highly uncertain, since they are in general based on evidence which does not even include returns from exploratory drilling. Against this, however, these are many areas of the UK zone which have not even been subjected to full seismic surveys. It is quite possible that any shortfall in the area between 56°N and 62°N will be offset by substantial finds in the other unassessed areas shown in Table 2.

Many outside economic commentators have tended to assume that the eventual total of reserves recovered will be at the top end of the official range—see for example recent work

TABLE 1. Oil production forecasts^a in millions of tonnes.

	1976	1977	1978	1979	1980	1981	1982	1983	1984	1985	1986	1987	1988	1993/94
Treasury Forecasts made in:														
1976	15–20	35–45	55–70	75–95	95–115									
1977		40–45	60–70	80–95	90–110	100–120								
1978			55–65	80–95	90–110	100–120	105–125							
1979				70–80	85–105	95–115	115–140	115–140						
1980					80–85	85–105	90–120	95–130	95–135					
1981						80–95	85–110	85–115	90–120					
1982							90–105	90–115	95–125	95–130				
1983								95–115	95–125	95–125	85–120			
1984									110–130	110–130	100–125	85–115	80–115	40–90
Outturn	12.2	38.3	54.0	77.9	80.5	89.4	103.2	114.0	–	–	–	–	–	
Simon and Coates Central Forecast									119	119	115	110	109	70

a. Including natural gas liquids (NGLs) and onshore production.

TABLE 2. Department of Energy estimates of initial oil reserves on UKCS.

million tonnes	Estimates made in	
	1983	1984
Fields in production or under development		
Proven	1,375	1,450
Probable	250	225
Possible	225	250
Discoveries not yet fully appraised		
Proven	75	50
Probable	225	225
Possible	400	375
Reserves in future discoveries		
North Sea 56°–62°N	200–750	450–1,900
West of Shetland	25–350	25–350
West of Scotland	0–550	0–550
Other UKCS	0–475	5–475
Totals of initial reserves		
Proven plus probable in		
existing discoveries	1,925	1,950
Possible in existing discoveries	625	625
Potential in new discoveres .	255–2,125	480–3,275
Production to end 1983	572	572

Source: Department and Energy "Brown Book" 1984.

done by Fred Atkinson and Stephen Hall (see note i). This optimism is partly based on exploitation experience elsewhere in the world, and partly on statistical probability distributions of future finds, allowing for the success ratio achieved in the North Sea so far. If this optimism proves justified, then fears of an imminent large decline in production certainly seem unduly alarmist.

Recent events, however, require a reconsideration of this comfortable conclusion. There are two main reasons for this. The profitability of future oil discoveries obviously depends on the price of oil, the tax structure, and the state of technology. Neither the outlook for price, nor for technology, can be accurately predicted. However, the likelihood of any increase in the price in real terms between now and the mid-1990s appears to be becoming more and more remote, both for supply and demand reasons. Furthermore, although technology is improving in continental shelf extraction techniques, the total costs of new fields under development will inevitably be much higher than those of the first few fields discovered mainly because they will be much smaller than the profitable Forties and Brent fields. Examination of the total costs of production shows that in some of the smaller fields now under consideration, capital plus operating costs might amount to at least £10–12 per barrel, compared with roughly £2 per barrel for the Forties field. Although this still leaves scope for profitable extraction, and with a fairly high tax rate, the profit/risk trade-off is clearly changing in a way which is damaging to future exploration and production.

The second major reason for concern is more immediate. At present three fields—Brent, Forties and Ninian—account for roughly half of North Sea production, but their combined total output will begin to fall this year. Other fields are scheduled to come on stream, but none of them is remotely comparable in size to the three fields just mentioned. There will thus be a built-in tendency for output to decline in the latter half of this decade even if a remarkable number of new smaller fields are rapidly brought into development. As the managing director of Shell UK (Exploration and Production) recently commented, around 90 small North Sea oil fields will need to be developed at a cost of more than £50bn if the UK is to be self-sufficient in oil until the turn of the century. With a constant real oil price, this appears somewhat improbable—but more to the point the chances of bringing such production on stream by 1990 are extremely remote.

In consequence, even allowing for the new estimates of reserves, it is now almost certain that total production will decline after 1985 or 1986, at least until the end of the decade. After that, prospects depend on price and technology, and there is an extremely wide range of possible outcomes. It is still just conceivable that production may stabilise or even begin to increase again at some point in the 1990s, but a prolonged tail-off looks much more probable, even on the assumption of stable, or slowly rising, real oil prices.

So far, these conclusions may not appear very different from those of Mr Lawson, and it is hard to disagree with him that the oil down-slope will be less steep than the up-slope. *However, the risks of any major divergence from this comfortable path seem definitely skewed, particularly on the profile for the real oil price.* The Treasury's assumptions on oil prices are shown in Table 3. After a decline of about 6% in the real price over the next five years, there is a highly convenient jump of 13½% in the following five. This latter increase is enough to safeguard the official production profile against the rising costs referred to above, making output profitable even if the average tax-take falls only slightly as smaller fields come on stream after 1988/89. (The Treasury's assumption is that the average tax-take falls by 1½ percentage points a year from 1988/89 to 1993/94.) But what would happen if, instead of rising, the real oil price continued to fall after 1988/89? New fields would become increasingly unprofitable on the present tax system, and average tax rates would presumably need to be reduced to maintain production. This would, of course, mean that the *tax* profile would fall away much more rapidly than the *production* profile, and would substantially undershoot the Treasury's projections shown in Table 3. What is worse, it is far from impossible to imagine shifts in the real oil price which could eliminate profitable production in most new North Sea fields, whatever the tax regime in force at the time. The present margin of spare capacity in the world oil market is probably around 22%, with the still-fragile OPEC cartel producing less than two-thirds of its theoretical capacity. In the last 12 months, during perhaps the most vigorous phase of world economic expansion, OECD oil demand has risen by only 2½%, and part of this can be explained by stock movements. A continuation of rapid OECD growth for many years (or political disruption in a major

TABLE 3. Treasury projections for North Sea output, prices and revenues, 1982/83 to 1993/94.

	1982/83	1983/84 Estimate	1988/89	1993/94
Real North Sea price (1982/83 £/tonne)	145	140	132	150
North Sea Oil and NGL production (million tonnes)	107	118	80–115[a]	40–90
Real value of oil and gas production[b] (1982/83 £bn)	16½	18	15	13
Total NS oil and gas revenues (1982/83 £bn)	8	8½	7½	5½

a. Refers to calendar year 1988.
b. Includes oil, NGL and gas production, and pipeline tariff receipts.
Source: HM Treasury.

producing country) would be needed to eliminate the supply overhang and force a large increase in the *real* oil price at any time in the next 10 years. If there is a dominant long-term risk to the present structure of real oil prices, it is therefore more likely to be on the downside, with a reversal in the world economic cycle, or a further trend reduction in OECD energy demand, being the trigger for unsustainable pressure on the OPEC cartel. Many independent forecasts, like the Treasury's, assume in their central case that this will not happen, and that the real oil price will remain unchanged in the 1985–93 period, with a slight dip in the middle. If so, then the Chancellor will probably be right in arguing that the re-entry from the oil economy will be more gradual than the original launch into it. But there is a large risk, ignored in the government's analysis, of a further trend decline in the real oil price, causing a much more precipitous drop in the opportunities for profitable production in the North Sea; and the government's rather cosy assumption of a cushioned re-entry would then be quickly smashed. This possibility makes it all the more important for the UK to make the most of whatever period of high oil production is left to it.

THE EFFECT OF RISING OIL PRODUCTION

The years in which North Sea oil production was beginning to build up coincided with a period in which the rest of the economy dropped into a prolonged recession, particularly in the manufacturing sector. It is tempting to view these two events as somehow linked, and several authors have in fact blamed the decline in manufacturing output on the arrival of oil production.[1] The argument runs as follows. If balance of payments equilibrium is to be maintained in an economy after the discovery of an exportable natural resource such as oil, those economic sectors which had previously provided the bulk of the economy's exports (mainly manufacturing in the UK) need to shrink as oil exports expand. It has now been clearly established that this argument is valid, but only if applied to the *relative* positions of oil and manufacturing in the economy: as oil increases its relative share of output, the relative position of manufacturing must decline if current account equilibrium is to be maintained in the long-term. However, this need not lead to any reduction in the *absolute* level of manufacturing output, provided that the whole economy grows rapidly enough to offset the sector's relative decline. Furthermore, it is possible to go further than this. If, as in the case of the UK in the 1950s and 1960s, the advent of oil substantially relaxes a balance of payments constraint on output, then it is possible for overall output growth to be boosted so much that manufacturing growth leaps ahead of its long-term trend, despite its declining relative position in the economy.

This certainly has not happened in the post-1979 British economy, as Table 4 shows. In the first three years of sizeable oil production, from 1976 to 1979, the traditional deficit on trade in oil was almost wiped out, and the balance of trade in non-oil products deteriorated accordingly. Although the exchange rate moved up slightly, and UK competitiveness began to deteriorate, there was no absolute decline in the level of manufacturing output: manufacturing and other tradeable goods lost their share of GDP, but continued to expand in absolute terms. After 1979, however, the combination of oil price increases with the advent of a new government led to a much sharper rise in sterling, and to a further deterioration in an already adverse competitive position. At this stage, manufacturing output dropped into a period of absolute decline which was so severe that GDP as a whole also fell, despite a continuing sharp rise in oil output. The existence of oil therefore deflated the non-oil economy, mainly via the exchange rate, and this eventually brought down the level of wage increases and price inflation. Since the declining sectors of the economy were employment-intensive, while the expanding oil sector was not, the aggregate number of jobs fell sharply, and unemployment rose. There was no decline in the economy's appetite for manufactures

TABLE 4. The oil economy.

	1976	1979	1983
Oil output (million tonnes)	12	78	114
Balance of trade in oil (£bn)	–3.9	–0.7	7.1
Indices (1976 = 100)			
Real GDP (O)	100.0	109.1	107.3
Manufacturing output	100.0	102.3	89.0
Energy output	100.0	165.3	190.6
Output per head	100.0	107.5	113.2
Consumers' expenditure	100.0	110.3	115.7
Private investment	100.0	119.6	118.4
Public investment	100.0	77.0	68.5
Real disposable income	100.0	111.8	111.7
Public consumption	100.0	103.1	109.2
Employees (000)	22,524	23,139	21,063
Unemployed (000)[a]	1,249	1,242	2,970
Retail price inflation (%)	16.5	13.4	4.7
Average earnings (%)	19.8	15.5	8.4
£-effective (1975 = 100)	85.7	87.3	83.3
Relative unit labour costs[b]	100.0	123.2	133.8
Import volume of manufactures[b]	100.0	143.0	170.8
Import volume of consumer goods[b]	100.0	144.3	172.8
Output of consumer goods[b]	100.0	105.1	93.1
Non-oil trade balance (£bn)	0.0	–2.7	–7.5
Oil tax as % of GDP	0.0	1.2	3.4
Total tax as % of GDP	39.1	39.6	45.5
PSBR as % of GDP	7.2	6.5	4.0

a. definitional changes have affected this series.
b. 1976 = 100.
Source: Simon and Coates.

but this appetite was translated into imports rather than domestic production, mainly because of the adverse competitive position. From 1976 to 1983, the volume of imported manufactures rose by 70%, but domestic production fell by about 11%. Despite the decline in overall economic activity, which cut non-oil tax revenue, the government was able to reduce the public sector borrowing requirement (PSBR) as a share of GDP at about the same pace as oil revenues climbed. Excluding oil revenues, the PSBR remained roughly constant in proportion to GDP.

After 1979, the government therefore chose to translate rising oil revenues into a reduced rate of price inflation via an appreciation in the exchange rate. Instead of attempting to protect UK output by holding the exchange rate down, fiscal policy and the level of interest rates actually contributed to the rise in sterling which was anyway being induced by oil. The flow of oil revenues into the Exchequer was used almost entirely to reduce public borrowing, rather than as a means of reducing taxation, or increasing public expenditure elsewhere. As the PSBR fell, real interest rates might also have been expected to decline, but instead they contributed further to sterling strength by moving to levels only rarely seen in previous UK history.

Oil was used as a lubricant to ease the impact on the employed labour force of the deflationary shock which the government chose to impart to the system. Without oil, still higher interest rates would probably have been necessary to drive the exchange rate up to the levels required to bring inflation down as sharply as the government desired. Furthermore, in the absence of rising revenue from the North Sea, non-oil taxation would have been savagely increased to bring about the desired cut in the PSBR. If the whole of this tax burden had fallen on the basic rate of income tax, an increase of 9p in the £ compared with the present rate would have been necessary (assuming, unrealistically perhaps, that everything else in the economy would have been unchanged in the absence of oil) to have brought the PSBR down to its present level.

In the Chancellor's Cambridge speech, Mr Lawson admits that the government has so far chosen to use oil revenues to soften the adjustment to the low-inflation, low-borrowing, economy which has now been brought about. However, he also argues that the trend reduction in manufacturing output had started long before the arrival of oil, and he hints that the government had no choice but to allow the economy to slip into recession after 1979 in order to squeeze inflation out of the system. Neither of these latter assertions is incontestable.

First, it is wrong to suggest that Britain's manufacturing industry was in relative decline before the arrival of oil. In virtually every economic cycle from the beginning of the industrial revolution up to and including the early 1970s, manufacturing was the fastest-growing sector in the economy, increasing its share of real output in the UK on a continuous basis; and in no sustained period before 1979 did the level of manufacturing production ever decline. The post-1979 experience has been completely different in type from anything that has gone before, and it is misleading to suggest otherwise.

Second, it is also wrong for Mr Lawson to argue that there was no viable alternative to the policies actually pursued after 1979. Indeed, the 1976–79 out-turn suggests that there *was* available an alternative strategy: holding down sterling by reducing interest rates with the aim of safeguarding the non-oil tradeable sector. Some rise in the exchange rate was probably inevitable after the oil price increases in 1978/79, but its extent and duration could have been minimised, rather than maximised, by changes in interest rates and fiscal policy. The improvement in inflation would then have been much less abrupt, but the level of output would have been much higher throughout the period. The decision to make the maximum short-term gains on inflation, almost whatever the output cost, was a political choice, not one rooted in immutable economic logic.

THE EFFECTS OF NORTH SEA DECLINE

Britain now enters the era of declining oil production with a manufacturing sector which has shrunk in size, and which is not at present capable of supplying the nation's still-strong appetite for manufactured goods. The balance of trade in manufactures has deteriorated from a surplus of £5bn in 1976 to a deficit of £5bn last year, and the trend is still worsening. Furthermore, investment in new capacity has slumped. Allowing for leased assets, new capital formation in manufacturing has dropped by over one-third since 1979 and official estimates of the total capital stock—which are almost certainly too optimistic—show that this new investment has been only just sufficient to offset capital depreciation in the past five years.

These trends will need to be reversed extremely sharply if, as the Chancellor suggests: "It is reasonable to expect that there will be some return to the traditional trade pattern of a surplus in manufacturing and invisibles offsetting deficits in food, basic materials and, eventually, fuel." Although the Chancellor goes on to admit that this will "probably require a real exchange rate somewhat lower than it is today", he does not indicate that any new policy initiatives are necessary to prepare for the shift. In fact, he adopts an extremely relaxed view of the prospects for the economy as oil declines.

This approach seems to be based on three main considerations. First, as noted above, the government believes that the likely rate of decline in oil output will be extremely gradual, offering a long adjustment period for the rest of the economy. Second, the government's overall philosophy prevents them from adopting a more direct interventionist policy to ease the industrial transition in any case—their laissez-faire approach requires this to be left to the market. Third, the oil era has in one very significant way helped to cushion the economy from the re-entry problem. Since the end of 1978, the counterpart of the oil-induced current account surplus has been a large capital account outflow which has resulted in direct acquisitions of overseas assets of more than £18bn. Exchange rate changes and capital gains have boosted the value of the UK's net overseas assets by still more than this—in fact by about £30bn between 1978 and 1982. Before the peak of oil production is reached in 1985, the overall increase in net overseas assets may exceed £40bn.

Assuming that long-term inflation in the world runs at 6–7%, and that the real rate of return on financial assets amounts to 2–3%, then the UK can look forward to a permanent nominal income flow of around £4bn a year from these assets. While Mr Lawson is certainly right to point to this as a major gain, its importance should not be over-emphasised. It represents less than one-third of the annual contribution of oil to the balance of payments. Furthermore, it is extremely small compared with the UK's total import bill—under 6% of this year's likely visible imports. Consequently, even if Britain's propensity to import has been only very marginally damaged on a permanent basis by the low level of capital investment at home since 1979, the impact of this deterioration could comfortably swallow up the income gains from £40bn of extra foreign assets, leaving the overall balance of payments no better prepared to face the period of declining oil production.

In fact, even from the point of view of balance of payments security in the long term, Britain may have been better off diverting its extra £18bn of direct investment into *domestic* fixed capital formation, rather than the acquisition of foreign assets. In the past, some economists have argued against doing this on the grounds that the real rate of return on foreign financial assets is likely to exceed that on domestic fixed capital. This in itself is questionable. However, it should also be borne in mind that maximising the rate of return is not necessarily the only objective to aim for: the need to promote high output and high employment is also important. If £18bn over four years had been diverted from foreign to domestic investment, gross domestic fixed capital formation could have been sustained at levels roughly one-fifth higher than actually occurred from 1979 onwards; and the total outstanding net capital stock (excluding dwellings) would by now have been boosted by roughly 3½% compared with the level actually attained. Making the (heroic) assumptions that the capital/output and capital/employment ratios would have been left unchanged by this addition to the capital stock then about ¾ million new jobs, and a continuing flow of extra output worth £10bn a year, could have been created. Roughly 40% of this would have needed to have been diverted into exports (or import substitution) to have provided the same balance of payments gains which have instead been derived from the income flows on overseas assets.

All this, of course, is based on the belief that a practical choice existed in terms of economic management options between investing at home and overseas. In order to have accomplished the switch towards domestic investment, it is almost certain that exchange controls would have been necessary throughout the period, and that a more expansionary fiscal/monetary stance would have been needed to ensure a competitive exchange rate. Some direct public sector role in investment creation would probably also have been required. Since these policy changes would probably have involved a worse inflation outturn than actually occurred, it is not surprising that they failed to commend themselves to the present administration.

POLICIES FOR RE-ENTRY

Many of the same policy choices discussed above still present themselves. On the government side, there is a strong belief that no major policy changes are needed now to prepare for the expected gradual re-entry from the oil economy. The existing combination of a basically tight fiscal stance with continuous moves towards economic de-regulation and privatisation is, the Chancellor believes, the best way of promoting the flexibility that will be required eventually to replace oil with flourishing new industries. Not surprisingly, the government's critics take a different view. They find it incomprehensible that domestic investment and employment have been allowed to slump just when the government has been given the resources to improve both through direct action. They argue that the decline in oil output may well be much sharper than the official projections suggest, and that the government has a direct responsibility for promoting alternative industries with the utmost urgency. This requires a series of policy changes: a more expansionary fiscal and monetary stance, a more competitive exchange rate and a higher level of public investment are normally among the minimum recommendations.

This policy debate obviously extends well beyond the narrow subject of oil, and indeed it covers the whole battleground of macro-economics. But the eventual need to replace a wasting asset brings an old debate into sharper focus, and makes its implications still more important for us all.

NOTES

(i) Hall, S. G. and Atkinson, F. *Oil and the British Economy*. Croom Helm, London, 1983. The approach used by these authors is to estimate a relationship between oil discoveries and search activity, which (as expected) produces a declining marginal product as search activity progresses. By extrapolating this declining marginal product into the future, the authors conclude that the official estimates of oil reserves are probably on the conservative side.

REFERENCES

1. Forsyth, P. J. and Kay, J. "The Economic Implications of North Sea Oil Revenues". **Fiscal Studies**, 1980.

23 The Missing Link

J. A. Miller

This article was published in The Investment Analyst *in July 1984. Jonathan Miller writes: It might be worth noting that the article was justified in its differentiation between broking and market making functions and justified also in pointing to the risks of over-capacity. It completely failed, however, to appreciate the dynamic effects of the opening of the market and the enormous increase in the volume of business that would follow Big Bang. Nonetheless, the issues raised on the role of brokers, dealers and central markets are very much alive in 1999 – if not more than ever alive with the growth of parallel dealing channels and the proposed regional mergers of stock exchanges*

Jonathan Miller was for 7 years an investment manager with the Sun Life Assurance Company of Canada, working in London and Montreal. He was 19 years with Fielding, Newson-Smith & Co., until it was acquired by the National Westminster Bank in 1986. For the last 10 years he has specialized in consulting on securities market development. In 1990, he was joint founder of GMA Capital Markets, where he was Managing Director until 1994; since then, he has been a freelance consultant. He has worked in over 30 countries, about half of them being transition economies of eastern and central Europe and the former Soviet Union; the remainder being in western Asia, southern Europe, Latin America, and Africa.

He was a Council Member of the SIA/IIMR for over 20 years, and from 1984 to 1986 he was a member of the Council of the London Stock Exchange. In 1988, he served on the Dearing Committee, which created the present framework for setting UK accounting standards. His publications include Dictionary of Financial Regulation *(Stock Exchange Press, 1989).*

Since this note was written there have been a number of fresh developments, notably the publication of the Stock Exchange Discussion paper in April 1984 which states that "almost everybody doubts that it (single capacity) can survive after the abandonment of fixed commission". Nevertheless, there is a case for continuing to question popular presuppositions, especially when an increasing amount of money is riding on them. There is still time to undertake the investigations necessary to validate or discredit them and to ensure that the foundations of a new market structure are properly constituted. There is no excuse for not attempting serious analysis of a subject upon which the livelihood of so many people depends.

At the heart of the current debate on the transformation of the securities market and the securities industry is the belief that there is a Link between abolition of fixed commissions charged by brokers and the maintenance of single capacity which separates jobbers as principals from brokers as agents. The announcement in the autumn of 1983 that fixed commissions would be abandoned by the end of the calendar year 1986 has precipitated a flood of recommendations to make other changes and has triggered a capital inflow from non-member to Stock Exchange member firms.

The purpose of this note is to argue that the Link between commission and capacity is not anything like strong enough to warrant the scale of changes being put forward and that, in fact, the pressure to introduce new practices in market-making has a different provenance. If it is accepted that this is so, then market-making reform need not be seen as **contingent** on commission reform and therefore the two may proceed in a properly, orderly manner along parallel paths. This, in turn, must be far more in everyone's interest than the terrible muddle towards which we now seem to be heading.

It must be stressed that the case put forward is entirely dependent on estimates of the relative scale of broking commissions and jobbing income. If the estimates are substantially wrong then the case fails. If they are right, the current conventional wisdom must be called into question. If nothing else, it is hoped that the presentation of a counter argument will stimulate the release of information which is essential to sensible commercial planning.

THE ECONOMICS OF THE LINK

The reason for the widespread misconception of the Link is the absence of financial information. Stock Exchange partnerships have always been reticent about their affairs and the reference of the Rule Book to the Restrictive Practices Court made them more so. The 1981 Commission Review, for example, which purported to justify higher commissions is a model of obscurity. The Stock Exchange Fact Sheet may say much about the market but it says precious little about the exchange. Perhaps it is natural that brokers and analysts should be more inclined to analyse other people's businesses than their own. At all events, there is not much to go on.

There is, however, something. At the simplest level, the clients have indicated and are indicating that they think Stock Exchange commissions are too high and that they support too much capacity. It is all Lombard Street to a China Orange that they intend to pay Stock Exchange members less as soon as they get the chance. It must therefore be assumed that the values of the market for broking services will contract. From this it is inferred, through a series of nonsequiturs, that brokers will have to take up jobbing and vice versa.

The Stock Exchange itself has contributed to this misconception by mentioning it as a possible line of argument in the RPC case; the implication was that separation of capacity was integral with proper supervision of the market and that deregulating commissions would threaten to impair the protection of investors. Interestingly, the arguments which originally justified the commission scale, when it was introduced in 1912 were quite different. At that time the Stock Exchange said "it is impossible to fully enforce the rule restraining a dealer [i.e. a jobber] from dealing with a nonmember if he is able to employ a broker at a nominal remuneration to pass his bargain through."

The current reasoning hinges on the economics of broking rather than the inclination of brokers and jobbers corruptly to collude. To quote from a leading commentator[1] ". . . it seems to me that there will, upon the introduction of negotiated commissions for domestic securities, be inadequate profitability for continuance of the disciplined acceptance of single capacity." This can only mean that either there are economies from integrating brokers and jobbers to reduce costs sufficiently to make the whole system viable or that brokers will have to recoup their losses from commission by taking a market-maker's turn at the expense of jobbers.

One can say with some assurance that there are no great economies from integration because the two types of business provide different services. There may well be some savings in overhead and settlement, but sales, research and making books would continue to require their own specialised personnel. It is clear from the reduction in the number of jobbing firms over many years that there are economies of scale in jobbing which make the small jobber, and by extension, the small broker/market-maker, non-viable.

On the revenue side, when assessing whether there is enough reward in market-making to offset reductions in agency commission, the position is less clear, though there are some clues. Chief among these is the article by John Robertson, Senior Partner of Wedd, Durlacher, Mordaunt & Co. in the July 1983 issue of *The Investment Analyst*. There he said that the average net turn on equity books was 0.11% and that on gilts 0.018%. Applying the former figure to the turnover in equities in the year to March 1983, implies a jobbing income of £50m. The broking income in the same period can hardly have been less than £350m. Of that broking income, about a third (on the basis of a private inter-form comparison) would have been generated by institutional business. (It has to be recognised here that, though institutions represent over half the turnover in equities, they enjoy much lower levels of commission on their bargains.) Clearly, if brokers are to suffer a reduction in commission scales sufficient to eliminate their profits (say 25% across the board) they would need to capture all the jobbing return to maintain their revenue and they would have to do so at zero cost to maintain their profits. To put it another way, if institutional commission averages 0.4% and if the jobbers net turn averages 0.1%, a 25% reduction in institutional commission equates with the market-maker's value added. However one looks at it, and whatever reservations one may have about the estimates, it is clear that there is not enough money in equity market-making to compensate for any serious level of commission cuts.

That said, the Link, in respect of equities, is discredited, save for the proposition that the clients would be willing to see an increase in the dealing turn as a counterpart to a reduction in commission. All things are possible, but it would be extraordinarily eccentric of the customers to insist on substitution of covert charging once price controls were removed for overt charging when they were in place.

THE CAPITAL MARKET COMMITTEE

The CMC in a paper issued in November 1983 produced variations on the Link argument, which concluded that there was a sufficiently strong presumption of connection to demand preparations for change in capacity simultaneous with a "big ban" on deregulation of commissions. Five interlinked arguments were produced:

(a) Investment houses . . . will be able to obtain stock from or sell stock to the market through a broker whose commission might be negotiated down to a very low level . . . This could enable investment houses outside the market to quote more favourable net prices to clients than could be quoted by brokers acting as agents and if this occurs the likelihood is that brokers will at once demand to be able to act in a dual capacity.

(b) Under the system of negotiated commissions, brokers may well come under compelling competitive pressure to preserve their business and make up for reduced margins by trading as principals . . . Once this happens and brokers start intervening by trading as principals with clients (for example, taking for their own account as principals the unmatched position of a block trade between two clients), jobbers will be prevented from transacting all the business of a centralised market.

(c) We do not think it would be possible to preserve the system of single capacity effectively by legislation against a background of these commercial pressures without an elaborate statutory structure.

(d) [If brokers are required to bring one side of every bargain on to the market and] if such requirements were to apply only to Stock Exchange members with commissions fully negotiable, it seems virtually certain that a parallel market involving principals quoting keener prices would soon develop outside the Stock Exchange.

(e) ... In the interval between the introduction of negotiated commissions and the end of the present single capacity system ... investment houses [outside the Stock Exchange], the most heavily capitalised of which are foreign, would probably obtain a large part of the business available.

Argument (a) presumably relates to argument (e). It is saying that, for example, Prudential Bache will trade through a "deep discount" broker to provide a cheaper service to the ultimate investor than that offered by the ordinary Stock Exchange broker, with the further implication that negotiated commissions will reduce both the price of the ordinary Stock Exchange broker's services and the volume of business available to him. The intensity of this pressure triggers argument (b) that brokers will be compelled to make up margins by trading as principals. Given that they cannot be adequately compensated by the rewards of *market-making*, their profits as principals must derive from *position taking* — trading for their own account — though the second part of (b) associates this with block-trading, which is identical in form but not necessarily in objective. (The block-trader positions stock on unmatched bargains as an adjunct to conducting a broking business, the position taker does it for its own sake.) It is well known that block trading in the US is not particularly profitable over time and it must be a delusion to presuppose that it would restore to broking margins here if they come under pressure from outside competitors who can provide a cheaper service and who are doubtless block-traders themselves. That is the logic of the situation, though it does not remove the desire of brokers to become block trading principals.

Even supposing that block trading positioning were adequately profitable, the implications would be perverse. The clients would be paying more than at present because satisfactory trading profits for the intermediaries would replace unsatisfactory jobbing profits and there would be a cross subsidy between those profits and broking commission. This both resurrects the "covert charging" argument mentioned earlier and raises the general point that if commissions are to be subsidised, why should it be by one activity rather than another — particularly an activity which is likely to be risky to the point of imprudence and intensely competitive.

PUT-THROUGHS

The answer lies in the existing artificiality of the put-through rules, a source of perennial irritation which at the margin increases the cost of bargains, quantifiably, as a trade-off against the non-quantifiable benefit of a central market. Jobbers gain from the put-through rules to a small extent from the turn they charge and to a much larger extent from the opportunity to acquire cheap stock and to be fully informed of what is going on. If put-throughs were conducted outside the market the turn on the remaining business would have to be bigger. This problem exists whether commissions are fixed or negotiable but, like so many other things, is generally thought to be integral with the "big bang" on commissions, partly because of US experience and partly because of inadequate information.

In the US commission deregulation was followed by a big increase in block-trading activity, but the circumstances were different. Dual capacity was already in place and, more important, there was no stamp duty. Furthermore, the broker/dealers would cross subsidise block-trading from their substantial retail businesses.

ADR'S

An extension of the US argument has been created by the expatriation of dealing in UK stocks into ADR's, which was initiated by the growth of US investment in UK securities.

The creation of a pool of US-owned stock naturally led to local trading and it was not long before UK investors spotted that they could participate too and not have to pay stamp duty. The CMC said that £335m of revenue had been lost to the UK in 1983/84 as a result of this, though "revenue" was not defined.

With or without negotiated commissions, the ADR threat would remain, being almost entirely dependent on stamp duty (the contribution of commission differentials between US and UK brokers being relatively small, particularly if the continuation concession is taken into account). ADR's are not of themselves a reason to alter capacity, but if they precipitated the abolition of stamp duty the position would change. (The ADR issue deserves fuller consideration, but that would extend well beyond the limits of this note.)

Abolition of stamp duty would remove the main barrier to competition with equity jobbers. Outsiders could make books on competitive terms. For non-put-through business, this would do no more than threaten the preservation of the central market. Brokers, or other intermediaries would continue to "broke" but would check their prices among a wider and different set of market-makers. Put-through business would rise as traders could "arbitrage" between stocks on much better terms and, it is asserted, brokers would therefore have to take stock on their own books to lubricate this business when buyers and sellers were not matched.

Before pursuing this argument, it must be emphasised that put-throughs are pre-eminently a "broking" activity because they require a major servicing capability which can find counterparties to an initiating order. Dual capacity only arises when orders are unmatched. Then the question is whether it would be more efficient for the broker to run his own book to accommodate the balancing long or short position, or whether he should lay-off with someone else in the market. It would be extraordinary if, even if he did run his own book, there were not many occasions when he did not lay-off elsewhere. If so, and assuming that the bulk of the business were matched anyway, the importance of "capacity" would be diminished to the issues of positioning as such, which has already been commented on, and the advantages of having the option to charge for services either via a commission or via a turn.

PRACTICALITIES

In practice it seems that the authorities would be reluctant either to abandon stamp duty revenue or to sanction a proliferation of "fair-weather" market-makers. In this latter prohibition they may well be wrong because, though the fair-weather brigade are thought to be the bane of the Eurodollar market, they do not seem to have done any harm to Wall Street.

If only "all-weather" market-makers are to be allowed and if they are to be afforded dual capacity, there will be a very powerful force for recartelisation of the Stock Market in fewer hands. The well-signalled direction of impending change has already stimulated large entities to prepare for entry into the market at a level of commitment that would not deter them from short term losses. Simultaneously, the small fry are being frightened into amalgamation with other big fish. Once the new generation of participants recognise that they cannot force their peers out of business by price competition there will be every incentive for them to discipline their price-setting because, in a high fixed-cost industry, everyone suffers from marginal cost renegades.

THE GILT MARKET

So far comment has been aimed almost entirely at the equity market which accounts for the bulk of the income of Stock Exchange members as a whole and in which single capacity is entrenched by stamp duty. Feelings run just as high, if not higher, in the gilt-market and the pressures for change are just as strong.

The position there, however, is less clear because it is dominated by the Bank of England and because it is less easy to derive turn and commission values from turnover data. Grossing up the Stock Exchange "Charge for General Services", which is a percentage of total chargeable revenue of member firms, indicates total income of £560m for 1982/83. If equities accounted for £400m of that, all other forms of activity generated £160m, the lion's share of which would have been in gilts. Jobbing in gilts is said to be more profitable than jobbing in equities so the balance between broking and jobbing revenues is probably less extreme than in equities. On the other hand, gilt jobbers do benefit from a special relationship with the Bank of England and the rewards to a broker from entry into market-making would depend on how that evolved. The Bank has made it clear that it does not feel that it can ignore the applications of experienced and well capitalised financial houses to deal direct with it and make markets in giltedged stocks, especially if single capacity is not maintained in other parts of the market. It now envisages the creation of a body of "primary dealers" analogous to those operating in the US market.

These views do not appear to flow directly from the perception of the Link presumed in equities, still less from a desire to remedy assumed deficiencies in the present method of operation. They are, rather, a continuum of the spirit of change evident in the equity market. Arguably, if the latter were to be discredited, the Bank might modify its policy. Either way, the reform of the gilt market remains at the discretion of the authorities and independent of ordinary commercial considerations.

THE WEAK LINK

Having established that there is no necessary connection between commission and capacity, it should not be concluded that there is no link at all. There is obviously a link in most people's minds which will drive their commercial decisions. If one is in an industry in which one area of activity is contracting, it is only natural to look for another into which to divert resources and maintain income. There must therefore be a link between reduced commissions and the pace of diversification.

CONCLUSIONS

In fact, the dynamics of the Link do not flow from commission, they flow from capacity. Brokers, frustrated by the put-through rules, want to be able to cross stock within their own offices and take positions to lubricate the flow. Legislators and others, keen to create a City environment in which large internationally competitive businesses are seen to grow and prosper, recognise that single capacity inhibits the amalgamations that they desire. Professional investors, impatient with the limitations to liquidity of a jobber controlled market want to see the introduction of more market-making capacity. Officials in the Department of Trade and the Bank must accommodate the joint pressures of the politicians and the commercial community. The Stock Exchange's capitulation on minimum commissions is, therefore, not so much a reason for changing the capacity rules as a catalyst for allowing all the external forces to become effective.

It may well seem rather petty and irrelevant to dispute the causal direction of commission to capacity or capacity to commission, but it does have important practical consequences. For a start, there is a timetable on deregulation of commissions. If the Link works from there, it will be necessary to make capacity reform simultaneous.

This creates two sets of risks. The first, and less important, is that the regulators will make a mess of doing too much at once. The second is that a large and unnecessary injection of capacity is brought into the broking system — because people believe that brokers should also be jobbers — just when it ought to contract. In the end the securities industry's charge for its services will reflect its average costs plus some margin. If the costs of the industry have been irrationally increased by surplus capacity which is sufficiently strongly backed not to be squeezed out by a few years bad trading, the public will end up paying more than they ought. In equities therefore the cure from the public's standpoint could be worse than the disease.

REFERENCE

1. . . . Richard Lloyd, Chief Executive and Deputy Chairman of Hill Samuel Ltd.

24 Macroeconomic Forecasting Models and Investment Analysis: A Review

P. STONHAM

In this article published in The Investment Analyst *in January 1986, Paul Stonham of the European School of Management in Oxford reviewed 21 major forecasting services of the UK economy in the light of the needs of investment analysts and fund managers.*

INTRODUCTION

This paper looks at 21 major organisations forecasting the UK economy, including the OECD, which is international. A list of those included is shown in the Appendix, together with details of their publications. The intention is to review the extent to which these forecasting models are of real assistance to investment analysts and fund managers. The emphasis is less on accuracy of prediction, important though it is, than on the kind of forecast provided, which is a function of the structure, detail and underlying assumptions of the models. All of the formal models are econometric in design, and computerised, but vary in such aspects as size (in terms of number of equations and variables), assumptions made, element of judgement, time horizon, and objectives (e.g. forecasting or policy-making).

THE MODELS

One can distinguish between institutions using large-scale macroeconometric models for forecasting, policy analysis, and testing economic theories, and other organisations, mainly stockbrokers, using quantitative techniques and smaller models to analyse and evaluate securities markets. The latter are characterised by more detailed treatment of financial and monetary sectors and by a wider-ranging input of assumptions and judgements. From the viewpoint of investment analysis, the interesting questions are the following: do the results of first group have relevance *per se* to portfolio management decisions? Or, at the other extreme, is it better directly to model securities markets and relationships in them e.g. to apply quantitative techniques to a formal asset allocation model of investment?

The larger models include Cambridge Econometrics, City University Business School, CBI, Data Resources Inc. (Europe), Henley Centre for Economic Forecasting, Scicon (the ITEM Club), Liverpool University Research Group in Macroeconomics, London Business School, NIESR, OECD, Oxford Economic Forecasting, and the HM Treasury Macroeconomic Model.

Smaller and less formal models with more specifically detailed components like the financial or companies sector include the stockbrokers Capel Cure Myers, Grieveson Grant, Hoare Govett, James Capel, Lang and Cruickshank, Phillips and Drew, Rowe and

Pitman, Simon and Coates, and Wood MacKenzie. The Society of Business Economists does not have a model, but produces regular UK economic forecasts based on questionnaires and consensus opinion.

The distinction between large and small models, in terms of size, is rather artificial. For instance, the Liverpool model has less than 20 behavioural equations and just over 50 variables. Cambridge Econometrics' Multisectoral Dynamic Model uses 5,000 equations, mainly because of the large number of individual industries and commodities it identifies. Phillips and Drew employ 86 equations and 100 variables, about half are exogenous. The Treasury model, with detailed treatment of the public sector, has 1,000 variables and 700 equations, although as the Treasury explains[1] size does not necessarily mean theoretical complexity. Naturally these numbers are constantly changing as the models are developed.

All the larger models describe relationships between variables in a mathematical way, and typically solve for variables like unemployment and wages, government spending, total output, prices, tax revenues, interest and exchange rates. The equations that determine these variables differ from model to model, and are specified by the interpolation of historical data and judgement about behaviour. A North Sea oil sector is nearly always included as a sub-model.

The major models are Keynesian in outlook (except Liverpool) and have a particular view of the causality of unemployment, output, and inflation. This says the economy is demand-driven, spending plans are realised, and markets cleared by changes in demand. Prices are cost-based. Private spending depends on income, not wealth, employment on output, and trade is demand-determined. Inflation is cost-based, and the exchange rate is endogenously determined by relative prices, interest rates, and the money supply, as main factors.

These assumptions about equations and variables, with adjustments for time, and judgements about exogenous and endogenous causality, are statements about how the economy is believed to behave. Five of the six ESRC-supported models, perhaps the most well-known large ones, are similar in this respect (Cambridge; CUBS; LBS; NIESR; Treasury).[2] Liverpool takes a different view of money. This model takes a "rational expectations" view of behaviour in which the general public behaves as if it was already aware of the framework and assumptions of the forecasting model. It is monetarist, in that the money supply influences inflation, not costs, wealth not income determines private spending, and interest rates and prices clear markets.

The Treasury model is worth describing in more detail, it is a very large quarterly model, and can be accessed by smaller models (e.g. members of the ITEM Club). It conforms to the national income identity. Final spending is demand-determined, with consumption split into durables and non-durables to differentiate the effects of changes in wealth, income and interest rates. Final consumption and public sector fixed investment are largely exogenous; industrial fixed investment depends on lagged output and nominal interest rates. Imports and exports are determined by relative competitiveness – prices, profitability and demand. In the labour market, employment and wages are specified differently; the former depends solely on wages, the latter on a range of supply and demand factors. Prices are mainly mark-ups on cost, and the exchange rate equation includes expected future values, the uncovered differential, and residual flows. In the monetary sector of the economy, sectoral financial surpluses and deficits generated elsewhere are allocated, together with stocks, between financial assets and liabilities. Among four financial sectors, the non-bank private sector is critical in producing net financial wealth. The supply of money (£M3) is demand-determined, and interest rates connected by mark-ups. The general level of interest rates is fixed either exogenously, or endogenously on the money supply.

FORECASTING

Assessing the success of forecasting models is not straightforward. The simplest way is to compare forecasts with actual outcomes. This is done periodically in the Financial Times, for example, and a "league table" is drawn up comparing forecasts by institutions with outcomes for variables like gross domestic product, consumer spending, exports, inflation and unemployment. Or, it can be done rather more scientifically[3], by ensuring consistency in information available to models, and explaining difficulties in forecasts in terms of judgements made, decisions about exogenous inputs, and differences arising from the structure and assumptions of the models themselves. The Financial Times, in July 1985, published a table of forecasts for 1984 and divergences from actual outcomes. The method used was to calculate percentage errors. As an average of major variables considered, e.g. GDP, consumer spending, and exports, the results varied widely from 5% for LBS to 47% for the Treasury, out of the 22 forecasts considered. Rather than evaluating the forecasts, Wallis[2] considered the variations between the six forecasting groups made in 1983 for periods up to 1991–95. They show great divergence in outturns between groups, even allowing the differences in assumptions about major exogenous variables and the role of judgement in assumptions about projected equation residuals. The main explanation appears to lie in their respective economic structures. Simulating shocks in exogenous variables, and allowing for time feedbacks to compare the overall properties of the models, also showed divergence in model responses. Barker[3] compared annual *ex ante* forecasts of recession and recovery made by non-government UK groups modelling the economy between 1979 and 1982 for variables like prices, production and unemployment. He concluded that no group was systematically better or worse than any other group, and that each tended to perform better in their chosen area of specialisation e.g. medium-term forecasting. In an OECD study[4] of years 1966–1982, annual forecasts of GNP for member countries were about half within one percentage point of the outcome and one-quarter between one and two percentage points – fairly comparable to national forecasts.

The weaknesses of these econometric models are fairly well known. Inadequate data, changing patterns of economic behaviour, the pitfalls of "data mining" (searching long enough for data to fit observed behaviour), little knowledge of the effects of forecasting information on expectations and therefore behaviour, lack of basis in fact for theoretical presumptions, and inability to cope with "shocks". Although some model relationships seem reasonably stable, like the consumption function and prices, others, like capital investment and interest rates, are quite the opposite. These, and other defects, contribute to popular doubts about the forecasting qualities of macroeconometric models.

Although reliable real quantity forecasts can assist investment analysts, more detailed financial and company sector modelling would be even more helpful. But it is not advanced in this group of macroeconomic models. In some, like NIESR, monetary aggregates play a behavioural role; here Sterling M3 is an influence on personal sector liquidity and therefore consumption. In others, like LBS, there is a detailed financial sector; here forecasts for all financial balances and for UK and US dollar short rates are fed from the main LBS model to its financial model as exogenous. There are 9 financial asset-holding sectors, and 17 types of financial asset stock variables. Each sector is assigned asset demand equations, and simple supply equations. Asset prices clear markets for the exchange rate, equities and gilts. The CUBS model, by contrast, has no monetary sector, and the exchange rate is exogenous. Britton[5] believes that monetary sector modelling will not develop until it can really be shown that financial variables influence spending; models of bank lending, currencies and public sector debt are, as yet, primitive. The company sector is everywhere treated inadequately, so that company financial decisions cannot be modelled. Most variables in the sector are obtained as residuals.

WHAT DO INVESTMENT ANALYSTS REQUIRE?

Investment analysts will look to macroeconometric models for forecasting results. This is the main weakness, they are policy-orientated and therefore concerned with very broad aggregates, like unemployment. Forecasts are not primarily aimed at matching outturns, since the purpose of many models is to provide a forecast with assumptions made about relationships and the behaviour of variables, and taking positions about the conduct of policy.

Stockbroker research is typically fundamental analysis, although it often takes a technical view as well. Most of the variables in macroeconometric models are of interest, from real GDP, inflation and outputs of main sectors, through consumption, investment and stocks, trade, labour market, oil, prices, trade and payments, to financial assets. PBSR, taxes and interest rates. The relevance of accurate forecasts of such aggregates is clear; what is less clear is the quantitative impact on portfolio or individual stock valuations way down the line. For example, reliable estimates of the exchange rate will influence short-term interest rates and interest rate differentials, which enter equations for capital flows and external finance. Such estimates will also influence views of investors on the possible capital gains to be obtained from investment in particular currencies. Estimates of UK and world inflation affect corporate profitability and the company sector financial balance through import/ export prices; corporate profitability affects manufacturing investment and stock building and so on.

Analysts are ultimately interested in risk/return assessment of securities investment and the fundamentals of stock appraisal. For government bonds, the aggregates, particularly monetary ones, of macro-models, are critical – exchange rate, PSBR, interest rates and differentials, balance of payments, inflation, and the trend in industrial production – are all relevant to low risk investment. Forecasting gilt yields must pay attention to possible changes in monetary and tax policy. The process is apparently simple, since there are fewer variables to consider than for equities, the variables are aggregated, and bonds are homogenous. The government is a monolithic borrower whose financial position is measured in easily available data, and whose policy may have some consistency.

The position is different in equities. Here, analysts and fund managers may be interested in large, diversified portfolios where market risk and therefore the influence of highly aggregated macroeconomic variables is important. But ultimately analysts are interested in security earnings and dividends. For small portfolios or individual stocks there is difficulty in relating market-wide factors such as inflation, GDP, or interest rates to earnings or dividend predictions, or to other balance-sheet information. The synthesis of this information is more likely to occur on the basis of qualitative judgement than formally through econometric relationships. A recent study by Chugh and Meadow[6] of 2,000 members of the US Financial Analysts Federation showed that some macroeconomic variables were used in the stock evaluation process. This was due in part to analysts emphasising the long-over the short-term economic and financial performance of a company. In the long run, analysts emphasised (1) expected change in earnings per share (2) expected return on equity (3) prospects for the relevant industry. In the short-run, the three most important variables were (2) and (3) above, plus general economic conditions; also, economic and industry conditions figured more than financial statement data. Company-specific data assumed greater importance in the long-run. In any period, earnings-related data was taken more seriously than dividend-related. Within the more important long-term perspective, analysts looked to qualitative factors like quality of management, market dominance and ability to achieve stated corporate goals, as critical in influencing the effects of quantitative financial and economic variables. Companies were appraised overall rather than by reference to any specific measure or event.

UK BROKER FORECASTING

Amongst brokers in the UK, macroeconometric modelling practices are generally smaller scale than those described so far. They vary from one which accesses the Treasury Economic model as a forecasting input to additional forecasting capability (Capel Cure Myers) to others which rely on own models plus large measures of judgement (e.g. Phillips and Drew, Simon and Coates). One, Wood Mackenzie, specifically operates stock valuation models.

A typical forecasting service (Simon and Coates) publishes monthly, one-year, economic forecasts based on a mixture of econometric equations and judgement. In these forecasts, UK aggregates include final demand divided between private/government spending, fixed capital investment/stockbuilding and exports. GDP and imports, industrial production, unemployment, prices and earnings, current foreign payments balance, and bank base rates complete the picture. Industrial output is broken down by sector. Disaggregated forecasts are then made for categories of UK domestic demand, inflation, balance of payments, and monetary variables. For the company sector, financial balances and profits are forecast. Forecasts for the equities and gilts markets are based on this econometric background and focussed down with qualitative comment on equity market sectors, general equity market ratings, fundamentals, market psychology and recommendations for investor strategy. Similarly macro-forecasts plus judgement on PSBR, bank lending and taxes, for example, allow comment to be made on the gilt market. North Sea oil production and revenue is also modelled, and forecasts made of Sterling competitiveness and major developed countries' GNP, industrial production, and consumer prices. An international portfolio strategy is mainly qualitatively based (markets/currencies) and accompanied by historical statistical data on equity indices, money market rates and bond yields, with forecasts for a range of exchange rates and nominal and real interest rates. Forecasts are then made for major economies like the US with comment on prospects for equities, sometimes highlighting good value stocks.

This blend of econometric forecasting and judgement is common to other brokers' forecasting. Institutional members of ITEM use the Treasury Model, but also determine input as a group, using a range of assumptions and judgements and reviewing the data output in detail for plausibility and consistency. A world economy model is bolted on, and ITEM forecasting is particularly detailed in the financial sector. The Phillips and Drew model is quite small, with around 160 variables, of which 50 are exogenous, and 86 equations. Particular attention is paid to the company sector and the following factors enter into the estimation of corporate profitability: price controls and policy, world industrial production and inflation, and UK inflation, these all input into company sector financial balances together with corporate tax, fixed investment, price of domestic manufactures, cost of materials and fuels, and stockbuilding. In this sector, forecasts are made for individual company dividends, earnings, external finance, liquidity, profits, sources and uses of funds and surpluses/deficits. The model also emphasises the money supply and flow of funds.

In another approach, Wood Mackenzie also provides a computerised model of the UK economy, covering the usual macroeconomic variables and ensuring consistency between forecasts for the real and financial balances of sectors of the UK economy. The model is not a large-scale econometric one like the Treasury's but is used to make two-year base forecasts for a number of variables such as exchange rate, sector inflation, GDP, sector output and financial balance, and industry cash flow. Commentary includes judgement in the company's forecasting. But it is WM policy to go beyond reliance on outside econometric models or on a mechanical application of quantitative techniques; it is considered worth concentrating on the company and financial sectors. Thus, assumptions are imposed which take account of short-run outcomes, like the effects of pay settlements on average earnings, making the outcome more pragmatically realistic. The way tax revenues are derived and stock appreciation allocated is another example of this approach.

WM sees more value in assisting investors by the application of quantitative techniques to securities markets than in macroeconomic fine tuning. These techniques include: appraising equity risk premium levels and the relative returns available on equities, conventional gilts, index-linked and cash; asset allocation models weighting domestic and international markets; contribution analyses at all levels; and stock evaluation systems including relative value and risk/returns, based on the dividend discount model.

The stock evaluation system used by WM is typical of quantitative analyses which start with the company. Under- or over-valuation of a stock depends on risk-discounted forecasts of dividends. The calculations are accounting-based, and would normally take little note of macroeconomic forecasts. But after some five years, forecasts are made for the factors determining profitability like margins and input prices which take into account the influence of broader economic factors. In order to bridge macro- and micro-analysis, WM breaks the forecasting process down into three 5-year phases: short-term, transition, and maturity or steady-state. Long-term means the period when there is constant real growth in dividend and earnings. Transition is the period of "smoothing out" of short-term forecast earnings. Diversifiable risk depends on variations in the following: gross cash flow, current liabilities, return on equity, relative historic yield, industry risk, and management risk. The last two (subjective) factors are determined by macroeconomic assessment.

This model is therefore not devoid of macroeconomic forecast input – through dividend and risk forecasts. But it might be held this is a small input, and that even in the short-run macroeconomic factors should figure more importantly (cf. Chugh and Meadows, above). Turning points will not have been anticipated, and too much emphasis placed on short-term accounting information.

CONCLUSIONS

The large computerised macroeconometric models of the UK economy are used for policy advice and forecasting. As far as investment analysts are concerned, the macro results are available for background information or actual input to own models. For portfolio management and advice there is an alternative or complementary approach via smaller-scale quantitative techniques, particularly stock valuation modelling. Neither adequately bridge the behavioral and theoretically measurable link between forecasts of macroeconomic variables and direct security valuation. Analysts frequently bridge by the use of judgement, but formal, quantitative relationships are not well developed. A promising way forward is a more detailed econometric treatment of financial and company sector forecasting either in large-scale models or in-house models and the incorporation of results in expanded or more imaginatively-conceived stock valuation models.

APPENDIX

Forecasting Institution and Publications

Capel Cure Myers	Bath House, Holborn Viaduct,	Economic Review	(monthly)
	London EC1A 2EU	Economic Indicators	(monthly)
		Portfolio Review Strategy	(quarterly)
Cambridge Econometrics Limited	P.O. Box 114 Cambridge CB2 3RW	Forecast Report	($\times$ 3 pa)
City University Business School	Frobisher Crescent, Barbican Centre, London EC2Y 8HB	Economic Review	($\times$ 2 pa)

Confederation of British Industry	Centre Point, 103, New Oxford Street, London WC1A 1DV	CBI Industrial Trends Survey	(quarterly)
Data Resources Inc., (Europe)	30, Old Queen Street, St. James's Park, London SW1 9HP	World Service US Macro Service Canadian Macro Service Japan Macro Service Latin Macro Service America Macro Service East Asia Macro Service European Macro Service	(quarterly) (monthly)
Grieveson Grant,	Barrington House, 59, Gresham Street, London EC2	Economic and Fiscal Review UK Economic Indicators US Economic Indicators	(monthly)
Henley Centre for Economic Forecasting	2, Tudor Street London EC4Y 0AA	Costs and Prices Framework Forecast for the UK Directors' Guide	(quarterly) (monthly) (monthly)
Hoare Govett,	Heron House, 319–325 High Holborn, London WC1V 7PB	Economic Outlook Gilt-Edged Monitor Currency Outlook Portfolio Strategy	(monthly) (quarterly)
James Capel	Winchester House 100, Old Broad Street, London EC2N 1BQ	UK Economic Assessment International Bond Currency Review Gilt News	(monthly) (monthly) (× 2 weekly)
Laing & Cruickshank	Piercy House, 7, Copthall Avenue, London EC2R 7BE	Economic and Monetary Review US Economic Monitor UK Economic Forecast Economic Indicators	(monthly) (monthly) (monthly) (monthly)
Liverpool Research Group in Macroeconomics	Department of Economics and Business Studies, University of Liverpool, P.O. Box 147, Liverpool L69 3BX	Quarterly Economic Bulletin	
London Business School	Sussex Place, Regent's Park, London NW1 45S	Economic Outlook Financial Outlook	(quarterly) (quarterly)
OECD	Economic Prospects Division 2, Rue Andre-Pascal, 75775, Paris, Cedex 16	OECD Economic Outlook	(July and December)
Oxford Economic Forecasting Ltd	Templeton College, Kennington, Oxford OX1 5NY	UK Forecast World Forecast	(× 4 pa) (× 2 pa)
National Institute of Economic and Social Research	2, Dean Trench Street Smith Square, London SW1P 3HE	NIESR Review	(quarterly)
Phillips and Drew	120 Moorgate, London EC2M 6XP	Economic Forecasts World Investment Review Currency Trends	(monthly) (monthly) (quarterly)
Rowe and Pitman	1, Finsbury Avenue, London EC2M 2PA	Economic Commentary Economic Briefing Key Statistics	(monthly) (weekly) (monthly)

Scicon Ltd (ITEM Club)	49, Berners Street, London W1P 4AQ	Subscription service	
Simon and Coates	1, London Wall Buildings London EC2M 5PT	Private Investors' Bulletin Economics Analyst UK Economic Indicators	($\times$ 5 pa) (monthly) (monthly)
Society of Business Economists Forecasting Group	11, Bay Tree Walk, Watford, Herts WD1 3RX	UK Economic Outlook UK Economic Trends	(annual questionnaire) ($\times$ 2 pa)
HM Treasury	Parliament Street, Whitehall, London SW1P 3AG	Economic Progress	(monthly)
Wood MacKenzie & Co	Erskine House, 68–73 Queen Street, Edinburgh EH2 4N5	Trade Prospects UK Economic Outlook Interest Rate Prospects Economic Monitor International Economic Review	($\times$ 2 pa) (monthly) (quarterly)

REFERENCES

1. HM Treasury, Macroeconomic Model Technical Manual, 1982, 14.

2. Wallis, K. F. (ed). Models of the UK Economy: a Review by the ESRC Macroeconomic Modelling Bureau. Oxford University Press, 1984.

3. Barker, T. S. Forecasting the Economic Recession, UK, 1979–82; a Comparison of Model-Based *ex ante* Forecasts. Paper GPP 517, University of Cambridge, Department of Applied Economics.

4. Llewellyn, J. and Arai, H. International Aspects of Forecasting Accuracy. OECD Economic Studies, 3, 1984.

5. Britton, A. (ed). Employment, Output and Inflation; the National Institute Model of the British Economy, Heinemann, 1984.

6. Chugh, L. C. and Meadow, J. W. "The Stock Valuation Process: the Analyst's View" *Financial Analysts Journal*, 1984.

25 Investor Protection and the Advertising Practices of Share Tipsters

S. M. KEANE

Since 1969, Simon M. Keane has been, respectively, Lecturer, Reader and Professor of Finance at the University of Glasgow. He has published numerous books and articles on investment matters.

Simon Keane's paper considers the issues facing investors in the light of their expectations. He discusses advertisers' standards, risk, the degree of research based evidence, sampling and 'fairness'. During the 1980s concern had been growing about investor protection, and it is perhaps ironic that this article was published in July 1987 – the peak of the bull market.

The purpose of this paper is to consider the advertising practices of investment advisory services, more particularly those of "share tipsters". A distinction may be drawn between security-selection advice for portfolio construction purposes and security-selection advice for the purposes of exploiting abnormal-return opportunities. The former is concerned with efficient management of the risk, taxation and transaction-cost aspects of the investment process. The latter can be characterised as a "share tipster" activity, and is the aspect of investment advice which is the subject of this paper.

The SIB rules stipulate that financial advertisements should not be misleading to "persons who cannot be expected to have any special understanding of the matter in the advertisement"[1]. The Advertising Standards Board similarly requires that such advertisements be "fair" and should "in no sense take advantage of inexperience and credulity"[2]. The paper considers the criterion of "fairness" and its interpretation in practice in the context of financial advisers' claims to superior investment skill.

THE IMPACT OF FINANCIAL ADVERTISEMENTS ON INVESTORS' EXPECTATIONS

It can be assumed that most investors are relatively unsophisticated in their awareness and understanding of the investment-performance research literature. Their expectations of security return opportunities will tend to be formed from anecdotal evidence and from the cultural conditioning of the prevailing belief system. The relevance of these influences is that if investors' expectations are raised to unrealistic levels, the consequences can be far-reaching both for the investors' performance and for the efficient operation of the companies in which they invest.

The fundamental issue facing investors is the choice between *passive* and *active* investment. If security prices are accepted at face value the optimal strategy is generally accepted to be a passive one consisting of international diversification and minimal portfolio turnover[3]. Alternatively, if prices are viewed as unrealiable estimates of value the optimal strategy is an active one consisting of concentration (imperfect diversification) and of periodic switching between securities, where the degree of concentration and frequency of portfolio turnover are ultimately determined by the level of the investor's expectations.

In addition to incurring the direct transaction costs and risks associated with pursuing mispriced securities, investors with high expectations are also likely to incur the additional costs of professional security-selection advice, and possibly of active fund management. If the investment intermediaries fail to fulfil these expectations there is a further possibility that they will exert pressure on companies to pursue the kinds of short-term decision criteria which are presumed to promote early share price increases to the detriment of the companies' long-term welfare. To the extent that the problem of short-termism is an issue of substance, it can be attributed mainly to unrealistic expectations by investors. It is clear, therefore, that the incremental costs and risks of excessive investment expectations can be significant, making it critical that the promotional literature of investment advisory services conform strictly to the fairness criterion.

It should be noted that unfair advertising has both specific and general consequences for investor behaviour. The exaggerated claims of one advisory service has obvious implications for investors' expectations of that firm's returns versus those from competing services. The exaggerated claims of advisory services in general, however, have far-reaching consequences for investors' expectations about the returns from active versus passive investment.

INVESTORS' EXPECTATIONS AND THE CONVENTIONAL PERSPECTIVE

The traditional belief system prevailing in the securities market springs from the notion that, because many investors are naive and have limited information-processing skills, share prices will tend at times to represent mediocre estimates of value. The prevalent culture is consequently sympathetic to the belief that it is not only worthwhile, but a mark of responsible investment; for investors to have recourse to professional advice to pick "winners". Beating the market is assumed to be a fundamental goal of investment, and the presumption is in favour of a professional adviser's ability to generate abnormal returns. It follows that, from the conventional perspective, if the issue is left to the casual scrutiny of advertising standards agencies, it is likely that the content of an advertisement which implies superior investment skill will tend to be accepted as fair unless it is manifestly outrageous.

INVESTORS' EXPECTATIONS AND THE RESEARCH-BASED PERSPECTIVE

The research-based perspective proceeds from the premise that, although many investors may be naive, it is possible that the consensus price prevailing in the market substantially reflects the judgement of a sophisticated minority. Moreover, it stresses that the issue of price-reliability can be resolved only by empirical testing. It is easy to be deceived by investment experiences, and an ability to outguess the market can be verified only from careful statistical analysis. Investment performance measurement is a complex task which cannot adequately be accomplished from the random impressions gained by investors even over years of experience. Distinguishing investment skill from chance requires a study of large data samples over significant time periods, with sophisticated adjustments for risk and transaction costs. An examination of the research methods employed in any recently published performance-evaluation study is sufficient to confirm the difficulty of the task[4]. Moreover, apart from being an inadequate basis for assessment, personal investment experiences tend to foster illusions of successful investment. A natural tendency for investors to attribute their "successes" to skill and to underplay their failures, makes subjective, non-statistical assessment procedures wholly unreliable bases for measuring investment skill. Within a research-based perspective no presumption exists in favour of any particular expert's ability to perform better than random.

EMPIRICAL EVIDENCE FOR INVESTMENT SKILL

The investment community may be viewed as composed of two classes of investor – professional traders and general investors. The first group includes specialists with ready access to relevant information sources and possessing a high degree of information-processing skill. The second group, the majority of investors, can be characterised as non-specialist consumers of processed information, possessing limited interpretative skills. The evidence overwhelmingly favours the conclusion that, although some members of the professional group are able to earn modest abnormal returns commensurate with their analytical skill and effort, the remainder, together with the general-investor group, are deluding themselves if they believe that they can systematically identify mispriced securities. If they have any prospect of doing so it is only by identifying those professional analysts who have the necessary share-selection skills.

An investor therefore seeking to achieve a superior performance faces two hurdles – he must identify an adviser with authenticated "tipping" skills, and he must be able to translate the advice into above-abnormal returns. To overcome the first, he needs to have documented evidence that the adviser has successfully passed an appropriate performance evaluation test, or he must himself possess the necessary skills to perform such a test, and have access to the relevant data. To overcome the second hurdle he must be able to respond to the adviser's recommendations before their value is eroded in the market. The evidence overwhelmingly suggests that very few professional analysts possess superior investment skills, and that those who do only to a very modest degree[5]. The evidence further suggests that, when professional advice contains new information or new insights, the market's response tends to be almost instantaneous[6]. It is within this framework that the concept of fairness must be judged.

The statistical support for an advertiser's claims may be *specific* or *vicarious*. Specific evidence is evidence based on independent tests of the abnormal-return generating ability of the individual adviser or strategy. Vicarious evidence is derived from the general performance-evaluation literature. It is not intended here to review that literature in detail although it is appropriate to note the particularly relevant findings of a recent survey of 30 studies of stock recommendations made by over 200 advisory services and stockbroking firms[7]. The survey in total covered nearly 50,000 individual recommendations made over a 50 years period. It was found that, the abnormal gains averaged about 2% for investors acting the day after publication – insufficient on average to cover transaction costs. These are of course average results, but although one or two services, such as Value Line, stand out as more successful than others, the expected abnormal returns even in these cases remain very modest[8]. These results indicate, therefore, the level of returns which an investor might expect to achieve from an advisory service for which he has no specific evidence.

INVESTMENT TIPSTERS AND THE RECENT ANOMALOUS EVIDENCE

It is possible to argue that the efficient market perspective has become discredited by the growing body of anomalous evidence reported in recent years, and that active investment policies have to some extent been validated as a result. This view, however, springs from a concept of efficient market theory as a simple true-or-false issue that awaits conclusive proof before it ceases to be more than of academic interest. In effect, the concept is assumed to collapse if a persuasive piece of evidence of a single market inefficiency is reported. It is important to stress, therefore, that market inefficiency is not like an infectious disease which either exists or doesn't. Rather it can be compared to high blood pressure – the greater the degree, the more significant the consequences. The issue at stake, therefore, is not whether the market is inefficient (ie whether prices fail to reflect economic values to the penny) but how inefficient. If the degree of inefficiency is sufficient only to give modest rewards to highly skilled information-processors for their research efforts, and too fleeting to be transmittible to the ordinary investor, then the market can be viewed as "operationally efficient". Its inefficiencies are in practice irrelevant to the general investor. If the degree of inefficiency is such that the general investor can readily secure expert advice to identify materially mispriced securities, then the market is operationally inefficient. Only then is the presumption in favour of the professional adviser.

It is clear, therefore, that the EMH literature need not be completely free of controversy for its findings to have significance for investment and institutional policy-making decisions. Although the reported anomalies of recent years are numerous, including such phenomena as the January effect, the Weekend effect, the Small Firm effect, the Price-Earnings Ratio effect, Value Line, etc., none of this evidence supports the basic premise of the conventional belief system that recourse to professional advisers can be expected to help the investor identify significantly mispriced securities.

It follows that what is at stake here is not whether security price behaviour patterns are at times difficult to explain, or even whether some pockets of market inefficiency appear to exist, but whether the popular view of the market, and its abnormal-return opportunities, is justified by the accumulated empirical evidence. That view is in fact overwhelmingly rejected by the evidence, and it follows that the decision as to what is fair cannot be left to the judgment of the "competent" observer. The concept of fairness must be judged in the context of the more objective evidence of the research literature. Even if conclusive evidence indicates that a particular "tipster" in the past has systematically and significantly out-performed the market, this evidence has relevance only to that individual. It does nothing to undermine the accumulated evidence indicating that the majority of professional fund managers and advisers tested have been found unable systematically to match an appropriate market index after allowing for all transaction costs, bid-ask spreads, etc.

In summary, the accumulated empirical evidence indicates that, despite the anomalous evidence of recent years, certain relevant conclusions can be drawn with a high degree of confidence: (1) The abnormal-return opportunities in the market are limited and, where they exist, the returns are modest. Few, if any, advisers can generate sufficient returns for an investor to cover the transaction costs of an active investment strategy. (2) The task of identifying a superior tipster is exceedingly difficult and is comparable to the task faced by the tipster in identifying a superior share. (3) The market tends to price away rapidly the commercial value of any published advice containing new information.

FAIRNESS

For a financial advertisement to be fair within the context of a research-based perspective it must be representative of the returns an investor can reasonably expect (in the strict actuarial sense of the word) to earn from following the adviser's recommendations. Not the returns that might be obtained if events turn out favourably, or those that happen to have been obtained from selected investment decisions in the past, but the mean expected returns which can be supported from the findings of rigorously controlled statistical studies.

It can be argued, therefore, that an adviser who has not been specifically tested is not acting fairly if he uses his impressionistic experience to displace the vicarious evidence. The research literature is based on tests of a wide spectrum of advisers, and the onus rests on any individual tipster to demonstrate that the findings are not relevant in his case. It also follows that an adviser's claims need not be explicit to be unfair. An advertisement may be unfair if it indirectly implies a reasonable expectation of generating higher abnormal returns than those supported by the vicarious evidence.

ADVERTISING STANDARDS IN PRACTICE

A survey of financial advertisements by UK advisory firms was carried out to test the above concept of fairness by observing the degree of tolerance accorded in practice to investment advertisers' claims. Although many advertisements are relatively restrained in their claims, it is reasonable to assume that advertising tolerance levels are reflected in the practices of the least restrained. The object, therefore, was not to ascertain how representative of the industry particular unreasonable practices might be, but to note the levels to which financial advisers are prepared to raise investors' expectations, and the quality of the evidence produced to justify their claims. This approach can also be justified by the fact that extreme claims by even a few advisers are likely to raise the general level of expectations, including those from firms whose advertisements make no explicit claim to abnormal-return generating power.

Two questions in particular, therefore, were addressed:

1. Do the advertisements of financial advisory services at times appear to raise investors' expectations to levels which are inconsistent with the results of general investment-performance tests?
2. Where claims to exceptional investment skill are made, are they always supported by the results of a specific performance test conducted with the same rigour as the standard research study?

THE LEVEL OF INVESTMENT EXPECTATIONS

Although no advertisement was found which suggested that future returns could be guaranteed, most tended to suggest that the probabilities of obtaining significantly superior returns are materially enhanced by the advice offered:

"Penny Share Focus helps you to spot the next Penny Share winner and keeps you clear of the losers."
"You can often identify a fantastically under-valued share and get it on the ground floor" – The Penny Share Guide.
"How you can turn £1,000 into £140,000 in just 14 years – in Unit Trusts" – the Unit Trust News Letter.

Again no advertisements were found which attempted to quantify the actual returns that might be expected above those from a purely passive strategy, but several implied a level of return which was clearly in excess of the average that could reasonably be earned from a random selection:

"Which Penny shares will triple in 1987? . . ." – Penny Share Focus.
"Why you didn't turn £500 into £94,474 in less than four years" – Stockmarket Confidential.

It is clear, therefore, that a casual reader of tipster sheet advertisements is frequently given the impression that the opportunities for systematically outperforming the market are widespread and significant.

SPECIFIC EVIDENCE IN ADVERTISEMENTS

The second issue is whether the specific evidence produced in support of claims made is soundly based. The prerequisites of a valid performance evaluation test are that it should be based on an adequate sample of investment decisions spread over a significant time period, with due allowances for risk characteristics, transaction costs and the speed of price adjustment on transmission of the advice. A number of firms attempt to avoid the problem of proving investment skill by basing their case not on their performance record but on the intrinsic superiority of their selection process. For example, more than one advertisement in the survey implied an intrinsic advantage to a strategy of following the transactions of insiders. Others claimed access to inside information which is both legal and commercially valuable. Another alleged a comparative advantage in selecting European shares by virtue of "its range of contacts across Europe with the ability to pinpoint European growth stocks ahead of the field". Others imply an inherent advantage to investing in certain classes of share, eg:

"There is one undoubted factor in favour of low-priced shares, namely that most people can afford to buy them. And the more people that buy a share, the greater its chance of rising."

The majority of services surveyed, however, founded their claim to investment skill on past performance. Frequently this amounts to no more than a statement of having "a proven record". Where evidence of this record was reported, the statistics were characteristically flawed in one or more important aspects of the performance measurement process, ie in terms of the sample size, the time period, the impact of risk, or the effects of transaction costs:

Investment Sample

It is impossible to specify precisely what constitutes a statistically significant sample for an investment record to be representative. Under certain circumstances it may require the outcome of hundreds, and possibly thousands, of investment decisions to control adequately for the effects of chance. It is considerably easier, however, to recognise a statistically insignificant sample. It is not uncommon, for example, for an advertisement to highlight a single outstanding investment decision as evidence of future potential:

"Did you buy Amstrad in 1980? £5,000, now worth £450,000."

A similar strategy is to cite the returns of one client who happens to have had the good fortune to have chosen the most profitable of the advisers' recommendations:

" 'I turned £1,800 into £11,725' . . . so wrote Mr SCT of Wolverhampton . . . all that was accomplished by closely following our advice, month after month, week after week, proving once more that investment in 'Penny Shares' is not just luck."

Although these are examples of obviously unrepresentative samples, some advertisements are designed to give a spurious impression of representativeness. For example, Stock Market Confidential states that

"it is all very well knowing what to buy – the real secret is knowing what to sell. This is our full 'sell' record since May 1986: . . ."

and then lists about 30 sales all showing a substantial profit. Such a record is superficially impressive and, despite the small sample, appears to indicate effective investment advice. It lacks validity, however, on three grounds: (1) the period preceding the sames was characterised by a significant market-wide price rise, (2) it is possible that the firm adopted a deliberate strategy over a six month period of selling only their most profitable recommendations for the specific purpose of being able to exploit such a list in a subsequent promotion campaign, (3) the claim to have the "secret" of knowing what to sell was not borne out. When prices were checked some three months after the advertisement it was found that most of the shares had risen in value significantly since the sale date.

Time Period

Even a sample of thousands of investment decisions may be inadequate for an effective performance evaluation test if the time period is too short. Studies have shown that when performance tests are carried out for periods of less than 10 years, there will always be some fund managers who appear to have performed better than chance. But when the review period is extended beyond 10 years the virtual elimination of chance effects reveals that superior performance rarely exists. However, even the results of 10 or 20 years may be misleading. For example, some advisers advocated investment in a portfolio composed mainly of Japanese securities on the grounds that they predicted that the increase in Japanese productivity in the following five or ten years would be significantly greater than the increase implicit in Japanese share prices. Whatever number of individual companies the adviser might successfully recommend under such a strategy, he is in effect "betting" against a single event – the level of future Japanese productivity. It might be necessary to have a hundred or more years' data to confirm the existence of skill in making such cyclical predictions systematically. It is common practice, however, for fund managers and tipster sheets to cite investment results for one to five year periods as evidence of investment skill.

Risk

Adjusting for differences in investment risk is the most difficult element in the performance measurement process. Some analysts argue that making such an adjustment is misplaced on the grounds that share price volatility represents "opportunity rather than risk". However, most investment theorists believe that a positive risk-return relationship is inherent in the securities market as evidenced by the higher average returns of equities relative to bonds. Therefore, failure to adjust for risk raises serious doubt about any evidence presented to support superior investment skill, particularly in the light of the research evidence that, where skill does exist, the average excess return is likely to be very modest. Yet, the most common approach to risk observed in the survey was to ignore its existence entirely. For example, some advertisements use the higher returns from equities relative to building society deposits to imply a superior investment performance, rather than as a simple illustration of the risk-return tradeoff process. No single example was found where the advisory service made specific adjustments for risk in evaluating the firm's own performance.

Transaction Costs

None of the advertisements surveyed gave an adequate indication of the incremental costs of following the firm's advice, including commissions, bid-ask spreads, advisers' fees, and cash-holding costs. Although a few mentioned the impact of one or other of these costs, most implicitly encouraged investors to pursue perceived bargains without regard for the cumulative effect of the round-trip costs of transferring into and out of the recommendations.

Finally, in addition to the above flaws in performance evaluation, there was a general failure to recognise the difficulty faced by investors in implementing the advice before the market price adjusts. Although a few firms acknowledged the need for investors to act quickly, even to the extent of transmitting the advice by telephone, most ignored the issue. One adviser even dismissed the market's speed of reaction as a transient phenomenon suggesting that investors wait before acting until the immediate price activity "settles down" on the grounds that "the reasoning behind the recommendations is not going to change if you act straight away".

RECOMMENDATIONS

Given the limited abnormal-return opportunities indicated by accumulated research findings it has to be concluded that conventional faith in professional tipster skills is substantially misguided. The survey of the advertising practices of investment advisory services confirms that claims to such skills are at times materially inconsistent with the empirical evidence of investment performance studies. Because of the opportunities open to financial "experts" to exploit investors' unrealistic expectations, it is proposed that some reform in the regulation of advertising practice is desirable. One possibility is to prohibit all claims to superior selection skills unless the skills have been verified by an independent performance evaluation test. This solution, however, remains open to manipulation, and may be slow to alter the popular belief system about the abnormal return opportunities in the market. If investors are to achieve realistic expectations there is no real alternative but for them to acquire the perspective of the accumulated research literature. This perspective can never be acquired simply from personal experience, and, without it, investors will continue to be deluded by appearances. It is suggested therefore that investor protection agencies should require a mandatory note to be published with every tipster advertisement distilling from the literature the elements that are virtually beyond dispute. An example of such a note, extending the present requirement to warn investors of the riskiness of equity securities, is contained in Table 1.

TABLE 1. Warning note.

All equity securities are risky but some of the risk can be avoided by diversification.

Empirical tests have shown that:

* Very few professional analysts when tested have been found able systematically to identify shares which are likely to earn abnormal returns in relation to their level of risk.

* If an analyst has been shown to possess share-selection skill, the abnormal returns are modest, and share prices tend to adjust to his recommendations before investors can take advantage of them.

* Holding a well-diversified portfolio and engaging in as few transfers between shares as possible is likely in the long run to be the most profitable strategy for the majority of investors.

SUMMARY AND CONCLUSION

For investors who hold unrealistic expectations about the market's abnormal-return opportunities the consequences in terms of transaction costs and avoidable risks can be significant. Although the advertising practices of share tipsters are only one of several influences affecting investors' expectations, they can be assumed to be a significant factor in sustaining the popular perception of investment as fundamentally "to beat the market".

The traditional belief system of the market accords a high degree of tolerance to the claims of professional advisers, but whether the investor perceives the object of investment to be to beat the market or to optimise the return per unit of risk, the evidence indicates that investment tipster services are unlikely to provide value for money. In terms of "picking a winner", a pin in the paper is cheaper generally and no less effective. In terms of optimising risk-return trade-off, a passive broad-diversification strategy has been shown to provide the maximum benefit in the long term. If investors are to achieve more realistic expectations about risk-return prospects and to make informed choices about their basic investment strategy, there appears to be no alternative but for them to secure a greater awareness of the accumulated research evidence. Reform of the advertising practices of professional investment advisers is proposed as an essential preliminary step in creating awareness of this evidence. There is no reason to believe that the efficient operation of the market depends on the evidence for its efficiency being withheld from market participants[9].

REFERENCES

1. Regulation of Investment Business, Securities and Investment Board, Rule 7.05 (1).

2. British Code of Advertising Practice C.vii 1.2.

3. See Investments by W. Sharpe (Prentice Hall) 1985, Ch.7.

4. Cranshaw, T. E., "The Evaluation of Investment Performance", Journal of Business, October, 1977.

5. Firth, M. A., "The Investment Performance of Unit Trusts in the Period 1965–75", Journal of Money Credit and Banking, Vol. 9, 1977.

6. Foster, G., "Briloff and the Capital Markets", Journal of Accounting Research, Spring, 1979.

7. Dimson, E. and P. Marsh, "An Analysis of Brokers' and Analysts' Unpublished Forecasts of UK Stock Returns", Journal of Finance, (Vol. 39, 1984).

8. Copeland, T. and D. Mayers, "The Value Line Enigma (1965–78)", Journal of Financial Economics (November, 1982).

9. For the market to be perfectly efficient it would of course be necessary for some information-processors to be fooled. But it is possible for the market to be operationally efficient with all investors recognizing that a minority of professional analysts can earn economic rewards for their efforts without being able to transmit the benefits to other investors.

26 Group Accounting, Funds Statements and Cash Flow Analysis

T. A. LEE

This article was published in The Investment Analyst *in October 1987. Professor Lee analysed the funds flow statements in the context of takeovers and the distortions that arise when operating cash flows are confused with long-term investment. The paper considered the particular example of the acquisition by Guinness of Distillers. At the time of publication, Professor Lee was teaching in the University of Edinburgh.*

INTRODUCTION

The use by investment analysts of published funds statements with which to obtain cash flow information has been described in detail (Lee, 1983 and 1984). And the technique has been demonstrated in a number of corporate analyses, most recently in relation to the takeover of Distillers by Guinness (Lee, 1987a and 1987b). These analyses have also been the subject of a national newspaper feature (Ferguson, 1987), in which the finance director of Guinness was reported to be highly critical of the use of cash flow analysis in a takeover situation.

The major point at issue in this context is believed to be of considerable importance to investment analysts assessing corporate liquidity and cash flow performance. It reveals a means by which the operating cash flow of companies involved in takeovers can be seriously distorted. This is achieved by classifying what would be regarded normally as an operating cash outflow as if it were a long-term investment of a similar nature to capital expenditure. The result is an overstatement of post-takeover operating cash flow which could mislead analysts unless they were aware of the cash flow consequences of the accounting classification applied by the reporting company.

OBJECTIVE OF THE PAPER

The objective of this paper is to outline and discuss this problem within the context of a simple illustrative example. This will be followed by a comment on the 1986 cash flow results of Guinness in which the distorting classification has been applied. From these discussions, it will be demonstrated that the use of funds statements for cash flow analysis purposes is a function which requires a great deal of care and attention to the data. Fortunately, it is relatively easy to allow for any distortions, and this will also be explained.

IDENTIFYING THE PROBLEM

Put simply, the problem exists when one company acquires control of another through takeover. The usual situation is that the net assets of the acquired company are purchased and, for accounting and reporting purposes, are consolidated with those of the acquiring company. Part of the net assets acquired will usually include working capital relating to operating activities (that is, stock plus debtors minus creditors).

Following takeover, the first annual reporting of the expanded group will involve an accounting for the net assets acquired and the post-takeover profits and losses which relate to the latter. Consolidation of these matters is complex and can involve contentious issues. But it is relatively well documented in the accountancy literature (Taylor, 1987) – at least so far as concerns profit statement and balance sheet data. Consolidated funds statements are discussed to a lesser extent, and virtually nothing has been written on their post-takeover use to derive cash flow information.

At the first post-takeover reporting of funds flow, there is a problem of how to account for the net assets taken over (subsequent changes in net assets are consolidated normally in the group results). From a casual observation of annual reports, there appear to be a number of ways of doing this:

- Consolidate the individual increases in those items comprising net assets taken over with other group changes, and (usually) note these increases in the notes to the accounts (for example, as in the 1986 funds statement of Rank Hovis McDougall).
- Disclose the acquisition of net assets by takeover as a single use of funds – either without supporting detailed notes (as in the 1986 funds statement of GKN) or with a suitable note (as in the 1986 funds statement of Bunzl).
- Separate the individual items comprising the net assets taken over from the other funds movements, by inserting a separate column (as in the 1986 funds statement of Guinness).
- Disclose the acquisition of net assets by takeover, exclusive of working capital, and consolidate the latter in the overall group change in working capital (as in the 1986 funds statement of Ultramar).

EFFECTS OF ALTERNATIVES

As previously demonstrated (Lee, 1983), the funds statement can be used to derive cash flow data to assess corporate liquidity performance. One of the key adjustments in this process is netting profit (before non-cash additions and deductions) with the periodic change in working capital relating to operations. The result is a figure for operating cash flow which is the net cash surplus or deficit realised from profitable (or non-profitable) trading activities. The primary problem in this respect is the working capital adjustment. Unless the full change for the period is netted with the relevant profit figure, the operating cash flow datum will not reflect the total net cash flow relating to the operating activity of the period.

This is not usually a problem until there is a takeover – that is, when there is an increase in working capital due to one transaction. The first and the last treatments of working capital taken over, and described above (that is, of Rank Hovis McDougall and Ultramar), are not likely to create a problem. The reported change in working capital will include the increase due to takeover, and the operating cash flow will be reported or can be derived as if the acquisition had been a normal trading transaction (which, in essence, is what it is; stock, etc. being acquired in one lump sum rather than by a series of daily transactions).

The problem arises in the second and third treatments – that is, as in the cases of Bunzl and Guinness. Separating out the acquired working capital (either because it is part of a reported figure for the total cost of an investment in a subsidiary company acquired or because it is disclosed as part of such an investment), and excluding it from the main group working capital change, will provide a cash flow distortion. Profits (including those of the subsidiary since takeover) will be "matched" with a change in group working capital exclusive of that taken over. The usual effect will be to overstate operating cash flow if the working capital taken over is positive. In the funds statement of Guinness for 1986, where operating cash flow is calculated and reported, the distortion is quite explicit, and potentially amounts to nearly £900m to be spread over a number of years.

ILLUSTRATING THE EFFECT

To emphasise the points made above, it is useful to provide a simple illustration which will help to explain the distorting effect on operating cash flow of a takeover. Assume the following situation and transactions:

- ABC plc has an opening financial position of:

	£
Stock	1,000
Cash	2,000
	3,000
Equity	3,000

- During the first period, it purchased further stock for cash (£4,000), and sold stock for cash (£9,000). The latter had an original cost of £3,000.
- Also during this period, ABC plc acquired 100% of DEF plc for £10,000 in cash. DEF plc's sole asset on acquisition was £10,000 of stock.
- During the period, one half of DEF plc's stock of £10,000 was sold for £15,000 in cash.

Assuming conventional accounting practice, these transactions would result in the following financial statements at the period-end:

Profit Statement for first period.

	£	£
Sales (£9,000 + 15,000)		24,000
Less: opening stock	1,000	
purchased	4,000	
taken over	10,000	
	15,000	
Less: closing stock:		
purchased	2,000	
taken-over	5,000	
	7,000	8,000
Profit for first period		16,000

Balance Sheet at close of first period.

	£
Stock (as above)	7,000
Cash (£2,000 + 24,000 – 14,000)	12,000
	19,000
Equity (£3,000 + 16,000)	19,000

Funds Statement for first period (assuming no separations due to takeover).

	£
Source of funds	16,000
Profit for period	
Use of funds	
Increase in working capital:	
Stock (£7,000 – 1,000)	6,000
Increase in cash (£12,000 – 2,000)	10,000

Funds Statement for first period (assuming no separations due to takeover).

	Acquisition of DEF plc	*Relating to Operations*	*Total*
	£	£	£
Source of funds			
Profit for period	–	16,000	16,000
Use of funds			
Increase in			
working capital	10,000	(4,000)*	6,000
Increase in cash	(10,000)	20,000	10,000

* This figure comprises the increase in ABC plc's original stock of £1,000 (£2,000 – 1,000) minus the decrease in DEF plc's stock taken over of £5,000 (£10,000 – 5,000).

The important issue in these illustrations is the alternative funds statement treatments due to takeover, and their effect on deriving measures of operating cash flow. The first alternative above provides an operating cash flow of £10,000 (£16,000 – 6,000). The second alternative produces a "normal" operating cash flow of £20,000 due to the segregation of the stock acquired by takeover. What is being argued in this paper is that the £20,000 alternative is an overstatement of group operating cash flow. It contains the cash proceeds from the sale of the stock taken over (£15,000 in the first period), but with no "matching" of the equivalent cash cost (£10,000 on takeover).

The effect becomes even more distorted in subsequent periods when the remaining stock taken over is sold:

- Assume that the stock remaining at the end of the first period is sold in the next period for cash – £6,000 for ABC plc's original stock and £15,000 for DEF plc's stock taken over.
- Also assume the respective costs of sale are £2,000 and £5,000 (as in the first period-end balance sheet).
- Assume no other transactions.

This would then result in a funds statement for the second period of:

Funds Statement for second period.

	£
Sources of funds	
Profit for period (£21,000 – 7,000)	14,000
Reduction in working capital:	
Stock (£0 – 7,000)	7,000
Increase in cash (£33,000 – 12,000)	21,000

There is therefore reported an operating cash flow of £21,000 (£14,000 + 7,000), of which £15,000 relates to the DEF plc stock taken over. The overall operating cash flow effect for the two periods would be as follows, assuming the two alternative treatments of stock taken over:

	First Alternative	Second Alternative
	£	£
First period operating cash flow	10,000	20,000
Second period operating cash flow	21,000	21,000
Total	31,000	41,000

Thus, it may be concluded from this example that, if the working capital of a subsidiary recently acquired is either separately dealt with in the funds statement (as, for example, in the Guinness case) or hidden in an overall figure for the acquisition cost of the subsidiary (as, for example, in the Bunzl case), the effect will be to report a periodic change in group working capital which is incomplete. In turn, if this figure is netted against group profits to provide operating cash flow data, it will seriously distort the latter (a £10,000 overstatement in the above illustration).

AN ANSWER TO THE PROBLEM

There are two potential solutions to the problem. First, it could be recognised for accounting, reporting and analysis purposes, that a cash outflow be treated as a cash outflow and netted against its equivalent inflow (irrespective of whether it was the consequence of one transaction – as in a takeover, or several – as in normal trading activities). Application of such a consistent principle would result in operating cash flow calculations giving a net figure allowing for all working capital movements of the group. Using the above figures, the two-period operating cash flow would always be £31,000 (and therefore reflect the existing reporting practices of companies such as Rank Hovis McDougall and Ultramar).

Second, the working capital acquired by takeover could be disclosed separately but, if so, then any subsequent profits and working capital movements should be treated similarly. This would allow the short-term operating cash flow effects resulting from the takeover to be reported and assessed separately. Using the above figures, the results would be:

Funds Flow	Acquisition of DEF plc	Related to Other Operations	Total
First period	£	£	£
Source of funds			
Profit for period:			
(£15,000 – 5,000)	10,000		
(£9,000 – 3,000)		6,000	16,000
Use of funds			
Increase in working capital:			
Stock (£5,000–0)	5,000		
(£2,000 – 1,000)		1,000	6,000
Operating cash flow	5,000	5,000	10,000

Funds Flow	Acquisition of DEF plc	Related to Other Operations	Total
Second period	£	£	£
Source of funds			
Profit for period:			
(£15,000 – 5,000)	10,000		
(£6,000 – 2,000)		4,000	14,000
Reduction in working capital:			
Stock (£0 – 5,000)	5,000		
(£0 – 2,000)	2,000	7,000	
Operating cash flow	15,000	6,000	21,000
Total	20,000	11,000	31,000

Of the two solutions, the second appears to provide the greatest amount of information, and reflects the cash flow resulting immediately from the takeover. Either approach, however, is preferable to the situation of overstatement characterised by Guinness.

THE GUINNESS EXAMPLE

The problem delineated in the previous sections is not a serious one when the working capital acquired by takeover is small in relation to all other relevant data. However, in a situation such as in the Guinness takeover of Distillers, the effects are large and will influence a number of periods due to the nature of the working capital taken over (it largely consisted of maturing whisky).

Guinness has been reporting its funds flow in cash terms for a number of years. It netts profits with periodic changes in operating working capital to derive a measure of operating cash flow (which is not, however, described as such). As mentioned previously, it also separates out the net assets acquired by takeover from other movements in funds items. The 1986 annual report contained the following data (which are a summary of the source and application of group funds on page 30 of the 1986 report).

	Acquisition of Distillers	Relating to Operations	Total
Source of funds	£m	£m	£m
Profits	–	364	364
Increase in working capital	653	112	765
	(653)	252	(401)
New share capital	429	4	433
	(224)	256	32
Applications of funds			
Additions to tangible and intangible assets and investments (less disposals)	539	(56)	483
Taxes paid	–	44	44
Dividends paid	–	30	30
(less disposals)	539	18	557
Increase in net borrowings	763	(238)	525

Applying the logic of the argument in the previous section to the above figures, the investment analyst would be advised to concentrate on the total column rather than the centre one. The latter does not include, and will never include, any deduction for the cash outflow incurred as a result of the acquisition of Distillers' working capital. But it does include the cash inflow from realisations of that working capital (note 18 on page 45 of the annual report indicates that a figure of at least £46m for the sale of Distillers' maturing whisky is included in the 1986 operating cash flow of £252m).

The total figure for operating cash flow of £(401)m is therefore believed to be the most meaningful. However, it is also affected by dubious matchings of profit and working capital changes. Within the figure of £653m for Distillers' working capital taken over is a net figure for long-term provisions of £225m (largely for future provision of re-organisation costs less taxation recoverable). This figure presumably reduced the fair valuation paid for Distillers by Guinness, and ought not to be brought into the working capital figure, and certainly should not be deducted from profits in arriving at an overall group operating cash flow. Ideally, it should be separately disclosed with the increase in net borrowings of £525m. The provision represents a net future liability of the group of an extraordinary, nonoperating nature. Thus, the overall operating cash flow deficit for 1986 of £401m would appear to be an understatement of the "true" figure of £626m.

The final point to be made about the 1986 Guinness cash flow results relates to the future cash flow effects of its 1986 treatment of Distillers' working capital. Allowing for the above £225m "misclassification", the operating working capital taken over in April 1986 was £878m, of which £881m was stock (£661m in maturing whisky). It is estimated that the latter represents approximately eight years' stock (Rowe, 1987). £46m was reported in 1986 as sold – thus, this estimate does not appear inappropriate. The whisky stock has been adjusted up and down in valuation in 1986 but remains at approximately the figure at which it was taken over. Note 18 on page 45 of the annual report states that this is approximately its replacement cost.

With all these points in mind, it is not unfair to remind investment analysts that the operating cash flows of Guinness in the years to come will benefit considerably from the realisation of this stock – nearly £900m in total, of which over two thirds will provide cash over a number of years. Under these circumstances, and because of the materiality of the figures, it is argued in this paper that there is a case for disclosing separately the cash effects of the Distillers takeover – not only in the year of takeover but also in the subsequent years when the working capital taken over is realised. In 1986, at least 18% of the "operating" cash flow of Guinness (£46m out of £252m) appears to relate to stock of Distillers sold during the period, but no separate disclosure is made nor has any deduction been made for the cash cost.

CONCLUSIONS

The funds statement has long been the subject of criticism regarding the variety of classification and disclosure practices associated with it. Its use for cash flow analysis is established. But the lack of firm guidance on funds statement classifications makes its use for cash flow analysis purposes a less than certain process unless extreme care is exercised in establishing the nature of each funds datum. This is particularly true in the context of takeovers, and the uncertainty and possible distortions in cash flow figures is accentuated by such transactions. The Guinness example vividly illustrates this. The time is ripe for analysts to be provided with funds statements which are subject to firm standards on matters of classification and disclosure. It ought not to be left as purely a matter of individual judgement and discretion for the reporting company or group. After all, in the case of cash flow data, there ought to be little question of the accuracy of the figures.

REFERENCES

Ferguson, C. 'Guinness Follows Disturbing Trend in Accounting Practice', *The Times*, 6 July 1987.

Lee, T. A. 'Funds Statements and Cash Flow Analysis', *The Investment Analyst*, July 1983, pp. 13–21.

Lee, T. A. 'SSAP 10 and Cash Flow Analysis', *The Accountant's Magazine*, June 1984, pp. 232–3.

Lee, T. A. 'Why Guinness Needed to Get Distillers' Cash', *Scottish Business Insider*, March 1987, pp. 4 and 6.

Lee, T. A. 'What Has Happened to the Strong DCL Cash Flow?', *Scottish Business Insider*, June 1987, p. 8.

Rowe, S. 'Accountants Hide Guinness's Missing Millions', *Investors Chronicle*, 5 June 1987, p. 57.

Taylor, P. A. *Consolidated Financial Statements: Concepts, Issues and Techniques*, Harper and Row, 1987.

27 Why Most Equities Always Appear Cheap

P. THOMPSON

This article appeared in The Investment Analyst *in April 1988.*

Using a simplified theoretical model of an equity market to underline the title of his note, the author then explains why many indices can give a misleading picture of value, and concludes that shares that often look 'cheap' should, in fact, be sold.

At the time of publication, Peter Thompson was with Barclays de Zoete Wedd.

A major problem when an investor believes that the market is overvalued is that the majority of shares still appear cheap. They are valued on P/E ratios below the market average and their earnings are expected to grow as fast as the average. This note explains why these shares are frequently overvalued and should be sold.

It is probable that most investors are unaware that the mechanics of constructing indices virtually assure that the majority of shares are valued below the market index. This occurs because the index is weighted in terms of market capitalisation and the highly valued shares have a disproportionate impact on the index because of their high P/E ratios.

It is possible to illustrate why most equities always appear cheap in a simplified theoretical model of an equity market which is not greatly different from the FT Actuaries Industrial Index (excluding oils). This simplified market consists of ten shares in companies of equal size in terms of the assets they employ (or it may be more helpful to regard these companies as each representing 10% of the shares in the FT Actuaries Index). 60% of the shares in the model have a return on equity (ROE) of 15% – broadly in line with the London equity market. They are valued on a P/E ratio of 15. 20% of the companies are using their assets less profitably and the shares are valued on a lower P/E ratio and 20% are using their assets more profitably and are valued on a higher than average P/E ratio.

Of the less profitable shares 10% achieve half the average return on their assets and are valued on half the average P/E ratio, while the other 10% earn 2/3 of the average and are valued on 2/3 of the average P/E ratio.

Similarly half the highly rated profitable shares (10% of the total) are achieving one and a half times average profit on their assets and are valued at a P/E ratio one and a half times the average value. The most profitable 10% earn twice the average and are valued at twice the average P/E ratio.

Table 1 shows that with this simple model, although 60% of the companies are valued on the average P/E multiple of 15, the P/E ratio on the index (calculated by dividing the market capitalisation by the total earnings) is 18.2. This was almost exactly the P/E ratio on the FT Actuaries Industrial Group Index near the market peak, when the calculations were made. The P/E ratio is now nearly 30% lower but this does not affect the argument.

The model makes two facts clear:

1. mathematical logic ensures that shares in the median company must stand on a P/E valuation approaching a 20% discount to that on the index, and

TABLE 1.

Asset Value	Return on Equity	Earnings	P/E Ratio	Market Capitalisation	Percentage of the market	P/E Relative
100	7.5%	7.5	7.5	56	2	41%
100	10.0%	10.0	10.0	100	4	54%
600	15.0%	90.0	15.0	1350	46	82%
100	22.5%	22.5	22.5	506	17	124%
100	30.0%	30.0	30.0	900	31	165%
1000		160.0	18.2	2912	100	

2. a small number of highly rated shares have a disproportionate effect on the index P/E ratio.

In practice, the valuation of shares in the London market is skewed towards high P/E ratios with few companies on very low P/E ratios. Indeed not one of the 100 largest companies had a P/E ratio less than 10. This happens because the market tends to value low profitability companies on high P/E ratios on account of their recovery or take-over potential. This factor tends to accentuate the bias. Of the 225 largest companies in the industrial group, only 3% were on a P/E ratio of 10 or lower. In total 30% were on P/E ratios of 20 or more, 15% on P/E ratios of 12 or less, and the remaining 55% on PE ratios between 13 and 19, averaging around 16. Thus the impact of high P/E stocks on the Index is even greater than in the model.

The impact of a single highly rated company can be seen by looking at the 10 largest companies in the Industrial Group Index in terms of market capitalisation. These had an aggregate P/E ratio of 18.4, very close to the average for the whole Industrial Group Index.

Glaxo, with a P/E ratio and ROE of around 30, fits closely to the very highly valued company in the model. If Glaxo is omitted from this list the P/E ratio drops to 16.7. Glaxoi accounts for 17% of the market value of the companies in the list but less than 5% of the asset value. Marks & Spencer, with a P/E ratio of 22.5, fits as the second most profitable company in our model. If Marks & Spencer is also omitted the remaining eight shares are valued at 16.3 times earnings viz 85% of the index P/E. The list includes BAT Industries, on a P/E of 10.7, with the other seven companies being valued between 13 and 17. Similarly, it is noteworthy that the P/E ratio of an index of the ten largest UK industrial companies selected on an assets basis (a list which includes Marks & Spencer) had an average P/E ratio of only 16.

As long as investors are prepared to value highly rated companies on P/E ratios between one and a half times and twice that which they require on an average share, more than 60% of shares will be valued at less than the index and the average share will always stand at a discount of between 10 to 15% on the index.

This discount to the market average P/E ratio is often used during a bull market to provide a rationale for claiming that shares, which will be achieving market average earnings growth, are cheap. All that needs to happen is that investors become persuaded of this fact and the market will rise as these shares try to catch up with the market P/E. The correct P/E ratio for the market is very much a matter of convention and, as investors come to accept the higher P/E ratio for the market average, these average shares still look cheap. This is one of the mechanisms by which bull markets keep on rising.

If a company is expected to achieve market average earnings growth, its shares should probably be standing at a discount of between 10% and 20% to the index P/E ratio. This rule is particularly important in a bear market because it explains why it is often wise to sell shares in companies with average prospects despite the fact that they appear undervalued on a P/E relative basis.

Part IV
The 1990s

28 Volatility and the Big Bang Factor

P. POPE, D. PEEL AND P. YADAV

An increase in programme trading and the ending of dual capacity following the 'Big Bang' of 1986 were popularly believed to have created greater volatility in stock market prices. The authors examined the evidence for this belief, making due allowance for changes in global markets, the most dramatic of which was the October 1987 crash. They found that market 'folklore' was 'not entirely correct'.

Professor Pope is Director of the International Centre for Research in Accounting at Lancaster University; David Peel is Professor of Economics at Cardiff University; Pradeep Yadav is Professor of Finance at Strathclyde University.

When their article was published in May 1990, Peter Pope and Pradeep Yadav were both teaching at Strathclyde, as respectively Touche Ross Professor of Accounting and Lecturer in Finance. David Peel was Professor of Economics at the University College of Wales, Aberystwyth at that time.

One commonly held belief in the City is that the London stock market has become significantly more volatile since the deregulation that occurred with Big Bang in October 1986.

Two reasons have been suggested for this perceived increase in volatility:

The first is the increase in programme trading since Big Bang; the second, and more important, reason given is the ending of restrictions on dual capacity. The move away from the Stock Exchange floor to largely screen-based dealing has made trading decisions more visible and this visibility is alleged to have increased price volatility.

The point was summed up by Michael Sargent, head of market making at Warburg Securities, who said: 'Visibility has increased volatility. People tend to chase each other's tail, then they leap-frog. They chase each other all over the screen.'

There are three main reasons why we should be interested and concerned about stock market volatility:

- First, when prices fluctuate sharply, sometimes in periods as short as one day, investors may find it hard to accept that the explanation of the changes lies in information about fundamental economic factors. They are more likely to presume it is the result of excessive speculation and the irrationality of the market. If this impression grows it could arguably lead to a general erosion of investor confidence and a flow of capital away from equity markets.
- Second, increases in volatility will tend to increase the risks faced by market-makers and which would then lead them to charge correspondingly more for the liquidity they provide.

- Third, if volatility increased over a long period then it is possible that regulators and providers of capital might require securities firms to allocate a larger percentage of available capital to cash.

But why should price volatility occur in an efficient stock market? Factors which affect stock prices would include: expectations of future dividends, growth opportunities, interest rates and the perceived risk premia. As these expectations are based upon available information then new information about significant variations may affect price volatility. If new information arrives more frequently, or the impact on expectations increases, then volatility is also likely to increase.

As Professor Edwards at Columbia Business School noted: 'In general, the quicker and more accurately prices reflect new information ... the more efficient will be the allocation

TABLE 1. Descriptive statistics for daily index returns (%).

MSWI	*Mean*	*Std Dev*	*Max*	*Min*
3/1/84–1/7/88	0.08	0.88	–12.65	8.08
Pre-Big Bang	0.08	0.63	–2.56	2.88
Big Bang–16/10/87	0.14	0.70	–1.95	1.89
19/10/87–01/07/88	–0.04	1.64	–12.65	8.08
Post-Big Bang	0.07	1.19	–12.65	8.08
19/10/87–11/12/87	–0.46	3.22	–12.65	8.08
14/12/87–1/7/88	0.08	0.69	–2.88	1.96
FTA				
3/1/84–1/7/88	0.06	1.02	–12.12	5.66
Pre-Big Bang	0.07	0.75	–2.59	2.64
Big Bang–16/10/87	0.17	0.78	–2.26	2.12
19/10/87–01/07/88	–0.11	1.86	–12.12	5.66
Post-Big Bang	0.05	1.35	–12.12	5.66
19/10/87–11/12/87	–0.88	3.47	–12.12	5.66
14/12/87–1/7/88	0.11	0.90	–3.31	2.37
FTSE (O)				
3/1/84–1/7/88	0.05	1.20	–14.85	5.02
Pre-Big Bang	0.06	0.94	–2.92	3.88
Big-Bang–16/10/87	0.15	0.99	–4.23	2.72
19/10/87–01/07/88	–0.12	2.08	–14.85	5.02
Post-Big Bang	0.04	1.55	–14.85	5.02
19/10/87–11/12/87	–0.87	3.74	–14.85	5.02
14/12/87–1/7/88	0.10	1.19	–9.07	3.25
FTSE(C)				
3/1/84–1/7/88	0.05	1.13	–13.03	7.60
Pre-Big Bang	0.06	0.87	–2.83	3.35
Big Bang–16/10/87	0.15	0.86	–2.45	2.31
19/10/87–01/07/88	–0.12	2.01	–13.03	7.60
Post-Big Bang	0.04	1.46	–13.03	7.60
19/10/87–11/12/87	–0.83	3.78	–13.03	7.60
14/12/87–1/7/88	0.09	0.98	–3.45	2.45

Notes: MSWI = Morgan Stanley International Capital World Index
FTA = Financial Times Actuaries All Share Index
FTSE(O) = FTSE-100 opening prices
FTSE(C) = FTSE-100 closing prices

of resources. More asset price volatility ... may be a manifestation of a well functioning market. However, price volatility greater than that justified by objective new information ... makes prices inefficient by definition.'

Edwards also went on to say, however: 'Stock market volatility changes significantly over time. Despite many attempts to explain changes in volatility, we know very little about the factors that cause volatility to change.'

The question of whether deregulation, like Big Bang, increases price volatility is, essentially, an empirical question. To examine this theory we looked at the recent behaviour of the *Financial Times* Actuaries All Share Index (FTA), the FTSE-100 Index and 68 individual stock price series, on a daily basis from 1984 to 1988. The individual stocks are those shares that have continuously belonged to the FTSE-100 over the period being analysed.

In assessing the behaviour of the London market it seemed important to make allowances for changes that have occurred in all markets around the World. An obvious example of this is the crash of October 1987, when dramatic falls occurred in all the World's stock markets. Allowance is made for movements in global factors by examining the behaviour of the indices and the individual stock prices relative to movements in the Morgan Stanley Capital International World Price Index (MSWI).

An examination of the 60-day moving average of the daily volatility (variance) of the FTA from 1970 to 1988, suggested that Big Bang had no perceptible effect on volatility prior to Black Monday. In *Table 1* are shown the characteristics of daily returns in the FTA, FTSE (opening and closing prices) and MSWI indices, both before and after Big Bang. The results are also shown for the periods between Big Bang, Black Monday and afterwards.

The standard deviations of all four index returns series display an increase between the periods before and after Big Bang. Consequently, there seems to be evidence of increased volatility in both the UK and World markets since Big Bang. As the increases in volatility in the UK and World indices are of a comparable order it would suggest that the increase cannot be attributed to factors specific to the UK.

In the period between Big Bang and Black Monday there was only a marginal change in the volatility of the UK indices. However, post-Black Monday there was significantly higher volatility for all series. The conclusion that volatility has increased since Black Monday seems to be robust.

Also examined are the intra-day variance for the FTSE-100 index in the various subperiods. (The authors used Parkinson's high-low volatility estimator, which is theoretically five times more efficient than the usual variance calculated from closing or opening prices.) It is interesting to note that this intraday variance shows a significant increase in volatility in all sub-periods after Big Bang, including the period prior to Black Monday.

A formal comparison of the returns variances is presented in *Table 2*.

The main conclusion's drawn from these results are:

- First, the increase in volatility after Black Monday is significant and does not appear to be driven by a few outliers associated with the crash.
- Second, in the period between Big Bang and Black Monday, only the intra-day volatility showed a significant increase. Inter-day volatility did not change significantly.

As a further check, stock returns series for 68 individual stocks which were continuously included in the FTSE-100 index over the sample period were investigated. The results, shown in *Table 3*, indicate that while there was little change in the volatility of the main indices in the period up to Black Monday, this was not necessarily true of individual stocks. Many individual stocks do seem to have experienced significant increases in returns variance even before Black Monday.

Although the FTA and FTSE-100 indices have different distributions in the period

TABLE 2. Direct comparison of volatility

	Ratio of Variances	P-Value of F-Statistic
Pre-Big Bang vs. 27/10/86 to 16/10/87		
MSWI	1.221	0.0313
FTA	1.062	0.2894
FTSE(O)	1.112	0.1618
FTSE (C)	0.975	–0.3975
FTSE Intra-day	1.361	0.0021
Pre-Big Bang vs. 19/10/87 to 01/07/88		
MSWI	6.831	0.0000
FTA	6.050	0.0000
FTSE(O)	4.916	0.0000
FTSE(C)	5.289	0.0000
FTSE Intra-day	5.418	0.0000
Pre-Big Bang vs. 27/10/86 to 01/07/88		
MSWI	3.585	0.0000
FTA	3.174	0.0000
FTSE(O)	2.718	0.0000
FTSE(C)	2.798	0.0000
FTSE Intra-day	3.060	0.0000
Pre-Big Bang vs. 27/10/86 to 11/12/87		
MSWI	26.174	0.0000
FTA	21.087	0.0000
FTSE(O)	15.830	0.0000
FTSE(C)	18.725	0.0000
FTSE Intra-day	19.346	0.0000
Pre-Big Bang vs. 14/12/87 to 01/07/88		
MSWI	1.214	0.0791
FTA	1.424	0.0054
FTSE(O)	1.603	0.0004
FTSE(C)	1.255	0.0494
FTSE Intra-day	1.381	0.0098

following Black Monday there is *prima facie* evidence that it might not be appropriate to attribute the increase in variance to Big Bang, as the MWSI seems to undergo similar changes.

In other words, it seems that there were systematic changes occurring Worldwide over the sample period.

After using a market model to take into account World influences, it was found, once again, that the UK market was no more volatile in the period between Big Bang and Black Monday than it was prior to Big Bang. However, evidence was also found of increases in volatility in a significant number of individual stocks.

Moreover, since Black Monday the UK market did become more volatile, even after taking into account the influence of the increased volatility resulting from changes in global factors.

Subsequent tests showed that the proportion of total UK market volatility attributable to global volatility, increased sharply for a brief period after Black Monday, but then gradually settled down to earlier levels.

TABLE 3. Summary measures of returns variance ratio F-Tests on individual stock returns series.

-	Significant decreases	Significant increases	Insignificant changes	Total
Pre-Big Bang v Big Bang-16.10.87	9	32	27	68
Pre-Big Bang v 19.10.87–11.12.87	0	68	0	68
Pre-Big Bang v 14.12.87–1.7.88	5	27	36	68
Pre-Big Bang v 19.10.87–1.7.88	0	68	0	68
Pre-Big Bang v Post-Big Bang	0	63	5	68

It would appear that the folklore of the market being more volatile in the period prior to Black Monday and post-Big Bang was not entirely correct. The failure to find significantly higher volatility in the period prior to Black Monday makes questionable the attribution to Big Bang of the increase in volatility since Black Monday.

* Stock price data – Datastream
Dividend data – Extel
(Further details of the subsequent tests are available from the authors)

29 Goodwill to All Men?

A. SUGDEN AND G. HOLMES

This article was published in Professional Investor *in September 1990. Messrs Sugden and Holmes highlighted the anomalies that existed in the treatment of goodwill by UK companies. They found much that was purely subjective, and suggested that the best answer would be to require companies to take purchased goodwill on to the balance sheet and review it annually.*

At the time when this article was published, Alan Sugden had spent over 15 years in the City both as an investment analyst and as a fund manager. He is a Sloan Fellow of the London Business School and a former director of Schroder Investment Management Limited.

Geoffrey Holmes, FCA, FTII, had recently retired after more than 20 years as editor of Accountancy, *the monthly journal of the Institute of Chartered Accountants in England and Wales. As* Double Takes *was being prepared for publication, we heard of the sudden death of Geoffrey Holmes in mid-January 2000.*

How on earth did we get into this mess? As far as we can remember, the foundations of the present system of 'Immediate write-off' (purchased goodwill normally being eliminated from the accounts immediately on acquisition against reserves – SSAP 22 para. 32), were laid early in 1971, when the holders of Rolls-Royce debentures called in the receiver.

A major factor in Rolls-Royce's failure was the capitalisation of very large amounts of R & D expenditure on the development of a new engine, the RB 211, for the Lockheed Tristar. This gave the company's balance sheet a far healthier appearance than the technical risks of the development justified.

Thereafter most people, including ourselves, made it a rule of thumb in their own calculations to write off all intangibles if the company had not already done so. But times have changed in two important respects since 1971: firstly the shift in the UK economy away from manufacturing to service industries which, by their very nature, employ few tangible assets and a great deal of goodwill, and secondly the marked increase in growth by acquisition in the last few years which, in some cases, has created huge amounts of purchased goodwill.

CURRENT PRACTICE

Although a handful of companies have chosen to adopt SSAP 22's alternative method of treating goodwill, capitalising it in the balance sheet and then amortising it through the profit and loss account over its useful economic life, most companies have chosen immediate write-off direct to reserves to avoid the cost of amortisation hitting their earnings per share.

But immediate write-off does have one serious drawback: it can play havoc with the balance sheet, eg Smith Kline Beecham, with a current market capitalisation of well over £3 billion had negative shareholders funds at 31st December 1989 of £296.5 million. So some

FIGURE 1. Companies with large negative reserves.

Year Ended	Company	(a) Negative reserves £m	(b) Shareholders funds £m	$\frac{-a \times 100}{(b-a)}$	Remarks
31.12.89	WPP Group	(797.8)	(692.4)	756.9%	(a) Goodwill reserve (b) Excluding £350 m of Intangibles
28.01.90	Lowndes Queensway	(205.7)	(159.4)	444.3%	(a) Goodwill (£128.0 m); Profit & loss account (£77.7 m) (b) Excluding convertible loan notes
31.12.89	Alexander Proudfoot	(85.5)	(32.4)	161.0%	(a) Other reserves: Merger reserve (£78.1 m) and currency translation reserve (£7.4 m) (b) Excluding £1.7 m of Intangibles
31.12.89	SmithKline Beecham	(995.5)	(296.5)	142.4%	(a) Goodwill reserve
30.09.89	Saatchi & Saatchi	(434.6)	(87.7)	125.3%	(a) Goodwill reserve (b) Includes £176.5 m preference share capital of a subsidiary
31.07.89	Shandwick	(81.6)	(9.9)	113.8%	(a) Goodwill reserve
31.08.89	Bleinheim Exhibitions	(72.5)	0.2	99.7%	(a) Goodwill reserve
31.03.90	Erskine House	(98.7)	3.4	96.7%	(a) Goodwill reserve
31.12.89	United Newspapers	(146.1)	44.7	76.6%	(a) Other reserves: Goodwill, currency translation and issue costs (b) Excluding £136.3 m of Intangibles
31.12.89	TI Group	(360.5)	243.1	59.7%	(a) Goodwill written off
30.09.89	Tate & Lyle	(394.9)	316.5	55.5%	(a) Goodwill reserve

companies have created a 'goodwill reserve' against which to write off purchased goodwill, to help explain to shareholders why their funds (net of goodwill) have diminished dramatically, see Figure 1; this is very helpful. A few companies, like Guinness, show a detailed historical analysis, see Figure 2, which is even more useful.

Some companies have, however, found a crafty way of having their cake and eating it, by putting a 'fair value' on intangibles other than goodwill acquired. These other intangibles, eg brand names, are then not normally amortised, although they may be reviewed annually. A classic example is Ladbroke, which in 1987 acquired Hilton International and wrote off purchased goodwill against reserves. Then in their 1988 accounts they jumped on the brand name bandwaggon by deciding 'to attribute the premium arising on acquisition ... to the Hilton International brand name', and wrote £276.7 million back into the group balance sheet as an intangible asset.

Figure 3 lists leading companies with a significant proportion of reported shareholders' funds represented by intangible assets. Note that RHM has gone one step further by including brands, both acquired and created within the Group, at their 'current value to the group'.

But as Sir Adrian Cadbury said at his valedictory AGM last year, 'The market value of a company's own brands can only be established objectively when their ownership is transferred. Any other form of valuation is, by definition, subjective.'

FIGURE 2. Guinness note on goodwill.

Note 24 Goodwill Reserve
The goodwill reserve comprises goodwill on acquistions as follows:

	Year of acquisition	1988 £m	Additions £m	Transfers £m	Restatement £m	1989 £m
LVMH	1988/1989	45	147	–	–	192
Schenley	1987	92	–	–	–	92
Distillers	1986	326	–	77	(197)	206
Arthur Bell	1985	19	–	–	–	19
New Era Beverages	1989	–	24	–	–	24
Buckley's	1988	13	–	–	–	13
Other		59	25	(26)	–	58
		554	**196**	**51**	**(197)**	**604**

This has since been demonstrated by SmithKline Beecham's disposal of Marmite, Bovril and Ambrosia for £157 million. Who, at the date of the last balance sheet, could have put a reasonably accurate value on the brand name element in this disposal? And if, like RHM, brands are included at 'current use value to the group', is this an indication of the price above which the company would sell them? As Sir Adrian also said 'It could be a hostage to fortune'.

Brand valuation, like Current Cost Accounting, gives far too much scope for subjective judgment, and deserves the same fate.

CURRENT PROPOSALS

ED 47 Accounting for goodwill, issued by the Accounting Standards Committee last February, proposes to outlaw Immediate write-off; this is a complete U-turn on SSAP 22, where it is the preferred method. In addition, ED 47 wants to see purchased goodwill amortised over a maximum of 20 years, 'except in rare circumstances . . . where a period in excess of 20 years would be more appropriate', in which case the maximum should be 40 years. This is likely to go down like a lead balloon with the finance directors of acquisitive companies; but are they being reasonable, or just fighting their own corner?

The Exposure Draft also says that the amount attributed to purchased goodwill should not include any value for 'identifiable intangible assets', which are assets capable of being disposed of without disposing of a business. It isn't clear to us whether they too will have to be amortised if ED 47's proposals go through.

If brands are to be amortised, then companies are likely to resist strongly. As the finance director of Grand Metropolitan put it to the Financial Times; 'We are very committed to our brands and we put considerable resources into sustaining them . . . we don't believe there is any need to depreciate them'. Anthony Tennant takes the same view in his 1989 Chairman's Statement: 'Guinness believes that the inclusion of acquired brands in the balance sheet at historical cost is appropriate and that they should only be written down if their value is reduced. We will continue to add our voice to those of other companies who regard as misguided the proposed changes in accounting standards which would introduce automatic writing down. We dispute the logic of suggesting that a brand like Johnnie Walker which has been going strong since 1820 and gaining value year by year ought properly to be written off over, say, the next 40 years'.

Cadbury Schweppes takes the same line: Intangibles represent significant owned brands acquired since 1985 at historical cost. No amortisation is charged as the annual results

FIGURE 3. Companies with significant intangibles.

Year ended	Company Intangible assets £m	(a) Shareholders funds £m	(b)	$\frac{(a)}{(b)} \times 100$	Remarks
31.12.89	WPP Group	350.0	(342.4)	–	(a) Corporate brand names JWT, Hill & Knowlton and Ogilvy and Mather
31.03.90	Maxwell Comm Corp	2,162.7	1,006.3	214.9%	(a) Publishing rights, titles and benefits £2,151.0m Development expenditure £11.7m, amortised over the periods expected to benefit therefrom
31.03.90	Reed International	1,516.2	1,374.4	110.3%	(a) Publishing rights and titles, databases, exhibition rights and other similar intangible assets, at fair value on acquisition. Having no finite economic life, amortisation is not provided. Annual review, permanent impairment of value written off against profit.
30.09.89	Grand Metropolitan	2,652.0	2,810.0	94.4%	(a) Brands, including £1, 763m for Pillsbury (b) £1,724m of goodwill written off in 1989
2.09.89	Ranks Hovis McDougall	740.0	902.6	82.0%	(a) Brands, both acquired and created within the group, at 'current use value to the Group'. Cost is not subject to amortisation, but is reviewed annually.
31.03.90	EMAP	79.4	104.1	76.3%	(a) Acquired publishing rights, titles and exhibitions which have no finite life are stated at cost less provision for permanent diminution in value
31.12.89	United Newspapers	136.3	181.0	75.3%	(a) Publishing rights and titles at Directors' valuation at 31 December 1985 at £133m, estimated realisable value. Development expenditure £3.3m, amortised over 5 years or life of the project if shorter
31.12.89	Cadbury Schweppes	307.4	595.3	51.6%	(a) Significant owned brands acquired since 1985, valued at historical cost. No amortisation is charged as the annual results reflect significant expenditure in support of these brands. Values are reviewed annually
31.12.89	Guinness	1,375.0	2,838.0	48.4%	(a) Acquired brands at cost (b) Net of £604m negative goodwill reserve
31.12.89	Ladbroke	792.5	2,433.9	32.6%	(a) Betting shop licenses £415.8m, at estimated current cost for shops opened in 1984 and earlier. Brand names: Hilton International £276.7m; Vernons £100.0m

reflect significant expenditure in support of these brands but the values are reviewed annually with a view to write down if a permanent diminution arises'. We think they have a point. Conversely, if brands do not need to be amortised (providing they are capable of being sold separately), the 'Hilton International' dodge will ontinue.

But who is to say whether an intangible asset is capable of being sold separately? Presumably the directors. Looking at Figure 3, publishing rights frequently change hands, so United Newspapers, EMAP and Cap'n Bob are all right. Betting office licenses change hands too, though Ladbroke puts them in at estimated current cost for shops opened in 1984 or earlier, which more than doubles the total figure, but could Ladbroke really sell the Hilton brand name on its own and change the name of their hotels – to Stein International perhaps?

And could WPP sell the JWT name without any of the staff, or could Mr Kipling be disposed of without his plant and premises? Perhaps so; whisky brand names have been sold off separately in the past, as Guinness had to do to satisfy the MMC in acquiring Distillers.

'Ok, ok' you say, 'you've made your point, but what would you do about it?' Good question: we won't dodge it, but let's look first at the analyst's point of view.

THE ANALYSTS' VIEWPOINT

From an analyst's point of view, immediate write-off is grossly misleading and makes a nonsense of investment ratios designed to measure the return on capital. In this context it has been sad to see companies of undoubted integrity unintentionally pull the wool over the eyes of their shareholders by proclaiming an improvement in their return on capital which has been caused mainly or entirely by writing off purchased goodwill. For instance Unilever, with the acquistion of Chesebrough-Pond's in 1987, wrote off purchased goodwill of £1.288 billion and then showed in its annual report's 'Financial Highlights' an increase in the return on shareholders' equity from 17.8% in 1986 to 25.4% in 1987. A pretty impressive improvement, but if purchased goodwill had been included in the calculation, the return would have been only 17.7%, marginally down on the previous year.

So one thing we would like to see is the clear display, on the face of the balance sheet itself, of the cumulative amount of shareholders' money that the directors have spent on intangibles, net of any amount that has been written off through the profit and loss account. This could either be done by including net purchased goodwill as an intangible fixed asset, or by showing it as a negative reserve, clearly labelled Goodwill. If the latter, the reserve must be solely for cumulative purchased goodwill, excluding other items such as currency translation adjustments (as in United Newspapers), and must not be reduced by partial write-off direct to other reserves, nor credited with other items (as in WPP, which credited £14.3 million of premiums on shares issued for acquistions to its merger reserve in 1988, as well as debiting that reserve with a further £75.5 million of purchased goodwill).

ED 47 proposes that 'purchased goodwill that has previously been written off to reserves immediately on acquisition in accordance with standard accounting practice at that date, need not be reinstated to the balance sheet on the introduction of this standard'. We do not agree; we would like to see all that purchased goodwill reinstated, at least for the last five years.

OUR PREFERRED SOLUTION

Whichever solution is reached, two things are quite clear, even to a couple of old fuddy-duddies like us: firstly that if companies are given a choice in the way they treat purchased goodwill, it will inevitably lead to companies choosing the method that helps their figures, regardless of 'true and fair' considerations. This is the way life is, as has been demonstrated by companies' 'pick-and-choose' use of the merger accounting/acquisition accounting methods (soon to be stopped, we hope, by the adoption of ED 48, the recent draft on Accounting for acquistions and mergers).

Secondly, if the new rules leave a loophole (like brand names being able to avoid any amortisation that applies to purchased goodwill), then some companies will drive a coach and horses through it, and auditors will be powerless to stop them.

An attractive answer, in the cause of international standardisation, would be to adopt the US maximum period for amortisation of 40 years. If companies whinge at the prospect of amortising the cost of goodwill over that period, they should be told firmly that any acquisition so finely pitched that it would be scuppered by an extra say 2% per annum charge on the overall cost (assuming 80% is goodwill), then they shouldn't be doing the deal in the first place.

But perhaps the best answer of all would be not to insist on amortisation, but to require companies to take purchased goodwill on to their balance sheet, and to review it annually. Any permanent diminution in value would then be charged to the profit and loss account. This solution would have four advantages:

- ☐ Companies can't reasonably object to it.
- ☐ Dodges to avoid amortisation become redundant.
- ☐ Companies would not be lumbered with a charge to their profit and loss account which is not deductable for UK tax purposes (although it is deductable in some other countries, most notably in the US).
- ☐ If companies spend huge amounts of shareholders' money gunning around buying goodwill, then their return on shareholders' funds will be hit if the money is not well spent.

Anyway, what's the point of fussing about amortisation over 20 or 40 years, when the real value of purchased goodwill in the balance sheet will probably be halved by inflation over the next 10, or sooner if we have a change of government before the year 2000.

30 Economic Policy

W. GODLEY

In this 1991 essay, Professor Godley questions the assumption that there is an underlying equilibrium to the economy that remains intact, despite external shocks and buffetings. In fact, he argues that since 1979 the British economy has shown 'progressive failure' and the fluctuations of the 1980s masked an endemic decline. His conclusion is sombre: a continuation of the deterioration, at least in the medium turn.

Professor Wynne Godley has worked as Economic Adviser to the Metal Box Company and for 14 years at HM Treasury. From 1970 to 1985 he was Director of the Department of Applied Economics, and from 1972 Professor of Applied Economics at Cambridge University. He now teaches and does research work in the USA.

The question people should now be addressing is nor when a recovery from the present downturn will occur but whether any recovery large enough to reverse the present rise in unemployment is in prospect at any stage.

A severe recession, to use no stronger word, is certainly upon us. It was expected by no-one except for (what has been christened) 'the unholy alliance' of monetarists and Cambridge Keynesians. What is disturbing about the general response to the downturn is that, notwithstanding the failure of the forecasts, no-one seems to have the slightest sense that their system of ideas is under any threat or in need of overhaul. Surely they should be learning something from such serious mistakes?

In asking this question I am not being mischievous. There is a point of great importance to be made. I believe that most people who follow the economy have a notion that there exists all the time an underlying equilibrium which is stable and which has powerful self-righting properties. There may well be shocks to the economy which disturb its equilibrium and these shocks cannot, of their nature, be forecast by economic models. But when they occur it is only a matter of time before natural forces bring the system back to its equilibrium. Whether or not this is a fair description of how most commentators think, I am pretty clear that the great majority do assume that a severe recession of the kind we are now witnessing will inevitably right itself in one way or another. And it is this assumption that I wish to question further.

People's perception of the long-term evolution of the British economy has been distorted by the astonishing fluctuations in demand and output which have occurred during the last sixteen years and, more particularly, the last eleven years. This is borne out by the figures in Chart 1, which shows manufacturing output and total unemployment ever since 1950.

It is still something which turns up endlessly in answers to exam questions as well as in second-rate political journalism, that the 50s and 60s constituted the classic period of 'stop-go' which new thinking had forever made redundant by the mid-seventies and eighties.

CHART 1. Manufacturing output & (total) unemployment.

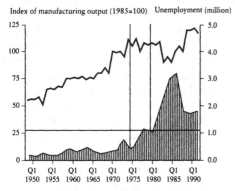

Source: Economic Trends (unemployment for fifties & sixties linked by author)

CHART 2. Labour productivity in manufacturing with a single (fitted) trend of 3% pa.

Source: Economic Trends

CHART 3. Balance of trade in manufacture and total balance (as a percent of GDP).

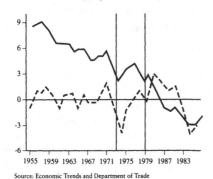

Source: Economic Trends and Department of Trade

CHART 4. Manufacturing balance & measures of competitiveness.

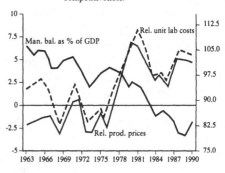

Source: Economic Trends & Department of Trade

But just look at the chart. The switchback really starts with the Heath–Barber boom of 1972–73 closely followed by the Healey recession. These fluctuations were already far larger than any that had previously occurred. However it was the Conservative government's medium term financial strategy, designed to provide the stable environment for long-term growth and the creation of 'real' jobs, which was the signal for all hell to break loose. To begin with we have the first real recession of the post-war period, with manufacturing output falling nearly 20 per cent in two years and unemployment rising towards three million. Then we have the Lawson boom which I have compared to a joy ride by Mr Toad, in which he drove a stolen car at rates far exceeding the speed limit, hooting and cheering whenever he overtook anybody until he finally crashed and had to be arrested. Now, of course, we have Messrs. Major and Lamont faced with a renewed downturn.

I have a serious purpose in rehearsing all this. What I want to draw attention to is that notwithstanding these hysterical fluctuations in demand and output, we can and must still try to identify the main long run, structural trends. And this is the part which makes pretty grim reading. For taking the whole period since the beginning of 1979, and ignoring the roller-coaster, we have a growth rate far lower than in any other period of comparable length prior to 1979. The average growth of manufacturing output was about one half of one per cent per annum. And unemployment, not very surprisingly, was considerably higher, about 300,000 higher, at the end of 1990 than it had been at the beginning of 1979. Yet in spite of the very slow growth of demand and output over the period as a whole, inflationary pressure is still, apparently, excessive. As Chart 2 shows, the growth of productivity in manufacturing industry for so long claimed as the one clear and indisputable indication of the success of the Thatcher supply-side policies, has not been significantly better than it was on average during the earlier post-war period (and, as I have already pointed out on many occasions, there would be, in any case, no merit in having an improvement in the growth of productivity if there were not also an improvement in production or some other measure of achievement). And then, the balance of payments is in considerably worse shape now than it was in 1979, despite the fact that the balance of trade in oil is still better now than it was then; there was a surplus in our balance of trade in manufacture in 1979 equal to 2 per cent of GDP which had become a deficit of 1.5 per cent in 1990.

The major point that I want, above all, to emphasise is that our perception of the whole periods and, I believe, of the short- and medium-term prospect now before us, would be entirely different if we had reached the present position by even stages. It would be clear to everybody that the underlying condition of the British economy had throughout the period been one of progressive failure. The wild fluctuations of the eighties – down, up and now down again – could not then have obscured the perception that the structural evolution of the economy was one characterised by endemic depression and decline. Those who think of the economy in terms of an equilibrium subject to unpredictable shocks have, as I said earlier, a strong tendency to suppose that whatever unpleasant things are now happening will automatically be reversed in due course. But any forces for self-equilibrium have clearly failed over the last decade, taken as a whole.

The question I want to ask now is whether we have the slightest reason to suppose that the adverse underlying trends of the past will now be reversed. Why on earth should they be? The effect of the slump at the beginning of the eighties was almost certainly adverse with respect to the structural matters. The Lawson boom was quite certainly destructive, not merely because it was excessive and landed us with one of the highest inflation rates in Europe, but because it gave all the wrong signals to industry, causing heavy investment in the wrong sectors – ie not nearly enough in manufacturing industry and far too much in distribution and financial sectors.

Why then should the economy perform any better in the future than it has in the past? What reason can we have for supposing, whatever happens in the short term, that the growth of output over the next decade will be significantly larger, or the growth of unemployment significantly slower, in the future than it has been in the past?

THE SHORT TERM

Although my main concern is with structural trends, I am not going to duck the question of what is going to happen in the very short term. I emphasise once again that although short-term developments dominate the news, make or break the lives of individual human beings and firms and profoundly affect the behaviour of politicians and voters, in a more fundamental sense they have secondary importance.

The impression I have is that what happens this year and next will be dominated by two new features of the economy, which because they are new, are very difficult for those who do their thinking mainly through econometric models to handle sensibly. The first is that personal consumption has been, to a much greater extent than usual, financed by borrowing, with very heavy indebtedness having been incurred by the household sector. My understanding is that it was a fall in net borrowing by households (and a consequent rise in saving) which was largely responsible for the initial decline in total demand. But while the growth of indebtedness has slowed down it has remained very rapid and I very much doubt, particularly with asset prices still in the doldrums whether a re-acceleration is on the cards.

So personal saving may go on rising, thereby preventing any significant recovery in consumption even if real wages rise as inflation falls. The other unwelcome feature of the situation is the financial deficit of the corporate sector; the figures show that borrowing at unprecedented rates is necessary just to keep existing flows of outlays on dividends and interest, as well as investment, going. As with household debt, the corporate deficit is a new feature of the situation which no-one knows how to interpret reliably. My own conclusion which is, of course, strongly reinforced by the results of industrial surveys, is that a very heavy fall in investment is in prospect. More problematic, because less easy for the outsider to keep track of, is the possibility that, as falling demand and real income interact in a downward spiral, firms go out of business on a scale at least as large as in 1979–81.

From all this I tend to the conclusion that we are in for a recession of the same order, at least, as in 1979–81 though spread more evenly across regions and industries and with more alarming consequences for the survival of firms – often good, well modernised firms – that are caught out by the need to borrow excessively. If forced to give figures, I would say there will be a fall of 3–5 per cent in output between 1990 and 1992 with unemployment rising above three million before the end of next year. The balance of payments, measured *ex post facto*, should improve a lot, but only because of the slump. This is all conditional, of course, on the existing policy stance being maintained – in particular on interest rates continuing to be held at whatever rate keeps sterling within its present band inside the ERM.

WHERE WILL THE RECOVERY COME FROM?

Government spokesmen, when asked what they are going to do about unemployment, invariably reply that nothing can happen until inflation comes down. It is not clear, and I think it is not really meant to be quite clear, whether this is prediction or a kind of threat. These and other comparable statements do however fall far short of constituting a coherent policy either for the short or for the medium term. In fact it is now completely impossible to discern what the government thinks it is up to. All its previous policies have palpably and tragically failed. The position we now find ourselves in was, one must charitably suppose, completely unforeseen by them and they clearly don't know what to do next.

Where then is the recovery supposed to come from? In a recent article in the *Financial Times* ('How lower inflation will bring recovery' Jan 7th 1991) Samuel Brittan concluded that 'The blame for prolonged recession lies neither in German policy nor in British interest or exchange rate policy, but in the rigidities of the domestic labour market; in the vernacular plain bloody-mindedness'. What arguments are used to support this strong and important conclusion? According to Mr Brittan, '... Nominal GDP has been growing at just over 8 per cent per annum. A very slight tilt downward is in prospect ... So long as this path is observed, a fall in the inflation rate will automatically {sic!} lead to an output recovery. On the other hand, so long as pay and price increases continue on their present scale, recession will deepen'. The explicit assumption behind all this is 'that total spending in cash terms is maintained, either through natural forces or through the actions of governments and central banks', although this conditionality is lost both in the title of the article and in its main conclusion (contained in the first passage quoted above).

This is all very silly. In the first place the conclusion would only hold if it were actually in the power of the authorities to make money income rise by about 8 per cent per annum irrespective of inflation; and also if they undertook to make it do so. But to predetermine the growth of money income, if possible at all, would require a complex technical apparatus (perhaps along the lines proposed by my colleagues Martin Weale and James Meade) which simply does not exist at the moment. Moreover no undertaking of any kind has been given that the authorities are even going to try to behave in this way.

But there is a more fundamental point. Even if the authorities could do it, they would be seriously mistaken if they tried to engineer a growth of money income as large as 8 per cent if inflation fell to 5 per cent. This is because the mere convergence of our inflation rate to Germany would do no more than stabilise our international competitiveness without actually improving it.

So the rise in domestic demand brought about by the successful implementation of Mr Brittan's proposal would run us straight back to unsustainable balance of payments deficits. Mr Brittan's proposition that, given any particular growth of 'money GDP', real output will grow by that amount less the inflation rate is a correct piece of arithmetic, and it possibly may make him feel better to place the blame for unemployment on British bloody-mindedness rather than on Mrs Thatcher or Nigel Lawson, but as a policy prescription it is vacuous at best.

RECOVERY HAS TO BE GENERATED BY NET EXPORT DEMAND

As the only way in which sustained growth can be achieved is through the agency of net exports, we are finally bound to face the question of whether we have joined the ERM at the correct rate. But first consider the magnitude of change in competitiveness (compared with the past) now required. Some sense of the problem is given by the figures illustrated in Chart 3, which shows how the balance of trade in manufactures (expressed as a proportion of GDP) has moved ever since 1955. The story is one of remorseless deterioration, with occasional remissions due to depression or devaluation. The chart also shows the total balance on current account. It is particularly to be noted that other factors, in particular the rise in the balance of trade in oil between 1974 and the mid eighties, offset, and therefore masked, the deterioration in manufacturing. But since 1988 or thereabouts, with the balance of trade in oil and the other components of the current account (like services) performing very badly, the manufacturing balance has come to dominate the scene.

I have heard it said, for instance by Gavyn Davies, that the present external value of the Pound can be justified by inspection of the published measures of international competitiveness, which shows that we are, in this particular sense, more competitive than in 1981 and not much different from our long-term average position.

But this is not nearly good enough! In Chart 4, two official measures of competitiveness (relative producer prices and relative unit labour costs – and note that an upwards movement means less competitive) against the balance of trade in manufactures over the whole period since 1963, are plotted. Nothing can be positively proved of course, but I can draw no comfort at all from the fact that measured competitiveness is no worse than on average during the eighties seeing that there was such a spectacular deterioration of performance during that period.

CONCLUSION

The conclusion I reach is an extremely sombre one. As a general principle I do not believe, using the evidence of the past or on the basis of an economic theory, that 'natural' forces making for failure – or for that matter success of industrial economies – are anything other than self-reinforcing ones. In the absence of some entirely new policy initiative, therefore, I expect the process of endemic deterioration to continue in the medium term. So far as the short term is concerned we are faced with an extremely severe recession. But there is much less scope for short-term remedial measures than there used to be, even if these were what the Government were disposed to apply. This is because, with inflation still high, the balance of payments still in heavy deficit and with no oil spout to act as *deus ex machina* the long term constraint has become binding in the short term.

31 The Money-Go-Round

T. CONGDON AND A. SUGDEN

This article was published in Professional Investor *in October 1993. The intellectual battles over the role of money supply in inflation control were at their most intense in the 1980s, but remained unresolved in the early 1990s. In this interview, Professor Tim Congdon argues that the focus of monetary policy should be on broad measures of the money supply, not narrow measures, and that the growth of the broad measures of money should be influenced by interest rates, debt management policy and an appropriate fiscal policy. Other monetary economists hold different views on these complex subjects.*

Professor Tim Congdon is one of the City of London's leading economic commentators. He first starting working in the City in 1976, at the time of the International Monetary Fund's visit to the UK. His work has emphasized the need for control of monetary growth and sound public finances in order to achieve low inflation and economic stability. He served on the Treasury Panel of Independent Forecasters ('The Wise Men') under the last Conservative Government. He is a visiting professor at Cardiff Business School and City University Business School.

Alan Sugden – see Chapter 29 for biographical details.

Alan Sugden: *Could we start by talking about the various measures used to monitor the money supply, MO and so on.*

Tim Congdon: The helpful way of looking at this question is not to think in terms of MO, M1 and so on, but to say that money consists of those assets that can be used to pay for goods, services and assets. It takes two principal forms. One obviously is notes and coin, but the bulk of payments nowadays are made by writing cheques. Cheques are written against bank deposits. So the second kind of money, bank deposits, is the dominant form of money in a modern economy.

The expression 'money supply' is perhaps rather unfortunate, because people often think that the money supply means new bank loans. It does not mean that, it means the stock of notes, coin and bank deposits that exist in an economy in a country at any particular time.

The government targets MO, but has abandoned M3?

As far as I am concerned, MO is not a measure of the money supply; it is simply a subcategory of the broader total. The notion of notes and coin having some relevance to behaviour is clearly a misunderstanding. If the amount of notes and coin that you, I or a company holds exceeds the level that we would like to hold, we pay the loose money into our account. It doesn't affect our decisions to spend.

If you want to understand fluctuations in economic activity in a modern economy, you don't look at statistics for notes and coin in circulation. You don't go there because the big fluctuations are virtually all in spending on capital items. For the corporate sector all these things are paid for by cheque. And in the personal sector, the volatile items are not groceries and newspapers. The volatile items, the ones that really swing around, that really cause the fluctuations, are spending on houses, cars and consumer durables. Now one of the characteristics of these items is that payments are virtually always done by cheque against bank deposits, and credit is often involved.

So if you want to understand these fluctuations, you simply don't go to M0. It is just a complete misunderstanding of how the economy works. I think a certain school of so-called monetarists has done immense damage to the cause of good monetary policy and the understanding of monetary economics in general by pretending that M0 can matter to anything very much.

Would you favour going to M3 or M4?

The M3 measure of money, which includes bank deposits, is the conventional broad money measure adopted around the world. The only difference between it and M4 is that M4 also includes building society deposits. M4 is dominated by the M3 part of it, so it is noticeable that they normally move together (see Figure 1).

Is is possible to demonstrate that if money supply is excessive, then you get inflation?

There are a number of ways of answering this question, but the simplest one is to say that the price level is the value of money and the value of money, like the value of anything else, is determined by supply and demand. Now if the demand to hold money balances in real terms is relatively stable then fluctuations in the supply of money will not change the real quantity of money balances that people want to hold, they will only change the price level. So if too much money is supplied, the value of money will fall and the price level will rise.

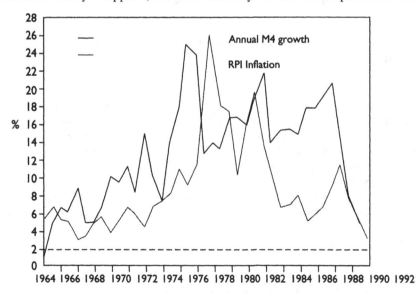

FIGURE 1. Annual growth of M3 and M4.

One of the problems that I think people in Britain have with this argument is that we have never actually been through a hyper-inflation. But for any nation that has been through it, it is so obvious that it hardly needs discussion.

That seems straightforward common sense, but how do we apply it to analysing the economy in any relatively stable two or three year period?

The crucial principle of monetarism is that the demand for real money balances is relatively stable. The quantity of money balances that people, companies and financial institutions in aggregate wish to hold doesn't actually vary a great deal from year to year; it changes, but it doesn't vary dramatically.

The best way of thinking about this is to think about your own behaviour. You know you've got so many assets, your house, your investments, some money in the bank, you've got your spending, and the whole time you are juggling the amount of money you have in the bank with how much you have in other assets. You don't want your bank balance to be some enormous proportion of your wealth; on the other hand you don't want to have nil in the bank.

But if there is a sudden and sharp change in the quantity of money, it takes time for us to bring our money balances back to right level. Friedman's golden rules, based on looking at data over the very long run and for several countries, are that large changes in monetary growth affect output with a lag of about six months or a year and inflation with a lag of about two years.

If we look back at the Barber boom, the inflation of 1978–80 and the Lawson boom, they were all preceded by excessive increases in the money supply, broad money (see Figure 2). How does the Government change the quantity of money in the economy?

The first thing to say is that the principal kind of money in a modern economy is the total of bank deposits, so the growth of the money stock or money supply depends on the growth of bank balance sheets.

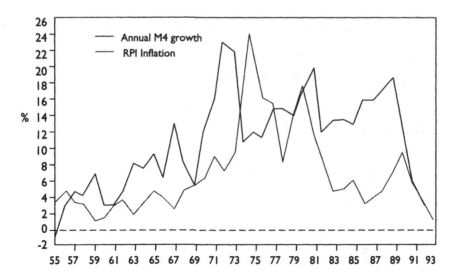

FIGURE 2. Inflation and broad money growth.

Now banks are profit maximisers, and they will expand their balance sheets if they can make a profit out of it. So the main influence on monetary growth most of the time is the extension of bank credit to the private sector. In my view, the Government cannot control this process exactly, they can only influence it. They influence it largely by Central Bank operations in the money markets, which set interest rates.

The Central Bank can control short term interest rates because it is the monopoly supplier of a special type of money, namely notes and coin. The key point here is that notes and coin are legal tender, while bank deposits are not. The fact that they are legal tender is crucial. The banks have to preserve the convertibility of their deposits into legal tender to remain in business as banks. They therefore always need to keep legal tender in their balance sheets. They always have a demand to hold cash.

The fact that the Central Bank is the monopoly supplier of legal tender means that it can control the price, the interest rate. But notes and coin and bank deposits are totally interchangeable, so when the Central Bank sets interest rates in the market that it fully controls, this sets short term interest rates throughout the system.

This then means that the Central Bank can exert considerable influence over the rate at which the banking system extends credit, because at any one time there are only a certain number of borrowers who are prepared to borrow at a certain interest rate. The higher the interest rate goes, the fewer the borrowers.

I think one of the things that has emerged in the last 20 years is that variations in interest rates are extremely powerful in their effects on the economy. That shouldn't come as a great surprise. But there was an important tradition in British macroeconomics which claimed that interest rates were not important as an influence on demand, and the last 20 years have shown that this is *not* true.

The trouble with using interest rate to influence the money supply is that if you also use it to try to control your exchange rate, you get into trouble.

Yes, if you are trying to do both at the same time, you get into a muddle. Of course this is what happened when Nigel Lawson was Chancellor. In trying to shadow the Deutschmark he had interest rates too low all through 1986 and 1987, and in early 1988 he reduced

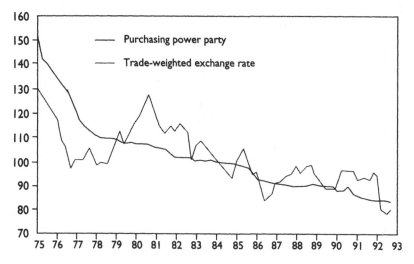

FIGURE 3. Strategy's Trade-weighted exchange rate and Purchasing power party.

interest rates at the peak of a very strong boom. The effect was that real domestic demand grew by 8 per cent in one year, which is ridiculous. A normal rise in real demand is about 2.5 per cent, in line with the growth in GDP, therefore the result was catastrophic.

But if you are using your interest rate to control your money supply, do you just let the exchange rate go where it wants?

In general that is certainly the system that I would like. I think the main reservation is that one clearly wants to avoid extremes. I am in favour of an override, so that if the exchange rate became seriously undervalued or overvalued relative to the purchasing power parity of the trade-weighted index, you could override the monetary target.

The question then is how often would these exceptions occur in the real world. The answer is very infrequently because despite all the exchange rate fluctuations of recent years, on the whole the trade-weighted exchange rate has been within 10 per cent of its purchasing power parity value (see Figure 3).

In our last interview you explained how the amount of money in the economy can be influenced by the way the Government finances its budget deficit, by its funding policy. If it sells to non-banks it reduces the money supply; if it sells to banks it doesn't. When would you use funding policy to influence the money supply?

Always. I am all in favour of using what we might call funding policy – call it debt management policy, call it open market operations, all valid expressions for the same thing – to change the quantity of money in order to get it closer to a target level.

This aspect of the subject seems to me to be plain common sense. It is certainly what we used to do in the early eighties and, indeed, for decades before that.

You say open market operations?

There are two types of open market operations. There are open market operations between the Central Bank and the banking system, which are intended to allow the banks to adjust their balances of high powered money (notes, coin and their balances with the central bank, also known as the 'monetary base' or the 'reserve base') to the desired level. These are known as 'daily money market operations'. The second kind is gilt edged sales. For the most part these are sales of government debt to non-banks.

I would use interest rates and funding policy to influence monetary growth. But that reflects the tradition of monetary policy I come from, the British tradition.

What else could you do? Place controls on the banks?

There is a school of thought which says that the Central Bank can control the quantity of money if it controls the quantity monetary base. People say that you can achieve a precise arithmetical link between the monetary base and the quantity of money, because banks have got to have some base in their balance sheets to meet deposit withdrawals.

My answer to that is no, that is not what happens. What happens is that banks decide how large they want their balance sheets to be on the basis of their own profit maximising decisions, and get whatever amount of cash they want from the Central Bank. The Central Bank meets their needs because it is their banker. That's actually how the world works. To say that this ought to be changed to some text book ideal of monetary base control is simply to misunderstand what a Central Bank does, its functions, its purpose and its history.

Another method, which has become very important recently, is capital control, where the banks must keep a certain relationship between their capital and their liabilities. I can see why, on prudential grounds, that makes sense. The difficulty with that is, to the extent that the banks are required to maintain more capital in their business than they wish, they will try to expand their balance sheets in ways that aren't captured by the control, or aren't followed by the regulators. That's another big subject.

You are not in favour of either theory?

No. May I summarise my philosophy? We live in a free economy, fortunately. There are no direct quantitative restrictions on bank lending any more and there are no exchange controls. I hope that this continues.

In our kind of economy the banks are free agents and like any other business they should be able to carry out their operations as they see fit. Not entirely, of course. Every business organisation is subject to various kinds of regulation and control, but as far as possible they should be free agents.

Now the Central Bank's job is to maintain monetary stability. In my view this means maintaining a stable growth of the quantity of money, making sure that it is in line with the growth of output, so that the value of money doesn't fall or rise. In my view the Central Bank can reconcile these objectives with a free banking system if it operates in the way I have described, through changing interest rates if credit growth is excessive or inadequate, and supplementing this through funding operations.

And in both money market operations and in open market operations at the long end, all the transactions are at arms length between free agents. The advantage of trying to control the quantity of money in this way rather than through capital controls or monetary base control or some other way, is that it actually reflects the wishes of the people concerned. I think that this is the great merit of this approach.

ADDENDUM

	M4 YoY% Nominal	M3 YoY% Nominal	RPI YoY%		M4 YoY% Nominal	M3 YoY% Nominal	RPI YoY%
1955	3.9		3.96226	1967	6.03	2.63	3.57
	2.2		4.1433		8.20	5.06	2.53
	0.6		4.08351		10.35	7.41	1.66
	−1		5.8285		12.10	10.22	2.12
1956	0.1		5.53702	1968	11.84	10.22	3.02
	0.8		6.55124		11.36	10.73	4.53
	1.7		4.66407		8.95	8.07	5.66
	2.6		3.24498		8.29	7.25	5.59
1957	3.1		3.81679	1969	7.63	6.15	6.22
	3.6		2.3407		4.97	1.75	5.41
	4		4.14491		5.15	1.73	5.06
	4.5		4.46313		4.87	1.96	5.12
1958	4.4		3.61253	1970	4.94	1.32	5.04
	4.4		4.5108		8.51	6.70	5.86
	4.3		1.91163		10.61	8.54	6.84
	4.2		1.98142		12.02	9.51	7.72
1959	4.9		2.12897	1971	14.41	12.88	8.57
	5.5		−0.3343		13.77	11.06	9.84
	6.1		0.55351		14.09	11.05	10.10
	6.7		0		16.21	14.00	9.21
1960	5.7		−0.4532	1972	17.85	16.00	7.96
	4.8		1.0979		21.22	21.94	6.17
	3.9		1.52905		21.75	23.90	6.46
	3		1.85185		21.60	24.23	7.71
1961	3		2.36722	1973	21.61	25.03	7.93
	3		3.01659		20.93	22.60	9.32
	3		4.15663		22.93	26.91	9.21
	3.1		4.23249		22.34	26.22	10.27
1962	3.5		4.71539	1974	19.45	23.71	12.88
	3.9		5.62958		15.72	19.11	15.88
	4.4		3.84037		11.18	12.21	17.01
	4.8		2.6487		11.28	10.60	18.17
1963	5.7		3.14961	1975	11.88	8.83	20.30
	6.5		1.56625		13.20	8.88	24.29
	7.4		1.31336		14.94	10.72	26.56
	8.2		2.11449		12.45	5.81	25.32
1964	9.10	7.09	1.5133	1976	12.54	5.50	22.45
	8.70	6.54	2.79		12.42	6.77	15.98
	9.10	7.53	4.35		12.60	8.00	13.66
	7.80	5.70	4.49		11.92	8.83	14.93
1965	7.76	6.17	4.50	1977	10.16	7.46	16.51
	7.88	6.96	5.17		10.81	8.00	17.41
	7.91	6.32	4.80		10.91	6.31	16.57
	9.62	7.51	4.57		14.63	9.36	13.07
1966	11.15	8.98	4.42	1978	18.41	15.58	9.50
	9.65	6.06	3.84		17.20	15.43	7.69
	8.82	5.81	3.69		16.60	15.73	7.85
	6.59	3.39	3.82		14.92	15.18	8.10

	M4 YoY% Nominal	M3 YoY% Nominal	RPI YoY%		M4 YoY% Nominal	M3 YoY% Nominal	RPI YoY%
1979	13.10	11.73	9.57	1989	17.69	20.79	7.71
	13.97	13.26	10.59		18.17	21.77	8.19
	14.56	13.35	15.97		17.12	19.70	7.71
	14.44	13.01	17.25		18.07	20.09	7.58
1980	14.20	12.90	19.09	1990	17.79	18.60	7.76
	15.23	15.48	21.54		16.92	17.33	9.66
	15.65	16.30	16.36		14.83	13.99	10.43
	17.27	18.61	15.28		12.18	10.71	9.98
1981	17.11	17.97	12.70	1991	9.70	7.80	8.70
	16.88	16.86	11.70		7.80	5.22	6.01
	16.48	16.92	11.26		6.60	3.95	4.76
	14.08	13.55	11.90		5.93	3.60	4.15
1982	13.34	14.35	11.13	1992	5.52	3.00	4.10
	11.82	11.31	9.35		5.10	3.07	4.17
	11.95	8.92	7.98		4.83	3.15	3.63
	12.57	8.90	6.17		3.73	1.98	3.05
1983	13.95	12.49	4.97	1993	3.31	2.70	1.81
	14.13	12.44	3.78		3.02	1.68	1.27
	13.01	11.49	4.65		3.40	2.31	1.63
	12.99	11.11	5.05		4.70	6.03	1.55
1984	11.56	8.18	5.15	1994	5.70	6.96	2.38
	12.26	8.05	5.14		5.40	5.97	2.58
	12.86	9.24	4.71		5.00	4.80	2.31
	13.14	10.13	4.84		4.50	2.93	2.63
1985	13.80	11.88	5.51	1995	5.00	5.33	3.40
	12.89	11.83	6.97		6.52	7.15	3.41
	13.14	14.09	6.32		8.53	12.49	3.67
	13.19	13.41	5.53		9.50	15.78	3.16
1986	14.57	16.92	4.94	1996	10.12		2.77
	16.01	18.90	2.77		9.93		2.25
	15.38	19.00	2.61		9.60		2.16
	15.59	19.25	3.41		10.41		2.62
1987	14.67	19.55	3.94	1997	10.75		2.70
	14.34	19.44	4.19		11.07		2.66
	15.39	20.07	4.31		11.60		3.48
	16.59	22.30	4.12		11.10		3.68
1988	17.13	21.01	3.36	1998	10.43		3.40
	17.17	20.31	4.25		9.77		3.99
	18.65	22.42	5.45		9.37		3.32
	17.44	20.27	6.52		8.50		2.96
				1999	7.20		2.21
					6.63		1.41

Regression relationship between increases in M4 and M3
1. M4 independent variable, M3 dependent variable
Regression Output:

Constant	−4.1112
Std Err of Y Est	2.2946
R Squared	0.87386
No. of Observations	126
Degrees of Freedom	124
X Coefficient(s)	1.26928
Std Err of Coef.	0.04331

2. M3 independent variable, M4 dependent variable
Regression Output:

Constant	4.38505
Std Err of Y Est	1.68994
R Squared	0.87386
No. of Observations	126
Degrees of Freedom	124
X Coefficient(s)	0.68847
Std Err of Coef.	0.02349

Source: Economic Trends

32 The Rewards of Virtue?

R. SPARKES

This article was published in Professional Investor *in March 1994. In 1984 Friends Provident launched the first ethical unit trust. Ten years on, Russell Sparkes examined the growth of direct ethical investment and its increasing popularity with savers. He also assessed the relative performance of the major funds in the sector. His overall conclusion was that ethical investment was becoming 'more complex and difficult to do'.*

Russell Sparkes is Fund Manager, Central Finance Board of the Methodist Church. Russell has worked in the investment field for over 22 years and for the last five years for the Central Finance Board of the Methodist Church and also its associated company Epworth investment Management. He is also Secretary of the Joint Advisory Committee on the Ethics of Investment. He writes and lectures on ethical investment, and his book The Ethical Investor *was the first UK book on the subject published by a mainstream publisher.*

In the last 18 months, emerging funds have captured the investment limelight. A new collection of funds seems to appear daily, enticing investors with promises of high returns. However, behind the scenes, another trend is catching on in a quieter, yet steadier fashion – ethical or environmental investing. (See table 1 and figure 1, which illustrates the growth of direct ethical investment since the end of 1984 and its changing composition).

Since 1984, when Friends Provident launched the first ethical unit trust, the growth rate has been 35% per year, or a doubling every two and a half years over the last nine years. The growth spurt seen in 1987–1990 appears particularly impressive given how bleak that period was for many unit trusts. It should be noted that the above statistics refer only to funds such as unit and investment trusts, and life funds in which the public can invest directly. Indirect funds that are ethically constrained include church and charity funds, and some local authority pension funds that amount to around £15bn.

Although ethical investment has enjoyed increased press coverage over the last year – not least in *Professional Investor*, and *Money Which* – some in the investment management profession may still be unclear about the specifics. Put simply, it means investment funds where non-financial criteria of an ethical or ecological nature are an essential part of the investment policy.

TABLE 1.

Year (31 Dec)	1984	1987	1990	1993
No of Funds	3	11	30	42
Funds £m	54.6	143.1	317.2	801.5

FIGURE 1. Growth of ethical investment £m.

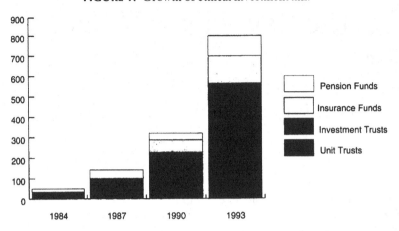

Positive ethical criteria might include supporting good employment practices or companies that make significant charitable donations, while such funds would avoid unacceptable industries like the arms trade or tobacco. Environmental funds select energy conservation and recycling, and shun polluting industries and companies that harm the environment or perform unnecessary experiments on animals.

Recent years have seen a rising number of funds with an environmental bias, but in practice most funds use both sets of criteria. Late 1993 saw new funds such as Friends Provident's Ethical Investment Trust and an Opportunity 2000 fund to promote the role of women in the workforce make their debut. This year has kicked off with the launch of the Equitable Ethical Trust, the first venture of Equitable Life in this area.

GROWING POPULARITY

It is easy to see why the sector is popular with savers. The 1990s seem to be seeing a reaction against the 'greed is good' mentality and the blatant consumerist ethos of the 1980s. For example, in May 1992 Co-operative Bank took an ethical stance of non-involvement with tobacco companies, oppressive regimes, companies which maltreat animals etc. This was considered a brave move in the more competitive and price sensitive world of retail banking, yet it was rewarded by a 13% increase in deposits to £1.24bn. after a period of stagnation. These new customers tended to be the key class A,B,C1 aged 24–40. The Body Shop also pricked the upmarket consumer's conscience with its organic products. Now other retailers such as Sainsbury and Tesco are riding the 'green' wave with a host of environmentally correct products.

Environmental liabilities have also become both real and substantial following 1992's Rio Summit and the Government's call for the polluter to pay. The Chartered Association of Certified Accountants published Accounting for the Environment at the end of 1993, while David Lascelles in last month's *Professional Investor* discussed how markets might assess and ultimately price environmental risk.

Last November, EC proposals indicated stricter liability on business to pay for pollution, while the then Environment Minister, Tim Yeo, stated that public funds could not bear the costs of environmental clean-ups if a company was unable to foot the bill. That liability might extend to the company's bankers so it is no wonder that the major banks have established environmental management units.

THE REWARDS

Companies are not the only ones to have benefitted. Fund managers have also gained from adopting an ethical or ecological stance. In the US where ethical investment began in the early 1970s, there is significant data showing that such constraints actually add to investment performance. In the UK, Barra, which conducted a five year study of ethical investment indices to the end of 1988, found a small outperformance with a slightly lower beta than one. The WM company recently published a paper *The Implications of Ethical Constraints on Investment Returns* indicating how ethical investment can produce above average returns.

The author of this article has also done a preliminary study of an 'ugly index' (tobacco, defence, companies operating in oppressive regimes, alcohol and gambling) comprising about 30% of the FT All Share Index in December 1988. It shows an erratic but clear trend of underperformance for the five years ending 1993. The outperformance of ethical indices is highly significant for the charity sector, where the Charities (Consolidation) Act 1993 is liberalising investment policies, and ethical values, unlike a pension fund, are at the heart of their activities.

It was interesting that last November's *Investor's Chronicle* annual review of the charity sector devoted three of its forty-odd pages to a special section on ethical investing – the first time this subject featured in its own section. This article also highlighted Friends Provident's claim that '400 ethically screened All Share index stocks have out-performed their other funds.'

Assessing the investment performance of actual ethical unit trusts is difficult because the sector's rapid growth limits the number of funds with a statistically valid track record. There are, however, nine trusts with a minimum three-year investment performance rating. See table 2.

TABLE 2. Performance (quartile rankings) UK equity growth sector

	Size £m	1991	1992	1993	3 Years	Agg Score
Abbey Ethical	20.6	1st	3rd	2nd	1st	0.337
Allchurches Amity	17.6	3rd	2nd	4th	4th	0.426
Eagle Star Envir Opps	12.4	1st	1st	4th	1st	0.375
Fidelity UK Growth	75.5	2nd	1st	1st	1st	0.181
Friends Provident Steward	154.4	2nd	3rd	2nd	2nd	0.309
NM Conscience	12.3	1st	3rd	4th	2nd	0.422
Scot Equitable	12.6	2nd	3rd	4th	3rd	0.403
Sovereign Ethical	8.3	2nd	4th	3rd	4th	0.433
TSB Environmental	21.4	1st	3rd	4th	2nd	0.386
Sector Ave % change		+7.4	+10.0	+20.7	+62.4	
No of Funds			146	144	132	

Data derived from that published in *Money Mangement* magazine.

Note for table 2
1) The Eagle Star Environmental Opportunity Fund is the one example of an environmental fund that is neither an ethical or ecological one. It simply aims to make money by investing in companies active in the environmental field. Given that its ultimate owner is BAT Industries, this would appear to be an appropriate stance.
2) The Fidelity UK Growth Fund was launched in 1984 as the Fidelity Famous Names Trust. It was formed in accordance with the British Medical Association to create a vehicle that avoided investing in tobacco companies, and despite its name change in 1991, it still does.
3) The aggregate score is a measure of the mean percentile ranking adjusted for the standard deviation.

PERFORMANCE

With three first quartile funds (out of nine) over three years, and three second quartile funds, it is clear that investors have reaped superior returns from ethical/environmental funds. This is particularly true on a weighted basis, since the six outperforming funds included five of the largest funds, and the six in total amounted to 87% of the sample at the end of the period, or 92.6% at the beginning of the three years under review. Put simply, if an investor had invested on a weighted basis in these nine funds at the beginning of 1991, he would have enjoyed a hefty 66.2% rise in value by the end of 1993, compared to a 62.4% increase in the average UK growth trust over this period.

The Friends Provident Stewardship Trust is such a large chunk of the UK ethical unit trust universe that it probably makes sense to analyse its performance separately. At the beginning of 1991, it had a market capitalisation of £89.6m, which amounted to 59.9% of the nine UK ethical funds then in existence. Over the three years its value jumped by 65.1% which has not skewed the results.

Unit trust investors and their advisors are increasingly interested not just in the position of funds in performance league tables, but also in the volatility of those positions. The aggregate score in table 2, which measures both of these, reveals that the larger funds have a more consistent performance than the smaller ones. The Fidelity UK Growth trust was outstanding, although its ethical constraints are considerably less than those of its peers. The Friends Provident Stewardship Trust, in second place, reflects the Stewardship fund's fairly steady position in the middle of the second quartile. While the Abbey Ethical fund and the Eagle Star Environmental Opportunity fund both boasted better absolute returns over the period than the Friends Provident trust, their greater volatility pushed them down the tables.

Interestingly the smaller trusts appear to show a distinct deterioration in relative performance with each year, which is not apparent in the three largest funds – Friends Provident, Fidelity, and Abbey Ethical. This seems strange given the heavy bias of most ethical funds to smaller companies. UK smaller company funds recovered in line with the economy last year, with the average UK smaller companies trust increasing in value by 31.8%, 11.1% more than the average UK growth trust.

PATIENCE IS NEEDED

The reasons behind the larger funds' outperformance may reflect the recent explosive growth of information about environmental costs and liabilities as well as the increasing variety of demands from ethical investors. Ethical and ecological screening is an essential and time consuming part of any ethical fund manager's life. It is becoming more so. As long ago as 1989, Peter Sylvester of Friends Provident said 'It's taken five or six years to evolve, but the managers here have become adept at finding the companies that meet the positive criteria and avoid the negative criteria.'

The press are also fairly quick to criticise any fund that they suspect is using ethical/ environmental investment purely as a marketing tool. In short, ethical investment is becoming more complex and difficult to do – it is an asset class in its own right, and one that requires the allocation of adequate resources to do it well.

This does not necessarily mean that ethical funds have to be run by a large group, only that there must be a commitment to the field and an awareness that the required high staff overhead may have to be funded for a while before the funds become big enough to cover it – which if the performance is good they certainly will.

Fund managers can take heart from Jupiter Tyndall Merlin, who established the Merlin

Research unit as the City's first specialist environmental research department in 1988. A year later the company stated that 'not less than 10% of the Merlin Ecology front-end load goes to fund the research unit, and the fund absorbs 60% of staff overheads. But we all believe that it is going to get big so we are prepared to loss-lead on the trust.' Merlin's foresight was justified. It now directly manages £60m in the Merlin International Green investment trust and Merlin Jupiter Ecology unit trust, as well as managing green funds for Citibank and Skandia Life.

Another example is the Co-operative Insurance Service (CIS), which, like Jupiter Merlin, is a small manager of unit trusts. As with its sister company, the Co-operative Bank, there can be no doubting its commitment to what it calls socially responsible investment. In just over three years the CIS Environ trust has reached £24.7m of assets, with a three year performance record just outside the first quartile. About 85% of the Environ fund's assets are in the UK, making this an excellent performance in an international growth sector which is currently dominated by emerging market funds.

33 Adjusting to Uncertainty

D. BROBY

This article was published in Professional Investor *in May 1995. Daniel Broby writes: Political risk became a topic for finance research as a direct consequence of the drive for international portfolio diversification. Time-varying risk, as a result of the political process, was not covered by the traditional Capital Asset Pricing Model derived by Sharpe (1964) and Lintner (1965). In this two-period framework, the ongoing activities of domestic and international politicians could only be attributed as random. In reality, as my article explains, the political process, in a multiperiod context, is not random but probabilistic.*

Since undertaking the research that provided the background to the article, a great deal of work has been done on conditional Capital Asset Pricing Models that helps to put such issues into a multiperiod context. My own research interests have changed as a result. I am now working with Durham University on the conditional CAPM in order to explain structural shifts in the various European benchmark indices as a consequence of the political process within Europe (and in particular the introduction of the single European currency). The increasing integration of financial markets and the ongoing political process makes me believe that such work is more, not less, important than when it was initiated. Since 1995, my own personal interests have also migrated from a UK focus to a European focus. I am now physically located in continental Europe, applying finance theory in the successful pursuit of positive alpha.

Daniel P. Broby is Chief Portfolio Manager at Unibank Investment Management. He was educated at Stirling University and Brunel University, and holds an MSc in Investment Analysis and an MPhil in Economics. He has worked in the fund management industry since 1985. Prior to joining Unibank Investment Management, he was a Director of Quilter Fund Management in the UK. He was elected an individual member of the London Stock Exchange in 1990 and is a director on the Council of the Institute of Investment Management and Research. He has produced numerous publications, and is the author of 'The Changing Face of European Fund Management' for the Financial Times *and is a contributing author to* Financial Reporting 1995–1996: A Survey of UK Reporting Practice by the Institute of Chartered Accountants in England and Wales.

On Friday 7 April, the news that the Conservative Party had lost control of every council in Scotland, whilst the Labour Party recorded its biggest ever vote in local government elections, resulted in some short term volatility in the exchange rate but otherwise had very little effect on asset prices. The reason the news was largely ignored was that it had been already discounted by the financial markets. With opinion polls indicating that, were we to have a general election today, a change of government is likely, understanding the effect of political instability on securities pricing becomes an important fund management tool.

Academic investigations into the efficiency of the UK securities markets has placed little emphasis on the effect of political instability. The reason for this is that instability is short term in nature and its manifestations in the UK do not affect the cash flows of a company to the same degree as in developing countries.

To address this deficiency the author of this article undertook a research project for Brunel University during the 1992 elections. A questionnaire was developed and distributed to the members of the Institute of Investment Management and Research. The results of this research will contribute to our understanding of this important area and the conclusions will assist fund managers, analysts and investors in their market timing and investment decisions.

At the time of sending out the questionnaire, the Conservatives had been the ruling party in government since Mrs Thatcher's victory on 3 May 1979, following the winter of discontent. Commentators collectively agreed that the result of the election would be extremely difficult to predict. They ignored previous academic research which concluded that the political business cycle is already discounted in the voters' minds and security prices.

Consumer confidence was particularly poor. The country was experiencing the longest period of recession since the second world war. Against this background both parties confirmed their commitment to reduce the inflation rate to the average of the ERM member countries and keep it down. Future company earnings were less likely to be influenced by the different macro economic variables.

The level of political instability was reminiscent of February 1974. That election was conducted under the backdrop of the three day week. The Conservatives polled 37.9% of the vote and Labour 37.1%. The Conservatives failed to form a government and resigned in favour of a coalition led by Harold Wilson, the Labour leader. Following the announcement of the election to the actual election the FTA All Share Index rose 7% on the back of voting indications biased towards a Conservative win.

The result came as a surprise and the FTA All Share Index fell by 22% within a month of the result. The memory of this outcome, attributed to political instability, weighed on the market. Finance theory had no predictive model to encompass such a scenario which explains why we set about constructing one.

The model that was developed as a result of the research was relatively simple. It was hypothesised that perceived political risk (Ri) is a function of the expected likelihood of loss of an earnings stream (EL). This can be on a company specific level as well as a global systematic level. This in turn is correlated to the actual estimated probability of an adverse event (P). Perceived political risk is also correlated to the estimated magnitude of the likely loss of earnings. (M)

In addition to an expected loss or gain, political risk is also a function of attributes, such as the extent to which companies exposed to political risk have knowledge about that risk. (K) In addition to attributes of political risk perception, judgmental bias may creep in. This will be influenced by individuals' previous experience and understanding of the effect of political risk on the earnings of the company. (E) In addition, there may be systematic, sectoral or sample population differences in risk perceptions. (D) These functions create a simple model of the individual political risk perception as shown below:

$$Ri = f\{EL(P),M,K,D,E\}$$

The outcome of the election, a Conservative victory which resulted in the FTSE 100 Index bottoming at 2,382.7 on 3 April and rising in short order to 2,737.8 by the 11 May, was conclusive enough to provide a robust test of the above model. The questionnaire enabled us to make various predictive conclusions which this article will explain.

In order for an investor to buy a security he must be satisfied that a given risk premium gives adequate compensation for that investment's risk. Investors have differing utility functions. Political risk is an integral part of economic activity. The pricing of securities does not take place in a vacuum. Political activity, where the parties and interest groups constantly battle for special economic privileges, distorts the allocation of economic resources. The inter-relationship of the various factors makes measurement all the more difficult.

Theoretically, in well developed capital markets, such as the London Stock Market, the value of a security at any given moment should be equal to the discounted value of the stream of income that it will generate over its lifetime. The discount rate used to calculate the present value of the future net receipts of such a security has to reflect the risk and uncertainty that these cash flows will not develop as predicted. The existence of risk and uncertainty results in variance in the returns on such investments.

This trade-off must be based on his knowledge of the probabilistic outcomes of the different scenarios he envisages. To do this in a scientific way he must use a quantitative proxy for risk, such as the variability of return around an expected average. If the market is efficient it must reflect all available information. As a result, such a proxy of risk must include all significant functions of risk. If political risk is significant, then for the UK stock market to be efficient, it must be included in such a proxy of risk.

The most widely accepted models of securities valuations are the Capital Asset Pricing Model and the Arbitrage Pricing Theory. Neither the Capital Asset Pricing Model nor the Arbitrage Pricing Model specifically mention political risk. That said, just because the term political risk does not appear in the models does not mean that it is not factored into them in some way.

Political risk is defined in the context of an implication of unwanted consequences of political activity. This activity has the ability to affect the relative prices and costs of all the cash flows of the firm on the micro-economic level. On the macro-economic level, it can affect the equilibrium output and price levels and even influence adaptive expectations and open economy capital flows.

LOSS OF CONFIDENCE

Instability could possibly result in the inefficient pricing of an asset. These are caused as a result of the uncertainty that surrounds instability. Uncertainty makes investors and market makers less confident in their valuation of a security. Firstly, investors can delay or cancel a sale or purchase and secondly, market makers in securities can increase the bid-offer spread that they are prepared to deal at.

At its most extreme such political risk manifests itself in the form of expropriation or nationalisation. Under such circumstance the future cash flows attributable to the firm are only equivalent to the discounted compensation that may or may not be agreed with the owners of the firm.

Risk and uncertainty create future outcomes whose conclusion is imperfectly known. Risk implies that there is a degree of known objective probability in such outcomes. Uncertainty caused by political instability refers to a situation which is unique. As a result the frequency distribution of possible outcomes cannot be objectively specified. The difference between uncertainty and risk can be identified by the informational content. The more information one has on uncertainty, the more it becomes measurable, insurable and avoidable. Once quantified in this manner uncertainty can be described as risk.

What exactly is political risk? Previous academic investigation into the subject has limited its search to definitions of governmental or sovereign interference with business and commonly restricting these to private investment. Political risk arises from the actions of national governments which interfere with or prevent business transactions, or change the terms of agreements, or cause the confiscation of wholly or partially foreign owned business property.

The Efficient Market Hypothesis is not necessarily at odds with a political risk premium. On a company specific level, likely political changes would be factored into the market price. On an macro economic scale any political business cycle, as previously explained with reference to the CAPM, would be discounted across the market as a whole.

Political business cycles were identified in the late sixties. Governments can actively create them in order to improve their election chances. Voters reward income growth and punish unemployment and inflation. They also appear to ignore all information other than that of the recent past.

One of the common systematic elements of political risk common to most UK stocks is country risk. This incorporates factors influencing the stability of the host country's political, economic, social environment, as well as its governmental actions pertaining to capital repatriation credit, equity ownership restrictions, legal requirements, tax codes, patent protection laws, local persons and product usage, and bureaucratic procedures.

Fund managers can hedge country risk through diversification and stock selection. The UK's performance in international trade, economic leverage, and various measures of liquidity, under a different government should all be assessed in determining if the stocks selected reflect the correct degree of political risk.

On a more company specific level, what is political risk for one firm may not be political risk to another. Abrupt changes in the regulation of the water industry by OFWAT is political risk to water supply companies, and may even have some correlation to how regulation of the electricity industry is perceived, but it is not political risk to a food manufacturing company.

Political risk, in the money market, is impersonal but the response is negotiation between teams of negotiators. It is a dynamic situation susceptible to surprise. One way in which companies avoid the risk involved is to shield their transactions from the reach of governments and become multinational. The risk of a potential change of government will theoretically result in greater overseas diversification.

The voting market, like the stock market, was found to have no memory. Voters are only concerned with permanent, rather than temporary, effects of policy. A number of other academic investigations into the topic in the UK confirmed this view. Peel and Pope (1983), in their work on British Elections between 1960 and 1979 found no systematic relationship between the price rise in the week prior to the election and opinion poll results. In their study Thompson and Ioannidis found only a weak relationship.

On the other hand, Manning (1987), who used a company specific analysis, did find a relationship. His paper was based on Labour's repeated threat to re-nationalise British Telecom at the price which the public originally paid for them.

The results that we obtained from the questionnaire enabled us to confirm Manning's conclusions. We compared post-ante share price movements with hypothetical estimates made by the respondents as well as the implied option volatility of British Telecom with the predictive results. We found that once uncertainty was removed, the stock adjusted to a more demanding rating but with a lower implied volatility.

This demonstrated a quantifiable political risk that we then analysed using conventional multiple scenario spreadsheets to estimate the cash flows of the company under differing political regimes. The results confirmed that the earlier stated simple model was robust enough to use in the context of political risk.

The quantification of political risk remains problematic. Future research must concentrate on ways of improving the quantification of the risk and the required return to compensate for it. One of the conclusions that may help that increased probability of political change results in greater political risk.

The UK market appears to focus on impending or current change. The election and the Gulf war clearly focused investors' minds. The political risk that was identified required a corresponding higher expected return to compensate for it.

DISRUPTIONS

Unanticipated disturbances in the financial markets such as the Gulf war or an election, caused by political uncertainty, may disrupt the capacity of the financial system to allocate capital. The correct political risk premium model does not belong to either the GARCH or DYNAMIC families. Political risk only becomes measurable when uncertainty is removed. Event studies are therefore the best way to achieve quantifiable results.

Political instability results in lower rates of economic growth. It is advisable for fund managers to identify if this is factored into share prices. It is possible that political instability causes an avoidance of an investment. Were one to buy a portfolio of such 'over-looked' investments it would be possible to spread the risk and achieve a greater return. Conversely, markets appear to reward parties with perceived better economic policies.

Recent and impending political change, such as an election, is the most acted upon political risk factor. As a result of the questionnaire going out during an election it was possible to conclude that a certain election is better than an uncertain result for share prices. This would be the case regardless of which party won that election. Fund managers with their own political bias should be aware of this when making their investment decisions.

The questionnaire confirmed that social unrest is more likely to make people invest abroad, and that political lobbying works to the benefit of the 'establishment'. Unsurprisingly, it was also concluded that armed conflicts affect share prices.

By building a profile of the respondents it was possible to show that fund managers have a bias for Conservative governments which is reflected in their investment decisions. The expected outcome of a possible Labour government's action on the topic of the privatised companies was more reasoned. The most likely effect was perceived to be breaches of prospectus agreements and contract discrimination.

The respondents were more concerned with other political considerations less close to home. Africa is seen as having the most missed opportunities due to concern about political risk followed by the CIS and Middle East.

The work done on sectors showed that utilities are considered the most responsive sector to a monetary induced political shock while the breweries are the least responsive. It was also reveals that the less cyclical a company's earnings stream and the higher its payout ratio, the more susceptible it is to political risk.

Based on previous research, a number of factors were identified which could put companies at greater political risk:

- Periodic external requirements for new technology.
- Competition with other companies in the same field.
- Dependence on natural resources.
- Investment effect on the economy.
- Monopolistic characteristics
- Social desirability of the product.

Political risk is clearly a complex subject, awareness of which will enable fund managers to add value in turbulent times. The most important conclusion for fund managers was that even when abrupt political change occurs, a market equilibrium will develop.

34 Buying Growth Shares Using Value Filters

J. SLATER

This article was published in Professional Investor *in February 1997. Jim Slater writes: Recent market conditions have not favoured value investors. By value I mean buying growth shares at a reasonable price using value filters. These market moods do, however, change frequently, and I have no doubt that their time will come again.*

Jim Slater is a Chartered Accountant who for the 10 years from 1964 to 1974 was Chairman of the legendary financial conglomerate, Slater Walker Securities.

Since then, he has written a number of children's books while concentrating upon his private business interests and perfecting his system of stock market investment. He is generally recognized as an authority on stock markets with an uncanny ability to identify undervalued companies and read market trends.

More recently, Jim Slater has devised Really Essential Financial Statistics (REFS) *in conjunction with Hemmington Scott.* REFS *is a monthly investment service that is popular with private investors and institutions alike. In January 1998, he also founded a monthly investment newsletter* Investing for Growth.

I have always been attracted to growth shares, particularly those that can be purchased at what I perceive to be a discount to their proper value. I use a number of sieves to ensure that value is present as well as growth. In his recent paper 'Value or Growth?', Michael Lenhoff of Capel-Cure Myers referred to my style of investing as a hybrid of value and growth, or GARP – 'Growth at a reasonable price.' I prefer to describe it as buying growth shares using value filters to provide a margin of safety.

The task of devising, and helping Hemmington Scott to develop our monthly investment service, *Company REFS*, removed many fuzzy areas from my mind. All calculations had to be carefully defined and some difficult points needed to be resolved very precisely before the computer software could be written.

The first and most important question was to define growth shares and to eliminate cyclicals and recovery stocks from our growth share universe. In my view, the main characteristic of a reliable growth share is that it should be able to produce increasing EPS year after year, almost irrespective of general economic conditions. In the UK, few companies qualify.

Our aim was to catch mature growth companies, and nascent ones, before all the action was over. We also wanted to eliminate major cyclicals. After many months of trial and error, we finally settled on these parameters for defining a growth share:

- There must be broker forecasts.
- There must be four years of consecutive EPS growth, including any forecast periods. In practice, this means that a company can make the grade if it has two years of past EPS growth and two years' future growth forecast by brokers.

- Each of the past five years' results must have been profitable. None may show a loss.
- Where four periods of growth follow a previous setback, it must have achieved, or be expected to achieve, its highest normalised EPS in the latest period out of the last six.
- All property companies and investment trusts are eliminated.
- Companies in the highly cyclical Building & Construction and Building Materials & Merchants sectors, and those in the Vehicle Distribution sub-sector, are required to meet the above growth criteria. However, they are also required not to have incurred a loss, or suffered an EPS reversal, in any of the last five years of reported results. This last criterion eliminates most of the companies in those sectors, but leaves the few that are arguably genuine growth companies.

In the FT-SE All-Share about 300 companies qualified, 50 in the FT-SE 100, 90 in the Mid-250 and 160 in the SmallCap.

The next task was to ensure that the financial statistics of all companies were synchronised, so that they could properly be compared with each other. The term 'prospective price-earnings ratio' is bandied around too glibly. It usually refers to the current year and that is fine if the year has just begun. However, if the term is used when the year is almost over, it is clearly much less pertinent.

We resolved this problem by compiling all growth statistics on a rolling 12 months ahead basis. To make this calculation on, say, 1 October, for a company with a calendar financial year, it is necessary to take a quarter of the current year's brokers' consensus forecast and three quarters of the consensus forecast for the following financial year. By adopting this approach for all companies, chalk and cheese are converted into chalk and chalk, enabling tables to be prepared and meaningful comparisons to be made.

Once the characteristics of a growth share have been defined, the first value filter I apply to the resultant universe is to establish that the growth company's price-earnings growth factor (PEG) is attractive. The PEG is calculated by dividing the rolling 12 months ahead price-earnings ratio (PER) by the rolling 12 months ahead EPS growth rate. A share with a PER of 15 and an EPS growth rate of 10% per annum would therefore have a PEG of 1.5, which is about the average. The lower the PEG the better and to provide a margin of safety, I usually invest in companies with PEGs of well below 1.0.

To my mind the PER is a one-dimensional and very limited measure, especially when it is used to compare companies with widely differing financial year ends. I like to know exactly how much growth I am getting for my multiple and I like to be able to compare any share I am considering with every other share in my universe of growth shares.

The level of the PEG gives an instant fix on the growth you should get for your money in the coming 12 months. For longer periods the trend of EPS does, of course, have to be taken into account.

I eliminate any shares with rolling 12 months ahead PERs of over 20. In a few years' time, those PERs usually regress to a more normal level and the resultant fall in the rating then has to be amortised over the life of the investment.

EPS growth may more than offset the fall in the PER. However, a company with a very high PER must have a very high (and therefore probably unsustainable) growth rate to justify a low PEG. For example, a share with a PER of 30 and an estimated EPS growth rate of 50% would have a PEG of 0.6. A 50% growth rate would be too high to be maintained for many years. A far better proposition would be a company with the same 0.6 PEG but based on a prospective PER of 12 and an estimated EPS growth rate of 20%. The margin of safety would be much better as the 20% growth rate might be sustainable for many years and the PER would be far more likely to be upgraded than downgraded.

My next value filter is to ensure that a company's cash flow is in excess of its EPS for the last reported year and for the average of the previous five years. If a company is expanding rapidly it can sometimes justify a one year deficit of cash flow per share in relation to EPS. However, it is noticeable that most great growth companies seem to have strong cash flow and as a consequence usually have net cash in their balance sheets.

My next sieve – positive relative strength over the previous 12 months and previous month – cannot be described as a value filter. It is, however, very effective and there is a clear reason why positive relative strength is such an important factor when buying shares with low PEGs. The intention when investing in them is to benefit from their above average EPS growth and from the status change in their PERs when the market re-rates them. Positive relative strength is important because it indicates that the market is already beginning to appreciate the virtues of the company, so the wait for the re-rating should not be unduly long.

Usually, EPS growth might account for 20%–25% of an annual capital gain, but the status change in the multiple compounds this and is often far more significant. Take for example a company which had a share price of 120p, EPS of 10p, and a prospective growth rate of 20%. It therefore had a PER of 12 and a PEG of 0.6. If, after a year, EPS rose to 12p as expected, and the PER was re-rated to 18, the share price would increase to 216p. In that event, the resultant capital gain would be 96p, of which 75% would be due to the re-rating of the PER, and only 25% to the increase in EPS.

I use further sieves, but first see how well the basic method has worked since the inception of *Company REFS*. We have back-tested 14 six-month periods at monthly intervals ending on 28 October 1996. The average gains are set out below:

	Gain %
FTSE All Share	6.44
PEG 0.6, or lower	22.21
PEG 0.6, or lower and cash flow per share greater than EPS	23.62
PEG 0.6, or lower, cash flow per share greater than EPS and positive one month and one year relative strength	33.01

We decided upon six month test periods because they bridge either interim or annual results. This gives all of the companies a few days in the spotlight and allows time for their PERs to be reappraised by the market.

The average universe of shares with PEGs of under 0.6 was 27. This was reduced to seven shares by applying all three sieves. Of course, a much wider universe could have been obtained by simply lifting the very demanding level of the PEG above my preferred threshold of 0.6 or slightly relaxing one of the other criteria.

We found that the cash flow sieve is far less effective with FTSE 100 stocks. With small companies it can underwrite their survival prospects, but with leading companies survival is rarely in doubt.

Critics often argue that with leading companies it is much more difficult to outperform the averages. We ran another test simply taking, from each monthly edition of *REFS*, the growth share with the lowest PEG in the FTSE 100 Index. As is apparent, over the same 14 six-month periods, *with no other sieves*, the average gain was astoundingly good:

	Gain %
FTSE 100 Index	6.39
Growth share with lowest PEG in FTSE 100 Index	27.37

Low PEGs also work well with the Mid-250 Index, but the results were less dramatic. We selected all growth shares with PEGs of under 0.75, and compared them with the index over the same 14 periods of six months each. The higher level of PEG was selected to obtain a worthwhile universe of shares:

	Gain %
Mid 250 Index	8.86
PEG 0.75 or lower	20.77

Further evidence of the effectiveness of this approach is provided by the performance of the Johnson Fry Slater Growth Unit Trust managed by my son, Mark. For the last year he has been managing the trust using my three sieves as his *primary* criteria. The trust is now comfortably at the top of the UK Growth sector and it has beaten the market by a wide margin:

12 months ended 31.10.96 – offer to offer.

	Gain %
Johnson Fry Slater Growth Unit Trust	62.32
Best other unit trust in UK Growth sector	43.06
UK Growth sector unit trust average	18.39
FTSE All Share Index	17.45
(Source: Hindsight)	

Of course, the test periods in all of the above cases are relatively short and market conditions have been very favourable for growth shares. That is why I drew particular comfort from Jim O'Shaughnessy's new book *What Works on Wall Street*. He was given access to 43 years of data from the S & P Compustat database and researched a 40 year period testing one criterion after another.

Some of the results of his research are set out below and as you will see they support my argument:

Compound annual return %.

	Low Value Group	High Value Group
Price-to-Book Value (PBV)	14.4	7.5
Price-to-Cash Flow (PCF)	13.6	6.8
Price-to-Sales Ratio (PSR)	15.4	4.2
Price-Earnings Ratio (PER)	11.2	8.4
EPS up five years in a row and best relative strength	16.86	
PER below 20 and high relative strength	16.66	
High one year relative strength and low PSR	18.14	
High one year relative strength	14.03	
Low one year relative strength	1.78	

To put these figures in perspective the compound annual return for all shares over the 40 year period 1954–94 was 12.5%.

O'Shaughnessy did not research the use of PEGs because forecasts were not available over the whole period. Also he considers brokers' forecasts unreliable. Despite their shortcomings, I prefer to invest with the benefit of knowing the consensus forecast, rather than fly blind.

You will notice from the table above that although shares with low PERs out-performed those with high PERs, their performance was below the market average. This does not surprise me as many shares with low PERs thoroughly deserve them. Far more meaningful than a low PER is a low PEG, which indicates that the prospective PER is low *in relation to the estimated future growth rate*.

O'Shaughnessy suggests that it is unwise to switch methods and the best results are obtained by sticking to a sound discipline that can be honed by experience. He agrees with my view that the best overall approach is to concentrate on growth shares using value filters. However, his research indicates that in the aftermath of a vicious bear market, positive relative strength can be a dangerous criterion. In those comparatively infrequent and short periods, shares with poor relative strength in the previous year usually perform better than those on which large profits have been made. It looks therefore as if followers of my approach could have a difficult period ahead in a bear market before the averages reassert themselves.

I mentioned that I also use other supplemental and mandatory criteria. They are set out below:

- Gearing of under 75%, unless cash flow is particularly strong.
- An identifiable competitive advantage.
- The absence of directors selling in a cluster.

In addition, there are some highly desirable bonus factors which provide me with additional comfort:

- Accelerating EPS is one of the most encouraging indicators, especially if the source (eg cloning a proven activity) can be identified.
- A cluster of directors buying more shares.
- My personal preferred range of market capitalisation is £30 m–£250 m, so the SmallCap Index is usually my first hunting ground.
- I give preference to companies that pay dividends. The level of payment is an extra indicator and it is a pity to preclude the institutions, which require dividend yields, from joining in the buying that will eventually create the status change in the PER.
- A low PSR is probably the best value filter.
- Something new such as a change of chief executive, new products or a major acquisition can often enhance EPS and trigger the reappraisal of a company's PER.
- A low price-to-research ratio is an attractive feature with technology stocks.
- A low PBV provides a little comfort, but with growth stocks it is one of the least important filters.

Many of the above criteria can enhance returns substantially. In particular, a cluster of directors investing can be a wonderful buying signal and so can rapidly accelerating EPS, especially if it is based on the capacity to clone proven activities.

O'Shaughnessy found a low PSR to be effective when coupled with high relative strength in the previous year. But a degree of caution is necessary when applying these kinds of value filters to growth shares. If the PSR requirement is too demanding it will eliminate most exceptional growth shares. Very few great growth shares have low PSRs – they tend instead to have high margins arising from their competitive advantage and higher than average PSRs. A good example is Rentokil in 1995 just before the bid for BET. It had a PSR of 4 and margins of 24% against BET's PSR of 0.72 and its miserable margins of only 6%. It is easy to imagine how keen Rentokil's management must have been to get their hands on BET.

When assessing PSRs, the level of gearing does, of course, also have to be taken into account and allowance made for the type of industry. In particular, distributors usually have very low PSRs and margins.

To use a low PSR as a sieve when searching for value (as opposed to growth) stocks, I would suggest below 1.0 as an appropriate level. When using a low PSR as a *value filter for growth stocks* I would suggest 1.5 or even 2.0. I do not consider a low PSR to be a mandatory criterion for buying growth stocks – it is more in the nature of a reassuring comfort factor, similar in many ways to a low PBV.

In conclusion, a low PEG is a far more meaningful measure than a low PER. I also believe that using 12 months rolling ahead statistics is the most effective way to compare growth stocks, once they have been defined. My basic method of selecting growth shares with low PEGs, strong cash flow and high relative strength seems to me to be a formula that should work well in most market conditions and almost certainly will do so on average.

Time will tell.

35 Asset Allocation: Too Important to Be Left to Money Managers

S. FOWLER

This article was published in Professional Investor *in February 1997. Stuart Fowler writes: When I wrote the article, I was conscious the fund management industry and its customers had got the whole process upside down. We typically overweight the implementation decisions where results are random and underweight the strategic decisions where there are at least a few reliable assumptions about market behaviour that act as a foundation for planning. The then recent Pensions Act has changed the balance slightly, but in the private client area the problem of poor investment planning awareness is compounded by very high implementation costs.*

After training as a securities analyst, Stuart Fowler worked as a European equity broker in the 1970s before switching to international portfolio management, first at Touche Remnant and later at Hill Samuel. In 1989, he co-founded Valu-Trac Investment Management, a quantitative boutique that pioneered the active passive style of management, mainly working with US pension funds. Since 1996, he has acted as a consultant in the field of quantitative, strategic, investment planning.

Professional money managers in the UK have for the most part indirectly excluded themselves from the highest level in the decision hierarchy: the allocation of a fund's capital between different types or classes of asset and between different markets within each asset class. These are the decisions that account for most of the return and risk characteristics of any balanced portfolio.

They have excluded themselves in an obvious way by clustering around a consensus asset mix and in a more subtle way by adopting an intellectual platform which is gnostic, geared to demonstrating to clients and potential clients an ability to satisfy exacting performance standards. This intellectual platform is inconsistent with the stochastic nature of asset class returns: a vast range of potential outcomes, expanding over time, within which most shorter term absolute and relative returns are random and not forecastable.

In avoiding asset allocation decisions they have been acting rationally. Clients seemed happy to accept a standard and largely passive asset mix and it suited managers to avoid the risk of sticking their neck out and getting it wrong because it is such a high and unmanageable risk. The frequent failures of any gnostic approach over the timescales for which expectations were unreasonable would be exposed by the lack of diversification potential. There are not enough classes, too many common trends and too few weak correlations to do a good job of averaging the absolute and relative return variances of the individual building blocks in asset allocation. Managers have also been acting rationally in promoting instead the concept of rewards to their own expertise in policy implementation, particularly security selection, because this plays on the susceptibilities of their clients, even though the academic evidence suggests that their clients are wrong.

Now several developments are taking place that will change the customer's assessment of investment priorities. They raise new questions about the need for asset allocation arrangements that are particular and dynamic instead of standard and passive, such as: who is responsibile, is in control; who is best suited to provide help; what form should outside help take; and what is it worth?

This article puts forward a case that money management firms will need to reposition their investment thinking and remould their performance credentials in order either to demonstrate appropriate asset allocation expertise or to promote themselves as specialist policy implementers. At the margin, these developments offer opportunities for non-manager asset allocation services based on 'actuarial' approaches. These are defined as combining the flexibility to handle complex client specific inputs and the discipline of a long term framework of expectations about the behaviour of asset returns.

By offering performance targets that can realistically be met, these approaches escape the trap that managers have set for themselves in pursuing what they thought was in their best commercial interests. Money managers will not escape the trap by offering Tactical Asset Allocation products: their lack of commercial impact among pension fund sponsors is consistent with the observation that an active management approach which promises much is simply not viewed as credible when applied to asset allocation.

CHANGES IN CLIENT FOCUS

In pensions management, the big change is the Minimum Funding Requirement (MFR) of the new Pensions Act. This increases and brings forward the investment risks borne by the sponsor of a defined benefit scheme. Sponsors will need to choose between several alternatives that have not so far seemed like important issues: transferring the risk off their books onto the members by switching to defined contribution or money purchase schemes; accepting the risk but bringing it, like other business risks, under their own control; delegating management of the risk to a new third party or leaving it to their existing money managers' discretion.

For consulting actuaries, the increased importance of fund specific detail on the liability side and temporary declines in market values on the asset side calls for dynamic rather than traditionally static solutions. This applies equally in the context of their conventional consulting work and their growing business of asset/liability modelling.

If they have to come up with a solution for this anyway, logically they may then want to go further and provide a dynamic solution for return enhancement within the tight constraints for asset allocation that they will already have defined. Having the client base and a solution, why not put their hat in the ring and seek to attach to themselves the function, and high economic value, of ongoing policy determination at the expense of money managers? The consulting profession is surely sensitive to the disparity in the fees charged by each of the two parties to the process.

In private client management another radical change is occurring with implications for asset allocation responsibilities. It is the long overdue and apparently successful attack on British unit trust charges by new competitors. This high cost umbrella has sheltered the typical Independent Financial Adviser (IFA), affording a feast of rebated selling commissions. Faced with losing this easy option, they can either risk going out of that business or ensure they offer a service worth a fee.

There has always been a need for genuinely independent investment advice informed by both a knowledge of the behaviour and principles of financial markets and familiarity with the other aspects of financial planning such as tax and insurance. The 'mis-selling' scandal, exposure of the high costs of many financial contracts and the expected growth in personal provision for retirement incomes and long term healthcare all point to increasing awareness of this need. Some IFA firms are positioned to offer a high standard of service. Many are not.

Like the actuaries, the most ambitious can leverage their natural advantage of proximate relationships with the ultimate investor and take for themselves the top tier of the decision hierarchy. They can then hope to take advantage of the falling costs of investment policy implementation, via unit trusts, to raise a fee in proportion to the importance of the asset class decision, including the qualitatively superior option of an asset-based fee.

THE DECISION HIERARCHY

'Too important' in the title of this article is based partly on observations of the client's changing needs and partly on statistical approaches to quantifying 'how important' are the different types of decision in a portfolio. The statistical evidence of a hierarchy of descending orders of importance is well documented and quite widely accepted although it is often presented in a more self-serving way by money managers and so is worth summarising here.

The most extensive evidence comes from the US and applies regression analysis to samples of balanced funds: Brinson, Hood and Beebower (*Financial Analysts Journal*, July/August 1986) and Hensel, Ezra and Ilkiew (*Financial Analysts Journal*, July/August 1991). Regression analysis offers us measures of the strength of the association between achieved returns and the passive returns that would have been given by a particular asset mix, excluding any contribution from security selection or timing effects. Both studies regressed actual portfolios on combinations of benchmark returns representing the main asset classes held by US plans: dollar bonds, domestic stocks, foreign stocks and property.

They showed that respectively 94 and 98% of the return variance was explained by the asset mix. In the more recent study, based on a sample of portfolios measured by the Russell Company, a split was made as to 97% being the proportion explained by a naive policy mix equivalent to the average in each class and only 0.51% being the contribution of the average of the managers' judgement to hold a different mix. This is a valuable distinction.

The traditional approach to performance attribution that appears in most performance reports to clients requires that a systematic market return, equivalent to the reward for exposure to the various asset classes, be ascribed to one or other contribution, usually that of asset allocation or market selection, where it biases the results. If the decision to bear the systematic risk associated with a typical mix of assets is taken by the sponsor then it follows that the return contribution should also be attributed to the sponsor rather than to the manager's judgement.

The naive policy mix is used in the Russell analysis as the measure of systematic risk and return accepted by the sponsor. The study also reveals a dominant contribution by the naive policy mix to absolute quarterly returns: 3.75% per quarter compared with 0.49% for the managers' actual allocationbutions (all below ± 0.23%) for other judgemental contributions including timing and security selection.

The maximum contributions were also skewed in favour of the sponsor's contribution to asset allocation at 4.43% compared with the largest of any of the contributions on the managers' side being just 0.85%.

In the UK, where the mix is different but with a bias to less rather than more diversification (a concentration in equities at the expense of bonds), and where approaches to security selection are broadly comparable, one might expect a similar dominance by the asset allocation decision and by the sponsor's decision to hold a typical mix rather than the manager's judgement about which particular mix. Only the performance measurers have the data to perform a similar analysis using actual portfolios.

However, I have found that a Monte Carlo approach to randomly constructed UK portfolios is supportive of the high proportion of explained variance for asset allocation decisions relative to security selection shown by the two US studies (with an R^2 almost exactly between the two revealed by the US studies).

The analysis was based on a large sample of randomly selected portfolios all lying within the arbitrary but perhaps typical constraint of a 5% band either side of The WM Company average balanced pension fund allocation in each class (excluding property). It would be interesting to see real portfolio analysis for the UK along the same lines as the Russell study, for a large sample and a long period.

POLICY AND IMPLEMENTATION

Multiple regressions of randomly constructed international equity portfolios can also be used to determine the importance of the country decision, which some sponsors might not be sure about treating as policy or implementation. The evidence suggests it is part of the policy framework. Regressions based on multiple randomly selected portfolios of 50 stocks in any of 18 MSCI World Index constituent markets over a 12 year period from 1980 show that 85% of the US dollar return returns are explained by the country decision and the high proportion of explained variance holds in most years (Valu-Trac Investment Management, 1993).

Happily, the existence of active and index tracking country-specific funds, as well as index futures, allows investors to implement country allocation decisions as easily as asset class decisions.

THE ACTUARIAL APPROACH

For the purposes of this article an actuarial approach is one that makes assumptions about future returns, long term rather than short term, based on a combination of long histories of asset return behaviour and some general framework of explanatory macro-economic theory. It is agnostic in avoiding specific short term forecasts either for economic variables or for returns themselves. Its statistical foundation is time series analysis. It may or may not disaggregate nominal total returns (income and capital) by reference to series for inflation and dividends. Time series for nominal total returns, real total returns, price indices and dividends show different characteristics but ones that are generally agreed upon by statisticians.

An actuarial approach seeks to accommodate the high degrees of uncertainty implicit in the different time series histories and the commercial need for long term planning decisions. It does not offer solutions for uncertainty itself but accepts it as a condition of the environment and does not belittle its significance in the minds of its customers. It is this characteristic which above all has allowed actuaries to avoid the trap of excessive expectations on the part of their clients.

Accepting the evidence of the distribution of returns an actuarial approach will tend, explicitly or implicitly, to highlight the unusual: a form of management by exception. This is important in explaining why there is no loss in ignoring valuation inputs not derived from return series, including those valuation measures most used by money managers. The existence of unusual valuations, if real, will in almost all cases be confirmed by unusual past behaviour of returns and, in the absence of the latter, spurious judgemental observations of unusual investment opportunity can be safely discounted.

Judgemental approaches to investment thought to be successful should not really be seen as deriving their success from the precise inputs, which is what money management sales personnel would have us believe, but rather from the fact that their construct manages in an approximate way to harness the natural powers of financial market behaviour – which is just as smart but is not seen as a good sales pitch. In an actuarial approach, the natural powers and the rough appropriateness of the construct are the sales pitch.

There is a general belief that different actuaries will come up with broadly similar assumptions on which to base their valuations of long term funds or their recommendations of asset/liability matching strategies. This is partly because of common interpretations of the data but also because actuaries themselves are not immune from a consensus approach to handling the business risk implicit in significant differences in assumptions.

For the purposes of calculating MFR surpluses, conformity will be given a further boost by the use of standard assumptions given by the DSS. For whatever reason, a uniform characteristic of an actuarial approach is a broadly consistent discipline over long periods of application that is well protected from the psychology of the marketplace.

MATHEMATICAL MODELS

This discipline comes in part from the reliance on a mathematical framework. Actuaries enjoy relatively little client suspicion of their use of mathematical models and have not so far been under pressure to justify either their general or their particular approaches. The profession has a real competitive advantage in being able to apply quantitative techniques without calling into question a firm's judgemental skills and experience and without having to produce unreasonable proof statements. However unfair, this advantage is not immediately available to money managers even if they now start to emulate the same techniques.

Whether IFAs can successfully adopt the same quantitative mantle may well depend on how they have already positioned themselves in terms of the balance between promoting gnostic and agnostic approaches or short and long term approaches to financial markets.

For many, if not most, it would be an uphill struggle.

ACTUARIAL SOLUTIONS

Lest I am accused of skipping the hard part of the case for an actuarial approach, it is worth pointing out the particular features that are likely to arise.

One is that there will be no easy solution for the key allocation between equities and bonds. Time series data for returns for UK bonds and equities (more so than in most other countries) are extremely difficult to interpret because of the divergent trends in nominal and real long term interest rates as a function of an unusually long period of unusually large rise followed by fall in the rate of change in the price level. It is this, rather than exceptional instability in the rate of return on equities, that makes it difficult to derive a sensible assumption about the risk premium from the data.

The obvious solution is to use index linked gilts as the benchmark for measuring the risk premium from all equity exposure, domestic and foreign, but the history is too short. However, there is a felicitous fit between the relatively narrow range of the risk premium for UK equities since index linked gilts were first issued and the premiums typically earned in the last century and first half of this when conventional gilt yields contained no inflation risk premium (see Wilkie, *The Risk Premium on Ordinary Shares*, 1994) [Fig. 1, re share yield minus Consols from 1918 and minus index linked since 1982].

FIGURE 1. The risk premium on UK equities: yield differences.

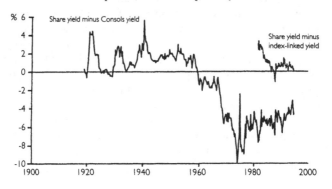

This is an example of a sensible approach to handling data limitations with an appropriate blend of economic theory and common sense. Although it runs counter to the new emphasis on nominal returns imposed by the MFR, it is the most logical approach to the inflation risk run by any long term saver and in that sense an index linked government bond is the risk free asset against which other asset classes should be judged.

Though an important decision for balanced fund performance, the bond/equity mix will in any event usually have some exogenous inputs, such as the need for income or, for defined benefit plans, the need to avoid unpleasant MFR surprises. If in future the mix is to be defined more precisely by the liability side of the model inputs, there is less need for a really robust solution on the asset side for managing or rebalancing the bond/equity mix.

A solution for equity market selection is arguably much simpler. This is because of the mean reverting tendencies of absolute returns and the stationary long term nature of relative returns from different equity markets (with little difference as between local currency and currency adjusted returns). Over the short and medium term, returns are highly dynamic and widely distributed but appear mostly random. Return differences also appear not to be explained by reference to factors such as economic growth rates, and even if they were the factors themselves are not forecastable.

In this dynamic environment, exceptional past return behaviour can be shown to be systematically exploitable without giving up any diversification benefits. As examples, Exhibits A, B and C explore the non-random, long memory tendencies of absolute real returns in the UK equity market and relative nominal returns for all of the developed equity markets.

The information that should be sought from the equity data by the asset allocator is about both returns and risk. It should highlight exceptional future returns, taking into account the error associated with that assumption, based on observations of exceptional past behaviour in the return series. It should also highlight genuine rather than spurious opportunities to smooth the variance of the overall portfolio by including markets that have displayed and are for good reasons likely to display low correlations with other assets in the portfolio.

Two concepts are introduced here that are not necessarily a part of all actuarial disciplines. The first is that the covariance matrix made up of the cross correlations between all the asset building blocks available to the asset allocator is dangerous in its raw form if derived solely from past observations in a single period. The second is that the best basis for differentiating among all the expected returns is to polarise the outliers and compact the normal ones.

EVIDENCE OF NON-RANDOM ELEMENTS IN EQUITY MARKET RETURNS

1. Long Term Mean Reversion in Total Returns for a Single Market: UK Equities

EXHIBIT A. Term structure of serial correlations based on rescaled range analysis: UK Equities Real Return Series (Source BZW) 1919–1994 detrended (using best fit for entire period of 6% pa). Regressing the log of the cumulative peak to trough ranges (rescaled by dividing by the standard deviation of the observations) on the log of time, a positive gradient of 0.5 is indicative of a random walk. Deducting 0.5 from the rescaled range (Y axis), a positive gradient is indicative of positive serial correlation or trend persistence and a negative gradient is indicative of negative serial correlation or mean reversion. Evidence for the UK implies inconsistency with the efficient market hypothesis over periods below about seven years and longer than about 17 years and an approximate balance of opposing forces of long memory between about seven and 17 years.

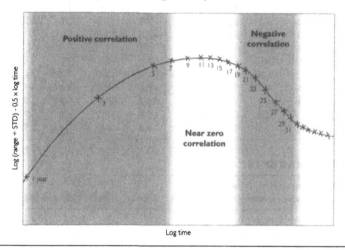

EXHIBIT B. Negative serial correlation for real returns detrended: 10 years forward vs 20 years back 1939–1984 (Source: BZW)

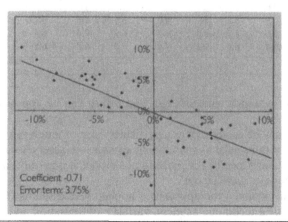

Both are broadly consistent with modern portfolio theory. They accept that most return behaviour is random but seek to exploit those systematic currents of mean reversion which are associated with skewed returns; they also accept that there are opportunities for useful risk reduction through averaging the variances of different assets, even if they share

2. Medium Term Mean Reversion in Relative Returns of International Equity Markets

EXHIBIT C. Annualised local currency total returns in subsequent periods for top and bottom decile markets by return in past periods versus average of 20 markets from 1970 to 1995 (Source: MSCI Indices from Micropal).

Negative serial correlation or mean reversion is indicated for top decile past performing markets by a negative sign and for bottom decile past performing markets by a positive sign. Values above ±4.0% are highlighted. Second and ninth deciles show similar patterns.

TOP DECILE MARKETS

All periods	Subsequent relative return									
	1 mth	3 mths	6 mth	9 mths	12 mths	18 mths	24 mths	36 mths	48 mths	60 mths
1 mth	17.3	3.9	4.0	4.7	3.1	2.9	1.0	1.1	−0.5	0.9
3 mths	13.3	9.5	7.7	10.9	6.8	5.0	2.3	0.1	−1.3	0.0
6 mths	18.3	11.1	10.9	8.6	5.0	3.6	1.5	−2.2	−2.7	−0.5
9 mths	19.5	15.6	11.1	8.9	5.5	4.5	1.8	−2.4	−3.3	−1.6
12 mths	17.2	11.9	9.9	8.8	5.1	4.6	3.1	−3.7	−3.1	−2.0
18 mths	11.4	7.2	5.8	4.9	3.0	1.0	−3.3	**−7.4**	**−6.0**	**−4.5**
24 mths	9.3	2.4	2.2	3.4	0.1	**−5.0**	**−8.0**	**−9.4**	**−9.6**	**−7.5**
36 mths	−1.3	**−6.0**	**−6.1**	**−7.7**	**−8.9**	**−10.2**	**−10.5**	**−9.6**	**−7.5**	**−7.5**
48 mths	**−6.9**	**−7.7**	**−6.0**	**−6.2**	**−6.5**	**−7.6**	**−8.7**	**−9.5**	**−7.1**	**−4.7**
60 mths	**−4.2**	**−4.2**	−2.1	−3.3	**−4.0**	**−4.9**	**−6.9**	**−5.6**	−3.6	−2.8

BOTTOM DECILE MARKETS

All periods	Subsequent relative return									
	1 mth	3 mths	6 mth	9 mths	12 mths	18 mths	24 mths	36 mths	48 mths	60 mths
1 mth	2.3	2.6	−0.3	−3.0	−2.8	−0.7	0.8	0.3	2.4	2.1
3 mths	7.3	2.3	0.7	−2.7	−1.1	0.6	0.8	3.0	**−4.3**	**4.1**
6 mths	−1.0	−1.0	**−4.1**	**−5.4**	−3.5	−0.5	0.6	3.2	**4.9**	**5.7**
9 mths	−3.7	**−4.6**	**−5.9**	**−6.0**	−3.5	−0.8	0.7	3.5	**7.0**	**6.6**
12 mths	**−6.1**	−3.6	−2.6	−2.3	−1.5	0.9	1.4	**4.6**	**6.5**	**6.7**
18 mths	−3.5	−0.9	−1.9	−2.6	−0.7	1.3	1.8	**4.8**	**7.2**	**7.6**
24 mths	**−5.5**	−0.6	0.7	0.6	2.2	**4.4**	**4.5**	**7.3**	**8.9**	**8.9**
36 mths	**4.2**	**6.5**	**5.2**	**4.1**	**4.0**	**6.6**	**7.5**	**8.7**	**9.4**	**8.2**
48 mths	**7.3**	**5.6**	**3.2**	**4.4**	**4.7**	**6.9**	**7.0**	**6.8**	**6.5**	**6.4**
60 mths	**8.4**	**10.4**	**6.0**	**7.2**	**7.4**	**7.6**	**6.8**	**6.4**	**6.8**	**8.9**

common longer term trends, and that risk and return can be approximately optimal by some definition.

These concepts may be thought of as a particular form of 'intelligence' that is applied to the data or the algorithms used in a modelling approach to asset allocation. Without some form of intelligence, informed by the purpose of a model, it is merely an engine and subject to the rule of 'garbage in, garbage out'.

In this particular example, the approaches applied would sanitise the weakness in the standard mathematical technique of mean variance optimisation and allow it to be combined with a dynamic solution for either rebalancing or reoptimising. Thus, optimal portfolio allocations could run without rebalancing as long as their return path is not unusual, so that activity is filtered to capture only trades which are likely to enhance long term returns relative to a static policy or to arbitrary rebalancing to the static policy at fixed time intervals. This return enhancing rebalancing discipline would be an essential purpose of the model and a key selling point. Such an approach would meet the need to recognise the dimension of variability in returns, in this case with a specific solution based on the elimination of spurious correlations. Analysis of the stability of correlations over time and tests for co-integration (ie for common trends that reduce diversification benefits) might be used to dictate these adjustments.

There is also a need for judgement, such as the assumption that data for emerging markets based on periods when they were undiscovered or emerging is not valid for a period after they have emerged.

DIVERSE TECHNIQUES

Within the broad church of an actuarial approach we can expect to see a diversity of specific techniques for dynamic asset allocation unified by a common commitment to discipline, consistency, sensible approximation, active management by exception and long term planning.

These characteristics are most likely to satisfy the customer's needs for tightly controlled asset allocation that will tend over time to add value.

They can potentially support: advisory services to clients who wish to retain or increase their control over policy; software driven products that empower clients to manage their own policy; methods for either judgemental or fully systematic asset allocation by non-managers, particularly actuaries and IFAs. They can also be used by money managers themselves but they will face the added challenge of changing both their own attitudes to investing and their clients' attitudes to performance reports and quantitative techniques.

Money managers have some time, if they start now, and collectively they have lots of talent but too many firms in the UK have also shown a rather stubborn attachment to the old ways of doing things and to the sales pitch that justifies them. This is what in the end may cost them their hold on the asset allocation decision.

36 Intellectual Property

S. MACPHERSON

When Professional Investor *published this article in February 1998, Intellectual Property was rapidly becoming one of the hottest subjects within the business community. Gradually the importance of this business asset was being both recognised by companies and at the same time fiercely protected. The response to Shonaig's article, which examined the valuation of intellectual property, attracted widespread interest, which remains unabated today.*

Shonaig Macpherson heads McGrigor Donald's intellectual property unit, which deals with intellectual property and information technology matters for a wide range of clients. In addition, the Technology Unit advises on fundraising and large corporate transactions.

Shonaig's own specialism relates to the protection and exploitation of intellectual property rights, advising on all aspects of research and development, joint venture, licensing and fundraising. The Technology Unit plays a major role in transaction support services for large corporate transactions undertaken by McGrigor Donald's Corporate Finance Team, such as the investment buy-out of Grampian Pharmaceuticals Limited and the flotation of Core Group plc. The Technology Unit also advises on electronic commerce and information technology matters to systems providers, major financial institutions and companies in Scotland and beyond. Shonaig is Company Secretary of the Scottish Biomedical Research Trust, a member of the Licensing Executive Society, Society for the Computers and Law and International Trade Marks Association. A regular speaker at International Conferences on intellectual property matters, Shonaig was appointed as a Visiting Professor of Heriot-Watt University in 1997 with specific responsibility to devise a module for Master Students in Engineering upon Intellectual Property. She is qualified and practises as both an English and a Scots lawyer, enabling her to deal with cross-border infringements and cross-border matters regularly. Shonaig's time is increasingly spent in devising International IP strategies and developing innovative solutions for exploitation of intellectual property rights.

In recent years there has been a growing recognition of the importance of intellectual property or, as it is becoming known, intellectual capital, as a strategic business asset. Despite this recognition intellectual property assets of companies are commonly undervalued and under-utilised.

Intellectual property is of strategic importance in shaping the global economy. The ability to protect inventions, copyright work, brand names and trade secrets around the world is of key importance to those companies that now compete on a global basis. For businesses seeking to expand around the world, one of the key factors in determining whether or not to locate in a country will be that country's recognition and enforcement of international law on intellectual property. The New World Trade Organisation (formerly GATT) now requires member countries to establish a minimum infrastructure of intellectual property protection, not only to attract foreign and inward investment, but to enable countries to protect and foster their own indigenous industries.

As a result of this requirement, pressure from the US relating to trade disputes and its own desire to be accepted into the world economy, China is now taking steps to protect intellectual property by the introduction of legislation. However, China must now make greater efforts to properly intellectual property rights, particularly against infringers.

Businesses have begun to expend much more money, not only in acquiring intellectual property rights, but in enforcing them. A recent example is the patent dispute between Intel and Digital Equipment relating to semiconductor chips which resulted in Intel acquiring a Digital Equipment's semiconductor manufacturing operations for £432 m as part of an out of court settlement.

Similarly there are constant battles to protect trade names and brands whether as a result of misappropriation by domain name hijackers on the Internet or copycat look-alike products placed on the market either in advance of the brand owner penetrating the market, or to acquire market share such as Asda's *Puffin* biscuit which compared with United Biscuits *Penguin*.

Despite this increased recognition and continuous battles, there are few companies able to properly evaluate the importance or worth to their businesses of intellectual property rights.

In the past some businesses such as Grand Met have sought to ascribe a value to their brands and would argue that their R&D expenditure reflects the value of their intellectual property. But this is not a true indication of the real value of intellectual property. As more companies emerge in technology fields seeking investment, whether through venture capital routes or the markets, the ability to value intellectual property rights will become of increasing importance.

PROTECTION STRATEGY

The majority of companies have limited intellectual property protection strategies in place. The primary purpose of their strategies is usually to protect a single use or product. Intellectual property rights, whether patent, know-how or trademark, are not seen as independent assets with an intrinsic value that may be separate from the value of the product for which it is applied. The intellectual property itself could have application for other uses or products, whether for the owner or for other businesses. Therefore the owner of the intellectual property rights may not realise the rights' true potential, as it only uses them in limited circumstances. The managers of intellectual property rights in most companies are traditionally lawyers and/or patent agents who will not be particularly interested in exploring whether or not the intellectual property rights are capable of generating further benefits to the business, beyond its use for a core product.

Recognition of under-exploitation of patented intellectual property in the pharmaceutical industry has become a source of assets and revenue for some small young biotech companies, particularly in the US, who are desperate to secure an income stream during the inevitably long period in which their own biotech product is being developed or obtaining regulatory approvals. Many of them have acquired rights to use patented intellectual property that the larger pharmaceutical companies have decided not to use or are only using for one particular product.

There are now several financial methodologies that are utilised to evaluate intellectual property rights. In the main these models are not dissimilar to the models used to evaluate other business assets. A key difficulty does present itself in that for the majority of other business assets, there is access to data in the public domain as to the value of assets of the type in question. Traditionally, intellectual property owners do not publish details of the income or profit that is derived directly from exploitation of intellectual property rights, particularly for secondary streams of income from non-core licensing activities of core non-intellectual property assets.

Further an acquirer of the intellectual property rights might argue that the intellectual property asset is only of value as a result of the acquirer's use of it, and that accordingly the owners valuation of it should be discounted.

The valuation of intellectual property rights will be based upon several factors including:

What type of intellectual property is being acquired?

- There are several categories of intellectual property rights, including patents, know-how, trade marks, copyright and design right. The life of each of these rights differs radically from 20 years for patents to up to 70 years for some copyright works.
- To obtain patent protection there are processes and costs involved not associated with know-how or copyright.
- Patents arise on a country by country basis and only if the applicable procedures are undertaken on a country by country basis. No such difficulties arise with copyright.

Will there be any limitation upon the acquirer's ability to use the intellectual property rights?
For example, the acquisition of new facilities, equipment, personnel or distribution networks.

- The owner may have already granted rights to use the intellectual property rights to a third party which could result in it having limited rights to use in certain fields of use, territories or time periods.
- This also raises the question of control over the intellectual property rights and the ability to ensure that enforcement of those rights is effective. The value of any licence to use intellectual property rights will be diminished where the user has limited power to ensure that any unauthorised user of the intellectual property rights is prevented from such use and appropriate damages are sought.

Has the intellectual property been subject to challenge in the past?

- If there has been a history of litigation in relation to use of the intellectual property this would discount the value as there may be continuing costs in use of the rights.

Are there any similar transactions that are comparable? Are there comparable products?

- This will only apply where information is available in the public domain. There is limited information available for sale of intellectual property rights per se but data is available regarding acquisition of technology companies and there are now market valuations too for technology companies.

Will any additional investment be required to exploit the intellectual property rights?

- Companies often have vast portfolios of patients and trademarks which are redundant in the sense that the patents and/or trademarks are no longer being used as the product has moved on technically, and is now protected by a newer patent. However, the patent may be valid and capable of being licensed to third parties, generating income for the owner.
- There are costs associated with maintaining intellectual property rights, particularly patents and trade marks. While the importance of maintaining these rights is recognised by companies, as in many of them responsibility for that maintenance is devolved to a central administrative function rather than to operational functions, the additional revenue potential of intellectual property is overlooked.

These are a few of the factors that should be taken into account in evaluating intellectual property rights.

As stated above, one of the difficulties in ascribing an accurate value to intellectual property rights is that in the majority of companies, intellectual property rights are seen as subsidiary to the key product, processor service that they underpin. The ability to apply the intellectual property rights to other users which are non-core to the owner's business is overlooked. Once the intellectual property has been acquired and protected it is often overlooked until perhaps issues occur over misappropriation by a third party.

An audit of intellectual property rights is advisable as it may result in identification of opportunities for new income streams from, or even disposals, of existing intellectual property rights. The secondary income streams are a low cost benefit for companies which inevitably need to maintain and enforce intellectual property rights for their core business.

Similarly, the true financial potential of intellectual property rights is undervalued. Intellectual property rights are of importance to the emerging high technology business whether in biotech or electronics and to all businesses, all of which to varying degrees will own some form of intellectual property.

37 Underestimated and Undervalued

J. NEWLANDS

This article appeared in Professional Investor *in April 1998. John Newlands came upon the fascinating history of the investment trust industry while attending Edinburgh University Management School as a mature student in the mid-1990s. He remarked at the time: At first sight, investment trusts appear rather dry and unadventurous. Yet delve a little deeper, and a tale of inspiration and insight, full of extraordinary stories, and of even more extraordinary characters, comes to light. I was quite unaware of how capital was raised during the industrial boom years of the nineteenth century by the jute weavers of Dundee, the lawyers and architects of Edinburgh, and the financiers and railway barons of London to fund much of the infrastructure of the United States, Canada, Argentina and elsewhere. I could not comprehend how an industry, which today manages well over £50 billion, could have developed with minimal publicity, negligible marketing and a generally poor level of public understanding. That was why I wrote the book – and why, a year or so later, during a period of unprecedented and often ill-informed criticism of the sector, I attempted to spring to its defence in '*Underestimated and Undervalued,' my article for* Professional Investor *magazine.*

John Newlands is a writer with a particular interest in investment trusts, their history and their analysis. A former Royal Naval missile engineer, he turned to full-time writing after completing a mid-life MBA degree at Edinburgh University and then working as a managed funds analyst in the City of London and in Edinburgh.

His first book, Put Not Your Trust in Money, *was commissioned by the Association of Investment Trust Companies (AITC) and published in September 1997; it was followed by a second, 'F&C' – A History of Foreign & Colonial Investment Trust (written with Neil McKendrick) almost exactly two years later. Newlands, who also writes articles and reviews for* Professional Investor, *the McHattie Group and the AITC, is currently (autumn 1999) working on a consultancy basis for the stockbroking firm of Williams de Bröe plc.*

Cubic tomatoes and rectilinear cucumbers are a packaging consultant's dream. But the chances of their tasting as good as the old, quirky, knobbly varieties are about the same as those of seeing the Lord Chancellor pushing a trolley through the flat-pack furniture department at B&Q.

Investment trusts, it seems to me, are at the quirky, knobbly end of the managed funds' spectrum. And having studied their history in some detail, I have concluded that their leathery closed-end wrappings, their robust constitutions and their idiosyncratic capital structures have been underestimated and undervalued for 130 years.

THE TEST OF TIME

Take 'the Foreign & Colonial' itself. The grandfather of the industry, still going strong today, with £2.2 bn under management at the time of writing, was launched in March 1868 by three remarkable men. Philip Rose was a City lawyer so astute that he defeated George Hudson, the legendary Railway King, at his own game, and thereby secured the biggest railway project the country had seen; and, in his spare time, he even managed to straighten out Benjamin Disraeli's tangled financial (and other) affairs. Samuel Laing was the shrewdest of stockbrokers, and a co-founder of Laing and Cruickshank; and the trust's first chairman, Lord Westbury, has been described as 'the most brilliant barrister of his generation . . . a man who was as respected for his integrity as he was feared for his intellect'. Small wonder that their brainchild has stood the test of time.

Yet the imminent demise of the industry was being predicted even before the first trust had been subscribed. *The Economist* was not alone in its sentiments, when it observed that Foreign & Colonial's intended investments in Danubian, Egyptian and Turkish government securities amounted to: 'loans to semi-civilised states, which will go on borrowing as long as they can, and when they cease to borrow, they will also cease to pay interest . . . the promises are far too sanguine to ever be performed'. Two years later, the price of trust certificates had advanced from 85 to 95, excellent dividends had been paid, reserves had been put aside, and the first of several follow-on issues was being prepared. *The Times* acknowledged that the issue had: 'been welcomed by a large class as a means of imparting as much safety as is practicable in such investments'. The concept, in short, was a resounding success.

The trust was based on the then pioneering principle that high risks in the emerging markets and government stocks of the day could be rendered acceptable through diversification. But its founders, well aware of the low regard with which stock market investment was, with some justification, held in the 1860s, went further. They were determined that their new venture would be presented as the very epitome of trustworthiness, reliability and integrity. The adherence to these ground rules has well served the trust, the industry and its shareholders ever since. On the few occasions when the sector's reputation has nose-dived, such as during the 1888–1890 'trust mania', it has invariably been caused by deviations from these founding principles.

Foreign & Colonial's founders thus established the sector, forged its reputation for probity and professionalism, and pioneered the skilled diversification of risk. But the great catalyst to the dynamic long-term performance of investment trusts – gearing – would not be used by Foreign & Colonial until 1879.

One of the earliest proponents of gearing was an Edinburgh lawyer – William Menzies, Writer to the Signet. Menzies, who in 1873 founded The Scottish American Investment Company Limited, known to this day as 'SAINTS', knew that his clients fell into two categories. Wealthy investors sought above average returns, for which they were prepared to tolerate a measure of risk. Other clients needed a safe and steady income. To meet these diverse needs, SAINTS was structured not as a legal trust but as a limited company, with ordinary shares for risk-tolerant investors, and debenture stock paying 5.5% interest for the 'widows and orphans'. This twin-pronged structure was to provide handsome rewards in years to come.

The next bout of criticism followed the 1890 Barings crisis. The popularity of trusts had soared in the late 1880s, especially after 1888 when Mr Goschen, the Chancellor of the Exchequer, reduced the yield on Consols from 3.0% to 2.75%. All kinds of speculators started jumping on the bandwagon, in an era of negligible regulatory control, and new trusts, of a highly dubious nature, were formed at an alarming rate. Nor did it help that it became harder and harder to find quality securities in which to invest, although there did seem to be plenty of willing sellers of South American bonds.

The 'trust mania' was reaching its peak when the Barings crisis broke. The old and respected firm of Baring Brothers had over-reached itself in Argentina, just as revolution hit the streets of Buenos Aires. Two years earlier, Barings had underwritten the Buenos Aires Water Supply and Drainage Company Loan for £25m, only to find the issue massively undersubscribed. Worse, Barings had guaranteed contractors' payments in gold, and when the paper peso went into freefall, the bank was in serious trouble. To meet its commitments, Barings had to borrow more and more, at ever increasing rates of interest, until even these borrowings were refused.

The news caused the worst stockmarket crisis since the Overend, Gurney bank collapse of 1866. Barings itself was saved by the intervention of William Lidderdale, Governor of the Bank of England, but market confidence was severely shaken, and prices fell sharply. Some of the newer, more speculative trusts formed in haste during the 'mania', and with no reserves to fall back on, went to the wall. The financial press had a heyday, although *The Economist* of 8 September 1893, while not mincing its words, did at least defend the older trusts which, it said, had 'suffered in the estimation of unthinking investors by being classed with a set of companies which had come to stink in the nostrils of the public'. The well founded trusts did indeed weather the storm, as they have done time and again since. These trusts, such as Alliance, Foreign & Colonial, and Railway Debenture, continued to pay dividends of between 5 and 8% before, during and after the Barings crisis.

It is even more instructive to look at the performance of River Plate & General Investment Trust during the Barings debacle. River Plate, despite being set up in 1888 specifically to invest in the Argentine economy, survived the crisis with fortitude, met all its commitments, and by 1892 was even able to increase its reserves from £16,000 to £18,000. River Plate's investments in Argentina, quite unlike those of Barings, were well diversified, being spread between railways, water and drainage schemes, industrial companies, mortgages, provincial government bonds and municipal bonds, and comprised not more than 60% of the trust's total portfolio. The structure of a soundly-run investment trust had made all the difference in the world.

The First World War's effect on the City has been likened to 'a bludgeon descending on a watch'. The Stock Exchange, for example, closed for five months when war was declared. The New York Stock Exchange was hit even harder, not reopening for nine months. Yet investment trusts, a number of which had been salting away reserves since the Baring crisis, survived. Dividends continued to be paid, and in some cases increased, during the war years. Reserves were almost totally wiped out, and market values frequently fell below book cost, but the robust 'closed-end' structure of the trust company, in times of trouble, had been proved once more.

WILLING TO EVOLVE

The long-term success of investment trusts is not just about durability, it is about the sector's ability, and willingness, to evolve. Major changes took place in the 1920s, when the introduction of Corporation Profits Tax led trust managers to seek franked income – income on which tax had already been paid. Taken with the onset of inflation, the trek towards equity investment had soon begun, such that by 1929 a typical trust would be equally invested in debentures (including bonds), preference shares and ordinary shares.

It is worth taking stock of what the best elements of the 60-year old sector had achieved by 1929. In his book *The Scottish Investment Trust Companies*, published in 1932, George Glasgow quotes the case of an investor who had put £1,000 into the ordinary shares of a leading trust – SAINTS – back in 1873. Despite an era of very low inflation, during which the protection of capital was less of an issue than today, and all the crashes and conflicts in between, both capital and income had performed handsomely for more than 50 years.

'A calculation has been made of what would have been the case of a man who in 1873 had invested £1,000 in the Ordinary Stock of The Scottish American Investment Co Ltd.

Assuming that he held his stock, never adding another penny to it; that he took up and kept his bonuses; that he exercised his rights to new capital by borrowing from his bank and then selling enough of the resultant new stock to repay the bank – assuming, in short, that he did not put any of his benefits into his waste-paper basket (a contingency not unknown to experience, surprising as it may be), that happy investor's original £1,000 would in 1929 have been worth about £70,000, and his income would have risen from an original £40 a year to £3,000 a year in 1929. Not a negligible half-century's reward for a man who did nothing more than invest his money wisely in the first place and refrain from changing his investment thereafter.'

George Glasgow, The Scottish Investment Trust Companies, 1932

It seems a little ironic, therefore, that the use of gearing, which had produced decades of strong performance, would be criticised when the Great Depression came.

The Wall Street Crash, in September 1929, marked the beginning of a vicious decline in which the Dow Jones Index fell from a peak of 386 in 1929 to a lowly 41 in 1932 (*see graph*). Despite the mayhem in New York, during which there were so many suicides that hotel concierges famously asked whether rooms were required for sleeping in or jumping from, UK investment trusts were not unduly savaged by the crash itself. But no-one could avoid the depression which followed because, to quote George Glasgow once more: 'A combination of circumstances arose which mostly, if temporarily, defeated the efficacy of the "distribution of risk" principle in its geographical element, for the whole world went wrong at the same time.'

In a 20-page benchmark review of the sector carried by *The Economist* in December 1934, sub-titled 'Whither Investment Trusts?', it was estimated that the market values of trust portfolios declined by 17% between 1929 and 1933, although this figure needs to be regarded with caution, owing to the valuation practices of the day.

The ordinary shares of some trusts fell by much greater percentages owing to the capital

Wall Street Crash.

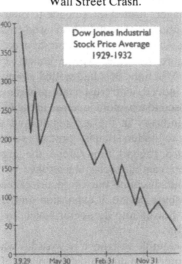

gearing employed. It was not unusual, at that time, for potential gearing to be as much as 350% for investment trust ordinary shares, although this figure was significantly offset, in reality, by the de-gearing effect of investments in fixed interest securities. I have calculated that the average actual gearing employed in 1929 was around 13%, but as in 1890, it was the extreme cases which blighted the sector's name. Trusts formed in the 1920s trust boom, with expensive borrowings, ultra-high gearing, and few reserves fared badly, and a small number failed to recover. But as oft times before, those trusts which had stayed true to the tenets of Messrs Rose, Fleming and Menzies held their ground, ready for next phase of recovery and growth. Before that, however, a new problem arose: coupons in default and, in particular, a scant regard for the rights of cumulative preference shareholders. An industry body was desperately needed to take a concerted stand, on behalf of the trust companies and their shareholders, in such matters.

On 29 September, 1932, the Association of Investment Trusts (now the AITC) was formed, at the suggestion of Foreign & Colonial's Arthur Crichton, for that very purpose. In the years which followed, aided by the campaigning efforts of the AIT, a slow recovery was maintained until the Second World War.

Fast forward, if you will, to the 1970s – the decade, above all others, in which the demise of the sector began to be postulated as a one-way bet. But along the way, spare a downwards glance at one of the greatest growth phases in trust history. Between 1945 and 1965, investment trust share prices, their growth supercharged by low-cost gearing obtained in the 'cheap money' era, multiplied no less than 14 times, outperforming equities by a factor of more than three over the same period. Tracker funds, had they then existed, would have been left for dust.

Now, however, the Grim Reaper really was hovering outside the AITC's front door. Trusts were reeling from the quadruple whammy effect of the savage '70s bear markets, inequitable tax treatment, widening discounts (to more than 30%) and the predatorial circlings of the old nationalised industries. But there was life in the old rooster yet.

Darwinism, in the form of hostile takeover bids, took large chunks out of the sector, but the tide slowly turned, aided, especially from 1979 onwards, by the lifting of exchange controls, the removal of CGT on transactions within the trust, and later, the introduction of regular savings schemes, Personal Equity Plans and an AITC publicity drive.

The effects of 'Black Monday' and the 1987 crash were illusory. Not only was the FT-SE All Share index actually fractionally higher at the end than at the beginning of 1987, but shrewd investment trust managers turned the setback to their advantage. Instead of panic selling as markets fell, one leading trust actually borrowed £50m to buy quality stocks, such as ICI, at temporarily depressed prices and contentedly watched as the shares recovered and started to climb once more. No other type of collective investment vehicle has the flexibility to take such action. When the dust had settled, it was found that investment trusts had had a very good decade indeed, with trust share prices multiplying by no less that 6.7 times during the '80s, as opposed to a fivefold increase in the FT-A All Share Index over the same period. But with the industry in the ascendant, and discounts still at around an attractive 15–18% (attractive to bidders, that is), predators moved in once more, taking out TR Industrial & General (1988: £560m), then Globe, the largest trust of all, in 1990, that single takeover removing £1bn from the sector at a stroke.

Shareholders did not lose out; discounts narrowed, prices rose, and the newly pruned and invigorated sector entered a sharp period of expansion. In the boom year of 1994 alone, a massive £8 bn of new money flowed into the sector which, by the end of 1997, had record total assets of more than £60 bn.

Since the unseemly 1994 scramble to launch new issues while discounts were less than 5%, investment trusts have entered an uncomfortable phase of indigestion and oversupply.

Now, in 1998, with discounts widening (but only to 12–13%) and new breed of trust vultures not just politely waiting in the wings, but overtly hovering, ready to pounce on weakling trusts, that old press pessimism has returned. With the prophets of trust gloom sharpening their pencils once again, what does history tell us about the likely way ahead? Well, as Barry Riley said in last month's issue of *Professional Investor*, driving through the rear-view mirror can be a hazardous pursuit. But here goes.

Point one: investment trusts will still be around when the Millennium Dome is coated in 'Kurust' and listed as an ancient monument.

Secondly the present oversupply needs to be corrected, will be corrected, and arguably is an industry own-goal which never need be repeated.

Thirdly, history tells us that trust scavengers have always left the sector leaner and meaner than before. Their likely permanent presence from now on offers a self-correction mechanism, albeit a rudimentary one, which should ensure that ultra-wide discounts will never happen again. This potentially factors out, or at least reduces, the risk inherent in trust discount volatility.

Lastly, if trusts are to excel as in times gone by, they will have to bring to bear the unique attributes and advantages which gave them their glory days. This not only means using their closed end structure to take long-term positions where openended funds fear to tread, but building in capital gearing, either through borrowings or by adopting split capital structures. Whether 'post-Euro' convergence of interest rates will help this process, only time will tell. But if large generalist trusts neither stray far from a market weighting nor use any gearing, they are almost guaranteeing underperformance and might as well become OEICs and be done with it.

At least the tone of negative comment about 'the Trusts' has improved since 1907, when *Rialto* magazine said of one forthcoming trust launch: 'We need only remark that anyone who subscribes to the shares should, after so doing, consult some medical practitioner of repute who makes a speciality of lunacy cases.' That same trust, The General Investors & Trustees Limited, went on to achieve considerable success, multiply capital and income many times, and later merged into what is now Foreign & Colonial Pacific.

And looking at that 1977 magazine cover of an old investment trust rooster, I am reminded of Winston Churchill's famous wartime comment: 'Some chicken – some neck'.

38 Brands and the Balance Sheet

J. KNOWLES

This article was published in Professional Investor *in February 1999. In recent years, as Jonathan Knowles points out, the source of corporate value has moved decisively in favour of intangible assets. This article charts the changes that are taking place, including the dramatic development of new technologies, and analyses the value of brands in the modern world. Jonathan concludes his paper by calling for a new approach to the valuation of companies.*

Jonathan Knowles is a Director of Wolff Olins, one the world's leading corporate identity and branding firms. He is currently based in New York.

He specializes in financial services and in mergers and acquisitions. Since joining Wolff Olins in 1995, he has worked on a number of high-profile assignments, such as Diageo (the merger of Guinness and Grand Metropolitan), Credit Suisse, Lloyds TSB and Goldfish (British Gas's entry into retail financial services).

Jonathan has actively contributed to Wolff Olins' approach to corporate and service branding, and to the understanding of the role of brands in value creation. He is a regular speaker at conferences and business schools on issues related to the role of corporate identity and branding in business strategy.

Prior to joining Wolff Olins, he spent three years with Marakon Associates, a US-based strategy consultancy firm specializing in management for shareholder value.

He began his career at the Bank of England, spending six years in the International and Banking Supervision areas (including two years as Private Assistant to the International Director). He left in 1991 to do an MBA at INSEAD.

On 16 September last year, Microsoft overtook GE to become the most highly capitalised company in the world, a development symbolic of the meteoric rise in importance of intangible assets over recent years. The source of corporate value creation, which traditionally resided in the ownership of property and physical assets, has shifted decisively in favour of intangible assets.

Research by Citibank and Interbrand Newell & Sorrell published last year indicated that the proportion of the market capitalisation of the FTSE 350 represented by tangible assets had declined from 56% in 1988 to 29% in 1998.

This article explores three questions: Why has this shift in value occurred? What is it about brands that makes them so valuable? What are the implications for investment management and research?

FUNDAMENTAL CHANGES TAKING PLACE

The growth in importance of intangibles reflects the fundamental changes that are taking place in the nature and sources of competitive advantage. The relative stability of economic cycles and the predictability of the pace of introduction of new technologies have been replaced by an environment of constant and often discontinuous change. Traditional analytical approaches to strategy now appear inadequate. It is not so much change itself that is the problem, but the rapid pace and comprehensive nature of it which favours a different set of skills.

In this environment, learning, innovation and other 'soft' skills are becoming as important 'core competences' for an organisation to possess as are the traditional 'hard' skills, such as strategic planning and value chain management.

Our definition of 'corporate asset' needs to be expanded to include not only financial and physical assets but also intangibles such as knowledge, motivation and customer franchise.

For literally centuries, wealth creation was based on the ownership of the physical means of production. During the agrarian period, that meant owning land (and generally – as in feudal societies – the labour to work on it and a militia to defend it). The industrial revolution changed the primary source of wealth generation from land to the ownership of manufacturing capacity.

The advent of mass production and distribution created the preconditions for the emergence of some of the world's major brands. This was the era of the some of the greatest entrepreneurs and brand-builders – such as Messrs Procter and Gamble, Kellogg, Cadbury and Rowntree. They seized the opportunity offered by the possibility to mass produce goods to a relatively uniform quality, and to distribute them cost effectively, to end the natural local monopolies which existed for most goods.

Of the world's 50 top FMCG brands, 29 were launched prior to 1949 (and 13 of these were even launched prior to 1900!).

At this stage the primary role of the brand was as a guarantee of quality. The values of the brand were essentially functional – they were based on the promise that the product would perform a given function more effectively than any other.

But the ability to mass produce goods of a standard quality was open to anyone who could raise the finance from the newly established capital markets. Multiple mass producers of similar goods led to the increase of consumer choice and the commoditisation of the underlying products.

Improvements in manufacturing techniques and the quality movement have largely eliminated the performance and quality variances that used to characterise most manufactured goods and provide the basis for differentiation.

Producing a quality product is now simply the entry ticket to doing business, not a guarantee of business success.

This fundamental conformity of product functionality and quality has resulted in the elimination of many bad products and services (a good thing) and a proliferation of good ones (a welcome, but confusing, thing for consumers). It has blurred the concept of the 'best choice'. How are we as consumers meant to work out which is the best choice for us given the increasing perception that you can get more or less anything from anyone (Mitsubishi will supply you with anything from a steel mill to a bank account) and it will meet the necessary functional standards?

Before we discuss the implications of this, it is worth pausing to review the major factors which are driving the perceived commoditisation of most goods and services. I would suggest that there are four primary influences: advances in manufacturing; new technology; communications; and social and physical mobility.

ADVANCES IN MANUFACTURING

The post-war period has seen a persistent erosion in the cycle times of products based on the adoption of new approaches to manufacturing, and particularly the concept of lean production. In 'The Machine that Changed the World', based on a comparison of 29 'clean sheet' car development projects between 1983 and 1987, the authors report that a totally new Japanese car required 1.7 million hours of engineering effort and took 46 months from first design to customer deliveries. The equivalent figures for US and European projects of similar complexity required three million hours of engineering effort and 60 months. Best practice currently stands at less than 30 months (or 18 if an existing plattform is used). These advances have been mirrored by improvements in quality standards. As recently as the early 1970s the notion of a quality Japanese car was a joke. Now Toyota is regarded as the world's most advanced car manufacturer. In automobiles, quality has converged to such an extent that the industry now averages one defect per vehicle (as calculated by J. D. Power surveys). In fact, the industry-wide average in 1996 is better than the performance of the best company in 1989 (when the average defects per vehicles was around 4.7 and the figure for the best manufacturer was 1.5). This convergence of capabilities and standards has eroded the extent of differentiation that can be achieved from the manufacturing process.

NEW TECHNOLOGIES

Often associated with manufacturing advances is another feature of competitive markets – the relentless drive for new technologies which can lower the cost of doing business or accessing consumers. The inevitability of eventual technological obsolescence has always been present, but the rate at which new technologies have been introduced and adopted has accelerated dramatically over the past few decades (consider the increasing speed with which different forms of recorded music are being introduced – vinyl, cassette, CD, MiniDisc and now DVD).

COMMUNICATION

A succession of new technologies – radio, TV, internet – have added the necessary in-gredient of mass communication to the mix of mass production and mass distribution. Better informed consumers mean that any competitive advantage based on consumers' lack of awareness of the availability of choice has been largely eradicated. But this availability of this vast amount has created an overload of information. The average US consumer was exposed to 30,000 items of promotional communication a day in 1995 (in the form of advertisements, direct mail etc.), versus just 560 in 1971. No wonder that 61% of American polled in the 1996 Yankelovitch Monitor survey claimed to be 'overwhelmed by all the in-formation that is available today'. This overload of information has changed the way in which consumers make their choices. Rather than behaving as the 'rational economic agents' that economic theory would have them be (and which would predict value maximising behaviour), consumers are acting more as 'satisfiers' rather than 'maximisers'.

SOCIAL AND PHYSICAL MOBILITY

Greater access to information has led people to question traditional ways of doing things. This has accelerated the social trend, evident since the end of the Second World War, of the erosion of traditional affiliations – such as those of community, family and belief – and the lessening of social rigidities. Add to this the advent of mass travel plus the rapid growth of immigration and of labour mobility, and you have a society that is fundamentally more socially and physically mobile than ever before. This has had a profound impact on con-sumer attitudes. What is emerging is a much more fluid society in which people are ready to transfer their loyalties to organisations, even new ones, that they perceive will meet their needs. A more demanding, better informed but overwhelmed consumer population produces an environment in which trust, and the ability to generate a sense of belonging, are at a huge premium.

That is what brands are all about. Brands represent relationships with customers. They allow you to replace the complexity with simplicity, the confusion with clarity, and the cynicism with engagement. By adding an emotional dimension to the interaction between producer and consumer, they permit you to develop a relationship rather than simply execute a transaction.

WHAT MAKES BRANDS SO VALUABLE?

Essentially, brands have three simple functions: to help process large volumes of information; to provide security in purchase; to provide satisfaction in use.

Let us examine each in turn:

- *Processing information*
  The average supermarket now stocks 30,000 SKUs versus 7,000 ten years ago – we need something to help us make the choice between an increasingly bewildering set of alternatives. In the US, there are 200 different Tylenol products alone! Brands simplify consumer choice by making certain key attributes the property of certain producers (J&J for baby care; Tide for detergent; Kellogg's for cereal; Volvo and safety), making them the obvious choice in their category.
- *Security in purchase*
  As noted above, this was the most original role of the brand – to provide a mark of ownership and a guarantee of quality. It is still a fundamental function of the brand to reassure consumers that they are getting a quality product which will meet their needs. A recent study by McKinsey on the importance of the brand in the purchase decision across a number of product categories revealed a range of 7% to 39%. Not surprisingly, the higher percentage categories were those which involved more complex purchase decisions or higher value transactions.
- *Satisfaction in use*
  This provision is the growing function of the brand. If consumers begin from the standpoint that the quality of the products or services is essentially similar, the basis for choice between the alternatives shifts from tangible features to intangible ones. Once performance and functionality levels are met, considerations such as design, prestige and country of origin become relevant factors of choice. It is no longer so much a question of what that product does but how it makes you feel.

These are the sources of the value of brands – the ability to say a lot, simply and powerfully, and on a number of different levels.

The literature contains a bewildering taxonomy of brand dimensions – my preference is to think of any brand as communicating along three particular axes: 'what you get' – the pure functionality of what is being offered; 'how you feel about what you get' – the emotional overlay that means that your Levi's are not 'just another pair of jeans'; and 'who it is from' – the increasingly important dimension of the behaviour of the company behind the product or service.

It is this richness of communication which establishes a meaningful connection between a manufacturers and their customers, or between employers and their employees. Brands have become so valuable because they act as the manifestation of these relationships. They encapsulate our preferences in a way that enables the producer/employer to secure our loyalty and trust. That trust is often proving to be the decisive factor of choice in situations characterised by overchoice and information overload – such as in the case of whose running shoe to buy, or whose employment offer to accept.

Perhaps, even, whose stock to buy?

INVESTING IN INTANGIBLES

The importance which institutional investors place on non-financial measures was the subject of a recent study published by Ernst & Young entitled *Measures that Matter*. Based on a sample of 600 investment reports (split more or less equally between sell-side and buy-side reports) plus some investment simulation, they conclude that non-financial criteria on average account for 35% of the investment decision. For 70% of investors, at least 30% of their decision is attributable to non-financial performance measures.

According to the report, the five non-financial metrics to which investors attached the most weight were: strategy execution; management credibility; quality of strategy; innovativeness (sic.); and ability to attract talented people.

The interesting thing about these metrics is that they appear to place equal emphasis on *what* is done and *how* it is done. There is a fundamental loss of belief in the concept of one 'right' strategy (a concept better suited to the stable business environments of the 1960s and which formed the holy grail of a legion of strategic planning processes), in favour of a belief in constant experimentation and reinvention.

This reflects the development of management thinking, as reflected in the writing of Professor Henry Mintzberg (see particularly his 1994 book *The Rise and Fall of Strategic Planning*). He sees strategy as something that is uncovered though experimentation rather than something which is designed, then implemented.

In this environment, flexibility and inventiveness are at a premium and it is logical that value should shift from physical assets to human assets. Having the right physical assets is still vital, but how you use them is at least as important.

If the importance of intangibles – be they capabilities, processes or brands – is no longer in dispute, devising a methodology for valuing them has proved elusive. In many ways, they are to the asset side of the balance sheet what shareholders equity is to the liabilities side – i.e. easiest to define as the residual when the other, more quantifiable elements have been deducted.

Significant progress has been made in the last decade, principally in the two areas of performance, measurement and brand valuation. The recognition that purely financial measures are inadequate to explain superior corporate performance culminated in the development of the 'balanced scorecard' by Professors Norton and Kaplan. The goal of the 'balanced scorecard' process is to identify and monitor the variables believed to most influence corporate performance. These variables span four dimensions – financial performance; knowledge of customers; internal business processes; and organisational learning and growth. In so doing, the authors aimed to monitor the measures that best accounted for an organisation's success in both the short-and long-term.

VALUATION

The second area is in the valuation of brands. Early methodologies such as that of *Financial World*, a US financial magazine (now no longer in print), were based on a multiple of historic brand earnings. This involved two steps; first, identifying the earnings uniquely attributable to the brand (done by deducting from the earnings of the branded products what were the equivalent earnings of a generic competitor); and second, determining the appropriate multiple to apply based on the brand's strength. The results of *Financial World*'s 1996 Brand Survey are reproduced in the table opposite.

Later methodologies have adopted a discounted cash flow (DCF) approach to the valuation of the future brand earnings. These typically involve developing a five to ten year forecast of the earnings attributable to the brand, and then adding a 'terminal value' or 'annuity' to cover the brand's earnings beyond the forecast period. The second stage of the process is to determine the appropriate discount rate to be applied to the brand earnings based on the perceived robustness of the revenue stream.

The details of the methodologies of different practitioners vary, but the DCF approach has been endorsed by the ASB in Financial Reporting Standard 10 as the appropriate way of valuing intangibles on the balance sheet.

Notwithstanding the above, the impression remains that brands sit uncomfortably in the financial world. This world is one in which deductive reasoning and rationality reign supreme, and which is self-confessedly an abstraction from the real world. By contrast, brands belong to the real world – a fuzzy world in which emotion and reason, perception and reality, happily coexist. By acting as the ciphers of meaning, brands neatly bridge the complementary worlds of product functionality and affinity.

The role of brands is relatively well understood in the connection with physical product or service brands whose underlying 'reason for being' can be justified in terms of their basic functionality. Similarly, the value of such product and service brands is easier to estimate due to the price premium and/or faster growth that these products and services enjoy relative to their generic alternatives.

By contrast, the subject of corporate branding is less well understood, not least because the concept of the 'reason for being' of an organisation is less easy to encapsulate.

In their influential book *Built to Last*, Collins and Porras set out to research what made truly exceptional companies different from other companies. Their aim was to isolate the timeless principles of management which distinguished outstanding companies. In reading it, one can sense their frustration that the answer did not prove to be a complex algorithm of 'hard' management skills but rather an amalgam of annoyingly 'soft' capabilities. Key components appeared to be a sense of purpose, a set of shared beliefs, and the desire to be a part of something whose value could not be expressed simply in financial terms.

The authors' research caused them to shift their perspective in a fundamental way – they went from seeing companies simply as the vehicle for bringing their products to market, to seeing the products as the vehicle for the ongoing existence of the companies. In this sense, the greatest creation of the company is the company itself.

This new perspective suggests that the principal determinant of the value of a company is its ability to create and sustain relationships with its employees and customers more than the performance of its current product range. It also suggests that a continual stream of great products and services is the product of being a great company, rather than the requirement of becoming one.

In many ways, this is common sense. The fact that the companies comprise human beings whose search for meaning and purpose is often played out extensively in the work environment means that companies cannot be insensitive to the non-financial aspirations that they are seeking to fulfil in their workplaces.

THE IMPLICATIONS FOR INVESTMENT

The traditional forms of financial and strategic analysis are still valid. They articulate the requirements that need to be met in order to secure the continued survival of the company.

But they are generally inadequate to identify the qualities and capabilities that are required to ensure that the company thrives in the new competitive environment.

This involves a new approach to the valuation of companies – one that incorporates the variables that best explain the long term success of organisations. My feeling is that an extension of the 'balanced scorecard' concept might be one such approach – or the application of systems dynamics. Either way, it involves getting away from engineering-based views of organisations as machines to biology-based views of organisations as organisms. The focus must shift from measuring the efficiency of the machine in producing a predetermined volume of products to the effectiveness of the organism in adapting to, and thriving in, a changing environment.

Such capabilities are the newly emergent forms of 'corporate assets' and the reason why intangibles now account for such a significant proportion of the capitalisation of companies. Identifying the metrics to express the health of these assets is the challenge for the investment management community for the millennium.

Printed in the United States
By Bookmasters